FINANCIAL MANAGEMENT CASES

*

FINANCIAL MANAGEMENT: CASES

by

Lawrence J. Gitman
The University of Tulsa

and

Edward A. Moses
The University of Tulsa

West Publishing Co.
St. Paul • New York • Los Angeles • San Francisco

COPYRIGHT © 1978 By WEST PUBLISHING CO.
50 West Kellogg Boulevard
P.O. Box 3526
St. Paul, Minnesota 55165

Library of Congress Cataloging in Publication Data
Main entry under title:

Financial management.

     1. Corporations—Finance—Case studies.
2. Business enterprises—Finance—Case studies.
I. Gitman, Lawrence J. II. Moses, Edward A.
HG4026.F497   658.1'5'0722   77-26108
ISBN 0-8299-0167-1

1st Reprint—1978

To Our Families

*

TABLE OF CONTENTS

PART TWO   MANAGEMENT OF WORKING CAPITAL

PART THREE   FIXED ASSET MANAGEMENT: CAPITAL
BUDGETING AND LEASING   147

PART FOUR   SOURCES OF LONG-TERM FINANCING   225

INDEX OF CASES

PREFACE

The use of the case method of instruction in financial management courses provides a mechanism whereby students can experiment with and gain a real-world understanding of the theories, concepts, tools, and techniques of financial management. Cases can be viewed as a laboratory in which experimentation, analysis, and decision-making approaches can be tested and learning can take place. This desired learning is manifested in an ability to effectively apply "textbook knowledge" to "real world" financial problem-solving/decision-making. The success of this learning process of course depends upon a variety of factors such as: the students' grasp of financial theories, concepts, tools, and techniques; the quality of instruction; student interest; and the quality of the case studies available. *Financial Management: Cases* is designed to fulfill the need for high-quality cases that create a suitable environment for the development of a real-world understanding of financial management. Collaterally, the cases have been selected in order to stimulate student interest in real-world financial problem-solving and decision-making.

General Description

The collection of forty-seven cases included herein present real business decision situations that can be used to effectively bridge the gap between an understanding of the theories, concepts, tools, and techniques of financial management and an ability to effectively use such knowledge to solve problems and/or make decisions related to the financial management of the business firm. This book contains a "new" mix of high-quality cases for use in a variety of financial management courses. The cases depict real-life situations in which the primary problems/decisions are concerned with some aspect of the financial management of the firm. They have been selected on the basis of such factors as reality, readability, timeliness, clarity of the problems presented, and the quality of presentation. They contain a reasonable amount of financial data that can be used in solving the problems and/or making the required decisions. We have taken a great deal of care in including cases that provide sufficient background and other information necessary to permit examination of peripheral issues not directly related to the problem/decision at hand. While all of the cases present real-life problem/decision situations, the names of the company and persons involved have in some instances been disguised. Most cases present situations which confronted firms during the period between 1970 and 1975; the recent nature of these cases should allow students to more readily investigate and understand the economic environment prevailing at the time the decision must be made. All cases have been classroom tested in order to insure their pedagogical effectiveness.

Distinguishing Features

Aside from the timely nature of the cases presented, *Financial Management: Cases* offers a number of additional distinguishing features. It offers more cases in the area of cost of capital and capital budgeting than do competing texts. The cases relate to both small and large business firms. General questions for discussion are included at the end of each case. The casebook is well suited for use with nearly all financial management texts. The cases generally center around a key issue (noted as a subtitle in the Table of Contents) that must be dealt with by the student. Sufficient analytical as well as subjective data is provided to stimulate meaningful analysis and class discussion. In combination these factors are believed to provide a new and interesting group of cases for use in a variety of financial management courses.

Organization

The casebook is organized into six parts. The first part contains nine cases concerned with various aspects of financial analysis and planning. Part two contains six cases devoted to the management of working capital. The third part contains nine cases concerned with fixed asset management; specific attention is given to both capital budgeting and leasing decisions. Part four includes eleven cases concerned with a number of different types of long-term financing sources. Cases related to dividend policy and stock repurchases are also included in this part. The fifth part includes seven cases, each one dealing with some aspect(s) of capital structure, cost of capital or valuation. One case gives explicit consideration to the Capital Asset Pricing Model (CAPM). The final part contains five cases concerned with selected topics in financial management. Cases devoted to mergers as well as various aspects of international financial transactions are included. The cases are generally arranged within each of the six parts from the most straightforward and well-defined problems/decisions to those that are concerned with broader and more comprehensive issues.

Conclusion

Clearly recognizing the importance of good case materials to the development of a true understanding of how and when to apply financial theories, concepts, tools, and techniques, the authors strongly believe that the cases included herein provide the mechanism—both in form and quality—to permit achievement of such a goal. We applaud professors for using the case method and are hopeful that students find the case approach a useful mechanism for gaining a real-world understanding of financial management problem-solving and decision-making techniques.

Lawrence J. Gitman
Edward A. Moses

*

ACKNOWLEDGMENTS

The authors are greatly appreciative of the willingness of the large number of cases authors whom we contacted and who so graciously agreed to let us consider their case(s) for inclusion in this casebook. Although hundreds of excellent cases were reviewed, for a variety of reasons, one of which being a space limitation, not all of them could be included. A special note of thanks goes to the following contributors whose willingness to share their excellent cases is most appreciated.

Abdel-Malek, T.	University of Saskatchewan
Bateman, Merrill J.	Brigham Young University
Belt, Brian	University of Missouri—Kansas City
Clark, Albert H.	Georgia State University
Coleman, Alan B.	Southern Methodist University
Deal, Emit B.	Georgia Southern College
De Fatta, Joseph A.	Northeast Louisiana University
Dellenbarger, Lynn E., Jr.	Georgia Southern College
Ferner, Jack D.	Wake Forest University
Fitzpatrick, Dennis B.	Boise State University
Fortune, Bill D.	Texas A & M University
Grablowsky, Bernie J.	Old Dominion University
Haslem, John A.	University of Maryland
Huffman, Robert J.	American National Bank and Trust Co. of Chicago
Johnson, Robert L.	University of South Dakota
Johnson, Robert W.	Purdue University

Kuniansky, Harry R.	College of Charleston
Loesby, Rex	University of Washington
Longenecker, Justin A.	Baylor University
Longstreet, James R.	University of South Florida
Marks, Leonard, Jr.	Castle & Cooke, Inc.
McEnally, Richard W.	University of North Carolina at Chapel Hill
Modrow, William G.	University of South Florida
Mohundro, Charles W.	East Texas State University at Texarkana
Norgaard, Richard L.	University of Connecticut
Northwestern University	Graduate School of Business
Osteryoung, Jerome S.	Florida State University
Poland, Leo A.	Wichita State University
Rakes, Ganas, K.	University of Virginia
Southwestern Publishing Co.	College Department
Springate, David J.	Southern Methodist University
Stanford, Melvin J.	Brigham Young University
Stanford University	Graduate School of Business
Trivoli, George W.	University of Texas at Arlington
Truitt, J. F.	University of Washington
Upson, Roger G.	University of Minnesota
Wagner, Charles R.	University of South Dakota
Wheelen, Thomas L.	University of Virginia
Williams, John D.	University of Akron
Young, Charles W.	University of North Florida

The research assistance of Kersi P. Damri is greatly appreciated. We also wish to thank Margaret F. Ferguson and Patsy J. Raney for their excellent typing assistance. The editorial staff of West Publishing Company has been most cooperative and we would like to thank all who have worked on this book. A word of thanks also goes to Cobb/Dunlop Publisher Services.

Finally, we would like to thank our families for providing support and understanding during the preparation of this book. To them we are forever grateful and hope that this book will provide answers to their many questions.

FINANCIAL MANAGEMENT CASES

†

PART ONE
FINANCIAL ANALYSIS AND PLANNING

*

Case 1
Harper Brothers Company

Founded in 1895 in Westmore, Iowa, the Harper Brothers Company was originally established as a partnership of Fred and Tom Harper. The department store was originally located across the street from its present location. As was typical of many department stores of this nature at this time, the store carried the image of a general store, with much of the goods bought in large size lots and sold in various quantities as requested by the customers.

In 1903, with the passing away of Tom Harper, the store was incorporated. Two local citizens of Westmore were brought into the corporation as stockholders. A fourth stockholder was the store's manager. Fred remained as the majority stockholder, retaining approximately 90 percent of the outstanding stock.

It was the wish and desire of Fred and Tom that Harper Brothers Company should always remain as a closely held corporation. Therefore, in the event of a death of any of the stockholders, the stock could not be publicly sold, but rather the heirs of the stock were required to sell the stock back to the corporation. In 1928, the shares of stock of the two "outsiders" (the local citizens) were bought by the corporation, and it became an estate. By-laws were drawn up which stated that the corporation was to be family held; thus following the desires of the original owners.

Fred passed away in 1932, leaving his estate to his two daughters, Marie and Martha, and his son, John. John died in 1945, leaving his one-third of the estate to his two children, which was equally divided. Martha holds her shares of stock in connection with her son Robert Simpson. Thus, at the present time, there are five

This case was prepared by Mr. Roger E. Wells under the supervision of Professor Robert L. Johnson of the University of South Dakota as a basis for classroom discussion and not to illustrate either correct or incorrect handling of an administrative problem situation.

3

stockholders owning and controlling Harper Brothers. These five members serve on the board of directors. Robert is president of the firm. The general manager of the firm serves as vice-president. An attorney engaged by the firm is secretary of the board and Martha is treasurer.

The corporation experienced a successful growth throughout its history. In its early stages, it handled many of the functions of food processing itself, such as butter-making, egg-grading, meat-processing, etc. Eventually, these functions were replaced with more efficient means by outside firms specializing in these functions. Harper Brothers gained recognition and a fine reputation in the field for always presenting to the customers a good line of merchandise with the latest styles and innovations in products. They were respected by their competitors and managed to emerge from the Depression as a sound business establishment.

As time passed, Harper Brothers became more departmentalized until today the firm is comprised of nine stores broken down into 28 departments.

Store	Number of Departments
Dry Goods	2
Men's Wear	3
Shoes	3
Women's Ready-to-Wear	6
Variety (not departmentalized)	1
Hardware	4
Furniture	6
Groceries and Meats (combined)	3
Total	28

These departments are not completely fixed, but may vary slightly somewhat from year to year. For example, whereas the Furniture store formerly handled toys, these are now completely handled by the Variety store. Basically, however, the number of departments remain the same.

Each store is run by a store manager. These nine store managers report to the general manager who in turn is responsible to the president of the firm. Approximately 65 people are employed by Harper Brothers, which include store managers, clerks, and office personnel.

Inventory is taken twice a year, with the fiscal year beginning February 1 and ending January 31. This allows for the store to clear much of its Christmas inventories, which are very high in this type of retailing. A physical inventory is taken and checked against the inventory balances on the books. There has been some trouble in the past, with some of the store personnel taking merchandise home without paying for it.

The store draws its customers from approximately a 50-mile radius. Westmore is the county seat, with a population of around 5,000 people. The town is expanding and is continually attracting new industry to the community. Farming comprises the area's main industry, with this area being some of the richest farming land in the state. Consequently, the majority of the store's customers are farmers, and, therefore, the store makes a special effort to cater to this group. However, many of the customers are from Riverview (population of 90,000), which is located about 40 miles away. This group of customers should continue to increase upon completion of a new interstate highway system connecting the two towns. The store also receives considerable tourist business because Westmore is located on a well-traveled highway.

The store is located at the east end of the block and runs west along Main Street. It has a store front of approximately 130 feet and is approximately 65 feet deep on the east end. The main store houses Men's Wear, Women's Ready-to-Wear, Shoes, and Dry Goods. The Groceries and Meats are in the rear of the main store. Elevator service is provided for customers going upstairs to the Furniture store. Located next to the main store is the Hardware store, and located next to this is the Variety store. Customers can walk from one store to another inside. Free parking is provided in the rear of the store.

Post-World War II years found Harper Brothers beginning to experience difficulties in operations. A downward trend became quite evident in the middle fifties. Apparently, the source of much of Harper Brothers difficulty arose from faulty management. The general manager became very lax in his management policies. No control was exerted on the store managers, and they were left free to purchase goods as they deemed necessary for their stores. Before long, creditors were pressuring Harper Brothers to pay off its large accounts. Shelves were cleared of their inventories to raise necessary funds to meet payments. However, no new credit was extended to Harper Brothers to replace the sold merchandise, and, soon, low inventory stocks were depleted. Customers turned away when Harper Brothers could not supply them with the desired merchandise.

Because the general manager has been a long-time friend of the family, there is reluctance to replace him with a new manager. Other interfamily personal problems are also prevalent. Harper Brothers appears to be overstaffed with personnel, and much of the personnel are elderly people who are kept on the payroll because they have been "long-time, loyal employees." Thus, it seems that some employees are being kept on to a point beyond where they are producing sales efficiently. Added to this problem is the fact that the store's insurance and workman's compensation are higher than normal because of the large percentage of elderly people on the payroll. It should be noted also that there is a general rise in operating expenses, wages, and cost of merchandise.

Because Harper Brothers is a closely held corporation, no new capital is available for expansion and for present operations. The only capital available is that which is retained by the firm, and this amount is not very large because the stockholders withdraw most of it in dividends. The present store is badly in need of a modernization program—new fixtures, paint job, furnishings, store front, etc.

TABLE 1
Harper Brothers Company
Comparative Balance Sheets
as of January 31

ASSETS	1957	1958	1959	1960
CURRENT ASSETS:				
Cash on hand and in bank	$ 2,890	$ 8,434	$ 1,906	$ 5,110
Accounts Receivable—Trade	31,036	29,597	33,498	37,267
Contracts Receivable	6,213	6,585	1,865	1,874
Reserve for Bad Accounts	(5,581)	(5,427)	(5,304)	(5,871)
Accounts Receivable—Employees	11,315	6,144	8,868	7,344
Accounts Receivable—Stockholders		1,239	93	440
Inventory and Merchandise in transit	269,800	256,375	235,375	228,512
Miscellaneous Receivable	5,435	2,599	1,974	1,165
Prepaid Items	—	6,302	1,261	968
Total Current Assets	$321,108	$311,848	$279,536	$276,809
Land, Buildings, and Equipment—Dep.	70,524	65,391	67,391	61,906
Investments	23,682	16,006	15,452	14,626
Total Assets	$415,314	$393,245	$362,307	$353,341

LIABILITIES AND CAPITAL

	1957	1958	1959	1960
CURRENT LIABILITIES:				
Notes Payable—Bank	$ 12,500	$ 22,500	$ 20,000	$ 10,000
Trade Acceptances Payable	7,500		3,000	
Accounts Payable—Trade	37,829	37,820	38,631	102,121
Installment Contracts Payable			6,470	4,252
Accounts Payable—Stockholders	988	709	3,229	
Accrued Taxes and Other Items	13,068	12,332	11,965	13,766
Stock Purchase Account—Current	4,389	4,245	4,103	3,953
Total Current Liabilities	$ 76,274	$ 77,606	$ 84,398	$137,092
Stock Purchase Account—Deferred	26,000	23,000	20,000	17,000
Capital and Surplus	313,040	292,639	257,909	199,249
Total Liabilities and Capital	$415,314	$393,245	$362,307	$353,341

TABLE 2
Harper Brothers Company
Comparative Income Statements
for the Year Ending January 31

	1957	1958	1959	1960
NET SALES	$848,166	$819,195	$863,799	$869,684
COST OF SALES:				
Inventory, Beginning	250,265	258,403	248,513	229,897
Purchases	657,731	626,159	661,571	690,215
Freight and Express	10,766	9,518	10,270	8,493
	$918,762	$894,080	$920,354	$928,605
LESS: INVENTORY ENDING	258,403	248,513	229,897	220,826
	$660,359	$645,566	$690,457	$707,779
LESS: PURCHASES DISCOUNTS	8,423	7,429	7,051	3,264
NET COST OF SALES	$651,936	$638,137	$683,406	$704,515
GROSS PROFIT	$196,230	$181,058	$180,393	$165,169
LESS OPERATING EXPENSES:				
SELLING EXPENSES				
Advertising	$ 10,887	$ 7,019	$ 8,493	$ 9,662
Sales Salaries	82,296	83,540	87,594	90,350
Departmental—Direct	8,072	3,925	8,855	15,887
General Selling	31,506	40,093	39,644	33,141
	$132,771	$134,577	$144,586	$149,040
OTHER OPERATING EXPENSES:				
Buying	$ 1,870	$ 1,356	$ 1,376	$ 1,819
General and Administrative	46,046	40,968	45,072	45,933
Occupancy—Housekeeping	21,734	22,060	22,020	22,815
	$ 69,650	$ 64,384	$ 68,468	$ 70,567
TOTAL OPERATING EXPENSES	$202,421	$198,962	$213,054	$219,607
NET OPERATING LOSS	$(6,191)	$(17,904)	$(32,661)	$(54,438)
OTHER INCOME AND EXPENSES				
Dividends Received	$ 44	$ 44	$ 84	$ 45
Interest Received	541	843	1,113	107
Miscellaneous Income	752	249	844	(444)
Interest Paid	(1,391)	(2,466)	(2,942)	(2,920)
Provision for Federal and				
State Income Taxes	(15)	(150)	(10)	(10)
	(69)	(1,190)	(911)	(3,222)
NET LOSS	$ (6,260)	$ (19,094)	$ (33,572)	$ (57,660)

TABLE 3
Harper Brothers Company
Comparative 100% Statements
for the Year Ended January 31

	1957	1958	1959	1960
Net Sales	100.0%	100.0%	100.0%	100.0%
Cost of Goods Sold	77.9	78.8	79.9	81.4
Less: Purchase Discounts	1.0	0.9	0.8	0.4
Net Cost of Sales	76.9	77.9	79.1	81.0
GROSS PROFIT	23.1	22.1	20.9	19.0
Less: SELLING EXPENSES:				
Advertising Expenses	1.3	0.9	1.0	1.1
Sales Salaries	9.7	10.2	10.1	10.4
Departmental—Direct	1.0	0.5	1.0	1.8
General Selling	3.7	4.9	4.6	3.8
Total Selling Expenses	15.7	16.4	16.7	17.1
Less: OTHER OPERATING EXPENSES:				
Buying	0.2	0.2	0.2	0.2
General and Administrative	5.4	5.0	5.2	5.2
Occupancy—Housekeeping	2.6	2.7	2.5	2.6
TOTAL OPERATING EXPENSES	23.9	24.3	24.6	25.3
NET OPERATING LOSS	(0.7)	(2.2)	(3.8)	(6.3)
NET LOSS	(0.7)	(2.3)	(3.9)	(6.6)

TABLE 4
Harper Brothers Company
Comparative Merchandising Analysis Statements
For the Year Ended January 31, 1957

Store	Inventory Beginning	Purchases	Inventory Ending	Cost of Sales	Sales	Gross Profit
Dry Goods	$ 23,791	$ 40,630	$ 25,506	$ 38,915	$ 56,632	$ 17,717
Men's Wear	41,472	60,021	41,288	60,211	79,612	19,400
Shoes	19,522	29,305	23,329	25,497	27,758	12,261
Women's Wear	14,930	38,763	14,891	38,802	50,465	11,663
Variety	24,987	34,970	24,212	35,744	50,480	14,736
Hardware	47,801	107,222	47,334	107,688	151,078	43,390
Furniture	51,304	72,818	50,422	73,701	101,988	28,287
Groceries and Meats	26,458	284,762	31,420	279,801	320,152	40,353
TOTAL	$250,265	$668,491	$258,403	$660,359	$848,166	$187,807

For the Year Ended January 31, 1959

Store	Inventory Beginning	Purchases	Inventory Ending	Cost of Sales	Sales	Gross Profit
Dry Goods	$ 20,883	$ 36,926	$ 22,909	$ 34,900	$ 49,240	$ 14,340
Men's Wear	46,346	42,132	35,543	52,934	64,513	11,579
Shoes	23,468	18,991	21,271	21,188	30,411	9,222
Women's Wear	12,436	33,763	8,194	38,002	48,132	10,129
Variety	24,439	44,756	26,147	43,048	66,852	23,805
Hardware	48,200	102,933	45,626	105,506	142,908	37,402
Furniture	43,123	72,486	45,176	70,433	93,401	22,967
Groceries and Meats	29,618	319,854	25,028	324,445	368,342	43,898
TOTAL	$248,513	$671,841	$229,897	$690,457	$863,799	$173,342

TABLE 5
Harper Brothers Company
Typical Ratios
for Retail Department Stores

Ratio	National Average
CURRENT ASSETS TO CURRENT DEBT	3.53 times
NET PROFITS TO NET SALES	1.30%
NET PROFITS TO NET WORKING CAPITAL	6.34%
NEW SALES TO TANGIBLE NET WORTH	3.08 times
NET SALES TO NET WORKING CAPITAL	4.30 times
FIXED ASSETS TO TANGIBLE NET WORTH	25.9%
CURRENT DEBT TO TANGIBLE NET WORTH	29.4%
INVENTORY TO NET WORKING CAPITAL	69.7%
CURRENT DEBT TO INVENTORY	59.6%

Source: Dun & Bradstreet, *Dun's Review and Modern Industry.* November 1963, p. 39, Chicago, Illinois.

QUESTIONS

1. Analyze the financial statements of Harper Brothers Company. Indicate its strengths and weaknesses.
2. What action can be taken by management to rectify the situation?

Case 2
The First Forecasts

In March of 1969, Morgan Curtis, vice president of Midway Equipment Company, Inc., was faced with the task of preparing the first financial forecasts for the company. Midway was a new corporation which was just being formed to manufacture and sell a new type of amusement park ride vehicle that had been developed and tested over a period of several years by two imaginative mechanics in their spare time. The development of the new vehicle had taken place mainly in a garage-type workshop, and a patent application had been filed for the basic design, which employed several innovative principles. The inventors, Roger Hanley and Willard Martin, operated several of these vehicles on a demonstration basis at an amusement-industry convention, and this demonstration had led to some favorable publicity in a trade magazine. Messrs. Hanley and Martin felt that a good market existed for their new ride, but lacking experience in manufacturing and selling, they were not sure how to proceed other than to contemplate setting up their existing vehicles for local operation and building others in their workshop if somebody wanted to buy them.

The new ride caught the attention of Harry Sharp, an energetic salesman. After some marketing investigation on his own, he called on Messrs. Hanley and Martin and worked out an agreement with them to organize a manufacturing and sales enterprise. Mr. Sharp soon arranged for several of his associates to work with the new company, mostly part-time at first, with the idea of going full-time if the enterprise prospered, as Mr. Sharp, who immediately devoted his entire attention to Midway, was sure it would. Mr. Sharp and his associates invested $9,000 of their

This case was prepared by Professor Melvin J. Stanford of Brigham Young University as a basis for classroom discussion and not to illustrate either effective or ineffective handling of an administrative situation.

own money, and several other friends lent them $6,000, which they also invested. By late February, this money had been spent on organization and development costs, and Midway's management agreed that substantially more funds would be needed to go ahead on the scale they felt was feasible.

Mr. Curtis had a friend in an investment firm whom he planned to see about raising money. In addition, Fred Lyon, the production manager, knew an engineer at his regular job who was interested in new enterprises and who had some contacts at another investment banking house. In the latter part of February, Midway's officers met with the engineer, Albert Robbins, who was so favorably impressed with the new ride that he agreed to invest $5,000 cash of his own. Moreover, he felt that the investment banker whom he knew would probably be interested in providing whatever additional capital was required. On this basis, Albert Robbins and Morgan Curtis listed the following information which they thought would be needed in their discussions with potential investors.

1. Cash flow projection, one year by month, and a second year in total, at two levels of sales and production.
2. Pro forma income statements and balance sheets for the two first years' operations, with supporting detail on costs and marketing plans, at the two levels of sales and production.
3. A résumé for each member of Midway's management.
4. Color pictures and movies of the new vehicles in operation.
5. Written technical descriptions and specifications of the new vehicles.
6. Some letters of endorsement from potential customers, and the trade magazine article that had already been published.
7. Evidence of patent search and application.
8. Viable proof of incorporation.

Mr. Sharp and his associates set to work to put together all of the required information. Morgan Curtis, who was a Certified Public Accountant with some management experience, found that developing the detailed figures to use in the financial forecast was rather difficult at times because of the exuberant optimism of Harry Sharp. The latter, when asked about specific figures, would enthusiastically speak of sales forecasts that seemed too high to Mr. Curtis, who also thought Mr. Sharp's expense estimates were too low. By working many hours late at night and on weekends, however, in extended discussions with Messrs. Sharp, Lyon, and Herbert Jones (the executive vice president), and by adjusting some of their estimates to a more conservative basis, Mr. Curtis was able to develop what he felt were reasonable figures to use in the basic financial forecasts.

Harry Sharp was confident that he could personally sell 1,000 units a month to begin with, just as soon as they could be manufactured, in lots of 20 units. (It was considered that with adequate installation facilities, 20 vehicle units were about the right number to be run together.) The other members of management decided, however, that it was much more realistic to plan in terms of a salesman having to spend, on the average, about four days to sell 1 installation (20 units), which would amount to a monthly sales forecast of 100 units per salesman. Mr. Sharp agreed that he would primarily supervise the salesmen in their selling effort.

Initially, production would be a limiting factor of the number of units that would be available for sale. Sales promotion activities would also have to be built up to support the salesmen's efforts. Accordingly, it was decided that a realistic, yet conservative, total sales level would be 600 units per month as soon as production could reach that level. It was further agreed among the members of management that the lowest sales level they could imagine was 400 units per month, after production reached that level. Production would initially consist of assembling component parts purchased from other manufacturers. Later on, Midway would begin to manufacture any parts that it would be cheaper to make than to buy. Since the assembly process would require only moderately skilled workmen, Fred Lyon and Morgan Curtis calculated that it was reasonable to expect that 100 units could be produced in the month of April, 300 units in May, and 600 in June and thereafter. However, a more pessimistic alternative production forecast, which took into account possible startup delays as well as the lowest imagined sales level, was set at nothing in April, 100 units in May, 200 units in June, and 400 in July and thereafter.

Price of the units was initially set at $895 F.O.B. factory. This was below the price of competing ride equipment, and it was recognized that the $895 figure might need to be adjusted up or down at some later date, depending upon market acceptance and actual production and selling costs. Terms would be net 30, and Mr. Curtis estimated that 5 percent of sales would be ample provision for both bad debt expense and sales returns and allowances. Midway would sell direct to amusement park operators, with no dealers or middlemen.

Sales promotion plans centered around establishing and operating 12 company-owned locations, as subsidiary corporations, in various parts of the United States, as demonstrations to which salesmen could bring prospective buyers (or from which they could get referrals). The cost of each such location was estimated at $25,000, including $17,900 for 20 vehicle units (sold by Midway to its subsidiary) and the balance for installation facilities. (Midway officials expected to also develop profitable sales of installation platforms and accessories to buyers of vehicles, but little effort was being made to plan for this activity until after vehicle sales got under way.)

It seemed reasonable that the first such installation could be operating by late April, with two more added each month until a total of 12 were operating. The longest imaginable delay for this whole schedule was estimated as one month. Sales of these vehicles to subsidiary operating companies were included in the sales forecasts of 400 or 600 units per month.

Estimating revenue for these installations proved to be a problem because of the lack of adequate operating data. Exploratory calculations on the basis of 25 cents per ride and a maximum of 300 rides per hour (4-minute cycle time, 20 units), made the potential receipts look very attractive. Obviously, however, there would be some idle hours and seasons when receipts would be much lower. Moreover, Mr. Curtis wanted to be especially conservative with these receipt figures since they did not represent Midway's principal intended source of revenue. Accordingly, it was decided to forecast net receipts from each installation at $6,000 per month at the expected level and $3,000 per month at a minimum level, starting in the month following startup of each installation. These figures were net of all operating expenses but did not reflect any deduction for depreciation (estimated at 20 percent per year) on the $25,000 which would be invested in each installation.

Manufacturing costs were developed in detail by Fred Lyon and reviewed with Morgan Curtis. Component parts had cost the investors $350 per unit, but they agreed that this cost could be cut substantially by shopping around and quantity buying. After discussions with several suppliers, a $254 per unit cost of component parts was forecast to start with. Purchase terms were usually 30 days net, and a one-month inventory of parts was desired. In addition, Midway would have to purchase some hand tools and molds for $3,000, with an estimated three-year life. Other tools and equipment would be leased by Midway, and a factory building would be rented. It would cost about $2,000 in March to make the building ready for use. Total factory operating costs, including payroll, utilities, rentals, etc., were estimated at $4,000 for the first month of production; and in the second month $8,000 at the expected level (300 units), and $6,000 at the lower level (200 units); and in the third and following months $9,000 for 600 units, and $7,000 for 400 units of production.

General, administrative, and engineering expenses were forecast at the expected (600-unit) level, to be $11,000 for March, $13,000 in April, $16,000 per month for May through August, and $20,000 per month thereafter (except in December, $30,000). At the lower (400-unit) level, the forecast was $11,000 per month for March and April, $13,000 for May, $15,000 per month for June through August, and $18,000 per month thereafter (except in December, $20,000).

Marketing expenses, including sales salaries and commissions, travel expense, advertising, and miscellaneous (but excluding the investment of $25,000 per company installation) were planned at $5,000 for March. At the expected 600-unit level of operations, the estimate was $10,000 per month for April and May and $30,000 per month thereafter. At the lower (400-unit) level, the estimate was $10,000 per month for April, May, and June, and $20,000 per month thereafter.

A minimum cash balance of $30,000 was desired for March, with $50,000 for April and May, and $100,000 thereafter. However, Mr. Curtis felt that at the possible lower level (400 units per month) of operation, they could get along with a minimum cash balance of $10,000 in March and $50,000 thereafter.

A calendar year was thought to be satisfactory for tax and accounting purposes. However, Mr. Curtis wanted to prepare the cash forecasts on a fiscal year ending February 28 in order to show to prospective investors the projected cash flow of a full year of operations.

Common stock was to be issued at $1 per share. Messrs. Hanley and Martin were to receive 450,000 shares for their development work on the vehicle. They would continue to work on refinements of the vehicle design but did not wish to take an active part in management. Any patent rights would be assigned to Midway as intangible assets. The management group was to also receive a total of 450,000 shares of stock for its efforts in organizing and managing the enterprise, including what they had spent on organization costs, and for the effort to raise outside capital. A tentative balance sheet as of March 1, 1969, is shown in Exhibit 1.

After carefully reviewing the foregoing data, Mr. Curtis felt that he was ready to prepare the necessary financial forecasts. Whatever these forecasts showed the cash need to be, he knew that the four members of Midway management and the two investors wanted to get started as quickly as possible. He knew that they also wished to minimize the amount of equity sold to outside interests and would not in any event want to sell shares equal to more than 20 percent of the resulting total capital stock.

EXHIBIT 1
Midway Equipment Company, Inc.
Tentative Balance Sheet
March 1, 1969

ASSETS
Cash	$ 5,000
Tangible Organization Costs	15,000*
Patents and Intangible Organization Costs	885,000**
Total Assets	$905,000

LIABILITIES
Advance from A. Robbins	$ 5,000

CAPITAL
Common Stock, $1 per share	900,000
Total Liabilities and Capital	$905,000

*To be amortized over 5 years.
**To be amortized over 10 years.

QUESTIONS

1. Prepare cash flow projections for the first year by months (for fiscal year ending February 28, 1970), and for the second year in total (for fiscal year ending February 28, 1971).
2. Prepare pro forma income statements and balance sheets for the fiscal years ending February 28, 1970, and February 28, 1971.
3. Based on your analysis, should Midway proceed? Why or why not?

Case 3
Western Nursery, Inc.

Western Nursey was organized in 1957 by Mr. George Kearns. The business was initially centered around the raising of plants and flowers in a small greenhouse on George Kearns' property. From 1957, until 1972, the business was operated on a part-time basis, with some continuing development of the plant and floral lawn care service. Shortly after George Kearns' son, Dennis, returned from the military service in late 1972, the business was incorporated. Dennis and his wife were the incorporators. They soon established a retail facility, and offered major landscaping services as well.

In January, 1975, Dennis Kearns was to meet with Mr. David Shafer, the Business Loan Director, of Farmers Union Bank, in Omaha, Nebraska. The purpose of the meeting was to discuss short-term financing for Western Nursery during 1975. During the past three years, Dennis Kearns had borrowed from Farmers Union Bank to cover the firm's cash requirements, and to finance the Nursery's inventory of fertilizers, tools, plants, and pesticides, all of which were sold through the retail facility.

Prior to his meeting with Mr. Shafer, Dennis Kearns was reviewing the performance of his operation since its incorporation in early 1973—and also remembering Mr. Shafer's reluctance to lend the nursery short-term funding during 1974. Mr. Shafer had indicated during their last meeting that he was unhappy about the nursery's lack of financial planning, and that it would be more difficult to borrow in the future. Neither Dennis Kearns, nor his wife, had received any formal training in accounting or business finances. The nursery did employ the services of a

This case was prepared by James A. Kosse, MBA student at Creighton University, under the direction of Professor Charles R. Wagner of the University of South Dakota, as a basis for classroom discussion and not to illustrate either effective or ineffective handling of an administrative situation.

public accountant, who provided the owners monthly Profit and Loss Statements, and annual Income Statements and Balance Sheets.

Mr. Kearns felt that there were two primary reasons behind his need for heavy short-term financing: First, the seasonal nature of the business itself required him to borrow to finance the inventory of goods sold through the retail facility, and, second, a sizable portion of the annual revenue was generated through large landscaping projects. Mr. Kearns' usual practice was to bid on such projects, and then collect two payments (based on completion rates of 50% and 100%), over the life of the project. Generally, a heavy investment in retail goods, plus the need to invest large sums of money in landscaping projects for which no payment will be received until the projects are 50% complete, placed Mr. Kearns in the position of having to borrow heavily. Exhibit 1 presents the Balance Sheets that Mr. Kearns was reviewing prior to his meeting with Mr. Shafer.

Sales had grown steadily throughout 1972, 1973, and 1974. Figure 1 shows a summary of monthly sales for the period 1972-1974.

FIGURE 1
Western Nursery
Sales: 1972-1974

Month	1972	1973	1974
Jan.	$ 2,819	$ 3,320	$ 5,120
Feb.	3,166	3,805	5,395
Mar.	4,429	5,522	6,076
Apr.	7,051	8,717	11,694
May	12,052	15,127	18,857
June	10,522	13,111	16,906
July	12,093	15,179	18,922
Aug.	9,233	11,498	14,863
Sept.	8,043	10,164	12,218
Oct.	4,844	5,852	8,328
Nov.	3,042	3,960	4,439
Dec.	5,546	7,145	8,132
Total	$82,660	$103,400	$130,950

Dennis Kearns was expecting sales during 1975 to increase 10% over the 1974 level, and believed that because of increases in both retail store sales, and large landscaping projects, sales should reach $144,000 during 1975. However, he also knew that the sales figures for the years 1972-1974 included credit sales for large landscaping projects for which cash would not be received for 60 to 90 days after the sale was entered on the books. He therefore compared total sales for 1974 to actual cash receipts during the same period.

Mr. Kearns knew that Western Nursery's cost of sales had been 34.77% of total sales during 1974. He believed that this figure would remain the same throughout 1975. He also believed that sales of retail items would be at a dollar level that would result in a figure for percentage-to-total sales, which would be the same as in 1974.

Another area of concern to Mr. Kearns was that of Operating Expenses. Figure 2 shows monthly Operating Expenses for the period 1972 through 1974.

FIGURE 2
Western Nursery
Operating Expenses: 1972-1974

Month	1972	1973	1974
Jan.	$ 2,542	$ 3,095	$ 3,462
Feb.	3,206	3,754	4,538
Mar.	3,373	4,111	4,587
Apr.	3,667	4,474	4,982
May	5,120	6,233	6,972
June	5,779	6,747	8,203
July	5,682	6,662	8,034
Aug.	4,720	5,786	6,381
Sept.	4,269	5,036	6,001
Oct.	4,249	5,145	5,818
Nov.	3,479	4,069	4,932
Dec.	4,559	5,344	6,444
Total	$50,645	$60,456	$70,354

Because the expenses which comprised total Operating Expenses were for the most part fixed, except for labor, Mr. Kearns felt that 1975 Operating Expenses could be controlled to a level of $80,000 during the year.

Again referring to the Balance Sheet for December 31, 1974 (Exhibit 1), Mr. Kearns was concerned about a number of items. First, the inventory level of $8,347 was $5,000 higher than was necessary for Western Nursery to conduct business during the slow winter months of January, February, and March. One goal Mr. Kearns set for 1975 was to finish the year with an inventory level $5,000 below that of 1974. Second, a short-term note of $5,506 was outstanding to the Farmers Union Bank. Mr. Kearns knew that Mr. Shafer of the Farmers Union Bank would not lend him additional funds during 1975 until this outstanding note was paid. Approximately $11,000 was being carried in Western's cash account. Most of Mr. Kearns' cash reserves were being held to pay the $3,901 in accounts payable as of December 31, 1974, plus the $5,506 note owed to the Farmers Union Bank.

Mr. Kearns estimated that $45,000 in fertilizers, tools, pesticides, and other lawn care items would be required throughout 1975 to meet the needs of his retail store customers. He estimated, based on the buying habits and seasonal requirements of his customers, that his inventory would have to be replenished during the following periods:

April,	1975	$20,000
June,	1975	$10,000
August,	1975	$10,000
November,	1975	$ 5,000
Total Purchases		$45,000

Mr. Kearns was still dissatisfied at this point in his analysis. He knew that if he were to repay the note to the bank, plus pay off the nursery's accounts payable, he would have little trouble securing a loan from the bank for his spring inventory requirements. At the same time, Mr. Kearns was concerned that in depleting his cash reserves early in the year, he might have to secure additional financing, above the funds required for inventory, just to meet operating expenses and retain a cash balance of at least $2,000.

With the information assembled thus far, Mr. Kearns consulted his accountant, who prepared the following Pro Forma Income Statement for December 31, 1975.

FIGURE 3
Western Nursery
Pro Forma Income Statement
December 31, 1975

Sales	$144,000
Cost of Sales	50,069
Gross Profit	$ 93,931
Operating Expenses	80,000
Net Profit before Taxes	$ 13,931
Taxes (20%)	2,786
Net Profit After Taxes	$ 11,145

EXHIBIT 1

Western Nursery
Balance Sheet Summary

	Dec. 31, 1972		Dec. 31, 1973		Dec. 31, 1974	
ASSETS						
Current Assets						
Cash		$ 2,594		$ 705		$11,177
Accounts Rec.		3,471		9,978		2,893
Inventory		10,127		7,186		8,347
Other		3,320		126		713
Total Current Assets		$19,512		$17,995		$23,130
Fixed Assets						
Furn. & Fixtures	$ 1,578		$ 469		$ 5,195	
Res. for Depreciation	1,261	317	78	391	550	4,645
Mach. & Equipment	12,081		4,362		4,362	
Res. for Depreciation	6,575	5,506	631	3,731	1,510	2,852
Motor Vehicles	13,191		10,307		10,307	
Res. for Depreciation	8,946	4,246	2,528	7,779	5,643	4,664
Total Fixed Assets		$10,069		$11,901		$12,161
Other Assets		—		6,118		5,127
Total Assets		$29,581		$36,014		$40,418
LIABILITIES						
Current Liabilities						
Accounts Payable		$ 3,998		$ 5,329		$ 3,901
Notes Payable		—		3,800		5,506
Other		—		744		429
Total Curr. Liabilities		$ 3,998		$ 9,873		$ 9,836
Long-Term Liabilities						
Notes Payable*		—		18,826		16,826
Total Liabilities		$ 3,998		$28,699		$26,662
CAPITAL						
Capital Stock	$13,000		$ 500		$ 500	
Earned Surplus	12,583	25,583	6,815	7,315	13,256	13,756
Total Liab. & Net Worth		$29,581		$36,014		$40,418

*Payment of $500.00 required in March, June, September, and December.

EXHIBIT 2

Western Nursery
1974 Sales and Cash Receipts

Month	Year	Total Sales	Cash Sales	Credit Receipts 30 Day	60 Day	90 Day	Total Cash Receipts
Dec.	1973	$ 7,145	$5,359	—	—	—	—
Jan.	1974	5,120	3,584	$1,429	$ 198	$ 293	$ 5,504
Feb.	1974	5,395	3,776	1,024	357	198	5,355
Mar.	1974	6,076	4,253	1,079	256	—	5,588
Apr.	1974	11,694	7,016	1,215	270	256	8,757
May	1974	18,857	7,544	2,339	304	270	10,457
June	1974	16,906	6,763	3,771	1,169	304	12,007
July	1974	18,922	7,570	3,381	3,771	1,169	15,891
Aug.	1974	14,863	5,944	3,784	3,381	3,771	16,880
Sept.	1974	12,218	7,330	2,973	3,784	3,381	17,468
Oct.	1974	8,328	5,830	2,444	2,973	3,784	15,031
Nov.	1974	4,439	3,107	1,666	1,222	2,973	8,968
Dec.	1974	8,132	6,099	888	416	1,222	8,625
Jan.	1975	—	—	1,626	222	416	
Feb.	1975	—	—	—	407	222	
Mar.	1975	—	—	—	—	—	

QUESTIONS

1. Prepare monthly pro forma income statements for Western Nursery, Inc., for 1975.
2. Prepare monthly pro forma balance sheets for 1975.
3. Estimate the total bank credit required for each month during 1975.
4. Review the forecasts and the assumptions on which they are based. On the basis of these forecasts, should Western Nursery be given additional short-term financing? Why or why not?

Case 4
Joyce-Page Men's Clothiers

Prior to opening a retail men's clothing store, William Page and James Joyce had been good friends for fifteen years. This friendship had been the result of a chance meeting at a clothing manufacturer's fair. As a Tennett Company manufacturer's representative, Joyce had impressed Page and sold him a new line of suits and overcoats for the Ohio Clothing Store of Youngstown, Ohio. This friendship evolved into a working relationship.

Over the years, Bill Page had worked as a manufacturer's representative for the three largest men's clothing manufacturers in the United States and Canada. After traveling for twelve years, he settled down and opened a small retailing store in a shopping center in Youngstown, Ohio. His business was successful for two years but then began to slowly lose its share of the market due to competitive disadvantages. Cash shortages and inability to borrow large sums of money due to a lack of collateral impacted both his cash and inventory position. After two years of business, he liquidated the firm at a nominal profit of $36,000.

While living in Youngstown, Page and Joyce had gotten together many times, and business was occasionally discussed. Eventually, they considered a partnership and owning a business together. Joyce was a middle-aged, conservative clothing store salesman. Most fellow retailers readily admitted that Joyce was the most successful salesman for the Ohio Clothing Store and had made a good deal of money. However, Joyce was very disappointed in his upward mobility in the

This case was prepared by Thomas F. Connors, MBA Student at Creighton University, under the direction of Professor Charles R. Wagner, of the University of South Dakota, as a basis for classroom discussion and not to illustrate either effective or ineffective handling of an administrative situation.

corporation. Ultimately, Joyce and Page decided to make the move in the early fall of 1973.

William Page and James Joyce then opened a men's specialty store in suburban Youngstown. The store stocked men's top-quality suits, coats, slacks, shirts, and accessories for work, dress, or leisure. The owners felt that Youngstown lacked a personalized quality clothing store for men and that there was an unlimited demand for just such a service.

The store was located near the center of the metropolitan area and on a major arterial street. The building was a two-story colonial type which had access to an adequate amount of parking. Only the first floor was used for retail selling space, while the second floor was idle except for a couple of small offices. The atmosphere of the store was cozy, neat, and luxurious. Both the owners and sales personnel were efficient and attentive to the needs of all customers. The owners felt that personalized service for all customers was a necessity in order to maintain repeat business and growth. From the initial opening, the store proved to be a very successful operation. This could be attributed to both owners since both had been established retailers individually. When Mr. Joyce left the Ohio Clothing Store, he brought most of his clientele with him as well as a vast amount of expertise in the selling end of the business. Mr. Page gave the partnership a varied and complete knowledge of retailing. During the many years Page had acted as a manufacturer's representative for the three largest men's clothing manufacturers, he developed the ability to recognize style trends, better methods of merchandising, and the importance of special offers. Page's experience in an independent business operation had strengthened his previous knowledge of retailing.

The marketing strategy was based on the premise that only men who are successful and over age 30 would be willing and able to afford their products. All of the items in the store's inventory were top-quality and high-priced in accordance with this merchandising policy. The owners established the objective that any customer's purchase would project an image of being and looking well-dressed. If the customer was not satisfied after tailoring had been completed, the item could be returned at no cost to the purchaser. (This is the primary reason for the large returns indicated in the financial statements.)

Messrs. Page and Joyce use only the local newspaper as an advertising medium. Mr. Joyce has maintained that the sports section is the only logical place for advertising, and this is where all ads have been placed. Mr. Page has been told many times by personal friends and customers that they have never seen the company advertisement. This revelation disturbed him and forced him into studying marketing and advertising. After thorough analysis, he has determined that the ad should be alternated daily between the business and sports section. He intended to survey customer preference through personal contact. Mr. Joyce, not in full agreement, allowed the trial for one month before evaluation.

The owners had established their business in September, 1973. At the grand opening, many inventory lines had not been delivered by the manufacturers. This delay in getting stocked continued to slow operations during the first quarter. But both Page and Joyce felt that the company could reach sales of $300,000 during the first year in business and be very profitable. Exhibits I and II reveal that the store had been profitable and had reached the sales objective in ten months. The owners were very satisfied with the progress of the store in the short time the business had been opened.

It was during 1974 that the country was plagued with many economic problems. Mr. Page felt that the business was recession-proof because their clothing lines catered to the upper-middle-class professional and business people. Mr. Page felt that his and Mr. Joyce's clientele were successful age-30-or-over businessmen and professional people who were "solid fixtures of the local economy." He further stated that "these men will buy at least two suits a year regardless of the state of the economy." Mr. Joyce agreed that the business was sheltered by the clientele, but had a few reservations in regard to Page's clientele. Mr. Joyce felt that the clientele for each owner could be broken down as such:

Mr. Joyce's Clientele (40% of Sales)	Mr. Page's Clientele (45% of Sales)
1) Conservative dressers	1) Liberal dressers
2) Successful	2) Semisuccessful
3) Middle-age (40+)	3) Lower 30's - mid 40's
4) 50% Doctors	4) 90% Businessmen
5) 30% Businessmen	5) 10% Professional
6) 20% Professional	

Mr. Joyce felt that since his clientele were older, they would have lower household expenses and higher incomes, which would negate economic woes. This was not always the case with Mr. Page's clientele, who were younger, had house payments, and families to raise.

The owners received the twelve-month figures from their company bookkeeper and were very pleased with the performance. (See Exhibits 3 and 4.) The sales and net income before taxes were well beyond their best estimates when considering the recession and inflation during the past six months. It was then that the bookkeeper expressed her concern that the owners had just looked at the income for the year, that the company had lost money in August and that it was continuing to do so at present. Mr. Page expressed the opinion that such a case was impossible and she should recalculate all entries. Mr. Joyce stated that it was just a bad month and "we'll get it back and much more at Christmas time."

The bookkeeper was also asked to prepare cash budgets for September and October after the August Income Statement (see Exhibit 5) was presented to the owners. The owners agreed that sales for September would be near $22,000 and increase to $40,000 for October because of fall fashions and the holiday season. In the past, credit sales had averaged 60% of every sales dollar and 5% were uncollectible. Credit revenues were always collected the month after the sale.

A listing of all monthly fixed expenses was standard procedure for the company and is as follows:

Owners' Salaries	$4,166
Rent	770
Insurance	400
Security Services	132
Professional Service (bi-monthly, next payment October 1)	2,279

All other cash expenses were variable and had been increasing due to economic cost pressures. The bookkeeper estimated all items as a percentage of total sales and listed them as follows:

Employees' Salaries	6.0%
Advertising	5.5
Office Supplies	1.5
Interest	2.0
Utilities	3.25
Miscellaneous	7.5

The owners agreed that this was the maximum payout for the next two months, and although they showed concern over the amounts (dollars and percentages), they were both quite confident that the upcoming holiday season would increase their sales as they had estimated.

EXHIBIT 1
Balance Sheet
Joyce-Page Company (Unaudited)
As of February 28, 1974

Assets

Cash	$ 9,286	
Accounts Receivable	31,972	
Inventories	86,738	
Total Current Assets		$127,996
Equipment & Property	3,548	
Less: Accumulated Depreciation	402	3,146
Utility Deposit		275
Organization Expense (Net)		889
TOTAL ASSETS		$132,306

Liabilities & Owners' Equity

Accounts Payable	$17,329	
Other Current Liabilities	3,717	
Total Current Liabilities		$ 21,046
Notes Payable—Officers		27,500
Notes Payable—Bank		50,575
Capital Stock		5,500
Retained Earnings		27,685
TOTAL LIABILITIES & OWNERS' EQUITY		$132,306

EXHIBIT 2

Joyce-Page Company

Periodic Income Statements (Unaudited)

Period from September 1, 1973 - July 31, 1974

	First Six Months (Sept.-Feb.)	*Third Quarter (Mar.-May)*	*June*	*July*
Gross Sales	$204,207	$122,112	$40,337	$35,290
Less: Returns & Allowances	(19,311)	(14,035)	(5,324)	(6,701)
Other Income	1,650	—	—	—
NET SALES	$186,546	$108,077	$35,013	$28,589
Less Expenses:				
Cost of Goods Sold	99,279	60,161	18,268	15,838
Salaries	7,516	4,201	1,233	1,793
Travel	905	—	—	—
Advertising	5,940	3,649	1,188	1,401
Selling Supplies	1,375	1,014	186	620
Miscellaneous	9,264	5,666	1,592	2,563
Rent	4,510	2,310	770	770
Insurance	2,298	1,084	427	230
Donations	261	6	6	—
Security	264	132	—	132
Interest	2,633	1,405	408	518
Professional Services	2,279	2,279	—	2,279
Utilities	1,867	981	—	657
TOTAL EXPENSES	$138,391	$ 82,888	$24,150	$26,801
TOTAL INCOME Before Taxes	$ 48,155	$ 25,189	$10,863	$ 1,788

EXHIBIT 3
Joyce-Page Company
Balance Sheet (Unaudited)
As of August 31, 1974

Assets

Cash	$ 4,124	
Accounts Receivable	49,160	
Inventories	132,537	
Total Current Assets		$185,821
Equipment & Property	3,548	
Less: Accumulated Depreciation	548	3,000
Utility Deposit		275
Organization Expense (Net)		800
TOTAL ASSETS		**$189,896**

Liabilities & Owners' Equity

Accounts Payable	$ 46,020	
Other Current Liabilities	4,796	
Total Current Liabilities		$ 50,816
Notes Payable—Officers		26,000
Notes Payable—Bank		48,300
Capital Stock		5,500
Retained Earnings		59,280
TOTAL LIABILITIES & EQUITY		**$189,896**

EXHIBIT 4
Joyce-Page Company
Income Statement (Unaudited)
For the Year Ended August 31, 1974

Gross Sales	$430,460	
Less: Returns & Allowances	51,620	
Net Sales		$378,840
Add: Other Income		1,650
TOTAL REVENUES		$380,490
Less: Expenses	$211,751	
Cost of Goods Sold	16,393	
Salaries	16,393	
Travel	905	
Advertising	13,899	
Selling Supplies	3,345	
Miscellaneous	21,075	
Rent	9,130	
Insurance	4,269	
Donations	273	
Security	528	
Interst	5,626	
Professional Services	9,116	
Utilities	4,430	
TOTAL EXPENSES		$300,740
NET INCOME Before Taxes		$ 79,750

EXHIBIT 5
Joyce-Page Company
Income Statement for August

Gross Sales	$ 28,514	
Less: Returns & Allowances	6,249	
Net Sales		$ 22,265
Less: Expenses	$ 18,205	
Cost of Goods Sold	$ 18,205	
Cost of Goods Sold	1,650	
Salaries	1,721	
Advertising	1,721	
Miscellaneous	1,990	
Other	4,994	
TOTAL EXPENSES		$ 28,510
NET INCOME (LOSS) Before Taxes		($ 6,245)

QUESTIONS

1. Analyze the financial statements of Joyce-Page Men's Clothiers, indicating the strengths and weaknesses of the company.

2. What major factors have contributed to the decline in the profitability of the firm that occurred in August? Could these factors have been anticipated?
3. Prepare a cash budget for September and October 1974. Be explicit about your assumptions.

Case 5
Tape Town, Incorporated

Background

Peter Adams, III and Lee Bradford, seniors at Eastern University, wanted to start a business which would grow and mature while they were in graduate school. Their plans were to remain in Georgetown after graduation. They sought a business in which they could act as owners and hire a manager to supervise day-to-day activities. Close friends since childhood, both came from financially comfortable backgrounds. They hoped to restrict their investment to $10,000 to $15,000, unless an unusually inviting proposition presented itself.

One objective was to enter a field in which they could quickly become the area leader. Reviews were made of several franchise propositions involving (1) quick foods, (2) coin-operated laundries and dry cleaning facilities, (3) car rental services, and (4) a Datsun dealership. In their research, they came across a franchise for an auto tape center. After a thorough analysis of the franchise, they decided to enter this field, but with their own independent tape center rather than with a franchise company.

Peter and Lee proceeded to develop and analyze this business venture. They discussed it with their fathers, both successful businessmen, who were impressed with the project. At the suggestion of both parents, Marshall Johnson, President of the Georgetown National Bank, was contacted to discuss the prospects for a loan. On August 30, 1970, they met with Mr. Johnson, who appeared quite impressed with their enthusiasm and approach to selecting this new business. The banker was

This case was prepared by Professors Ganas K. Rakes and Thomas L. Wheelen of the University of Virginia, with student research assistance, as the basis for classroom discussion and not to illustrate either effective or ineffective handling of an administrative situation.

familiar with both families and asked, "Will your fathers be willing to endorse the loan if it is granted?" Peter responded, "No, Mr. Johnson, between us we have a total net worth of $25,000. I have $10,000 in securities and $5,000 in your bank, and Lee has $8,000 in securities and $2,000 in cash." Peter then added, "Neither of us needs our money for graduate school since this will be financed by our families." Johnson replied, "You are fortunate young gentlemen, and I am glad to see that you are attempting to make it on your own in the business world. Your fathers must be proud of you. I will be more than happy to review your loan application. Submit your formal proposal, and after a review, we can discuss it. Please feel free to call on the bank for any assistance." Peter and Lee agreed that they would submit the formal proposal within the next two weeks.

Loan Proposal

To: Mr. Marshall Johnson, President
         Georgetown National Bank
From: Peter Adams III and Lee Bradford
Subject: Loan Application for TAPE TOWN, INC.

We conceived this project after noting the claims of several business magazine articles that stereo tape cartridges and cassettes were revolutionizing the prerecorded music industry. Sales growth of 40% was predicted as commonplace, and the relatively small initial investment required to enter this industry was emphasized.

When we speak of prerecorded tapes, we mean tape cartridges and cassettes. The cartridge, highly touted as a replacement for the old reel-to-reel procedure, was developed in the mid-fifties, but did not become a commercial craze until 1962, when a four-track cartridge was introduced by Earl Muntz on the West Coast. The cartridge was vastly improved in 1965 by inventor Bill Lear (of Lear Jet), with the creation of an eight-track cartridge, capable of carrying eight tracks (four stereo tracks) of music instead of four. The first cartridge equipment was a player designed for auto use, which continues to be the largest use of tape equipment. The prerecorded tape industry was further revolutionized by a technilogical breakthrough, the cassette, introduced to the United States in 1966 by N.V. Phillips of Holland. The smaller cassette is an ever-increasing portion of prerecorded tape sales. Cassette equipment demand was, until recently, almost completely satisfied by the Norelco line of cassette players, manufactured by the American subsidiary of N.V. Phillips. Cartridge players hold the edge in the auto market, with cassette players capturing the greatest part of the portable and home market. Cartridge systems have not been very successful in homes because of their lack of recording ability and their inability to reverse the tape once a selection has begun. The cassette has its drawback too, though, in that it is recorded at a lower speed (1 ⅞ i.p.s.) and so has lesser fidelity than the cartridge. Technology, however, is rapidly closing the gap.

Tape equipment is also booming and was the fastest-growing consumer electronic product in 1969 (see Exhibit 1). Seventy-five percent of the equipment is made in Japan and Europe. Profit margins are almost as great on equipment as on tapes, and the future of tape equipment is as varied as the use of the tape itself.

EXHIBIT 1

Tape Town, Inc.

Tape and Equipment Sales (in millions)

Year	Tape	Equip.	Total
1968	$225	$367.5	$ 592.5
1969	401	549	950
1970	694	719	1,413

Source: Forbes, October 1, 1969.

We gained a tremendous amount of working knowledge by interviewing Mr. Tab Brown, the owner-manager of The House for Car Stereos in the large city of Athol. This is a franchise operation. Mr. Brown discussed inventory, finance, merchandising, and installation. We then visited an independent dealer, Tune Times, Ltd., also in Athol. Mr. Carl Ground, the manager, was most cooperative and described his business from an independent's point of view. It was after these two visits that we decided to become an independent outlet.

Appraisal of Competition

Georgetown has a city-county population of 75,000 and a projected annual growth rate of 10%. In addition, the local university has a population of 11,000 students and a projected yearly increase of approximately 7-8%. The age groups of the present population are distributed very nearly like those of the U.S. tape-buying population, and these age groups are estimated to have more disposable income than the national average. Georgetown is a regional buying area and attracts almost 6% of its retail customers from surrounding counties. There are 4,500 cars at the university alone, with only an estimated 1% of these cars equipped with auto tape players.

At the City Planner's office, we reviewed a 1969 market analysis of Georgetown that had been conducted by a national management consulting firm. This document contained detailed information concerning (1) population age breakdowns, (2) population projections by age groups, (3) disposable income, and (4) buying pattern analysis by age groups with respect to the three main shopping areas—Shopper's World (45 stores), downtown Georgetown (85 stores), and West Main Street, immediately adjacent to the university (15 specialty stores). We also found retail projections for each of these areas. We used this information as the basis for analyzing our present and potential competition and as a means of selecting a location.

We felt that prerecorded tape sales had a great future. But was it feasible in Georgetown? Our first impression, encouraged primarily by our knowledge of the tremendous record sales in Georgetown, was that such a business was indeed feasible. We realized, though, that a survey of the present tape sellers in town was needed. We compiled a list of nine dealers who, we felt, carried the most stereo tapes in cartridge or cassette form. None of these were solely in the tape retailing business, but, instead, ranged from a national discount store to a drugstore. We attempted to determine the approximate weekly sales of cartridges and/or cassettes, the average inventory (at least on the selling floor), the types of selections available, and the lines of equipment carried for each of the stores. The results are shown below:

Store	Weekly Tape Sales	Weekly Equipment Sales
1	35+	10+
2,3	15-35	3-9
4	15-35	
5,6	0-15	0-3
7,8	0-15	
9	0-3	

These data are approximate, and are, in some cases, our own estimates. Only one store carried a relatively full line of tape equipment, most of which was cartridge players. Only two of the men appeared to have a working knowledge of tape sales, which seems to reinforce our conclusion that no store was that intense about tape sales.

Several stores sold their tapes in boxed units quite different from those we intend to sell, so that we consider these tapes in a different market from ours. Tape sales to these people, we feel, are just an "add-on" value to the primary record sales or drugstore sales, whereas ours are to be our livelihood and chief interest.

Our final assessment of the competition was that no substantial competition now exists in Georgetown. We know that this city has been under consideration as a possible tape outlet by one franchise, and this indicates potential to us. We feel that our total commitment to tape sales aimed specifically at the Georgetown youth market will be a sufficient marketing advantage to allow us to compete profitably. Our specialization and a policy of selling at lower prices should provide sufficient volume to develop favorable relationships (quality discounts) with our suppliers. We will use substantial advertising to help develop this lower price-youth identification. The result should be a substantial share of the area demand for prerecorded music.

Market Analysis

We have examined the selling side of tape sales and feel reasonably assured that we can gain a substantial market share within our first year of operation. But what about customers? Is there enough demand to support our efforts?

First, we examined the profile of the tape customer nationally. At one extreme is the home tape enthusiast. This person is often a "classical" hi-fi buff who has used reel-to-reel tapes for several years and who owns component stereo equipment with hi-fidelity speakers. He is now turning to tape cartridges because of their ease of use and storage, but still expects his tape equipment to have good speaker and amplifier quality.

The intermediate unit is the eight-track cartridge auto player, primarily purchased by the young man who buys pop-rock music to play in his car. Eighty-five percent of this equipment is owned by people under 25 years of age. The largest segment of this bracket is the 16-25 group, for which the car is really home. The auto tape player is used to create a mood that no car radio can. The eight-track customer is primarily interested in a tape selection that is current and presently prefers the cartridge to the cassette because the cassette player is difficult to use in a car.

At the other extreme of the prerecorded tape spectrum is the cassette customer. He prizes his mobility because of the rapid pace of his life. His music goes where he goes, and high fidelity is less important than volume.

The youthful tape market is the market of today, but what of tomorrow? The adult customer is becoming increasingly important. The young customer may spend an hour in the store and buy only one tape, while his parents will buy five tapes in less time. Also, home equipment, aimed at the adult, represents a larger purchase per unit than auto or portable equipment. The displays and atmosphere of our store would take the adult into consideration while still maintaining "communication" with the younger set through pop selections and bright decorations (see Exhibits 2 and 3).

Location

Before we began the search for actual buildings in which to locate this company, we set up a few guidelines which we felt were necessary for any location. The first requirement was that the location be near ample parking facilities. We further felt that any location should have space available that could be used for our operations involving installations of auto tape decks. Finally, we felt it important that the location be on a major thoroughfare. We felt that these prerequisites were necessary to give the company an adequate drawing potential.

Reference to the Georgetown City Zoning Map revealed that a B-3 zoning classification would be necessary for our business. This restriction automatically limited our choices. Our first preference was the shopping center, but the space required would cost $700 per month plus a percentage of our sales. We felt this to be too costly. Also, several potential competitors were located in the center and could prevent our entry, since this was a provision in their lease contracts. We chose a building on a corner one block from the main shopping area of the city. The building in question is handled by Doyle Realty, Inc., and rents for $350 per month with utilities and air conditioning included. The selected location meets all of our initial requirements. It is on a main thoroughfare with an average daily traffic count of 6,710 in 1969 and a peak-hour volume of 642 between 5:00-6:00 P.M. In addition, it faces two one-way streets which have parking spaces on either side and a large downtown parking lot which provides free parking for shoppers. Another feature considered was the fact that the building contained garage space, with facilities for four to five cars. This was felt to be ideal for our auto tape installation sales.

Other factors considered in our choice of the location involved the relatively small need for renovation and the nearness to stores whose customers are in the same market segment that buy the most tapes and tape equipment. In addition, a restoration is under way by the Downtown Merchant's Association to improve this area. One other important factor weighed was the location's extreme "visibility" due to its corner location.

Store Renovation

Having made the location decision, we obtained information on renovation costs. These are listed in detail in Exhibit 4.

First of all, an examination will be made of the modifications necessary to refurbish the exterior of the structure. Exhibit 2 pictures the building as it will look after renovation. The blue and white colors were chosen for their attractiveness and eye-catching ability.

EXHIBIT 2
Tape Town, Inc.
Store Front

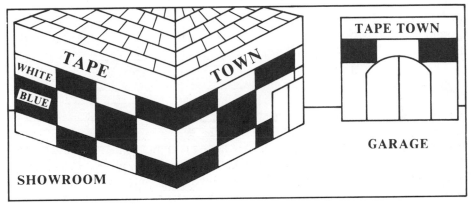

The interior of the store is depicted in Exhibit 3. (See p. 36.) The tapes will be displayed in the principal business area at the front of the store. Static electricity must be avoided as it could cause defects in the tapes. Thus, this area will have a mosaic tile on the floor rather than carpeting. The home equipment section will have wall-to-wall carpeting to give it a more comfortable atmosphere and appearance.

Inventory

The job of inventory selection and control will be extremely important. In the first case, we have limited display space, and, second, the music tastes of the "younger generation" change rapidly. Finally, we cannot afford to tie up working capital in stagnant inventory.

The first and most important thing for us to establish was the size of our initial tape and equipment inventory. By talking with The House of Car Stereos' management in Athol; Music, Inc., in Georgetown; and a distributor, we determined a feasible beginning tape inventory of 4,500 cartridges and 500 cassettes. The cartridges selected represent about 3,100 of the 8,000 titles available, and the cassettes cover about 380 of the titles released. The average cost of these tapes is $4.00 each, resulting in a $20,000 inventory. An initial cost for equipment was set at $3,000. We will carry the Tenna Ranger auto unit at $30.00, which is an

EXHIBIT 3
Tape Town, Inc.
Store Interior

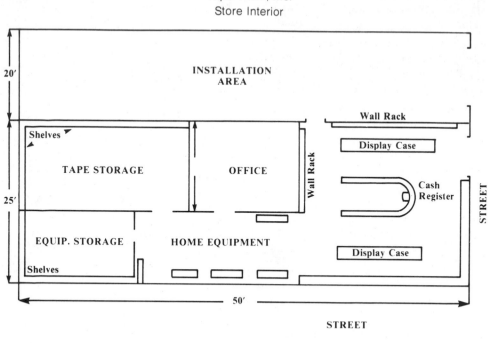

eight-track, two-speaker tape player. Home equipment will consist of two floor player units and two floor recorder units, with one player in stock. This equipment plays cartridges and retails for $35.00 and up. We will carry six to eight Norelco portable units on the floor and an equal number in stock. These units range from $19.95 upward. It is not necessary to carry great amounts of equipment because our distributors are close by and delivery is fast. Our total initial inventory investment is to be $23,000. This inventory will be serviced by two of the four largest distributors in the area. Equipment will be ordered directly from the manufacturers. We have developed an inventory control system for (1) reordering and (2) color dating to let us know how long the tape has been in stock.

Personnel and Organization

We will employ one full-time manager-salesman who will be fully responsible for daily operations. His starting salary will be $7,600 per year. One part-time clerk at $1.65 per hour and one experienced installer at $2.80 per hour will also be employed. It is essential that our manager be a mature, but youth-minded, person with experience in a position of business responsibility. To be a successful tape salesman, he must be very knowledgeable of today's music trends—the pop scene. He also must understand tape equipment and be able to discuss componentry and speaker quality with adult customers. The success of our inventory selection will depend upon how well our manager can predict the future music tastes of the 16-25 age group. Our manager will be given responsibility and salary increases commensurate with this ability. We have in mind Mr. Pete Burns, who has managed a record store in the past. He is very active in the local music scene as a musician and as a former disc jockey.

We intend to have two salespersons on the floor during the peak late afternoon and evening hours. The store will be open almost 70 hours each week (10:00 A.M. to 10:00 P.M. five days, and 10:00 A.M. to 6:00 P.M. one day), so that at least two salespeople are needed in order to arrange an acceptable work schedule. We will employ an experienced auto tape installer. A good installer can do the average job in 30 minutes. Average installation cost will be from $15 to $20. We will be satisfied initially if he makes seven to ten installations per week. As owners, we expect to visit the store frequently, but will not draw any salary or other benefits from the company until it becomes profitable.

Pricing

Pricing is somewhat flexible on tapes. Equipment is primarily list pricing. Stereo cartridges cost us $4.00 to $4.25, to which we will add a 40 to 50% markup. Cassettes cost about $1 less, but have a higher pilferage rate. We believe that we can capture a good part of the market by discounting our cartridges. Our prices will range between $5.95 and $6.25, while our competitors sell at $6.95. This discounting is important because much of the hesitancy to buying cartridges is due to the large price differential between stereo records ($4.98) and stereo cartridge tapes ($6.95).

Equipment has a slightly lower margin—30 to 37%. Auto units range in retail price from $20.00 to $60.00, the average being $30.00. We will promote the $30.00 unit. Portables in the $20.00 range will be our main sales item in this area. We would like a high turnover in portable equipment. Home equipment has the lowest margin and is carried mainly for prestige. Home player-recorders, however, have become more important since the introduction of cartridges with recording capability. Our revenue estimates are based on an average markup of 40% for both tapes and equipment.

Some of our home equipment customers will undoubtedly wish to buy the more expensive equipment on credit. We will install a simple credit system requiring the purchaser to have a Tape Town Credit Charge, BankAmericard, or Master Charge. The allowable credit on the Tape Town plan will be determined by the price of the equipment. The service charge will be 1½% per month on approved credit, and the credit period will be 30 days. We anticipate to be carrying 30% of gross sales in accounts receivable at the end of the first year. We expect to sell most of the auto and portable equipment for cash.

Advertising

Advertising is our most important marketing item. One of the most effective methods of promotion is one over which we have no control—word of mouth. Our eye-catching exterior and the visibility of our tape equipment contribute to the promotion of our store. We plan extensive advertising in the various types of media for the first six weeks—local newspaper, university paper, and spot announcements on the three local radio stations. Some of the advertising will be defrayed by the distributors through a cooperative advertising program. We will continue to use all media, but try to ascertain which provides us with the best results.

Finance

We were able to predict Georgetown tape and tape equipment sales. This was done by first deriving a factor that represented the fraction of U.S. retail sales that tape and tape equipment sales represent for the years in question, 1971-1975.

Tape Sales as a Fraction of U.S. Retail Sales

	U.S. Retail ($000,000,000)	U.S. Tape ($000,000)	Tape as % of Total
1971	$388.5	$ 777.3	.0020%
1972	411.8	870.6	.0021
1973	436.5	975.1	.0022
1974	462.7	1,092.1	.0023
1975	492.7	1,223.2	.0024

Equipment Sales as a Fraction of U.S. Retail Sales

	U.S. Retail ($000,000,000)	U.S. Equip. ($000,000)	Equip. as % of Total
1971	$388.5	$ 805.3	.0020%
1972	411.8	901.9	.0022
1973	436.5	1,010.1	.0023
1974	462.7	1,131.3	.0024
1975	492.7	1,267.0	.0025

The U.S. factors for the years 1971-1975 were then multiplied by the estimated Georgetown retail sales to obtain figures for tape and tape equipment sales in this city. Figures for Georgetown retail sales were obtained from the consultant's report previously cited.

Georgetown Tape and Equipment Sales 1971-1975

	Georgetown Retail ($000,000)	Georgetown Tape Sales	Equip. Sales
1971	$115.0	$230,000	$230,000
1972	121.0	254,000	266,200
1973	127.0	279,400	292,100
1974	133.0	305,900	319,200
1975	136.0	326,400	340,000

The final step in forecasting sales involves setting a reasonable market share that the business can obtain. It is felt that the business can obtain a share of 40% of Georgetown tape sales for several reasons:

1. There is no real competition in terms of similar stores.
2. Large quantities sold should allow undercutting prices of competitors.
3. Promotion is relatively inexpensive in Georgetown.

With such a market share, sales forecasts can be compiled for the years in question.

Sales Forecasts, 1971-1975

	Georgetown Tape Sales	Georgetown Equip. Sales	Mkt. Share	Sales Total
1971	$230,000	$230,000	40%	$184,000
1972	254,000	266,200	40	208,080
1973	279,400	292,100	40	228,600
1974	305,900	319,200	40	250,040
1975	326,400	340,000	40	266,560

We used this information to prepare a set of pro forma statements for the first five years of operation (see Exhibits 5 and 6).

EXHIBIT 4
Tape Town, Inc.
Startup and Rental Expenses

Costs of Renovation and Equipment:

Ceiling Hung and Lights	$ 400
Floor Tile	180
Pine Paneling	100
Painting Exterior and Sign	400
New Door	100
Carpets: Office	60
Home Section	45
Office Chairs, Desk, Cabinet	515
Safe	250
Cash Register	200
Adding Machine	99
Typewriter	125
Electric Drill and Complements	40
Tool Set	20
Saw	3
Storage Shelves	120
Total	$2,657

Rental Expenses:

Display Cabinets and Counter	$ 75/month
Telephone	18/month
Building	350/month

EXHIBIT 5
Tape Town, Inc.
Pro Forma Balance Sheets
1971-1975

	1971	1972	1973	1974	1975
Assets					
Cash	$36,954	$ 79,226	$136,049	$179,314	$236,938
Inventory	23,000	23,000	23,000	23,000	23,000
Accounts Rec.	10,133	13,186	15,003	16,398	17,669
Equipment	1,370	1,370	1,370	1,370	1,370
Total	$71,457	$115,412	$165,422	$220,082	$278,977
Liab./Equities					
Loan (Due 1980)	$25,000	$ 25,000	$ 25,000	$ 25,000	$ 25,000
Capital Stock	10,000	10,000	10,000	10,000	10,000
Retained Earnings	36,457	80,412	130,422	185,082	243,977
Total	$71,457	$115,412	$165,422	$220,082	$278,977

EXHIBIT 6
Tape Town, Inc.
Pro Forma Income Statements
1971-1975

	1971	1972	1973	1974	1975
Sales Revenue	$184,000	$208,120	$228,600	$250,000	$266,560
Cost of Sales	110,400	124,872	136,160	150,000	159,936
	$ 73,600	$ 83,348	$ 92,440	$100,000	$106,624
Oper. Expenses					
Salaries	$ 15,010	$ 15,911	$ 16,866	$ 17,878	$ 18,951
Advertising	2,000	2,000	2,000	2,000	2,000
Depreciation	274	274	274	274	274
Taxes	3,163	3,710	4,085	4,670	4,793
Rent and Utilities	4,200	4,200	4,200	4,200	4,200
Rental Equipment	900	900	900	900	900
Remodeling	1,285				
Incorp. Expenses	26				
Total Expenses	$ 26,848	$ 26,995	$ 28,325	$ 29,923	$ 31,118
Net Income (BT)	$ 46,752	$ 56,353	$ 64,115	$ 70,077	$ 73,506
Taxes	10,295	12,398	14,105	15,417	16,611
Income After Taxes	$ 36,457	$ 43,955	$ 50,010	$ 54,660	$ 58,895

QUESTION

1. Comment on the reasonableness of the forecasts made by Adams and Bradford.

Case 6
Baker Bros., Inc.

Early in September 1974, Jack Faulkner was starting his second week as Secretary-Treasurer of Baker Bros., Inc. An experienced financial manager, Mr. Faulkner was well aware that Paul Stewart, President of Baker Bros., had hired him to "put the company's financial house in order." However, despite a week of nonstop discussions with other company executives, all he had found out about Baker Bros.' financial situation was that suppliers were clamoring for payment and that cash was available to satisfy only the most pressing needs.

To help him understand Baker Bros.' financial situation, Mr. Faulkner had collected the summary financial information shown in Exhibits 1, 2, 3, and 4. As he was looking through some of the recent financial statements, the accounts payable clerk dropped a stack of overdue invoices on his desk. A note attached stated that cash was not available to pay the suppliers.

Company Organization and History

Baker Bros., Inc., was organized as a Florida corporation in 1944 with its headquarters in Jacksonville. Since that time, the company has become a major southeastern distributor of heating, air conditioning, and refrigeration equipment, parts, and supplies with 45 outlets in Florida, Georgia, Alabama, North Carolina, South Carolina, and Mississippi. Through the addition of sales outlets to expand its market area and broadening of its product line, Baker Bros. increased sales from $7.7 million in 1968 to $36 million in its fiscal year ended January 31, 1974.

This case was prepared by Professor Charles W. Young of the University of North Florida as a basis for classroom discussion and not to illustrate either effective or ineffective handling of an administrative situation.

Each sales outlet or "store" operated by Baker Bros. serves as a sales and distribution point for the full line of approximately 20,000 climate control and refrigeration products carried by the company. Each store is run by a manager who is responsible for the hiring and supervision of personnel and for sales, credit, purchasing, inventory, and cost control at the store level. Management feels that this delegation of authority and responsibility is a major contributor to the company's success, and managers are paid on the basis of the net profit generated by their stores. Decisions affecting company policy, selection of senior management, capital expenditures, and the addition of product lines are reviewed by corporate management.

Suppliers

Products sold by the company are purchased on a regular basis from approximately 250 manufacturers and suppliers. Special-order items are purchased occasionally from an additional 400 vendors. The largest single supplier of new air conditioning equipment and parts to the company provides approximately 15% of total purchases each year. The company has nonexclusive wholesale distributorship agreements with many of its suppliers. These agreements are generally informal and are subject to termination by either party on short notice. Most purchases are made on open account with terms of 2/10, net 30.

Customers

Sales are made to approximately 8,000 customers, consisting of mechanical, heating, air conditioning, and refrigeration contractors, institutions, governmental units, and a variety of commercial users such as supermarket chains. Substantially, all sales to customers are on open account, and no single customer accounts for as much as 1½% of total sales during any one year. Terms typically are 2/10, net 30, but extended terms are sometimes offered to gain a competitive advantage.

The company solicits sales from customers in both the new construction and the replacement and repair markets. New equipment sales provide relatively lower gross margins than sales of replacement parts. It is difficult for the company to monitor sales by market category; however, estimates of total sales contributed by products sold in the two markets during each of the past four fiscal years are as follows:

	1974	1973	1972	1971
New construction	35%	20%	15%	9%
Replacement and repair	65%	80%	85%	91%

Financial History

In 1964, the Allied Chemical Company acquired a 57% interest in Baker Bros., Inc., through purchase of common stock at an aggregate cash price of $302,550. Allied's ownership was increased to 80.7% in 1967, when the company purchased a substantial block of common stock from another shareholder. On June 10, 1971, in an underwritten public offering, Allied sold 358,092 shares of common stock, and the company sold 51,908 shares at $18.00 per share. This sale plus a private sale to Baker Bros.' management personnel liquidated Allied's holdings in the company. In mid-1974, after a 100% stock dividend in May 1972, the company had 1,109,574 shares of common stock issued and outstanding distributed among 588 holders of record. Selected high and low common stock prices are shown in Exhibit 5.

Long-term debt outstanding on January 31, 1974, was as follows:

Bank loan—7¾%	$ 810,000
Insurance Co. loan—8½%	2,000,000
Mortgage notes—5¾% to 8%	101,719
Other notes—8%	110,000
	$3,021,719
Less: Current maturities	203,785
Remainder	$2,817,785

The insurance company loan was closed on July 13, 1973, with part of the proceeds of $2 million applied to reduce the long-term bank loan from its previous high of $1.7 million. Principal payments on the insurance company loan are deferred until December 1, 1978, at which time payments of $100,000 will be due on each of the June 1 and December 1 interest payment dates until the note is paid in full on June 1, 1988. Covenants in the loan agreement require Baker Bros. to maintain consolidated net working capital of not less than $7 million and a consolidated current ratio of at least 2 to 1. Further, the company is precluded from incurring any funded or current debt except that short-term bank borrowing, not to exceed $1 million, is permitted providing that the company is out of the bank for 60 consecutive days in each fiscal year. A number of other negative covenants are also imposed by the loan agreement, but none of them appear to materially constrain the company's ability to operate as it has in the past. However, violation of any of the negative covenants, in addition to failure to make payments of principal and interest when due, gives the insurance company the option to declare the loan immediately due and payable.

Current Situation

While looking through the stack of reports and statements he had gathered on his desk, Mr. Faulkner notes that during the three years of public ownership the management of Baker Bros. has devoted most of its attention to promoting growth in both sales and earnings per share. In fact, growth was the major topic discussed by the President in his letter to shareholders in the fiscal year 1973 annual report. In this letter, the 33% increase in sales and 23% growth in earnings per share were highlighted, and continued growth was predicted for 1974.

Emphasis on growth was also apparent in the 1974 annual report. For example, the President's letter predicted:

"The Southeast as a whole—and Florida in particular—continues to be the nation's premier growth area. Management believes that exploitation of the market coverage we have achieved and continued efforts to control costs should result in another excellent year for the company."

This letter also mentioned the energy crisis that hit the country in late 1973— shortages, rising costs, and declining home construction as problems plaguing the industry in early 1974. The impact of these factors was predicted to be less severe in Florida because of the strength of the state's residential construction industry and because many expected construction to rise during the second half of 1974. (Data on building permits issued in the United States and the company's major market areas during 1972, 1973, and 1974 are shown in Exhibit 7.)

As Mr. Faulkner dug deeper into the financial information he had collected, he was surprised to find that the outstanding short-term loan was $700,000 over the limit imposed by the term loan debt covenant. Although a quick check provided information that the insurance company had agreed to the additional bank debt, their agreement had been obtained with the understanding that the loan would be reduced to $1 million by January 31, 1975. However, the insurance company had waived the requirement that Baker Bros. be out of the bank for 60 days during fiscal year 1975.

Analysis of the July 31, 1974, accounts receivable balance provided the aging schedule shown in Exhibit 6. When questioned about the overdue amounts, the accounts receivable clerk reported that most accounts overdue in excess of 180 days represented sales of new equipment to construction contractors.

Investigation of the inventory balance disclosed that the company had adopted a policy in 1974 to build inventory as a hedge against future shortages. About $1.6 million was added to inventory during fiscal year 1974 for this purpose and the build-up had continued into 1975. Further, it was found that there had been no significant inventory revaluations during the last several years to reflect obsolescence, deterioration or reductions of cost to market. Because purchases were initiated by store managers and all inventory was located at one of the 45 stores, there was little information available at the Jacksonville headquarters to identify either the unit composition of the inventory or its marketability.

As Mr. Faulkner continued to peruse the information he had accumulated, he knew that Mr. Stewart expected him to convert his impressions of Baker Bros.' financial situation into an analysis that would clearly identify the magnitude and urgency of the company's problems and to propose a plan for their solution.

EXHIBIT 1
Baker Bros., Inc.

Statements of Consolidated Income
for the years ended January 31
(Dollar figures in thousands)

	1971	1972	1973	1974
Net Sales	$15,284	$21,445	$28,454	$36,085
Cost of Merchandise Sold	11,542	16,289	21,544	27,737
Gross Profit on Sales	$ 3,742	$ 5,156	$ 6,910	$ 8,348
Operating Expenses*	2,427	3,415	4,548	5,786
Profit from Operations	$ 1,315	$ 1,741	$ 2,362	$ 2,562
Other Income	9	41	65	200
Interest Expense	(51)	(101)	(158)	(300)
Income Before Income Taxes	$ 1,273	$ 1,681	$ 2,269	$ 2,462
Provision for Income Taxes	606	812	1,158	1,239
Net Income	$ · 667	$ 869	$ 1,111	$ 1,223
Earnings per Share	$ .67	$ .81	$ 1.00	$ 1.10
*Includes:				
Provision for doubtful acc.	NA	NA	NA	$225
Depreciation and amortization	NA	NA	NA	$ 72

EXHIBIT 2
Baker Bros., Inc.
Consolidated Balance Sheets
January 31
(Dollar figures in thousands)

	1971	*1972*	*1973*	*1974*
ASSETS				
Current Assets:				
Cash	$ 315	$ 585	$ 559	$ 320
Accounts & notes rec.				
(net)	2,005	2,679	3,919	5,418
Inventories	3,913	4,325	6,711	8,336
Other current assets	21	5	19	101
Total current assets	$6,254	$7,594	$11,208	$14,175
Property, plant & equip.				
(net)	419	422	676	759
Goodwill	181	169	378	354
Other Assets	19	22	23	8
TOTAL	$6,873	$8,207	$12,285	$15,296
LIABILITIES AND STOCKHOLDERS' EQUITY				
Current Liabilities:				
Notes payable to banks	$ 10	$ 0	$ 521	$ 800
Current portion—LTD	103	212	297	204
Trade accounts payable	1,160	1,232	2,850	3,415
Accrued liabilities	1,164	792	960	899
Total current liabilities	$2,437	$2,236	$ 4,628	$ 5,318
Long-Term Debt	1,360	1,192	1,720	2,818
Stockholders' Equity:				
Common stock—$.10 par	50	55	111	111
Other paid-in capital	238	1,066	1,057	1,057
Retained earnings	2,788	3,658	4,769	5,992
Stockholders' equity	$3,076	$4,779	$ 5,937	$ 7,160
TOTAL	$6,873	$8,207	$12,285	$15,296

EXHIBIT 3
Baker Bros., Inc.
Quarterly Statements of Consolidated Income*
(Dollar figures in thousands)

	3 Months 4-30-72	6 Months 7-31-72	9 Months 10-31-72	12 Months 1-31-73	3 Months 4-30-73	6 Months 7-31-73	9 Months 10-31-73	12 Months 1-31-74	3 Months 4-30-74	6 Months 7-31-74
Net Sales	$ 5,754	$13,687	$21,552	$28,454	$ 7,649	$18,062	$27,625	$36,085	$ 7,981	$19,049
Cost of Goods Sold	4,378	10,422	16,455	21,544	5,870	13,905	21,301	27,737	6,178	14,584
Gross Profit	$ 1,376	$ 3,265	$ 5,097	$ 6,910	$ 1,779	$ 4,157	$ 6,324	$ 8,348	$ 1,803	$ 4,463
Operating Expenses	947	2,070	3,268	4,548	1,271	2,723	4,258	5,786	1,427	3,059
Profit from Operations	$ 429	$ 1,195	$ 1,829	$ 2,362	$ 508	$ 1,434	$ 2,066	$ 2,562	$ 376	$ 1,406
Other Income	11	24	36	65	12	73	136	200	89	150
Interest Expense	(36)	(79)	(108)	(158)	(44)	(97)	(162)	(300)	(81)	(176)
Income Before Taxes	$ 404	$ 1,140	$ 1,757	$ 2,269	$ 476	$ 1,410	$ 2,040	$ 2,462	$ 384	$ 1,380
Income Taxes	201	568	875	1,158	242	719	1,040	1,239	195	704
Net Income	$ 203	$ 572	$ 882	$ 1,111	$ 234	$ 691	$ 1,000	$ 1,223	$ 189	$ 676
Earnings per Share	$ .18	$ .52	$ .80	$ 1.00	$ .21	$ .62	$ .90	$ 1.10	$ .17	$ .61

*Unaudited

EXHIBIT 4

Baker Bros., Inc.

Quarterly Consolidated Balance Sheets for 1972, 1973 and 1974*

(Dollar figures in thousands)

	4-30-72	7-31-72	10-31-72	1-31-73	4-30-73	7-31-73	10-31-73	1-31-74	4-30-74	7-31-74
ASSETS:										
Current Assets										
Cash	$ 661	$ 496	$ 452	$ 559	$ 677	$ 598	$ 399	$ 320	$ 564	$ 416
Accounts & notes rec.	3,452	4,285	4,266	4,095	4,752	5,930	5,636	5,629	5,605	6,712
Allow. for bad debts	(158)	(230)	(301)	(177)	(243)	(313)	(413)	(211)	(233)	(276)
Inventory	6,055	6,368	6,312	6,711	8,642	9,773	8,762	8,336	10,655	10,132
Prepaid and other	8	17	29	20	8	17	30	102	21	34
Total current assets	$10,018	$10,936	$10,757	$11,208	$13,836	$16,005	$14,414	$14,176	$16,612	$17,018
Property, plant & equip.	834	939	967	953	1,006	1,051	1,077	1,103	1,131	1,154
Accumulated depr.	(289)	(302)	(316)	(277)	(291)	(306)	(324)	(343)	(362)	(376)
Net	$ 545	$ 637	$ 651	$ 676	$ 715	$ 745	$ 753	$ 760	$ 769	$ 778
Goodwill	395	394	383	377	372	366	360	354	348	342
Other Assets	29	22	18	24	41	24	25	6	31	22
TOTAL	$10,987	$11,989	$11,809	$12,285	$14,964	$17,140	$15,552	$15,296	$17,760	$18,160
LIABILITIES AND STOCKHOLDERS' EQUITY:										
Current Liabilities:										
Notes payable—bank	$ 334	$ 778	$ 547	$ 521	$ 800	$ 1,000	$ 900	$ 800	$ 800	$ 1,400
Trade accounts payable	2,867	3,222	2,883	2,850	4,909	5,726	3,768	3,415	5,657	5,379
Current portion—LTD	213	223	294	297	318	206	206	204	204	202
Accrued taxes	299	194	304	392	461	284	257	230	313	165
Other	371	341	376	569	472	370	560	669	622	453
Total current liab.	$ 4,084	$ 4,758	$ 4,404	$ 4,629	$ 6,960	$ 7,586	$ 5,691	$ 5,318	$ 7,596	$ 7,599
Long-Term Debt	1,877	1,833	1,697	1,719	1,833	2,926	2,923	2,818	2,815	2,725
Stockholders' Equity:										
Common Stock	111	111	111	111	111	111	111	111	111	111
Paid-in capital	1,055	1,057	1,057	1,057	1,057	1,057	1,057	1,057	1,057	1,057
Retained earnings	3,860	4,230	4,540	4,769	5,003	5,460	5,770	5,992	6,181	6,668
Stockholders' equity	$ 5,026	$ 5,398	$ 5,708	$ 5,937	$ 6,171	$ 6,628	$ 6,938	$ 7,160	$ 7,349	$ 7,837
TOTAL	$10,987	$11,989	$11,809	$12,285	$14,964	$17,140	$15,552	$15,296	$17,760	$18,160

*Unaudited

EXHIBIT 5

Baker Bros., Inc.

Common Stock Prices
(Traded Over the Counter)

	High	Low
1972	27¼	15¼
Quarter Ended		
4-30-73	21¼	15
7-31-73	20	15½
10-31-73	21	16¾
1-31-74	19½	6
4-30-74	6¾	4⅞
7-31-74	4⅞	3⅛

EXHIBIT 6

Baker Bros., Inc.

Aging of Accounts Receivable
July 31, 1974
(Dollar figures in thousands)

	Amount	%
Current	$2,685	40
Overdue:		
31— 60	805	12
61— 90	671	10
91—120	470	7
121—150	403	6
151—180	336	5
Over 180	1,342	20
TOTAL	$6,712	100
July Sales	$3,443	

EXHIBIT 7
Baker Bros., Inc.
Private Residential Construction
Authorized (14,000 Places)*

Number of Housing Units

	United States	South	Florida	Alabama
1972	2,218,922	905,426	278,145**	28,323**
1973	1,819,535	763,166	266,982	20,390
1972:				
Jan.	137,324	61,526	18,900	1,687
Feb.	148,069	63,682	17,454	1,610
Mar.	191,071	80,669	22,586	2,285
Apr.	191,792	74,066	18,425	2,704
May	206,919	78,770	21,237	2,242
Jun.	214,598	84,039	22,906	2,270
Jul.	179,637	72,317	21,050	2,094
Aug.	206,424	81,461	22,356	2,942
Sep.	190,570	82,793	34,602	2,895
Oct.	201,110	82,885	29,442	2,691
Nov.	176,842	69,791	22,617	3,272
Dec.	174,566	73,427	25,068	2,484
1973:				
Jan.	152,077	72,688	21,882	2,605
Feb.	145,696	70,066	22,564	1,970
Mar.	184,402	75,445	23,284	1,849
Apr.	185,386	74,923	26,230	2,077
May	191,707	78,943	26,756	1,976
Jun.	193,719	87,309	41,409	1,348
Jul.	157,326	60,286	21,435	1,405
Aug.	162,855	62,194	21,380	1,440
Sep.	125,190	50,274	14,376	2,424
Oct.	122,948	48,976	15,617	1,476
Nov.	107,160	44,377	13,069	873
Dec.	91,069	37,685	14,694	1,260
1974:				
Jan.	85,937	41,698	16,572	1,293
Feb.	85,528	41,262	15,171	1,120
Mar.	117,988	47,081	15,181	2,158
Apr.	128,084	47,717	13,778	1,278
May	114,043	39,994	11,180	984
Jun.	99,878	34,245	11,856	1,057
Jul.	93,606	32,850	8,279	842

*Source: U.S. Dept. of Commerce, *Construction Review,* various issues.
**13,000 places.

QUESTIONS

1. Analyze the financial data Mr. Faulkner has collected, and identify the factors that have caused Baker Bros.' cash crisis and forced it to rely heavily on trade credit.
2. How serious are Baker Bros.' financial problems? Which problems must be solved immediately and which ones can wait?
3. What policy or other structural constraints must Mr. Faulkner accommodate in developing his plans to work out the company's financial problems?
4. What actions should Mr. Faulkner recommend in order to solve Baker Bros.' financial problems?

Case 7
Allied Plastics, Inc.

In late January 1972, Mr. Nathan Leff, vice president of Allied Plastics, located in Atlanta, Georgia, was examining the company's balance sheet with an eye toward establishing a more stable liabilities schedule. In addition, he was considering the raising of additional funds to finance expansion of the firm's plastic operations.

Description of Firm's Products and Customers

Allied Plastics was founded in 1962 by Nathan and Jenny I. Leff, who were husband and wife. The firm was a small designer and fabricator of standard and custom plastic products. Their products included such diverse fabricated items as windshields for golf carts and plastic cubes, nameplates for individual employees, directional signs for office buildings and industrial machinery and equipment, plastic furniture, and indoor and outdoor nonilluminated signs of various sizes and descriptions. The company's customers included builders, industrial designers, architects, plus various industrial users of fabricated plastic items. Allied Plastics worked with all the standard materials of the industry, such as acrylics, styrene, vinyls, polyethylenes, acetates, and both rigid and flexible engraving stock.

The Company's Beginning and Early Years

The initial capitalization consisted of 300 shares of capital stock issued at $1 par, to Jenny I. Leff, who was designated president. Nathan Leff served as vice president and was the chief operating officer of the firm.

This case was prepared by Professor Harry R. Kuniansky of the College of Charleston as a basis for classroom discussion and not to illustrate either effective or ineffective handling of an administrative situation.

Mr. Leff, who was now in his mid-fifties, had previous business experience in the construction industry, but following a heart attack in 1961 his doctor had strongly advised that he not return to that line of work. At the time, Mrs. Leff was doing engraving work for Delta Plastics, a small Atlanta firm. Both Mr. and Mrs. Leff believed that the plastics industry was in its infancy in regard to signs with plastic bases with either engraved or applied letters. After advisement with Mrs. Leff's brother, Dr. Donald Stein, a local physician, they decided to enter the plastic sign business. Dr. Stein agreed to endorse a $5,000 note maturing in 12 months with Allied's bank, the Atlanta National, Polly Street Branch. These funds were necessary for working capital and the purchase of needed equipment.

The firm rented a vacant store owned by the father of Mrs. Leff. The location was ideal, as it was near the downtown business district, which easily afforded the Leff's the opportunity to contact possible sources of business such as engineers, architects, builders, and contractors. Sales involved two types of signs, engraving on phenolic plastic and glue-applied letters on acrylic plastic. Mr. Leff contacted prospective customers and brought the orders back to the store. Mrs. Leff, with the help of a part-time employee, completed the engraving orders while Mr. Leff did the applied sign work. Mrs. Leff handled the bookkeeping function, and a CPA prepared yearly statements and tax returns.

Sales for the first month were $350 and for the first year were in excess of $19,000. The firm suffered a negligible loss during the initial year of operations. In 1963, net profit before officers' salaries was $9,650 with officer salaries being $8,000.

The firm continued with the same product lines until mid 1965. At this time, both Mr. and Mrs. Leff noted the profit potential in the fabrication of plastics. Plastic was fabricated or shaped by heating the material with a stripheater to the desired temperature and then bending or shaping to the form needed. As an example, this technique enabled the firm to sell chartholders to the medical profession. In addition, Allied was able to secure the account of a large motel chain for which it made drapery arms out of acrylic scrap. The company added another engraving machine, and sales for the fiscal year ending February 28, 1966, were over $46,000.

During 1965, Allied received debt funds through the endorsement of a note by Dr. Stein, and repaid it within 12 months. Short-term funds were borrowed from the Polly Street Branch of the Atlanta National Bank. Mr. Leff had banked at this location for a number of years and had a warm personal relationship with the branch manager, Mr. Harvey Higgins. Mr. Higgins was quite amenable to continue short-term borrowings as the company needed them. He realized that some of the firm's needs were of a permanent nature. However, he did not believe this was the appropriate time to explore term debt. For his part, Mr. Leff had given some thought to term debt, as he believed this might facilitate the planning process. He believed that an inordinate amount of his time was spent on financial activities such as telephoning to inquire about outstanding receivables and worrying about whether deposits would cover outstanding payables. During some months it had been necessary to refrain from paying bills because there was not enough funds from collections to cover maturing payables. Mr. Leff thought a term loan might relieve him of some of these financial pressures, thus paving the way for him to spend more time outside the firm; namely, calling on prospective customers. He believed increased time on the sales function would enable the firm to grow at a faster rate, since personal selling played an important part in stimulating sales, espccially those of the applied letter variety. However, Mr. Leff thought a term loan to be somewhat risky because it committed the firm to repay debt for a period over one year. He was not at all sure that Allied was that firmly established in the Atlanta market to warrant such a commitment. Applied letter signs sales were almost totally nonrecurring. Engraving sales were dominated by two or three large customers. If either sign sales declined or one of his large engraving customers switched its account, he feared that the firm might have difficulty in meeting the installments on term debt. Mr. Leff, therefore, decided at this time to forego any attempt to negotiate term-debt arrangements.

By fiscal 1967, the firm's sales had risen to $54,000, with net profits before officer salaries of $12,200. By 1967, fabrication of plastic materials was responsible for about 60% of the company's output, while engraving accounted for around 25% and applied letters 15%. In addition, fabrication was growing at a faster pace than either of the other two product lines.

The Firm's Competition

Allied was especially active in producing goods for architects and builders. These items not only provided profits in themselves, but enabled this type of customer to observe the quality of Allied's workmanship. Accordingly, the firm derived additional business, such as from hospitals and hotels, by doing excellent work for these clients. The company, as it had from its inception, continued to stress quality work and strict adherence to the scheduled date of delivery. Mr. Leff strongly believed that any compromise with these goals would seriously impair the competitive position of the firm. Basically, the firm was in competition with two or three well-established Atlanta firms as far as engraving was concerned, and price was likely to play a major role. The applied sign competition was composed of numerous small firms scattered throughout the metropolitan area. Price played a lesser role in securing sales, as most customers were more concerned with appearance and durability. Allied continually pointed out that plastic signs would last a lifetime, whereas painted signs lasted between two and five years. Profit margins on applied signs were higher than either engraving or fabrication.

Competition for fabrication sales was intense, mainly from large national and regional firms situated in the Atlanta area. Accordingly, lower profit margins were the rule, especially on large-volume orders. However, Mr. Leff believed the securing of this type order was necessary, because it provided coverage of the firm's fixed cost. In addition, these orders tended to be repeaters and therefore provided the firm with a stable sales base.

The Growth Years 1967-1970

A large jump in sales, in excess of 30%, was recorded between 1967 and 1968. Contributing materially to this growth was the building boom occurring in the city of Atlanta (see Exhibit 7). The boom reflected the development of Atlanta during the 1960's as the leading city in the Southeast. In response to the sales increase, the firm added another fulltime production employee. Allied added a store adjacent to the present site, and remodeled it to meet its specifications. This expansion was financed by short-term loans and profits. In 1968, Dr. Stein made a $7,500 loan with no maturity date and no interest rate. This enabled the firm to pay off some long-standing accounts payable and to withstand an operating loss that occurred in fiscal 1969. The loss was primarily due to a decrease in sales and an inability of the firm to curtail expanding operating expenses.

In 1969, the firm widened its product line by securing the distributorship of Harrison Plastics of Bradenton, Florida, producers of plastic-injected molded letters of various sizes and shapes, and the Delcy Corporation of Santa Barbara, California, manufacturers of directory boards and their interchangeable letters. Previously, Allied had purchased all of its letters at a 40% discount from Garrison Plastics in Atlanta, which was the only local distributor of plastic letters. The company used these letters in its own sign-making activities and also sold them to the general public. Mr. Leff foresaw profit potential in two ways from the new distributorship. He believed that he could materially increase letters sales to the public because the Harrison distributorship provided him with a more varied and larger inventory of letters and Harrison gave the firm a 60% discount on all letters purchased. In order to secure this distributorship, Harrison required that Allied maintain a minimum inventory of $6,000 and remit to Harrison promptly on terms of net 30 days. In order to finance this increase in assets, the firm borrowed from its bank $8,000 on a 12-month note with a $5,000 balloon on the end. Approximately one-half of the note had been paid back by February 1970.

In January of 1970, Mr. Leff received pro forma income statements and balance sheets prepared by George H. Schafer, a nephew of Mr. Leff, and a professor of finance at a local university. Among other things these exhibits projected gross sales in excess of $200,000 for the year ending February 28, 1973. In addition, Mr. Leff noted that he and Mrs. Leff were already spending many weeknights at the office. Mr. Leff noted the increasing difficulty in trying to sell and also supervise production in the sign and fabrication sections. Mrs. Leff found it cumbersome to oversee engraving, bill customers, and do the necessary accounting work. Especially crucial was the prompt billing of customers for work performed. This activity had to be done daily or billings would lag and therefore collections would be delayed. In view of the firm's tight cash position, this lag would only make the present cash situation more pressing. Also, Dr. Stein had stressed the importance of growth if the firm was to continue to prosper. Dr. Stein believed that organizations either grew or declined and that it was impossible for a firm to maintain the status quo.

All of these factors reinforced the idea that Mr. Leff had been pondering for the past few months, namely, that Allied Plastics was passing or had already outgrown the "Mom and Pop" phase of its existence. Mr. Leff believed it imperative that a general manager be hired and given the complete responsibility for production, as well as supervising bids for the fabricating jobs. In all likelihood, this person would probably wish to upgrade the quality of labor in the fabricating and sign sections. Hiring and keeping skilled labor was an increasing problem, and as the customers' demands grew for more complex products, the necessity for workers who possessed the prerequisite skills for manufacturing quality work became more and more important to Allied Plastics. Mr. Leff grappled with the problem of finding the right man and how to finance the required salary. He believed it would require between $10,000 and $15,000 to attract a person of sufficient ability to get the job done. He also considered some form of profit-sharing or stock-purchase plan for the individual he would hire.

Financial Considerations and Bank Relationships

By June of 1970, the company's financial condition had deteriorated to such an extent that it was having considerable difficulties meeting its current maturities. Growth in sales was occurring, but this seemed only to aggravate the liquidity problem. The managerial difficulties were compounded by the growth situation. Mr. and Mrs. Leff decided that both of these problems must be met at once. Accordingly, Mr. Leff began searching in earnest for a top-flight production manager. He became aware of a change in management at a large diversified Atlanta-based plastics firm, and the subsequent availability of one of its experienced managers, Mr. Lyman Miller. Mr. Miller possessed over 20 years' experience in both the production and management functions of plastic fabrication. Additionally, Mr. Miller was well acquainted with numerous purchasing agents and buyers for some of the large users of fabricated products in Atlanta and other large cities. He believed he could bring a portion of this business to Allied Plastics. Mr. Miller was hired and began work as general manager in September of 1970 at an annual salary of $12,000, plus 2% of net profit before owners' salaries.

At this time, Mr. Leff was also determined to tackle his financial problems, especially his schedule of maturing debts. Mr. Leff had preliminary discussions with Mr. Schafer and Dr. Stein, and it was agreed that it was necessary to secure some form of term financing. Accordingly, Mr. Schafer prepared pro forma income statements and balance sheets (see Exhibits 3 and 4) to present to Mr. Lawrence Glacken, manager of the Polly Street Branch of the Atlanta National Bank. Glacken had replaced Mr. Higgins as branch manager at the first of the year. Although relations between Mr. Leff and Mr. Glacken had been acceptable, the warm personal relationship that had existed between Mr. Leff and Mr. Higgins had not developed. Nevertheless, if at all possible, Mr. Leff wished to continue doing business at Atlanta National because of past satisfactory associations, and due to the fact the branch was located in close proximity to the firm.

Mr. Leff and Mr. Schafer approached Mr. Glacken with a proposal for a term loan of from three to five years' duration in the amount of $15,000. Mr. Glacken seemed amenable to such a loan, as he felt the prospects of the firm warranted a long-term commitment by the bank. Mr. Glacken required that all parties provide personal financial statements, Dr. Stein co-sign the note, and Mr. and Mrs. Leff sign the note personally as well as officers of the corporation, and that Mr. Leff secure a life insurance policy for the value of the loan and assign this policy to the bank. The only requirement that disturbed Mr. Leff was the last one. He could not comprehend why he should obtain such a policy, since both he and Dr. Stein were signing the note, and their personal assets would be sufficient in case of default of the note. In addition, and more important than the cost of the policy, which would range between $330 and $600 yearly, Mr. Leff felt it showed a lack of confidence by the bank in Allied's future prospects. He asked Mr. Glacken if the bank would remove the life insurance proviso. Mr. Glacken informed him that he would give him the bank's decision within a week to ten days. In the meantime, Dr. Stein suggested that Mr. Leff inquire as to the possibility of securing the loan from another Atlanta bank. He suggested that Mr. Harold Bogan, branch manager of the Metropolitan National Bank, might be interested in making a loan on more favorable terms. Dr. Stein was a friend of Mr. Bogan and banked at Metropolitan. A conference was arranged, and Mr. Bogan informed Mr. Leff that he would lend $15,000 at a 6% add-on rate, to be paid back over 60 monthly installments. Personal endorsements of Mr. and Mrs. Leff and Dr. Stein were required, but no life insurance policy would be demanded. Before accepting the Metropolitan National loan, Mr. Leff informed Mr. Glacken of the terms of the loan. Mr. Glacken stated that he had discussed the loan with the bank's loan committee and they concurred in his judgment that a life insurance policy should be required. Accordingly, the firm accepted the Metropolitan National loan and switched its account to that bank.

Recent Managerial and Financial Considerations

The term loan alleviated the severe liquidity squeeze for the moment, but the underlying conditions of undercapitalization and sales growth soon placed the firm in a liquidity bind again. By the fall of 1971, Mr. Leff needed to borrow again. The bank secured the borrowings ($14,000) with firm purchase orders on fabricated products from Allied's well-established customers. At this time, Mr. Bogan suggested the firm look for equity financing as he felt the firm was severely undercapitalized. Mr. Bogan also suggested that the firm could benefit from managerial consultants who would assess the organizational strengths and weaknesses of the firm and report on the accounting and reporting procedures of the company. Mr. Leff was receptive to this idea as for some time certain internal managerial problems had continued to plague him. He especially desired to secure more accurate and comprehensive information about the relative profitability of the firm's various product lines. At present, no cost accounting system was in operation, and the financial reporting system and balance sheets provided only periodic and annual income statements. He wanted this cost information for two basic reasons: One was to insure that each product line was making the proper contribution to the overall profitability of the firm. Second, he felt that this type information would help Mr. Miller and himself in the pricing decision made by the firm. Mr. Leff believed strongly that improved pricing would greatly enhance the profitability of the firm. For example, in pricing fabrication jobs, he knew the firm could accept less profit than on sign jobs, but he was not at all sure of how much he could cut fabricating job profit contribution and still have it beneficial to the firm. Fabrication and engraved sign orders were much more competitive than applied signs, and he wanted to insure that the pricing policies of the firm were neither preventing Allied from getting profitable work or pricing the job so low as to make it unprofitable. In the actual pricing decision on fabrication jobs, Mr. Miller tended to be lower than Mr. Leff, and this sometimes led to inconsistently submitted bids.

By January of 1972, Mr. Leff had decided to employ a managerial consultant. This consulting team would install a cost accounting system and provide a part-time accountant who would prepare the necessary financial reports and Allied's income tax return. Mr. Leff estimated that the cost would be between $4,000 and $4,500 the first year and between $3,000 and $3,500 thereafter. In addition, Mr. Leff was investigating the purchase of a vacuum forming machine which cost in the neighborhood of $8,000. Vacuum forming is a method of sheet forming in which the plastic sheet is clamped in a stationary frame, heated, and drawn down by a vacuum into a mold.[1] Mr. Leff knew the purchase of this piece of equipment would enable the firm to produce such items as plastic cups, dinnerware, plastic toys, lamps, and skylights. He believed it would be essential to employ a full-time salesperson in order to exploit the output from the vacuum forming machine. He thought he could hire a competent person for $10,000 plus commission. Although competition was intense in this area, Mr. Leff believed the addition of vacuum forming would allow Allied to double its volume within two years. He thought the profit margin from vacuum forming was similar to that of fabrication.

Considering all these major changes, Mr. Leff thought it imperative to develop a capital structure that would enable the firm to support without undue risk a growing asset structure, and at the same time pay the firm's maturing debts within the 30 days' terms furnished by his creditors.

[1]*Source: Modern Plastic Encyclopedia* 1970-1971, Vol. 47, McGraw-Hill Publishing Company.

EXHIBIT 1

Allied Plastics, Inc.

Balance Sheets

February 28, 1967-February 28, 1971, and August 31, 1971

	2/28/67	2/29/68	2/28/69	2/28/70	2/28/71	8/31/71
Assets						
Cash	$ 1,006	$ 372	$ 399	$ 1,513	$(3,854)	$ 4,688
Accounts Receivable	4,328	9,462	5,690	13,836	20,077	26,237
Inventory	4,107	5,202	7,564	11,074	19,031	26,884
Prepaid Interest	1,334	698	416	251	425	340
Total Current Assets	$10,775	$15,734	$14,069	$26,674	$35,679	$58,149
Fixed Assets	10,091	10,880	12,219	13,822	19,326	20,994
Less Accumulated Depreciation	(2,715)	(4,811)	(7,015)	(5,551)	(8,452)	(7,153)
Advances to Stockholders	6,202	9,697	11,749	11,830	10,832[1]	11,694
Other Assets	525	525	525	932	1,389	1,217
Total Assets	$24,878	$32,025	$31,547	$47,707	$58,774	$84,901
Liabilities and Net Worth						
Accounts Payable	$ 4,263	$ 8,269	$ 5,729	$ 5,787	$14,741	$24,665
Accrued Taxes	604	801	643	1,694	1,518	2,039
Bank Loans Payable	9,868	5,884	5,431	9,123	12,515	25,855
Total Current Liabilities	$14,735	$14,954	$11,803	$16,604	$28,774	$52,559
Term Loans	0	0	0	0	13,500	12,000
Other Loans	0	0	7,500[2]	7,500	7,500	7,500
Total Liabilities	$14,735	$14,954	$19,303	$24,104	$49,774	$72,059
Common Stock, $1 par, 1,000 shares authorized and 300 shares outstanding	300	300	300	300	300	300
Retained Earnings	9,843	16,771	11,944	23,303	8,700[1]	12,542
Total Liabilities and Net Worth	$24,878	$32,025	$31,547	$47,707	$58,774	$84,901

[1]Retained Earnings charged with $4,508, and advances to stockholders credited with $4,508.
[2]Loan to be converted at some future time to 20% of outstanding shares.

EXHIBIT 2
Allied Plastics, Inc.
Periodic Income Statements
Period from March 1, 1966–August 31, 1971

	3/1/66-2/28/67	3/1/67-2/29/68	3/1/68-2/28/69	3/1/69-2/28/70	3/1/70-2/28/71	3/1/71-8/31/71
Gross Sales	$54,774	$73,649	$64,307	$105,397	$135,006	$111,956
Less Sales Discounts	701	881	1,083	1,149	1,430	1,168
Net Sales	$54,073	$72,768	$63,224	$104,248	$133,576	$110,788
Beginning Inventory	3,613	4,107	5,202	7,564	11,074	19,031
Purchase of Raw Materials	14,011	23,998	16,820	29,568	48,833	51,263
Tools, Hardware, and Subcontracts	1,506	1,930	2,478	3,204	5,335	2,939
Less Ending Inventory	(4,107)	(5,202)	(7,564)	(11,074)	(19,031)	(26,884)
Cost of Goods Sold[1]	$15,023	$24,833	$16,936	$29,262	$46,211	$46,349
Gross Profit	$39,050	$47,935	$46,288	$74,986	$87,365	$64,439
Operating Expenses						
Salaries[2]	$19,667	$24,354	$33,281	$39,990	$64,777	$40,219
Rent	2,400	2,400	2,600	3,600	5,800	3,200
Utilities	2,569	2,684	2,753	4,043	5,099	2,917
Sales Promotion and Advertising	1,305	1,089	1,119	1,100	1,284	510
Licenses and Property Taxes	1,689	2,160	2,001	2,609	4,003	3,539
Insurance	378	404	1,144	2,064	2,571	2,466
Depreciation	1,677	2,096	2,204	2,268	2,901	1,501
Other	4,211	4,969	5,118	6,916	9,520	5,100
Total Operating Expenses	$33,896	$40,156	$50,220	$62,590	$95,955	$59,452
Net Operating Income or (Loss)	$ 5,154	$ 7,779	$(3,932)	$ 12,396	$ (8,590)	$ 4,987
Interest Expense	887	851	895	1,037	1,505	1,145
Net Income or (Loss)[3]	$ 4,267	$ 6,928	$(4,827)	$ 11,359	$(10,095)	$ 3,842
Owners' Withdrawals	$ 8,000	$10,000	$12,000	$ 15,000	$ 15,000	$ 8,000

[1]Cost of Goods Sold does not include either direct labor or overhead.
[2]Salaries includes all labor costs whether incurred in production or operations and owners' withdrawals.
[3]No Federal or State Income Taxes as owners choose to be taxed as individuals under Subchapter S of the Internal Revenue Code. Under this section of the code, all profits or losses flow directly to the individual stockholders.

EXHIBIT 3
Allied Plastics, Inc.
Pro Forma Balance Sheets
Fiscal Years 1971, 1972, 1973

	2/28/71	2/29/72	2/28/73
Assets			
a) Cash	$ 2,500	$ 3,500	$ 4,500
b) Accounts Receivable	16,469	20,585	25,732
c) Inventory	12,164	15,206	19,007
d) Fixed Assets	13,270	18,270	23,270
e) Other Assets	1,500	1,500	1,500
Total Assets	$45,903	$59,061	$74,009
Liabilities			
f) Accounts Payable	$ 6,082	$ 7,603	$ 9,503
g) Accrued Taxes	2,000	2,500	3,125
h) Bank Notes Payable	11,353	13,333	14,148
	$19,435	$23,436	$26,776
Net Worth			
i) Common Stock	$ 7,800	$ 7,800	$ 7,800
j) Retained Earnings	18,668	27,825	39,433
Total Net Worth	$26,468	$35,625	$47,233
Total Liabilities and Net Worth	$45,903	$59,061	$74,009

Key to Pro Forma Preparation

a) Assumed minimum balance
b) Turnover 8 times or 45 days
c) Turnover 3 times or 120 days
d) Assumed net of depreciation $5,000 increase per year
e) Assumed figure
f) 60 days Cost of Goods Sold
g) 4% of salaries
h) Plugged figure
i) Loan payable of $7,500 converted to equity
j) 2/28/70 Retained Earnings $23,303 – $11,830 advance to stockholders written off equals $11,473

EXHIBIT 4
Allied Plastics, Inc.
Pro Forma Income Statements[1]
March 1, 1970-February 28, 1973

	3/1/70- 2/28/71[2]	3/1/71- 2/29/72	3/1/72- 2/28/73
a) Gross Sales	$131,745	$164,681	$205,852
a) Less Sales Discounts	1,436	1,795	2,244
Net Sales	$130,309	$162,886	$203,608
b) Cost of Goods Sold	36,493	45,617	57,021
c) Operating Expenses	78,125	97,656	122,071
Net Operating Profit	$ 15,691	$ 19,613	$ 24,516
d) Less Interest Expense	1,300	1,300	1,300
Net Profit Before Taxes	$ 14,391	$ 18,313	$ 23,216
Federal Income Tax at 50%[3]	7,196	9,156	11,608
Net Profits	$ 7,195	$ 9,157	$ 11,608
e) Dividends	$ 0	$ 0	$ 0

Key to Pro Forma Preparation

a) 25% increase in sales and sales discounts each year
b) 27.7% of sales as per year ending 2/28/70
c) 59.3% of sales as per year ending 2/28/70,

Includes withdrawals by principals

d) 10% x $13,000 average balance on term loan
e) No dividends planned during this period

[1]Prepared in September 1970.
[2]Includes actual data from March 1, 1970-August 31, 1970.
[3]Imputed, as owners are presently taxed as individuals.

EXHIBIT 5
Allied Plastics, Inc.
Revised Pro Forma Income Statements[1]
March 1, 1972-February 28, 1973

	A	B	C
Gross Sales	$279,980	$279,980	$279,980
Less Sales Discounts	2,920	2,920	2,920
Net Sales	$277,060	$277,060	$277,060
Cost of Goods Sold	110,824	115,811	96,971
General, Selling, and Administrative Expenses	138,530	148,504	124,677
Net Operating Profit	$ 27,706	$ 12,745	$ 55,412
Less Interest Expense	2,290	2,290	2,290
Net Profit Before Taxes	$ 25,416	$ 10,455	$ 53,122
Federal Income Taxes at 50%	12,708	5,227	26,561
Net Profit After Taxes	$ 12,708	$ 5,228	$ 26,561
Dividends	$ 0	$ 0	$ 0

Assumptions for Pro Forma Statements

A — 25% increase over annualized 8/31/71 sales and sales discounts, operating profit 10% of net sales, cost of goods 40%, and operating expenses 50% of net sales, respectively; interest expense double figure on 8/31 statement.

B — 25% increase over annualized 8/31/71 sales and sales discounts, cost of goods sold and operating expenses same percent of net sales as 8/31/71 income statement; interest expense double figure on 8/31 statement.

C — 25% increase over annualized 8/31/71 sales and sales discounts, cost of goods and operating expenses 35% and 45%, respectively, representing optimal levels of efficiency; interest expense double figure on 8/31 statement.

[1]Prepared January 1972 and does not include sales and expenses from possible acquisition of vacuum forming equipment.

EXHIBIT 6
Allied Plastics, Inc.

Monthly Sales for Calendar 1970 and 1971

	1970	1971
January	$ 10,277	$ 13,350
February	10,366	16,508
March	10,189	15,578
April	10,174	18,613
May	7,283	15,571
June	10,218	20,152
July	9,487	20,195
August	10,400	21,346
September	9,700	14,045
October	12,840	17,800
November	13,526	18,000
December	13,305	12,420
	$127,765	$203,578

EXHIBIT 7
Allied Plastics, Inc.

*Total Private Nonresidential Construction
Metropolitan Atlanta Area
(in millions)*

Year	Amount
1964	$140
1965	133
1966	172
1967	200
1968	169
1969	184
1970	238
1971	149
(Jan-Aug)	

Source: Construction Review, United States Department of Commerce, December 1970 and April 1971.

EXHIBIT 8

Allied Plastics, Inc.

Percentage Breakdown of Financial Information for 53
Manufacturers of Miscellaneous Plastic Products

Statements on or about June 30, 1970, and December 31, 1970[1]

	Under $250,000	$250,000 and less than $1,000,000
Assets		
Cash	6.9	5.4
Marketable Securities	.5	.4
Receivables, Net	30.5	25.6
Inventory	21.1	22.7
All Other Current	2.2	1.6
Fixed Assets, Net	33.3	37.4
All Other Noncurrent	5.5	6.9
Total	100.0	100.0
Liabilities		
Due to Bank, Short-Term	7.0	6.7
Due to Trade	24.0	17.6
Income Taxes	2.8	2.2
Current Maturities, Long-Term Debt	5.5	4.7
All Other Current	10.4	9.1
Total Current Debt	49.7	40.3
Noncurrent Unsubordinated Debt	12.7	15.0
Total Unsubordinated Debt	62.4	55.3
Subordinated Debt	4.8	3.1
Tangible Net Worth	32.8	41.6
Total	100.0	100.0
Income Data		
Net Sales	100.0	100.0
Cost of Sales	71.9	77.2
Gross Profit	28.1	22.8
All Other Expenses Net	25.3	20.4
Profit Before Taxes	2.8	2.4

[1]Source: *Annual Statements 1971*, Robert Morris Associates, p. 53.

QUESTIONS

1. Comment on the assumptions underlying the pro forma statements in Exhibits 3 and 4.
2. Given the additional financial information in Exhibits 1 and 2, what changes, if any, should be made in the pro forma balance sheets and income statements in Exhibits 3 and 4?
3. Estimate the amount of external funds required by Allied Plastics, Inc., in fiscal 1973 and 1974, assuming acquisition of the vacuum forming machine.
4. From what sources should Allied Plastics seek additional external funds?

Case 8
Tanner's Book Store, Inc.

Late Thursday morning, July 24, 1975, Ralph Blake, sole owner of Tanner's Book Store, Inc. (TBSI), sat in his office contemplating his present predicament and wondering what his next step should be. Mr. Blake had just returned from the local bank, where he had been informed that the bank could not grant his request for a $45,000 loan increase. Mr. Blake had submitted this request in June to provide cash for operations during the slack summer months and for building the textbook inventory prior to the fall-quarter sales rush. In his analysis, Mr. Blake intended not only to review his past financial statements (Exhibit 1) but also to study some recently acquired industry ratios developed by the National Association of College Stores, Inc. (Exhibit 2).

General Business Background

TBSI was located in rented facilities adjacent to a college campus in a southern town with a population of approximately 20,000 people. Enrollment at the college had been about 6,000 students for the last two years, and Mr. Blake expected it to remain at this level for the next few years. Mr. Blake estimated that 95% of the store's business was generated by students and faculty, and he believed the store's sales volume was tied very closely to the enrollment at the college.

Mr. Blake did not have a definite breakdown of sales by category, but he estimated that the 1975 sales volume of $238,000 (TBSI operated on a fiscal year

This case was prepared by Professors Lynn E. Dellenbarger, Jr., and Emit B. Deal of Georgia Southern College as a basis for classroom discussion and not to illustrate either effective or ineffective handling of an administrative situation.

ending April 30th) involved the following amounts, with about 26% of gross sales accounted for by items other than textbooks.

Art supplies	$ 15,000
Engineering supplies	2,000
Gift items, soft goods, and fraternity and sorority supplies	25,000
Student-oriented supplies such as paper, calculators, and pencils	15,000
Books other than textbooks	5,000

	$ 62,000	26%
Textbooks	176,000	74%
Total Sales	$238,000	

Mr. Blake recognized the importance of nontextbook items both because of the high margin involved and because of their somewhat nonseasonal nature. Textbook sales were highly seasonal with the bulk of the sales falling in the four months in which the college quarters started (see Exhibit 3 for monthly sales). The bulk of the sales within these four months was during a few days although this daily pattern was not typical for all months.

Sales for the fiscal years ending April 30th for the last five years were as follows:

Year	Sales (000)
1975	$238
1974	255
1973	231
1972	218
1971	258

Mr. Blake believed the drop in sales in 1972 was due to the college opening its own book store in a location directly across the street from TBSI (Exhibit 4).

Employees

Permanent employees consisted of Mr. Blake, who worked full time at the store, and two women who had been employed at TBSI at the time Mr. Blake acquired the store. One of these women was the bookkeeper, and the other handled operating details such as ordering. All other employees were college students who were paid 85% of the minimum wage under a special exemption for student personnel. The number of students employed varied from 1 or 2 during slack periods up to 15 during the two rush weeks at the beginning of a quarter when the store might be operating six cash registers.

Leased Facilities

TBSI occupies 5,150 square feet of leased space in a building directly across the street from the college campus and the college book store (see Exhibit 4). When TBSI first opened for business in this location, it occupied 1,800 square feet of space

(A). In 1969, it added (B) 450 square feet for storage space. In 1971, it added (C) 900 more square feet, and in September 1974, it added (D) 2,000 square feet when it took over the premises formerly occupied by a men's clothing store. Before the expansion in 1974, the monthly rental was $700. With the expansion in 1974, a new five-year lease was negotiated, and the monthly rental was increased to $1,100.

The property occupied by TBSI is managed by the trust department of an out-of-town bank. When Mr. Blake realized he was in financial difficulty in 1975, he immediately attempted to renegotiate the new lease, but the trust department was unwilling to consider any changes in the lease terms.

At the time of the September 1974 expansion, TBSI also increased its bank loan by $8,000 to provide funds for additional fixtures and inventory for the new space.

Acquisition by Mr. Blake

Mr. Blake purchased the stock of TBSI in March 1973. Prior to the acquisition, Mr. Blake had had a number of years' experience working in both institutional and private book stores in both large and small cities.

He purchased 40% of the common stock of the corporation from Mr. Tanner and 60% from Mr. Stone. The working difficulties that existed between these two men was a basic reason for the business being offered for sale. Mr. Blake purchased the stock for $45,000 in the following manner:

$ 8,500	cash supplied by Mr. Blake.
$14,000	note given to Mr. Stone to be repayed at the rate of $3,500 per year.
$22,500	loan from the local bank. This note was set up on a demand basis to be renegotiated every 90-180 days. The interest rate was initially set at 8%, but as of July 1975 it had increased to 10%.

In addition to the $22,500, the local bank also lent TBSI $2,500 on the same terms as the larger loan to provide the initial cash for operations. In addition to signing the above notes in his capacity as a corporate officer, Mr. Blake also personally signed these notes and has continued to personally sign all subsequent notes.

In the acquisition of TBSI, Mr. Blake received merchandise inventory, valued at cost, of $59,000, plus fixtures, a car, and other personal property valued at $6,500. Mr. Blake also assumed accounts payable on the corporation's books of $39,000. These invoices generally have 30-day payment terms, but Mr. Blake believed 90-day payment was the generally accepted practice in the trade. The trade payables account had increased to $88,000 by July 1975.

At the time of the acquisition, Mr. Blake anticipated that increased sales and an improved gross margin would provide the means for debt reduction. He believed that promotion and advertising would provide the increased sales and that better management of used textbooks would provide the improved margin.

Market Structure

Mr. Blake visualized the market for TBSI's merchandise in the following way. (Illustrations used throughout this section are based on a new textbook with a retail list price of $10.)

Textbooks Acquired from Publishers

Pricing policy—In the new-textbook market, discounts are quoted on the retail price, with 20% being the basic discount allowed. For example, if the publisher's suggested retail price was $10, and the discount 20%, the cost to the book store would be $8. In some very few cases, the discount might be 25% or 15%, but the general rule is 20%.

Return policy—There is no standardized return policy for new textbooks. The range in policy runs from 100% to no returns in some cases. A typical policy might be allowed returns equals to 20% of the number ordered. Mr. Blake kept constantly informed of these policies through means of several trade publications.

Postage policy—The book store absorbed the postage on both new books received and on new books returned to the publisher. The general practice in the trade requires the buyer to pay postage.

Textbooks Acquired from Students

The first case is one in which the textbook will be used the next quarter.

Book was new—If the textbook is repurchased from a student who bought the book new, the store will pay the student $5 (50% of the new book retail price) and resell the book for $7.50 (75% of list price). This produces a 33% margin based on retail price.

Book was used—If the textbook is repurchased from a student who bought a used book, the store will pay the student $3.75 (50% of the used book retail price) and resell the book for $7.50. This produces a 50% margin based on retail price.

The second case is the one in which the textbook will not be used the next quarter. In this case, the book store will refer to a textbook buyer's guide which rates books and provides the list price of the book, book rating (based on such things as edition date, extent of use nationally, publisher, author, and subject matter), and the wholesale price of the book. The wholesale price might be something like $2.00 when the new book retails for $10.00. The book store receives the wholesale price plus a commission of 10% or 15% if the book is sold to the wholesaler. In this situation, the book store will base its repurchase price from the student on the wholesaler's price. The student would normally receive the wholesale price or 25¢ less than the wholesale price.

The third case is the one in which the textbook is replaced by a new edition. The book store will not repurchase books in this case since a new edition kills the old edition.

Textbooks Acquired from Wholesalers

Before every quarter, TBSI sends several major wholesalers a complete list of every book that is being requisitioned by the college for the coming quarter and indicates the quantities of each book that TBSI will accept. The wholesalers in turn send invoices for the books they can supply at 50% of the list price (in some cases, they may send new books at a discount of only 30%). The book store sells new books received from these wholesalers at full list price and used books at 75% of list. There are no return privileges on books received from wholesalers.

TBSI also receives a weekly bulletin published by the National Association of College Stores, Inc. (NACS), which contains green sheets listing books for sale by various stores and wholesalers throughout the country. Some books are obtained from this source.

Disposition of Textbooks Not Sold to Students

Textbooks left on the shelf after the regular quarterly rush period may be dealt with in several ways.

1. If they are new textbooks, they may be returned to the publisher.
2. They may be held at the store for sale at a later date.
3. They may be sold to a large wholesaler at the wholesale price.
4. The weekly NACS bulletin also contains pink sheets listing books wanted by other buyers. If TBSI sells to these buyers, it is acting as a wholesaler and will charge 50% of list price if the book is used and 70% if it is new.
5. About twice a year, a buyer from a large wholesaler visits TBSI and will buy books at the time of the visit.

Acquisition and Pricing of Nontextbook Merchandise

There are no returns allowed on these items, and the suppliers do not set a suggested retail price as is done in the textbook field. In general, Mr. Blake prices such items to provide a gross margin of 40%. TBSI sells less than $5,000 of nontextbook merchandise.

Financial Reporting Problem

At the beginning of fiscal 1975, Mr. Blake forecast sales of $280,000 and undertook the previously noted expansion. Sales reports for the first four months of fiscal 1975 (see Exhibit 3) convinced Mr. Blake that the increased sales forecast was sound.

From the time of the acquisition in 1973, Mr. Blake normally received monthly cash statements of sales. In April 1974, Mr. Blake's regular accountant moved to another town, and Mr. Blake switched his business to another local firm. The new firm continued the practice of providing monthly cash reports through August 1974. At that time, due to a backlog of work at the accounting firm's office, the statements were delayed. Mr. Blake received no monthly cash sales reports from September 1974 through February 1975. In March 1975, suspecting his business was in trouble, Mr. Blake severed his relations with the new accounting firm and switched the work back to the original accountant. The data developed at this time indicated the business had lost approximately $30,000 in the period from January to March 1975.

Bank Financing

In addition to what Mr. Blake termed permanent financing, TBSI normally borrowed short-term money from the local bank to acquire textbooks for the large sales volume at the beginning of each quarter. These funds were normally repaid shortly after the rush period. However, in January 1975, TBSI was unable to repay the short-term loan made to finance the inventory buildup for the September 1974 sales peak.

As of April 1975, indebtedness to the local bank was roughly as follows (see Exhibit 1 for details):

$22,600	Initial loan
8,000	Expansion in September 1974
3,100	Installment note to acquire a printing machine
11,500	Loan to purchase 1 acre of land
43,000	Short-term loan for inventory buildup
$88,200	

Current Situation

Mr. Blake approached the local bank in early June 1975 to borrow $40,000-$45,000 more to finance operations during the summer and to provide funds for the textbook inventory buildup for the September sales rush. At this time, accounts payable to the publishers had aged to the point that they refused to send more textbooks unless payment was received. The last week in July, the local bank informed Mr. Blake that they would not advance the requested funds.

EXHIBIT 1
Tanner's Book Store, Inc.
Balance Sheets
April 30

	1975	1974	1973	1972	1971
ASSETS					
CURRENT ASSETS:					
Cash	$ 96	$ 5,011	$10,969	$ 7,907	$ 7,455
Accounts Receivable	7,075	4,406	1,315	2,058	18,006
Merchandise Inventory ..	112,876	84,410	59,255	54,178	63,402
Prepaid Assets	NIL	1,850	28	60	NIL
Total Current Assets ..	$120,047	$ 95,677	$71,567	$64,203	$88,863
INVESTMENTS (Note 1)	$ 13,078	$ 750	NIL	NIL	NIL
PROPERTY—At Cost:					
Furniture and Fixtures ..	$ 30,547	$ 23,771	$16,044	$16,044	$15,289
Automobile and Trucks .	2,245	2,245	2,875	2,875	2,875
Total	$ 32,792	$ 26,016	$18,919	$18,919	$18,164
Less Accumulated Depreciation (Note 2) ...	17,684	12,827	12,507	10,017	7,230
Property—Net	$ 15,108	$ 13,189	$ 6,412	$ 8,902	$10,934
OTHER ASSETS—					
Loans to Shareholder	$ 33,603	$ 10,541	NIL	NIL	NIL
TOTAL	$181,836	$120,157	$77,979	$73,105	$99,797
LIABILITIES AND SHAREHOLDER'S EQUITY					
CURRENT LIABILITIES:					
Accounts Payable	$ 89,138	$ 67,305	$39,272	$36,474	$27,180
Payroll Taxes Withheld and Accrued	4,012	292	769	455	382
Notes Payable— Bank (Note 3)	86,347	11,250	171	245	30,000
Total Current Liabilities	$179,497	$ 78,847	$40,212	$37,174	$57,562
LONG-TERM LIABILITIES —Equipment note payable (less current portion) (Note 3)	$ 1,875	$ 3,229	NIL	NIL	NIL
Total Liabilities	$181,372	$ 82,076	$40,212	$37,174	$57,562
SHAREHOLDER'S EQUITY:					
Common Stock (Note 4) .	$ 28,000	$ 28,000	$28,000	$28,000	$28,000
Paid-In Surplus	8,645	8,645	8,645	8,645	8,645
Retained Earnings (Deficit)	(36,181)	1,436	1,122	(714)	5,590
Total Shareholder's Equity	$ 464	$ 38,081	$37,767	$35,931	$42,235
TOTAL	$181,836	$120,157	$77,979	$73,105	$99,797

The Notes to Financial Statements are an integral part of this statement. Prepared from books and records without audit. No opinion is expressed hereon.

EXHIBIT 1
Tanner's Book Store, Inc. (continued)
Statement of Income
For the Years Ended April 30

	1975	1974	1973	1972	1971
SALES	$237,959	$255,391	$231,676	$218,285	$258,022
COST OF GOODS SOLD	163,169	172,894	177,462	166,605	203,365
GROSS PROFIT	$ 74,790	$ 82,497	$ 54,214	$ 51,680	$ 54,657
GENERAL AND ADMINISTRATIVE EXPENSES:					
Officers' Salaries	$ 24,950	$ 19,189	$ 5,600	$ 5,200	$ 5,200
Salaries and Wages	22,681	22,176	20,775	21,602	22,057
Payroll Taxes	3,785	2,048	1,742	1,744	1,793
Office Supplies	109	282	689	649	495
Operating Supplies	1,751	615	(352)	1,430	637
Utilities	3,280	1,713	1,206	1,291	1,389
Professional Fees	3,152	2,322	1,545	1,220	1,375
Telephone	4,576	2,666	854	1,028	1,144
Miscellaneous Services ..	311	458	34	52	84
Sales and Operating Taxes	8,082	7,477	6,939	7,143	7,173
Property Insurance	3,367	1,476	737	NIL	968
Depreciation	4,857	3,045	2,490	2,807	2,500
Repairs and Maintenance	607	856	112	63	423
Automotive Expense	2,372	1,270	451	407	563
Rentals	15,808	9,902	7,600	7,867	7,099
Advertising	2,724	3,317	1,846	2,073	1,099
Contributions	248	194	10	20	49
Dues and Subscriptions .	721	426	130	155	380
Travel and Entertainment	1,000	515	204	363	141
Freight	423	NIL	NIL	2,118	1,355
Bank Charge	578	193	105	124	132
Interest	6,699	1,342	1,327	1,195	1,422
Cash Short (Over)	84	466	NIL	NIL	NIL
Miscellaneous Expenses .	166	170	50	88	NIL
TOTAL	$112,331	$ 82,118	$ 54,094	$ 58,639	$ 57,478
NET INCOME (LOSS) FROM OPERATIONS ...	$ (37,541)	$ 379	$ 120	$ (6,959)	$ (2,821)
OTHER INCOME					
INTEREST	$ 66	$ 10	$ 42	$ 26	$ 9
NET INCOME (LOSS) ...	$ (37,475)	$ 389	$ 162	$ (6,933)	$ (2,812)

The Notes to Financial Statements are an integral part of this statement. Prepared from books and records without audit. No opinion is expressed hereon.

EXHIBIT 1
Tanner's Book Store, Inc. (continued)
Notes to Financial Statements

NOTE 1 — INVESTMENT

On June 5, 1973 an option was acquired to purchase one acre of commercial property in Baxter County, Florida adjacent to Baxter Junior College. This option was exercised on June 5, 1974 for a purchase price of $12,000. An additional option was acquired on another one acre tract adjoining the original acre. This option was exercisable on July 30, 1975.

NOTE 2 — DEPRECIATION

Depreciation for this period was calculated by the straight-line method.

NOTE 3 — NOTES PAYABLE

The following notes are payble to the local bank:

Type	Date of Note	Due Date	Amount	Interest Rate	Monthly Payments	Outstanding
Install-ment	Nov. 1, 1973	Dec. 1, 1977	$ 5,005.000	12.5%	$129.30	$ 3,125.12
Regular	July 2, 1974	July 2, 1975	12,000.00	10.0%		11,469.67
Regular	April 8, 1975	June 8, 1975	22,627.18	10.0%		22,627.18
Regular	April 8, 1975	June 8, 1975	38,000.00	10.0%		38,000.00
Regular	April 8, 1975	June 8, 1975	8,000.00	10.0%		8,000.00
Regular	April 8, 1975	June 8, 1975	5,000.00	10.0%		5,000.00

TOTAL $88,221.97

All assets of Tanner's Book Store Inc. are pledged as collateral on the above notes.

NOTE 4 — COMMON STOCK

$10 par value, authorized 5,000 shares; issued 2,800 shares.

EXHIBIT 2
Tanner's Book Store, Inc.
Operating Summary

A. By Size of Store

	35 Stores with Net Sales Below $250,000 (Total Net Sales $5,241,000)				81 Stores with Profit Range in Middle 50% (Total Net Sales $120,016,000)				39 Noninstitutionally Owned Stores (Total Net Sales $101,527,000)			
	—Percent of Net Sales—				—Percent of Net Sales—				—Percent of Net Sales—			
	Avg.	Low	Med.	High	Avg.	Low	Med.	High	Avg.	Low	Med.	High
Net Sales	100.0	100.0	100.0	100.0	100.0	100.0	100.0	100.0	100.0	100.0	100.0	100.0
Cost of Sales	76.0	54.4	75.3	102.7	73.1	66.0	75.4	85.6	71.7	66.0	74.6	80.1
Gross Margin	24.0	-2.7	24.7	45.6	26.9	14.4	24.6	34.0	28.3	19.9	25.4	34.0
Operating Expense	20.2	9.7	20.4	33.7	22.9	10.5	20.7	30.6	23.5	15.4	21.7	32.2
Operating Income	3.8	-26.4	4.3	13.4	4.0	-0.0	3.4	8.9	4.8	-6.2	3.9	11.1
Other Income—Net	0.2	0.0	0.4	4.1	0.9	0.0	0.9	3.5	0.9	0.1	1.1	3.5
Other—Expense	0.2	0.2	1.7	3.2	0.5	0.0	0.6	3.6	0.5	0.1	0.7	3.6
Net Income Before Income Taxes and Profit Distribution	3.9	-26.7	4.7	13.4	4.5	0.8	4.2	6.6	5.2	-6.2	4.8	11.7

*The ratios in this exhibit are reproduced with the permission of the National Association of College Stores, Inc.

EXHIBIT 2

Tanner's Book Store, Inc. (continued)

Operating Expense

B. By Size of Store

	25 Stores with Net Sales Below $250,000 (Total Net Sales $3,635,000)				38 Noninstitutionally Owned Stores (Total Net Sales $98,061,000)			
	—Percent of Net Sales—				—Percent of Net Sales—			
	Avg.	Low	Med.	High	Avg.	Low	Med.	High
Personnel	13.9	6.4	13.0	39.2	15.2	7.0	14.2	20.6
Occupancy	4.2	1.2	3.7	10.0	3.5	0.8	2.9	10.0
Advertising	0.2	0.0	0.1	2.3	0.6	0.0	0.3	2.3
Telephone and Other Communications	0.3	0.1	0.3	0.7	0.4	0.1	0.3	1.0
Stationery and Supplies	0.6	0.2	0.5	2.0	0.8	0.1	0.6	1.4
Data Processing (Other Than Salaries)	0.4	0.0	0.2	6.9	0.4	0.1	0.3	1.4
Furniture, Fixtures, and Equipment	1.0	0.1	0.4	7.9	0.5	0.1	0.5	2.2
Professional Services	0.2	0.0	0.3	0.6	0.4	0.0	0.3	3.6
Travel and Entertainment	0.2	0.0	0.3	1.1	0.1	0.0	0.1	0.6
Insurance	0.1	0.1	0.4	0.6	0.2	0.1	0.2	0.7
Other Taxes	0.2	0.1	0.2	2.3	0.3	0.0	0.4	2.9
All Other Operating Expenses	1.6	0.0	0.7	15.5	1.4	0.1	1.0	5.1
Total Operating Expense	22.9	9.7	20.9	69.9	23.8	15.4	21.3	32.2

EXHIBIT 2
Tanner's Book Store, Inc.
*Sales Per Square Foot
of Occupied Space
(Dollars)*

C. Per square foot of occupied space (Dollars)	22 Stores with Net Sales Below $250,000 (Total Net Sales $3,305,000)			
	Avg.	Low	Med.	High
Course Books (Total)	123.1	113.4	119.1	143.1
Selling Space	151.1	115.8	149.8	167.3
Storage Space	583.6	430.4	456.2	8729.3
General Books (Total)	21.8	3.9	28.0	38.3
Selling Space	21.8	3.9	28.0	38.3
Storage Space	0.0			
All Books (Total)	102.7	48.7	116.7	460.7
Selling Space	124.7	64.5	128.0	460.7
Storage Space	449.0	198.9	461.4	9176.3
Student Supplies (Total)	43.8	20.3	49.1	82.2
Selling Space	55.6	25.4	49.1	164.4
Storage Space	192.8	101.7	215.3	245.9
Other (Total)	59.9	24.4	58.8	123.3
Selling Space	75.6	34.3	76.7	123.3
Storage Space	245.8	59.5	102.9	471.0
All Departments (Total)	64.7	21.1	56.6	201.6
Selling Space	82.6	37.1	68.6	276.3
Storage Space	278.7	48.9	361.9	1811.7
Total Space (Including Offices, etc.)	60.8	21.1	55.5	337.3

EXHIBIT 2
Tanner's Book Store, Inc. *(continued)*
Sales Per Square Foot
of Occupied Space
(Dollars)

D. All Departments	15 Stores with Net Sales Below $250,000 (Total Net Sales $2,336,000)			
	Avg.	Low	Med.	High
All Books	3.7	2.4	4.0	4.4
Student Supplies	1.9	0.9	1.7	3.3
Other	2.9	0.4	1.5	12.8
All Departments	3.1	1.1	3.0	6.9

	36 Stores with Net Sales $1,000,000 to $3,000,000 (Total Net Sales $63,570,000)			
	Avg.	Low	Med.	High
All Books	3.7	1.5	3.7	6.3
Student Supplies	3.2	1.5	2.5	6.7
Other	5.2	0.8	2.9	18.4
All Departments	3.3	1.5	2.9	6.5

E. Books Only	10 Stores with Net Sales $500,000 to $1,000,000 (Total Net Sales $8,147,000)			
	Avg.	Low	Med.	High
Course Books	3.9	1.8	3.6	8.0
General Books	2.1	0.6	2.0	3.0
All Books	3.2	1.5	3.3	4.2

EXHIBIT 3
Tanner's Book Store, Inc.
*Monthly Sales and Book Repurchases from Students**

	Month	Sales on Cash Register	Purchases from Students
1974	August	$ 3,080	$1,902
	July	5,718	576
	June	22,604	5,226
	May	8,644	2,322
	April	12,272	1,047
	March	43,354	9,408
	February	8,023	654
	January	62,885	1,750
1973	December	4,376	9,356
	November	6,374	932
	October	11,172	1,035
	September	73,998	206
	August	2,646	2,980
	July	4,597	620
	June	26,892	2,122
	May	5,182	9,870

*Summarized from cash reports.

EXHIBIT 4
Tanner's Book Store, Inc.

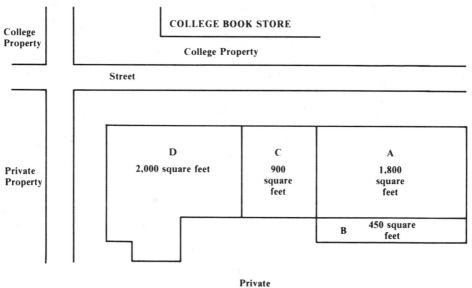

QUESTIONS

1. Analyze the present condition of TBSI and indicate the forces that have produced this condition.
2. Develop cash flows and financial statements for TBSI for the fiscal year ending April 30, 1976. Be explicit about your assumptions.
3. Based on your analysis, what are the options available to Mr. Blake?

Case 9
Willinson, Inc.

Development of the Company

Willinson, Inc., was a moderate-sized printing firm located in Mobile, Alabama. The company was founded in 1936 by George Willinson, a lifelong resident of Mobile. In the firm's early years, they printed a variety of items such as business cards, wedding invitations, letterheads, and envelopes. The firm experienced modest growth and by 1950 was doing an annual sales volume of $500,000. In 1955, George Willinson retired, and his son Jack Willinson took over the management of the firm. Sales in 1955 were approximately $800,000, with net profits of $20,000.

Jack Willinson decided to pursue a more vigorous policy concerning expansion of company sales. He believed that catalogue printing offered a potential growth market to the firm. Accordingly, he solicited retail and wholesale dry goods firms and began to develop a clientele in this area. Sales were of such magnitude that by 1959 the company was forced to increase its productive capacity by 100 percent. It did so by renting new facilities on the outskirts of Mobile.

Willinson experienced strong growth in the 1960's, and 1970 sales were approximately $4,000,000, with net profits in the neighborhood of $75,000. The company's catalogue business continued to increase and, in addition, Willinson had developed large accounts with distributors of personal cards, with special emphasis on Christmas cards. In fact, a significant portion of the firm's business was Christmas-related.

At this time, the company was owned 80 percent by Jack Willinson, with the

This case was prepared by Professor Harry R. Kuniansky of the College of Charleston as a basis for classroom discussion and not to indicate either effective or ineffective handling of an administrative situation.

other 20 percent belonging to key employees of long standing. No employee could sell their stock outside the firm unless it was offered to the company first. Since the company had always purchased all stock offered to it at book value, stock ownership outside the company was extremely unlikely. There was no public market in the stock, and dividends had never been paid. None were anticipated in the next few years.

Present Financial Situation

In early March 1973, Walter Hodgins, Willinson's controller, was initiating preparation of the firm's cash budget and a pro forma income statement for fiscal 1974 (April 1, 1973-March 31, 1974) plus a pro forma balance sheet as of March 31, 1974. Mr. Hodgins prepared the cash budget in order to determine the firm's cash needs or cash surplus for the coming year. He believed the preparation of both the cash budget and the pro forma statements facilitated company-wide planning, because it forced the firm to establish priorities in order to determine its cash needs for the next year. In additon, Mr. Hodgins felt that the presentation of the budget was helpful in its dealings with their bank, the Dauphin National Bank of Mobile.

Willinson, Inc., had banked with Dauphin National since the firm's founding, and relations with the bank were on a solid footing. Mr. Roland Norris, a bank vice-president, had serviced the account for the last three years and was well acquainted with both the financial and operational aspects of the company. Willinson had a line of credit with the bank necessary to cover its seasonal operations. The bank required the line to be cleaned up for at least two months of the year. Normally, the firm was out of debt in February and March of each year. In addition, the firm had financed capital additions on a term loan basis.

Preparation of the Budget

Mr. Hodgins realized that the sales forecast for the coming year was crucial, if the cash flow statement was to provide the company with a reasonable picture of its fund flows for the coming year. Therefore, he attempted to establish the condition of the economy in the coming year. He consulted various government publications as well as newsletters published by leading New York banks such as First National City and Manufacturers Hanover. The consensus of opinion was that in the next year the economy would remain strong and consumers would continue to gain confidence in the economy and spend more freely. In addition, unemployment would likely decline and capital spending by business would accelerate.

In relating this set of conditions to his own company, Mr. Hodgins believed the catalogue portion of the business would especially benefit from the predicted increase in consumer spending. Willinson's customers would demand larger and fancier catalogues, which would increase the firm's sales. Since the catalogues were printed mostly for dry goods firms, the sales increase would be felt mostly in the Christmas catalogues. Mr. Hodgins noted that the firm's sales had been flat for the last two years. In discussions with the sales manager, Mr. Sal Harkini and with the president, Jack Willinson, it was determined that a flat sales curve was not an acceptable company goal. In their view, Willinson's net sales should increase by approximately 10 percent next year. In light of this goal, Mr. Hodgins prepared a sales forecast by months (see Exhibit 5). He ascribed two-thirds of the firm's sales to the last six months of the year, as most of the growth was expected to occur in the Christmas-related cards and catalogues. Over the past five years, the July-December business ranged from 55 percent to 65 percent of total sales.

In order to ascertain the company's collection pattern, Mr. Hodgins prepared an analysis of the firm's collection experience over the past fiscal year. He discovered that on the average the collection period was 45 days. In other words, one-half of a month's sales were collected in the month following the sale and the other one-half in the subsequent month. Even though the firm sold on net 30-day terms, he believed the firm would not strictly enforce these terms and the 45-day collection period would hold. Noncollectible sales approximated 2 percent of net sales. He believed that this bad debt experience was a likely approximation of future uncollectibles. The firm's accounting practice was to charge off, on a monthly basis, 2 percent of sales as bad debts.

Based mainly on historical data, Mr. Hodgins estimated cost of goods sold to be 75 percent of sales. Exhibit 5 details forecasted raw material purchases and direct labor and overhead expenditures for the coming year. Terms for raw material purchases were net 30 days. The firm's policy was to remit within this period. Direct labor and overhead costs were paid in the period incurred. In view of a planned increase in capital expenditures, Mr. Hodgins believed yearly depreciation charges would be in the neighborhood of $120,000, spread equally throughout the year. All depreciation costs were charged to the manufacturing operation.

Mr. Hodgins and Mr. Willinson had been in constant communication concerning modernization of existing equipment. Both agreed that the firm must continue to acquire modern, up-to-date machinery in order to stay competitive and to insure adequate profits. Mr. Willinson expressed the belief that increased productivity was an important key to increased profitability. Accordingly, the firm had placed an order for $108,000 worth of machinery that was due to be delivered in April 1973. The firm planned to pay the seller in four equal consecutive installments beginning in April. The seller of the machinery would not charge any interest on the unpaid balance over this four-month period. Also, Mr. Hodgins expected to spend about $1,000 a month for small recurring capital needs.

In estimating his cash needs, Mr. Hodgins was on the conservative side. Although the firm had ready access to bank credit, Mr. Hodgins believed that it was unwise to try to operate with a bank balance that was extremely low, as the bank would tend to regard this as poor planning on the part of the firm. Last year, Mr. Hodgins felt that the firm had carried too small a balance in the peak months of September, October, and November. He believed that in these months more cash was needed, since cash balances were subject to larger swings in peak months. Hence, Mr. Hodgins decided that monthly average cash balances should be at least one-eighth of projected monthly cash outlays for raw materials, direct labor and overhead, and operating expenses. Although prepaid expenses had shown a steady reduction in fiscal 1973, Mr. Hodgins believed this asset would probably remain at its year-end level. Other assets would likely stay at the same year-end figure.

The estimation of operating expenses, which included approximate interest on short-term bank debt, had proved unreliable in the past. Previously, Mr.

Hodgins had assumed all operating expenses to be fixed. He decided to analyze these expenses, and he discovered that there was a definite variable element. He decided to budget operating expenses at $55,000 monthly plus 5 percent of projected sales. The 5 percent variable cost included 2 percent for bad debts expense. Although slightly more difficult to calculate, Mr. Hodgins felt the use of this formulation for estimating cash operating expenses would significantly reduce the budget variance that the firm had experienced.

On March 31, 1970, the firm borrowed $792,000, for five years at 8 percent, simple interest. The term loan was to be repaid in 20 equal, quarterly principal installments plus interest. Interest payments for the coming fiscal year would be $20,600. Mr. Hodgins estimated that the accruals account would hold at its year-end balance, and that monthly additions and subtractions to the accruals account would cancel each other out.

Income tax payments provided a difficult problem in terms of cash flow forecasting. Even though the firm's earnings were uneven during the year, Willinson paid their income tax based on their estimated earnings for the whole year. The firm paid one-fourth of their estimated taxes on July 31, October 31, and January 31. On April 30, the company paid the remainder of taxes due. Based on their actual earnings for the year, estimated income tax for fiscal 1973 was $80,000.

For fiscal 1974, projected taxable income was $239,400 with a resulting income tax of $108,400 (22% x $25,000 + 48% x $214,400). Quarterly tax payments of $27,100 would be remitted.

Mr. Hodgins did not foresee any purchases of either land or buildings during the coming year, as the rented space provided adequate capacity for the firm. Also, he did not foresee either any sale or repurchase of common stock during the next year.

Mr. Hodgins believed he could have the cash budget and the pro forma statements completed by the end of March. To facilitate preparation, Mr. Hodgins decided to estimate to the nearest hundred dollars.

EXHIBIT 1
Willinson, Inc.

Yearly Income Statements
Fiscal 1972 and 1973
(thousands)

	4/1/71- 3/31/72	4/1/72- 3/31/73
Net Sales	$4095.3	**$4185.0
Cost of Goods Sold	3090.3	3129.6
Gross Profit	$1005.0	$1055.4
Operating Expenses	932.9	881.8
Operating Profit	$ 72.1	$ 173.6
Interest on Long-Term Debt	46.0	33.2
Net Income Before Taxes	$ 26.1	$ 140.4
*Income Tax	6.0	60.9
Net Income	$ 20.1	$ 79.5
Depreciation	$ 109.2	$ 109.2

*First $25,000 taxed at 22%; all amounts over $25,000 taxed at 48%.
**Includes estimated income figure for March 1973.

EXHIBIT 2
Willinson, Inc.
Monthly Income Statements
April 1972-March 31, 1973
(hundreds)

	Apr.	May	June	July	Aug.	Sept.	Oct.	Nov.	Dec.	Jan.	Feb.	**Mar.
Net Sales	$2466	$2668	$2596	$3848	$4484	$4774	$5546	$5378	$3620	$1816	$2250	$2404
Cost of Goods Sold	1924	2092	1984	2836	3343	3485	3988	3806	2647	1546	1784	1861
Gross Profit	$ 542	$ 576	$ 612	$1012	$1141	$1289	$1558	$1572	$ 973	$ 270	$ 466	$ 543
Operating Expenses	688	715	718	733	798	801	875	819	747	610	655	679
Operating Profit	$(126)	$(139)	$(106)	$ 279	$ 343	$ 488	$ 683	$ 753	$ 226	$(340)	$(189)	$(136)
Long-Term Interest Expense	32	32	31	29	29	29	27	26	26	24	24	23
Net Income Before Taxes	$(158)	$(171)	$(137)	$ 250	$ 314	$ 459	$ 656	$ 727	$ 200	$(364)	$(213)	$(159)
*Income Tax	(76)	(82)	(66)	55	151	220	315	349	96	(175)	(102)	(76)
Net Income	$ (82)	$ (89)	$ (71)	$ 195	$ 163	$ 239	$ 341	$ 378	$ 104	$(189)	$(111)	$ (83)
Depreciation	$ 91	$ 91	$ 91	$ 91	$ 91	$ 91	$ 91	$ 91	$ 91	$ 91	$ 91	$ 91

*All amounts taxed at 48% except first $25,000 earned in July, which is taxed at 22%.
**Projected income statement for March 1973.

EXHIBIT 3

Willinson, Inc.

Yearly Balance Sheet
Fiscal 1972 and 1973
(thousands)

	As of March 31, 1972	As of *March 31, 1973
Assets		
Cash	$ 70.3	$ 59.4
Accounts Receivable (Net)	335.9	345.9
Inventory	322.2	309.3
Prepaid Expenses	69.5	60.4
Total Current Assets	$ 797.9	$ 775.0
Land	—	—
Buildings	—	—
Machinery and Equipment	$ 938.4	$ 955.0
Less Accumulated Depreciation	288.3	397.5
Total Fixed Assets	$ 650.1	$ 557.5
Other Assets	32.3	30.4
Total Assets	$1480.3	$1362.9
Liabilities		
Accounts Payable	$ 90.0	$ 79.9
Accruals Including Interest Payable	149.3	122.0
Notes Payable—Banks	0	0
Current Maturities of Long-Term Debt	158.4	158.4
Income Taxes Payable	2.0	.9
Total Current Liabilities	$ 399.7	$ 361.2
Long-Term Liabilities	$ 316.8	$ 158.4
Total Liabilities	$ 716.5	$ 519.6
Capital		
Common Stock	$ 42.6	$ 42.6
Paid-in Capital	48.6	48.6
Retained Earnings	672.6	752.1
Total Capital	$ 763.8	843.3
Total Liabilities and Capital	$1480.3	$1362.9

*Projected Balance Sheet.

EXHIBIT 4
Willinson, Inc.

Monthly Balance Sheet
April 1972-March 1973
(hundreds)

	Apr.	May	June	July	Aug.	Sept.	Oct.	Nov.	Dec.	Jan.	Feb.	*Mar.
Assets												
Cash	$ 281	$ 247	$ 276	$ 396	$ 462	$ 354	$ 396	$ 286	$ 393	$ 459	$ 756	$ 594
Accounts Receivable (Net)	3345	4002	4126	5167	6400	7183	7707	8170	6603	3929	3114	3459
Inventory	3304	3471	3504	2567	3107	3999	4392	4600	3896	3201	3066	3093
Prepaid Expenses	624	588	570	1110	1053	974	931	873	848	792	709	604
Total Current Assets	$ 7554	$ 8308	$ 8476	$ 9240	$11022	$12510	$13426	$13929	$11740	$ 8381	$ 7645	$ 7750
Land	—	—	—	—	—	—	—	—	—	—	—	—
Buildings	—	—	—	—	—	—	—	—	—	—	—	—
Machinery and Equipment	$ 9397	$ 9416	$ 9426	$ 9436	$ 9452	$ 9480	$ 9496	$ 9506	$ 9506	$ 9532	$ 9542	$ 9550
Less Accumulated Depreciation	2974	3065	3156	3247	3338	3429	3520	3611	3702	3793	3884	3975
Total Fixed Assets	$ 6423	$ 6351	$ 6270	$ 6189	$ 6114	$ 6051	$ 5976	$ 5895	$ 5804	$ 5739	$ 5658	$ 5575
Other Assets	364	382	348	382	538	538	409	355	379	479	350	304
Total Assets	$14341	$15041	$15094	$15811	$17674	$19099	$19811	$20179	$17923	$14599	$13653	$13629

*Projected Balance Sheet, March 1973.

(Balance Sheet continues on following page)

EXHIBIT 4
Willinson, Inc. (continued)

Monthly Balance Sheet
April 1972-March 1973
(hundreds)

	Apr.	May	June	July	Aug.	Sept.	Oct.	Nov.	Dec.	Jan.	Feb.	*Mar.
Liabilities												
Accounts Payable	$ 814	$ 973	$ 1046	$ 1573	$ 1802	$ 2427	$ 2634	$ 2543	$ 1180	$ 925	$ 824	$ 799
Accruals Including Interest Payable	1023	1050	1146	1089	1203	1333	1162	1149	1196	987	1060	1220
Notes Payable—Banks	668	1353	1374	1967	3173	3384	4000	3745	2605	705	0	0
Current Maturities of Long-Term Debt	1584	1584	1584	1584	1584	1584	1584	1584	1584	1584	1584	1584
Income Taxes Payable	(76)	(158)	(224)	(369)	(218)	2	117	466	562	187	85	9
Total Current Liabilities	$ 4013	$ 4802	$ 4926	$ 5844	$ 7544	$ 8730	$ 9497	$ 9487	$ 7127	$ 4388	$ 3553	$ 3612
Long-Term Liabilities	$ 2772	$ 2772	$ 2772	$ 2376	$ 2376	$ 2376	$ 1980	$ 1980	$ 1980	$ 1584	$ 1584	$ 1584
Total Liabilities	$ 6785	$ 7574	$ 7698	$ 8220	$ 9920	$11106	$11477	$11467	$ 9107	$ 5972	$ 5137	$ 5196
Capital												
Common Stock	$ 426	$ 426	$ 426	$ 426	$ 426	$ 426	$ 426	$ 426	$ 426	$ 426	$ 426	$ 426
Paid-in Capital	486	486	486	486	486	486	486	486	486	486	486	486
Retained Earnings	6644	6555	6484	6679	6842	7081	7422	7800	7904	7715	7604	7521
Total Capital	$ 7556	$ 7467	$ 7396	$ 7591	$ 7754	$ 7993	$ 8334	$ 8712	$ 8816	$ 8627	$ 8516	$ 8433
Total Liabilities and Capital	$14341	$15041	$15094	$15811	$17674	$19099	$19811	$20179	$17923	$14599	$13653	$13629

*Projected Balance Sheet, March 1973.

EXHIBIT 5

Willinson, Inc.

*Projections of Monthly Sales, Raw Material Purchases,
and Direct Labor and Overhead for Fiscal 1974
(hundreds)*

	Sales	Raw Material Purchases	Direct Labor and Overhead Cost
April	$ 2,500	$ 900	$ 900
May	2,700	1,000	1,000
June	2,700	1,000	1,000
July	4,300	1,500	1,500
August	5,000	1,700	1,700
September	5,000	2,100	2,100
October	6,300	2,100	2,100
November	6,000	2,100	2,100
December	4,300	1,500	1,500
January	2,200	800	800
February	2,500	900	900
March	2,500	900	900
	$46,000	$16,500	$16,500

QUESTIONS

1. Prepare a monthly cash budget for the period April 1973-March 1974 (round figures to nearest hundred dollars).
2. Prepare a pro forma income statement for fiscal 1974 and 1975 and a pro forma balance sheet as of March 31, 1974, and March 31, 1975.
3. Evaluate the reasonableness of the assumptions made by Mr. Hodgins in the preparation of the cash budget.

*

PART TWO
MANAGEMENT OF WORKING CAPITAL

*

Case 10
Houston Wire Rope Company

Late in 1967, Mr. Paul H. Rogers, major stockholder and president of Houston Wire Rope Company, faced the perennial capital-shortage problem of small business concerns.

Background of the Company

In 1951, Mr. Rogers, then a sales representative for a major producer of wire rope, conceived the idea of a business which would specialize in the purchase and resale of used wire rope. Acting upon the idea, he established his business in Houston, Texas, purchasing used wire rope from the oil fields and selling it to mining, logging, and marine companies. In addition to purchasing and selling, some processing of the used rope was required. This involved rewinding it onto new reels, inspection and grading of the rope, cutting out seriously defective pieces, and lubrication. The company quickly gained market acceptance and increased its sales volume each year.

In 1967, the Houston Wire Rope Company had attained an annual sales volume of $1,193,000. It had added new wire rope imported from Holland, Belgium, Germany, Italy, and Japan to supplement its lines of used rope. In fact, new rope had grown to account for almost 58 percent of total dollar sales volume. Approximately 40 percent of used rope sales were made to the marine industry (including substantial sales to large dredging companies), 25 percent to the logging industry, and 35 percent to the mining industry. Of the imported new rope sales,

This case was prepared by Professor Justin G. Longnecker of Baylor University as a basis for classroom discussion and not to illustrate either effective or ineffective handling of an administrative situation. Permission for use granted by Southwestern Publishing Company.

about 60 percent went to industrial customers, 25 percent to marine customers, and 15 percent to oil producers.

Sales were made to a nationwide market and even to a few accounts in Canada. Branch warehouses were also maintained in Jeanerette, Louisiana, and Oklahoma City, Oklahoma. A warehouse at Eugene, Oregon, had recently been closed. Although the major purpose of the branches was to purchase used rope from the oil industry in their respective areas, they also made sales in the same areas.

Need for Additional Funds

Throughout the history of the business, Mr. Rogers had felt the limitations imposed by inadequate capital. In starting each new branch, for example, a sum of $1,000 had been deposited in a local bank for use by the branch manager. This amount was increased as need developed for additional funds in the area. Competition had frequently been great, however, for all available funds.

The nature of the financing problem had changed somewhat over the years. In 1967, the company was being pressured by its bank to reduce short-term borrowing. In fact, the bank desired that outstanding loans be substantially reduced by a series of payments over the next few months. This pressure for reduction of short-term loans occurred at a time when the company was experiencing a need for all the working capital it could obtain. Working funds were required for normal operating requirements, and cash was also needed to pay income taxes and employees' bonus at the end of the year.

Relationships with Local Bank

The bulk of Houston Wire Rope Company's banking business was transacted with a relatively small local bank. Mr. Rogers was a stockholder and also served as a director of this bank. Although the company was free to deal with any bank, there was a normal expectation that the company would concentrate the major part of its business with this bank. Although Mr. Rogers owned stock, it might be noted that he was not a major stockholder of the bank.

The size of this bank was such that its maximum loan limit to any one business firm was $40,000. A limit of this type was not particularly burdensome to the firm when it was small, but it did present problems as the company grew in size and in its loan requirements. The local bank did arrange for additional loans from a larger Houston bank as the need for funds exceeded its own capacity. Such loans were negotiated through the local bank, although occasionally Houston Wire Rope Company personnel had direct contact with the larger Houston bank.

All notes payable to the local bank were secured by an officer's letter of guaranty. In effect, this meant that Mr. Rogers, the president, personally guaranteed every obligation of the corporation to the bank. This applied not only to unsecured loans, but also to notes supported by warehouse receipts (covering new wire rope) and installment notes secured by equipment. In effect, therefore, the loans were supported by the capital of the Houston Wire Rope Company, which amounted to a little more than $286,000, by collateral in the form of wire rope and equipment, and also by the personal signature of the president.

Unsecured Loans

The unsecured loans of the Houston Wire Rope Company amounted to $44,000 as of September 30, 1967. (This borrowing was supported by an insurance policy on the life of the president.) It is evident from the financial statements in Exhibit A that this type of borrowing had increased rather than decreased during recent years. Indeed, it had not been reduced to zero at any time during recent years.

The bank had expressed the opinion that this borrowing should be reduced to zero within the next few months. The bank took the position that it did not wish to provide intermediate or long-term capital for the company. The constant renewal of short-term notes, however, was equivalent to long-term financing.

As a result of pressure by the bank, Houston Wire Rope Company was attempting to reduce this loan by approximately $8,000 each month. It appeared that this would become increasingly difficult in view of the continuing demand for operating funds and the need for cash for income tax and profit sharing payments. This borrowing carried a 7 percent interest rate.

Borrowing Secured by Warehouse Receipts

Another type of bank borrowing used to finance inventory was secured by bonded warehouse receipts. New wire rope was placed in a bonded warehouse, and the bank proceeded to lend 80 percent of the cost value of this rope. As of September 30, 1967, this amounted to $60,092.80.

Only a part of the company's rope was housed in a bonded warehouse. All used rope and some new rope were kept in the company's warehouse and yard. The arrangement of keeping the wire rope in the bonded warehouse provided no great difficulty in meeting customer requests. In other words, the new rope could be obtained quickly from the warehouse as it was needed to fill customer orders. From a marketing standpoint, therefore, there was little problem involved in this method of financing.

The interest charge for this borrowing, to be computed realistically, would need to reflect not only the direct interest charge but also warehouse costs. When analyzed in this way, it appeared that the actual interest cost on this type of borrowing was between 9 and 10 percent per annum.

The larger Houston bank carrying the warehouse loan had expressed reluctance to continue the loan beyond the calendar year of 1967. From the standpoint of the bank, the element of danger in such a loan is determined by the stability or lack of stability in the value of the item being warehoused. According to the feelings of Houston Wire Rope Company personnel, new wire rope is not subject to extensive physical depreciation or obsolescence and thus should support a loan without undue concern to lending officials. However, the lending bank was pressuring for reduction of this type of borrowing.

Notes Secured by Equipment

Another type of borrowing was secured by equipment—primarily automobiles and trucks. As of September 30, 1967, such loans amounted to $18,153.93. These loans involved monthly installment payments. The rate of interest was 9 percent. In view of the installment basis of payment, however, the actual rate of interest was higher than the nominal rate.

Accounts Receivable

Trade accounts receivable constituted a substantial portion of the company's current assets, amounting to $157,873.42 as of September 30, 1967. Aging of these accounts for the last three years produced the following distribution:

Age	9-30-67	9-30-66	9-30-65
Current to 30 days	$ 90,411.52	$ 73,753.98	$ 84,303.97
30-60 days	24,614.62	30,184.44	35,760.14
60-90 days	14,149.65	15,577.69	15,768.63
Over 90 days	28,697.63	31,197.83	20,169.35
TOTAL	$157,873.42	$150,713.94	$156,001.99

Mr. Rogers felt that the growing age in accounts receivables was explained, in part at least, by the practice of selling to marginal customers, such as small oil drillers, who were frequently slow in their payments. There was no way to determine quantitatively, however, the extent to which this may have been responsible for the change.

Houston Wire Rope Company offered terms of sale of 2/10, n/30. In spite of the attractive discount for cash payment, however, the company was forced to carry the large accounts receivable balance.

Inventory Financing

The largest working capital item of Houston Wire Rope Company was that of inventory. As of September 30, 1967, the inventory account, both new and used rope, amounted to $252,344.01. Of this amount, $74,383.50 was pledged as collateral on notes payable. In other words, this represented new rope that was stored in the bonded warehouse.

The company was finding it increasingly difficult to control the inventory level of used wire rope. The supply of used rope had declined in recent years, making it more difficult to obtain quantities of used rope that at an earlier period were readily available. Accordingly, the company management felt compelled to take advantage of every opportunity to purchase used rope whenever it was available at a reasonable price.

Net Worth Financing

As is evident from the balance sheet presented in Exhibit A, the net worth of the company accounted for more than 50 percent of total liabilities and net worth. As of September 30, 1967, total net worth amount to $286,161.22. This amount has been built up over the years by retaining a portion of net income in the firm. A comparison of sales and net income retained in the business is presented in the following tabulation:

Year Ended	Sales	Net Income Retained in Business
9-30-67	$1,193,364.55	$17,405.30
9-30-66	1,240,073.05	20,328.11
9-30-65	1,080,803.33	33,693.14

The profits that were plowed back into the business provided the funds for expansion. In fact, Mr. Rogers had reinvested substantially all earnings over and above expenses. His personal assets were thus largely tied up in the business.

Income taxes had obviously reduced the funds available for expansion. In the last three fiscal years, a total of almost $27,000 had been required for income tax payments.

In addition, a cash bonus plan paid employees 25 percent of profits before income taxes, until 1967, when it was decided the reduction in profit would not justify any cash bonus. A profit-sharing (retirement) plan paid 25 percent of profits after bonus and before income taxes. Mr. Rogers felt that employees of the firm (28 in all) were in a large measure responsible for the success of the business and that these compensation plans were important in recognizing employee contributions. They obviously imposed a requirement for cash, however, that might otherwise have been available for other uses. They had received some criticism from the lending banks for paying out such a large percentage of profits to employees when they were needed as additional working capital in the business.

Key employees have the privilege of buying company stock at book value, and to some extent the cash bonuses had been used for this purpose. As of September 30, 1967, seven employees held approximately 11 percent of the outstanding stock and Mr. Rogers owned 89 percent. No stock was held by outsiders, and Mr. Rogers wished to avoid sale of the stock to individuals who were not directly associated with the business.

Term Financing

It is evident from the financial statements in Exhibit A that the Houston Wire Rope Company had no intermediate- or long-term debt financing. From time to time, it appeared logical that some long- or intermediate-term loans should be substituted for the short-term financing. This would not only facilitate expansion, but it would also reduce the pressure from short-term financing sources.

The possibility of obtaining longer-term funds had been explored only tentatively in the past. At one time, the company talked briefly with a representative of the Small Business Administration about the possibility of a Small Business Administration loan. It appeared to company management, however, that such a loan might impose unreasonable restrictions and reduce the flexibility of company management. As a consequence, the company backed away from such a proposal before exploring the prospects in detail. On another occasion, the company had discussed with a major insurance company the prospects for a long-term loan. The timing of this particular request was unfortunate, however. It had coincided with a decline in company net income and thus encountered questions on the part of the insurance company's loan examiner. The company management had not pursued either of these possibilities consistently or aggressively, however.

EXHIBIT A

Houston Wire Rope Company

Comparative Balance Sheet for 1967, 1966, and 1965

	9-30-67	9-30-66	9-30-65
ASSETS			
Current			
Cash on hand and in banks	$ 33,451.48	$ 17,745.45	$ 23,527.69
Accounts receivable:			
Trade	157,873.42	150,713.94	156,001.99
Employees & miscellaneous	642.64	950.15	1,580.73
Inventory			
New wire rope (partially pledged as collateral on notes payable)	206,226.53	171,483.47	238,706.85
Used wire rope	46,107.48	50,876.61	43,250.73
TOTAL CURRENT ASSETS	$444,301.35	$391,769.62	$463,067.99
Other			
Prepaid insurance	$ 8,289.19	$ 9,668.60	$ 10,661.72
Cash surrender value of life insurance	7,412.00	6,342.50	5,280.50
Club memberships	1,020.00	1,020.00	1,236.00
Airline and utility deposits	525.00	435.00	435.00
Prepaid interest	780.26	410.88	2,246.41
Prepaid rent	325.00	1,240.00	175.00
TOTAL OTHER ASSETS	$ 18,351.45	$ 19,116.98	$ 20,034.63
Property			
Automobiles and trucks	$ 72,484.18	$ 93,052.91	$115,976.16
Machinery & equipment	25,673.56	23,200.41	18,630.03
Office equipment	17,171.79	14,297.05	11,658.02
Leasehold improvements	15,616.01	15,616.01	1,062.60
	$130,945.54	$146,166.38	$147,326.81
Less Depreciation	57,488.05	67,246.56	58,329.57
TOTAL PROPERTY	$ 73,457.49	$ 78,919.82	$ 88,997.24
TOTAL ASSETS	$536,110.49	$489,806.42	$572,099.86

EXHIBIT A
Houston Wire Rope Company *(continued)*

Comparative Balance Sheet for 1967, 1966, and 1967

	9-30-67	9-30-66	9-30-65
LIABILITIES AND CAPITAL			
Current Liabilities			
Notes payable—Bank (secured by officer's letter of guaranty):			
Secured by insurance policy on life of officer	$ 44,000.00	$ 24,000.00	$ 23,000.00
Secured by warehouse receipts covering new wire rope	60,092.80	34,465.20	81,160.52
Monthly installment notes payable due within one year, secured by equipment	18,153.93	6,861.47	27,984.68
	$122,246.73	$ 65,326.67	$132,145.20
Accounts payable—Trade	96,217.77	108,032.89	123,788.51
Due to employees' profit sharing trust	7,268.43	8,842.71	16,684.59
Bonus payable to employees	— 0 —	10,604.55	15,141.00
Estimated income tax payable	4,934.58	6,535.60	16,500.00
Payroll, property, and sales tax payable	9,166.06	11,537.13	11,230.99
Accrued payroll	3,773.20	3,785.35	2,989.56
TOTAL	$243,606.77	$214,664.90	$318,479.85
Noncurrent Liabilities			
Installment notes payable due after one year	$ — 0 —	$ — 0 —	$ 4,564.60
Note payable—Loan on life insurance policy	6,342.50	6,342.50	— 0 —
TOTAL LIABILITIES	$249,949.27	$221,007.40	$323,044.45
Capital			
Capital stock	$234,270.00	$234,270.00	$234,270.00
Earned surplus	52,518.82	35,113.52	14,785.41
	$286,788.82	$269,383.52	$249,055.41
Less: Stock held in Treasury at cost	627.60	584.50	— 0 —
	$286,161.22	$268,799.02	$249,055.41
TOTAL LIABILITIES AND CAPITAL	$536,110.49	$489,806.42	$572,099.86

EXHIBIT B
Houston Wire Rope Company
Comparative Income and Expenses
for Years Ended September 30, 1967, 1966, and 1965

	Year Ended		
	9-30-67	9-30-66	9-30-65
INCOME			
Sales	$1,193,364.55	$1,240,073.05	$1,080,803.33
Less: Material cost	626,230.77	624,008.55	515,626.76
Gross profit	$ 567,133.78	$ 616,064.50	$ 565,176.57
Other Income	6,442.25	4,803.11	4,322.79
	$ 573,576.03	$ 620,867.61	$ 569,499.36
EXPENSE			
Advertising	$ 6,600.70	$ 8,201.07	$ 5,072.98
Auto, truck, and equipment leasing	36,119.72	17,089.48	356.36
Bad debts	6,537.74	7,827.51	8,516.76
Contract work	1,648.05	1,946.02	1,174.24
Contributions	305.00	178.90	492.50
Depreciation	26,268.88	33,681.62	32,852.56
Dues and subscriptions	1,568.30	1,397.00	1,398.65
Entertainment	2,099.45	3,481.10	1,901.26
Freight	35,370.37	38,814.53	32,698.42
Insurance—General	10,612.38	13,417.22	11,292.24
—Group	5,637.98	6,634.53	5,951.46
—Life	1,029.42	215.20	236.20
Interest expense	10,006.01	12,771.86	8,016.58
Legal and professional	10,385.53	9,397.61	8,281.10
Office expense	7,236.99	6,320.51	6,075.93
Pension expense	600.00	1,200.00	600.00
Reels & splicing	7,832.62	5,618.64	6,048.44
Rent expense	16,842.50	14,955.00	14,300.00
Repairs	4,359.37	3,240.91	3,220.01
Sales discount	14,045.60	15,423.15	11,831.28
Sales promotion	— 0 —	1,266.40	3,882.90
Supplies	10,234.59	9,905.80	10,375.40
Taxes	20,823.22	20,539.40	18,562.43
Travel expense—Moving employees	2,594.10	946.85	429.75
—Cars	15,001.83	21,637.93	13,168.77
—Trucks	28,631.34	35,959.64	32,699.53
—Salesmen	31,529.84	36,148.27	30,346.83
Utilities	15,530.03	16,228.45	13,623.35
Wages, salaries, & bonus	213,359.29	238,565.70	217,811.94
Bonded warehouse expense	1,691.45	2,486.49	1,543.13
	$ 544,502.30	$ 585,496.79	$ 502,761.00
Net Income Before Other Deductions	$ 29,073.73	$ 35,370.82	$ 66,738.36
OTHER DEDUCTIONS			
Profit-sharing plan	$ 7,268.43	$ 8,842.71	$ 16,684.59
Estimated income taxes	4,400.00	6,200.00	16,360.63
	$ 11,668.43	$ 15,042.71	$ 33,045.22
NET INCOME	$ 17,405.30	$ 20,328.11	$ 33,693.14

QUESTIONS

1. Analyze the financial statements of Houston Wire Rope Company, indicating the strengths and weaknesses of the company.
2. Are the banks justified in requesting that the outstanding loans be substantially reduced over the next few months?
3. As Mr. Rogers, what type of loan arrangement would you propose to a lender? What size loan is needed? What type of lender should you approach?

Case 11
Carton Industries Company

In early 1961, Robert Moore, a loan officer of the Illinois National Bank of Chicago, was reviewing a loan request from Carton Industries Company of Clearwater, Wis. Carton Industries had just purchased the Dairy Crate Company, a Chicago firm which had been a nonborrowing customer of Illinois National since 1949. It was at the request of the former owners of Dairy Crate that Illinois National was reviewing the loan application. Carton Industries desired a loan of $280,000 to finance the working capital needs of the combined companies.

The negotiations which resulted in the merger of Carton Industries and Dairy Crate Company had taken several months to complete. Carton Industries bought Dairy Crate for two basic reasons: (1) Dairy Crate's product line was competitive with Carton Industries' major product line, and (2) Dairy Crate had valuable sales associations and contracts in the metropolitan Chicago area. Carton Industries had developed a strong national market for its milk bottle and carton crates. These quality products enjoyed wide market acceptance. Dairy Crate Company had developed a similar acceptance of its milk crates in the Chicago market.

In 1960, Carton Industries leased a new 48,000-square-foot plant in Arkansas. This decision was based on a presentation made by the local Arkansas Chamber of Commerce to the president of Carton Industries during a vacation trip to the area. The annual rental was $15,000, but the completion of the plant was delayed by adverse weather. Carton Industries leased the plant to provide a centralized sawmill operation near sources of raw materials and low-cost labor.

With the newly merged operation, it was anticipated that 65 percent of sales

This case was prepared by Professor John A. Haslem of the University of Maryland at College Park and Mr. Robert J. Huffman as a basis for classroom discussion and not to illustrate either effective or ineffective handling of an administrative situation.

would be for wooden and metal milk bottle crates and wire milk carton crates. Other products manufactured and sold were bakery cabinets and refrigerating units (15 percent) and steel partitions fabricated for a large manufacturer of dairy wagons and milk trucks (15 percent). The remaining 5 percent of sales were air filters and small air-conditioning and warm-air heating units.

Carton Industries planned to move the Dairy Crate operation to its modern, efficient plant in Clearwater. The Carton Industries manufacturing facility employed 225 persons in a 70,000-square-foot leased plant. The annual rental was $28,000.

The company officers were:

Royal Strack—age 43: president and chief executive officer
Charles Brinker—age 47: executive vice president and general manager
Frank Strack—age 40: vice president (and a practicing lawyer in Milwaukee)
Clarence Strack—age 31: treasurer and sales manager
John Strack—age 37: secretary (and a real estate broker in Chicago)

Each officer's salary ranged from $15,000-$21,000. In addition, the company employed three full-time salesmen and six manufacturers' representatives.

The board of directors was made up of the Strack brothers and their mother, who held the 2,000 shares of outstanding common stock. The company was founded in 1921 by Royal Strack, Sr., who died in 1954. The family was the beneficiary of the Royal Strack, Sr., Real Estate Trust. The trust assets were profitable commercial and residential rental properties with a market value of $380,000.

Carton Industries had been a steady borrower at the First National Bank of Clearwater until the end of 1960, when the bank asked the company to seek other sources of financing. The Clearwater bank refused to extend additional credit because of Carton Industries' inability to retire its debt in recent years. The company's working capital position had worsened with the decline in sales and with losses suffered in 1959 and 1960.

The Clearwater bank's refusal to extend additional credit was precipitated by the merger with Dairy Crate. The bank felt the merger was unwise because Carton Industries had enough problems in meeting its current obligations without adding to the difficulty by purchasing a company which was unknown to the bank. Carton Industries currently owed the First National Bank of Clearwater $235,000.

Carton Industries requested the $280,000 loan to retire the outstanding loan at the Clearwater bank, to provide for start-up expenses at the Arkansas plant, and to pay some of the larger trade payables. The principals said they would support the loan with their available personal assets. Although this willingness suggested the owners were more optimistic than recent operating results indicated, Moore agreed to review the past financial statements, counsel further with the officers, and conduct various credit and trade inquiries before reaching a decision. The commercial loan policy of Illinois National Bank was to consider seriously all legitimate and reasonable credit requests of its present customers and prospective borrowers. Because of its large capitalization, Illinois National's legal loan limit was $2,750,000 compared to $300,000 for the First National Bank of Clearwater.

As a first step in the credit analysis, Moore asked the company to provide financial statements for the last five years on a combined basis (to reflect the merger with Dairy Crate Company). The statements were prepared by an accounting firm suggested by Moore, because neither firm had previously issued certified statements. Therefore, the CPA firm was unable to issue an opinion on the combined statements. These statements and some related notes, along with the personal net worth of the Strack family, are shown in Exhibits 1, 2, and 3.

EXHIBIT 1

Carton Industries Company

Balance Sheet (Combined)

	12/31/56	12/31/57	12/31/58	12/31/59	12/31/60
Cash[a]	$ 9,300	$ 41,400	$ 79,600	$ 44,500	$ 22,700
Notes Receivable	11,400	5,100	7,500		11,900
Accounts Receivable	158,100	158,900	169,900	150,800	172,700
Inventory	304,600	339,900	352,800	411,000	399,100
Other Accts. Rec.					23,500
Fed. Inc. Tax Refund					29,700
CURRENT ASSETS	$483,400	$545,300	$609,800	$606,300	$659,600
Investments			$ 1,000		
Machinery & Fixtures (net)[b]	$ 98,400	$126,100	138,100	$146,900	$207,700
Deferred Charges	13,100	7,500	7,500	8,000	10,300
Due from Officers	5,600	4,800	5,800		8,800
Other Notes & Accts. Rec.				7,100	
Cash Value Life Ins.[c]	28,800	34,900	49,900	46,600	53,400
TOTAL ASSETS	$629,300	$718,600	$803,100	$814,900	$939,800
Notes Payable—Bank	$ 40,000	$ 45,000	$ 95,000	$115,000	$200,000
Notes Payable—Ins. Co.[c]				40,100	40,100
Accounts Payable—Mdse.	36,900	41,500	62,400	80,100	247,400
Notes Payable—Officers	67,000	54,700	47,200	96,600	104,700
Accruals	53,600	59,200	59,500	58,000	56,200
Fed. Inc. Taxes	6,900	27,500	25,500		
CURRENT LIABILITIES	$204,400	$227,900	$289,600	$389,800	$648,400
Notes Payable—Bank					$ 35,000
TOTAL LIABILITIES	$204,400	$227,900	$280,600	$389,800	$683,400
Capital Stock—Common	$100,000	$100,000	$100,000	$100,000	$100,000
Retained Earnings	324,900	390,700	413,500	325,100	156,400
TOTAL LIABILITIES & NET WORTH	$629,300	$718,600	$803,100	$814,900	$939,800
[a]Average monthly bank balances	$ 39,000	$ 41,500	$ 44,000	$ 35,500	$ 16,000

[b]Fixed asset expenditures in 1960 were largely the result of equipping the Arkansas plant.

[c]The company has been paying for officer life insurance for many years; in 1959, part of the cash value was pledged to secure policy loans.

EXHIBIT 2
Carton Industries Company
Profit and Loss Statement (Combined)
(000 Omitted)

	1956	1957	1958	1959	1960
Net Sales	$2,005	$2,186	$2,315	$2,230	$1,995
Cost of Sales	1,603	1,724	1,869	1,863	1,791
Gross Profit	$ 402	$ 462	$ 446	$ 367	$ 204
Selling, G. & A., and Officers' Salaries	273	313	390	455	405
Operating Profit (Loss)	$ 129	$ 149	$ 56	$ (88)	$ (201)
Federal Inc. Tax (Refund)	63	71	26		(32)
Net Profit (Loss)	$ 66	$ 78	$ 30	$ (88)	$ (169)
Dividends	23	12	7		
Retained Earnings	$ 43	$ 66	$ 23	$ (88)	$(169)

Notes:

Sales pattern was fairly steady with a slight decline in January.

Sales terms were 1/10, net 30.

Collection experience indicated usually less than 2 percent of receivables over 90 days past due.

Total officers salaries averaged about $90,000.

EXHIBIT 3
Carton Industries Company
Strack Family Assets, 12/31/60

Assets	R. Strack	F. Strack	C. Strack	J. Strack
Stock in Carton Industries	$ 51,200	$ 51,200	$51,200	$51,200
Loans to Carton Industries	36,500	27,100	15,400	25,700
All Other (net)	94,300	39,700	22,400	18,100
Total Net Worth	$182,000	$118,000	$89,000	$95,000

Excludes beneficial interests in the R. Strack, Sr., Real Estate Trust of which Mrs. Royal Strack, Sr., is the prime income beneficiary during her lifetime (with provision for distribution of the assets to her sons upon her death).

QUESTIONS

1. Analyze the factors causing Carton Industries' need for additional working capital.
2. Would you, as Mr. Moore, approve the loan request to Carton Industries? If so, on what basis?

Case 12
Lady Patrician, Incorporated

Company History

Lady Patrician, located in Augusta, Georgia, was founded in December 1964 by Mr. Eric Strong, who assumed the title and duties of President. At that time, Strong was 32 years old. His career began ten years earlier, when a large cosmetic manufacturer hired him as a college graduate. Ultimately, he served this company as one of its district sales managers. He resigned this job to form Lady Patrician. Except for some aspects of the job as sales manager, history to that time left Mr. Strong's managerial and organizational talents untested. However, former subordinates described Strong as progressive and intelligent, but with a tendency to be overbearing.

The company's other principal was Mr. Clarence Twitchell. In 1964, he was 40 years old and had practiced in Augusta, Georgia, as a Certified Public Accountant for the preceding 15 years. After joining Lady Patrician, Mr. Twitchell continued as a senior partner in a local public accounting firm.

Lady Patrician was founded to manufacture and market a line of lipsticks, nail enamels, and nail care products. The firm's chief officers believed a strong demand existed for low-cost, high-quality nail products and lipsticks. Mr. Strong thought the key to success in cosmetic production and sales was mass distribution. He believed distribution cost could be lowered significantly through marketing in large volume. To achieve this type of distribution, Strong proposed to market the Lady Patrician line through manufacturers' representatives located throughout the

This case was prepared by Professor Harry R. Kuniansky of the College of Charleston as a basis for classroom discussion and not to illustrate either effective or ineffective handling of an administrative situation.

country. These agents would contact the large wholesale drug houses, who in turn serviced every significant drugstore within the continental United States.

Company Operations

Lady Patrician's basic terms of sale were 2/10, net 30. Frequently, however, terms of net 60 days were allowed. In many cases, sales were made on a so-called guaranteed basis. Under this arrangement, the right is reserved to the buyer to return the goods if not sold within a certain period of time. This differs formally from consignment[1] selling in that title to the goods passes to the buyer.

Production took place in a small one-story plant on the outskirts of Augusta. Production operations were simple. Only two skilled employees were needed. One was a foreman who supervised the combination of various ingredients. The other was a chemist, who tested the finished product for quality control purposes. Manufacturing costs per unit of product tended to be constant.

Mr. Twitchell was responsible for the maintenance of adequate accounting records, statement preparation, and the credit and collection function. The firm used an outside bookkeeping service to do its billing. This resulting in a usual four-to-seven-day delay from time of sale to billing date.

Bank Relationships and Company Financial History

The Community National Bank was Augusta's fourth largest bank as measured by total assets of $20,430,000. Its main office was located in the city's downtown area. Two branches were located in other parts of the city. The West Side Branch was situated in an industrialized area within two miles of Lady Patrician's offices and production facilities. Mr. Coltrane, a Vice President, was in charge of the office, and two Assistant Cashiers served mainly as loan officers. One of these was Mr. Charles Hicoxe. It was Community National's practice to extend to assistant cashiers and assistant vice presidents authority on secured loans to a limit of $20,000 and on unsecured loans to a limit of $10,000. Vice presidents had unrestricted loan authority up to $50,000. Above the $50,000 figure, all loans were referred to the bank's finance committee, which consisted of two senior loan officers, Mr. Jones, and Mr. Jennings, and a member of the board of directors (Mr. Hopkinson). Generally, the officer in charge of securing the loan participated in the finance committee's deliberations, but had no voting power as to the action taken

Bank policy encouraged lending on the security of accounts receivable but discouraged use of this type of financing for permanent requirements. However, a mandatory annual clean-up period was not required. Interest rates varied from 9% to 12% depending mainly on the quality of the receivables. Enforcement of loan liquidation schedules was left in the hands of responsible loan officers. Community National customarily limited its lending against assigned accounts receivable to 80% of their face amount. No receivables over 60 days old were accepted as security.

[1]Consignment is a delivery of goods from a seller or consignor to a distributor or dealer, who is to act as selling agent for the goods, without taking title to them at the time of delivery. Quoted from Donald T. Clark and Bert. A. Gottfield, *Dictionary of Business and Finance* (New York: Thomas Y. Crowell Co., 1957), p. 88.

The bank required a weekly report on assignments and collections and an aging schedule monthly. Periodically, receivable audits were conducted. The audit verified the borrower's receivables records by checking them against invoices and remittances. On a sample basis, it verified the accuracy of the assignment and collections report and the aging schedule.

At its inception in December 1964, Lady Patrician issued and had outstanding 4,000 shares of $1.00 par stock all held by Mr. Strong. An additional 5,000 shares were subscribed to by Strong. Two other individuals accounted for the remainder of the subscription of 11,000 shares. At that time, Mr. Strong had no definite plans to increase capitalization, although, if needed, several potential investors were held in mind. The rest of the financing, then, consisted of accounts payable, a $1,500 note due to Strong, and an automobile loan from a bank in another city.

In January of 1965, Mr. Strong approached Mr. Hicoxe of the Community National Bank with a request for a short-term loan to provide working capital "until receivables begin turning." Mr. Hicoxe agreed to lend $1,500 unsecured but endorsed by the two principals, and further agreed to refinance the automobile loan. At this time, Mr. Hicoxe expressed his willingness to lend up to $10,000, on a one-time 30-day basis. In the light of next year's (fiscal year beginning March 1) projected $1,000,000 sales volume, he noted the undercapitalization of the firm. Management was reminded also that bank lending was designed for short-term needs and not as capital.

In March of 1965, the bank loaned $5,000, endorsed and secured by specific invoices. An unforeseen manufacturing interruption contributed greatly to the need for the loan. By the end of August 1965, an additional $10,000 was lent for working capital needs. At this point, the relationship with Lady Patrician was considered satisfactory by the Community National Bank.

In September of 1965, Lady Patrician organized a wholly owned subsidiary to market nail polish remover, nail base, and nail hardener nationally to the mass market media, such as chain stores and discount houses. This shift in marketing strategy required a large increase in bank financing, mainly attributable to increased advertising costs. The August 31, 1965, balance sheet in Exhibit 1 pictures the company's condition prior to new bank financing. In September, the branch loan committee decided to extend a $70,000 line of credit secured by accounts receivable and endorsed by the two major stockholders. Mr. Hicoxe so informed the management, but said it would lend only 70% of accounts receivable instead of the customary 80%. An aging of the accounts receivable as of August 31, 1965, revealed that only 6½% were over 60 days old, but it was thought that the newness of the business warranted conservatism. Even though the company had an outside billing service, the bank informed management that it was responsible for accurate reports concerning collection and aging of the accounts.

February 1966 brought another increase in advertising costs, which necessitated an additional $20,000, bringing to $69,600 the bank loan outstanding. A routine accounts receivable audit by the bank revealed the company was overadvanced by $11,800 and that $21,000 of the receivables were over 60 days old. Both Mr. Twitchell, the treasurer, and Mr. Hicoxe expressed little concern over the amount of past due accounts because of the high credit rating of most debtors. The audit noted that weekly and monthly reports of aged receivables were consistently late. No other discrepancies were found. Payables were not audited. The auditor's recommendation to Mr. Hicoxe was favorable, but he suggested that the account be watched closely to insure that all reports were filed on schedule.

In February of 1966, the credit line was increased to $80,000, and the collateral margin was cut from 30% to 20%. The bank justified this increase to itself on the basis of expanding sales and profits from August 1965 through February 1966. During this time, additional capital was obtained. In March 1966, management decided to undertake direct sales. To implement this change, it was decided that manufacturers' representatives would be replaced with the company's own field personnel for an improvement in control of marketing.

Within a month thereafter, Mr. Strong applied for an increase in the company's line of credit, citing as the causes plant relocation to larger quarters, higher sales volume, the start-up expense of increased field personnel, and additional promotion costs. Mr. Hicoxe indicated no action could be taken until an independent certified audit of the company was obtained and the bank's factoring division had made its own audit. Strong was taken aback by this and expressed surprise in the light of the company's improving financial position. Mr. Hicoxe reiterated the position of the bank with respect to accounts receivable financing as a source of permanent capital. Mr. Strong stated that if the bank financed this phase of expansion, the company would generate enough profit to retire the accounts receivable loan since no additional large cash outlays were anticipated. Further, by September 1966, the company would be able to raise more funds through the sale of stock, although Mr. Strong was not at liberty then to name the potential buyers. Mr. Hicoxe ended this conversation by stating that he would inform the branch office loan committee of these intentions.

The Loan Decision

The committee met with Hicoxe to review the two audits. The independent certified audit disclosed the company's position as of May 31, 1966, and produced an operating statement from February 28, 1966, to May 31, 1966. The audit performed by the bank's factoring division was more detailed. An aging of the accounts receivable revealed that of $160,800 outstanding only $75,000 were current. The aging also disclosed that approximately 25% of these receivables originated from sales on a guaranteed basis. The auditors found a significant quantity of returned merchandise in the company's warehouse, for which no credit memos had been issued.

The adjustments to the general ledger for February were not posted. The accounts receivable ledger included no billings less than two weeks old. The bank accounts had not been balanced within the last four months. Various state and local taxes were in arrears.

Mr. Coltrane, the branch office loan committee chairman, voiced his opinion that the bank should continue the present accounts receivable financing, but an increase in the loan limit should be contingent upon a written pledge from Strong that he could raise additional capital. To the other committee members he recognized the risks in so doing but thought the receivables to be of sufficient quality, and he pointed to the loan's profitability. Mr. Jones strongly believed the bank should not increase accounts receivable financing, and, moreover, should try to remove itself gradually from the loan. Further, Jones had lost confidence in the managerial ability of Strong and Twitchell, and saw little chance of orderly loan liquidation. Mr. Jennings expressed no strong feelings but pointed out the bank's responsibility arising from its association with the company from its inception.

The committee asked Mr. Hicoxe to outline the general alternatives open to the bank and to recommend a suggested course of action.

EXHIBIT 1

Lady Patrician, Incorporated

Balance Sheets
(Fiscal Year Ends February 28)

	Jan. 1, 1965 (un- audited)	Feb. 28 1965 (un- audited)	Aug. 31, 1965 (un- audited)	Feb. 28, 1966 (un- audited)	May 31, 1966 (audited)
ASSETS					
Cash	$ 500	$ 5,300	$11,700	$ 26,900	$ 9,800
Accounts Receivable	4,500	6,600	49,700	196,000	160,800
Inventory					
Raw Materials	530	460	3,200	12,030	20,800
Finished Goods	1,270	3,140	11,200	50,870	81,700
Stock Subscriptions					
Receivable	11,000	3,500	0	0	0
Total Current Assets	$17,800	$19,000	$75,800	$285,800	$273,100
Noncurrent Assets	$ 4,200	$ 5,800	$17,700	$ 64,200	$123,000
Total Assets	$22,000	$24,800	$93,500	$350,000	$396,100
LIABILITIES					
Notes Payable (Bank)	$ 1,200	$ 1,500	$15,000	$ 69,600	$ 76,800
Accounts Payable (Raw					
Materials only)	2,300	1,000	13,600	50,200	81,800
Other Payables	1,500	1,500	13,348	62,716	52,065
Total Current Liabilities	$ 5,000	$ 4,000	$41,948	$182,516	$210,665
Long-Term Liabilities	$ 2,000	$ 1,900	$ 1,500	$ 700	$ 0
Total Liabilities	$ 7,000	$ 5,900	$43,448	$183,216	$210,665
Capital Stock $1 par—					
100,000 shares authorized	$ 4,000	$11,500[1]	$ 24,300	$ 85,000	$ 85,000
Capital Stock Subscribed	11,000	3,500	0	0	0
Undivided Profits	0	3,900	25,752	81,784	100,435
Total Capital	$15,000	$18,900	$50,052	$166,784	$185,435
Total Liabilities and					
Net Worth	$22,000	$24,800	$93,500	$350,000	$396,100

[1]Twenty-five hundred shares were issued for $2,500 cash. In lieu of officers' salaries, 5,000 shares were issued at a value of $1 per share.

EXHIBIT 2

Lady Patrician, Incorporated

Income Statements

(Fiscal Year Ends February 28)

	2 months ending Feb. 28, 1965 (unaudited)	6 months ending Aug. 31, 1965 (unaudited)	6 months ending Feb. 28, 1966 (unaudited)	3 months ending May 31, 1966 (audited)
Net Sales	$28,000	$156,000	$440,800	$200,400
Cost of Goods Sold				
Raw Material[1]	4,770	25,000	66,610	35,320
Direct Labor	5,640	31,630	86,900	39,590
Factory Overhead	3,790	20,370	62,790	26,990
Gross Profit	$13,800	$ 79,000	$224,500	$ 98,500
Operating Expenses[2]	8,800	49,476	116,748	74,588
Net Income before Fed.				
Income Taxes	$ 5,000	$ 29,524	$107,752	$ 23,912
Federal Income Tax[3]	1,100	7,672	51,720	5,261
Net Income	$ 3,900	$ 21,852	$ 56,032	$ 18,651
[1]Beginning Raw Materials				
Inventory	$ 530	$ 460	$ 3,200	$ 12,030
Purchases	4,700	27,740	75,440	44,090
Ending Inventory	460	3,200	12,030	20,800
Average Inventory	495	1,830	7,615	12,415
[2]Including Officers' Salaries	$ 5,000	$ 20,000	$ 70,000	$ 43,000

[3]22% of first $25,000, 48% of all amounts over $25,000.

EXHIBIT 3

Lady Patrician, Incorporated

Aging Schedules of Accounts Receivable at Various Dates

Days	Aug. 31, 1965	May 31, 1966
0-30	$24,500	$ 75,000
31-60	12,000	40,000
61-90	9,970	20,400
91-120	2,000	15,200
Over 120	1,230	10,200
	$49,700	$160,800

QUESTIONS

1. What adjustments, if any, would you make to the financial statements?
2. Analyze Mr. Strong's loan request from the bank's point of view.
3. As Mr. Hicoxe, what course of action would you suggest?

Case 13
Metro Contractors

Mr. John Harris, Vice President of the Citizens Bank of Houston (CBH), was examining the credit file on Metro Contractors, a fully licensed contractor offering service in all phases of mechanical construction. A request for an increase in a line of credit from $120,000 to $190,000 had been made by Metro, and Mr. Harris wanted to review the activity in the account since its opening in September, 1970. He was responsible for a recommendation at the next loan committee meeting.

Mr. Harris knew that in some respects Metro was typical of relatively new companies undergoing rapid growth. In his view, the company was under-capitalized and was substituting short-term bank credit for equity. Mr. Harris was also aware, from previous meetings with the loan committee, that they frowned upon a company continuously substituting bank debt for equity. In the past, they had been somewhat reluctant to grant credit extensions in such situations. As Mr. Harris began a thorough examination of Metro's file, he kept in mind this unwritten policy of the loan committee.

Company Background

Metro Contractors had been incorporated in December, 1969, as Morris Contractors, Inc., owned entirely by Mr. William C. Morris. Mr. Morris was well established in the construction trade, having four other branches located in the Southwest. Because of Mr. Morris's contacts, the company was able, from the outset, to work with several of the larger general contractors in the Houston area.

This case was prepared by Professor Edward A. Moses of the University of Tulsa as a basis for classroom discussion and not to illustrate either effective or ineffective handling of an administrative situation.

The company was a mechanical contractor, primarily engaged in heating, plumbing, air conditioning, and similar work on a subcontract basis. Most of its work was concentrated in the metro Houston area. Contracts entered into by the company generally provided that billings were to be made monthly in amounts commensurate with the extent of performance under the contract, with 10% retainage withheld until completion (see Exhibit 4).

Initial employment was 46 people, including Mr. Bob Robertson as general manager and Mr. Richard Hodges as assistant manager. Prior to working for Morris Contractors, Mr. Robertson had been employed as a representative of a mechanical contracting equipment manufacturer in the Houston area. Mr. Hodges, an engineering school graduate, was employed by a general contractor prior to his association with Morris Contractors.

In August, 1970, Mr. Robertson married Mr. Morris's daughter. As a wedding present, Mr. Morris gave Mr. Robertson his stock in the company and withdrew as an officer. Mr. Robertson, as the new president, changed the name of the company to Metro Contractors in September, 1970.

CBH's Relationship with Metro

Since its inception, the company had maintained a banking relationship with the Houston Bank of Commerce, one of the largest banks in Houston. At the time of Mr. Morris's departure, the company had outstanding a monthly repayment loan secured by equipment, and a $24,000 working capital loan. The company's account at the Houston Bank of Commerce had averaged in the moderate five figures, and the bank had found earlier loan experiences to be satisfactory.

Mr. Robertson had been a personal friend of Mr. Harris for a number of years. Shortly after he became president of the company, he discussed with Mr. Harris the possibility of switching Metro's account to CBH. Mr. Robertson was interested in this change because of his personal relationship with Mr. Harris, plus the fact that CBH was smaller and more aggressive than the Houston Bank of Commerce. The reputation of CBH as an aggressive bank was particularly important to Mr. Robertson as he had plans for rapid expansion. He felt that Mr. Morris had been too conservative in his estimation of job costs and that this had resulted in the company's bids being rejected on several large contracts. Along these same lines, Mr. Robertson realized that the present rented facilities would soon be too small, and he had taken an option to purchase additional land on the outskirts of Houston. Accordingly, on September 1, 1970, Mr. Harris advanced $30,000 to Metro, the purpose of which was to transfer the accounts and the working capital loan from the Houston Bank of Commerce to CBH. The loan was endorsed by Mr. Robertson and was due on November 30, 1970.

At the time of the initial loan, Mr. Harris pointed out to Mr. Robertson that the capital base was not strong enough to support the volume of anticipated contracts. He suggested that the company was in need of investor-supplied funds rather than increasing the bank debt to secure working capital. Shortly thereafter, Mr. Robertson invested $7,500 in the company.

On October 12, 1970, Mr. Robertson requested an additional loan of $45,000 from CBH for reducing trade payables. Mr. Harris turned down the loan request for a number of reasons. First, Metro had not used the proceeds of the loan from CBH to pay back the $24,000 working capital loan at the Houston Bank of Commerce. Second, the capital base was still too weak to support the volume of anticipated contracts. The cash flow was deemed inadequate for servicing trade suppliers and bank debt, given the scope of operations. Finally, although operations for the year ended September 30, 1970, reflected net income of approximately $17,600, the gross profit figures included almost $40,000 of estimated earnings on incomplete contracts (see Exhibits 1 and 3).

Shortly after Mr. Harris turned down the loan request, Mr. Robertson visited CBH. At that time, he informed Mr. Harris that since the statement date of September 30, 1970, the working capital loan at the Houston Bank of Commerce had been significantly reduced. In addition, Metro was able to handle its current needs through his additional investment in the company of $30,000 plus retainage payments received and thus did not need the requested $45,000 loan. Mr. Robertson was very optimistic about the future of the company, and he felt that Metro would have no problem in servicing the outstanding bank debt.

On November 15, 1970, Mr. Robertson approached CBH with a request for an extension of the $30,000 loan due on November 30, and an additional $24,000 loan for the purpose of reducing outstanding accounts payable. In his request, Mr. Robertson pointed out that by the end of March the company's cash flow should be improved from the receipt of receivables, which would allow him to pay the note in full. The bank agreed to extend the existing loan and granted the new loan. Both loans were endorsed by Mr. Robertson and due on April 5, 1971. The loans were repaid on March 18, 1971.

In early April, Mr. Robertson was granted a 60-day $42,000 loan from CBH for the purpose of current working capital needs. The original request was for a loan of $36,000, but Mr. Harris asked him to increase it to $42,000 in order to have sufficient funds to maintain his deposit account satisfactorily. At the time of the request, Mr. Robertson indicated that over the next two months his cash flow should be improved from receipt of retainage due and receivables, which would allow him to liquidate the loan. The company had approximately $84,000 of retainage due at the time of the loan request.

One week after the $42,000 loan was granted, Mr. Robertson requested an additional loan of $18,000 for current operating capital. He explained to Mr. Harris that Metro was approaching the construction season, and in order to insure that supplies would be available as required, the proceeds of this loan would be paid to major supply houses. Mr. Robertson again expressed confidence that the cash flow generated from accounts receivable would be sufficient to service the bank debt. Mr. Harris made the loan for 53 days, to mature on June 1, 1971, which was the maturity date of the previous credit. Both loans were endorsed by Mr. Robertson.

In late April, 1971, Mr. Robertson again visited the bank, asking for an additional loan of $24,000 for operating capital. Approximately one-half of the money derived from this loan would be used for paying accrued payroll taxes, and the remainder would be purely operating capital. Mr. Robertson reported that as of the end of April, 1971, Metro had total receivables of $230,000, of which $96,000 represented retainage on contracts and $134,000 was receivables due from work billed. There were two primary contractors which owed a total of $100,000. These contractors historically paid between the 10th and 15th of the month. According to Mr. Robertson, the month of April was the company's largest billing month, as construction was well under way on a number of new projects. Mr. Harris granted Metro the $24,000 loan, endorsed by Mr. Robertson, with the understanding that the total debt of $84,000 would be substantially reduced by early June, 1971.

On June 1, 1971, CBH's loan to Metro was classified as substandard by an F.D.I.C. examiner. The examiner commented:

> The loans consist of three unsecured notes all endorsed by Bob Robertson, principal of the firm. Credit information on the endorser indicated only nominal net worth outside of investment in stock of Metro Contractors. The bulk of the firm's receivables are due from large contractors, apparently of substantial means, and represents subcontracts performed by the debtor corporation. The business is obviously undercapitalized and does not have the capacity to carry such a large volume of receivables. It was indicated that an individual in Arkansas, who has substantial net worth, would indirectly support the debt. However, the bank holds no firm commitment in writing.

Upon being informed of the examiner's comments, Mr. Robertson agreed to a general assignment of all contract receivables. He also indicated that the summer months would put a heavy strain on operating funds due to the volume of work in progress and that he would have a need for an additional $36,000 for short-term operating capital during the summer months. Mr. Harris agreed to extend the $84,000 loan and to provide the additional $36,000 as needed, with the understanding that the loan would be substantially reduced by early August.

On August 6, Mr. Harris met with Mr. Robertson and Mr. Morris. A few days after the meeting, Mr. Harris wrote the following memorandum:

> The writer met with Bob Robertson and William Morris to discuss the status of Metro Contractors debt, which is now at $120,000 and was classified as substandard by the F.D.I.C. Since the classification, the bank has obtained an assignment of all contract receivables of Metro and a review of these contracts reflects that Metro is dealing with substantial contractors in the Houston area. Receivables as of July 31, 1971, amounted to $311,440, with retainages accounting for $140,553 of receivables. We are receiving monthly progress reports from the company and it appears to be operating on a satisfactory basis.

> At the meeting, Mr. Robertson requested a line of credit of $190,000 for the remaining months of 1971. In his request, Mr. Robertson indicated that the company was in a tight cash position due to the large amount of retainage on several jobs in the final stages of completion and that a substantial amount of the retainage will be used to retire the company's outstanding indebtedness.

> Mr. Morris agreed to execute a guarantee for $190,000, expiring December 31, 1971. Mr. Morris is chairman of the board of Morris Contractors, Inc., of Magnolia, Arkansas, and several other closely held companies. His personal financial statement as of May 31, 1971, reflects a net worth of $820,000, and although the statement is in joint name with his wife, Mr. Morris states that none of the assets are in her name. Approximately eighty percent of Mr. Morris's net worth is represented by the stock of these small companies.

> The guarantee would have an expiration date of December 31, 1971, with a maximum

amount of $190,000; however, Mr. Morris would review the Metro situation on December 1 and notify the bank of his intentions to continue the guarantee. At the same time, the bank would be committed to review the Metro account based on experiences to December 31 with the idea of releasing the guarantee at the earliest possible moment.

After the meeting with Mr. Robertson and Mr. Morris, Mr. Harris had agreed to present the request to the loan committee and promised to let Mr. Robertson know the bank's decision within a week. He felt that the loan committee would base their decision, to a large extent, upon his recommendation.

EXHIBIT 1

Metro Contractors

Statements of Income for the Periods Indicated Below

	Ten Months Ended July 31, 1970	Twelve Months Ended Sept. 30, 1970	Five Months Ended Feb. 28, 1971	Nine Months Ended June 30, 1971
Revenue	$455,220	$564,191	$527,366	$1,055,714
Cost	339,109	436,873	448,611	946,296
Gross Profit from Complete and Incomplete Contract Work (See Notes A, B, C)*	$116,111	$127,318	$ 78,755	$ 109,418
Operating expenses[1]	84,752	106,457	64,340	81,850
Operating profit	$ 31,359	$ 20,861	$ 14,415	$ 27,568
Other income	300	1,500	3,000	5,400
Other expenses[2]	3,982	4,765	5,065	11,864
Net Income[3]	$ 27,677	$ 17,596	$ 12,350	$ 21,104
[1]Includes:				
Amortization of organization expense	$ 65	$ 78	$ 33	$ 59
Depreciation	3,394	3,672	3,498	7,091
[2]Includes:				
Interest	$3,982	$4,765	$5,065	$9,198

[3]No provision for Federal or State Income Taxes as owners choose to be taxed as individuals under Subchapter S of the Internal Revenue Code. Under this section of the code, all profits or losses flow directly to the individual stockholders.

*Notes to financial statements are in Exhibit 3.

EXHIBIT 2

Metro Contractors

Selected Balance Sheets

	July 31, 1970	September 30, 1970	February 28, 1971	June 30, 1971
Cash	$ 3,464	$ 4,349	$ 3,092	$ 7,048
Receivables:				
Contracts	80,375	117,602	223,135	235,285
Other	3,600	10,500	4,254	6,852
Inventory	1,440	1,440	4,320	12,300
Prepaid expenses	660	1,330	1,574	1,574
Other	1,437	3,220	10,287	9,737
Cost and estimated earnings in excess of billings				
(See notes B and C)*			21,193	29,448
Current assets	$ 90,976	$138,441	$267,855	$302,244
Real estate	39,000	67,283	67,283	67,283
Fixtures and equipment	5,390	9,681	11,352	36,410
Automotive equipment	16,147	19,279	24,872	22,558
Less: accumulated depreciation	(4,358)	(4,292)	(7,790)	(11,383)
Net fixed assets	$ 56,179	$ 91,951	$ 95,717	$114,868
Total assets	$147,155	$230,392	$363,572	$417,112

*Notes to financial statements are in Exhibit 3.

EXHIBIT 2

Metro Contractors *(continued)*

Selected Balance Sheets

	July 31, 1970	September 30, 1970	February 28, 1971	June 30, 1971
Notes payable:				
Banks	$ 36,158	$ 60,062	$ 61,572	$109,999
Mortgage		5,722	5,722	5,722
Officers—stockholders		9,480		
Others		1,545	7,153	4,504
Accounts payable—trade	26,904	36,275	142,043	126,418
Accruals	4,140	4,028	11,189	27,212
Billings in excess of costs and estimated earnings (see note A)*		16,966		
Current liabilities	$ 67,202	$134,078	$227,679	$273,855
Banks	9,276	5,866	1,706	1,504
Mortgage	18,240	50,230	49,967	49,586
Other	12,600	2,962	4,614	3,807
Total liabilities	$107,318	$193,136	$283,966	$328,752
Capital stock	36,000	42,000	72,000	72,000
Paid-in-surplus		1,500	1,500	1,500
Retained earnings	3,837	(6,244)	6,106	14,860
Total net worth	$ 39,837	$ 37,256	$ 79,606	$ 88,360
Total liabilities and net worth	$147,155	$230,392	$363,572	$417,112

*Notes to financial statements are in Exhibit 3.

EXHIBIT 3
Metro Contractors

Note A: At September 30, 1970, gross profit includes $39,973 of estimated earnings on incomplete contracts, computed as follows:

Notes to Financial Statements

	1	2	3	4	5
Description	Percentage of Completion	Total Contract Price	Completed (2 x 1)	Estimated Contract Cost	Estimated Cost to Date (4 x 1)
Eastview School	50	$163,452	$ 81,726	$125,755	$ 62,878
J. H. Brown School	9	307,200	27,648	250,560	22,550
Rockwood Stadium	18	141,258	25,426	113,658	20,458
Furlow School	18	325,440	58,579	264,000	47,520
Totals		$937,350	$193,379	$753,973	$153,406

Total Revenue (column 3)	$193,379
Total Cost (column 5)	153,406
Estimated earnings on incomplete contracts	$ 39,973

Billings in excess of costs and estimated earnings at September 30, 1970, are as follows:

Billings on incomplete contracts		$191,065
Less:		
Costs	$134,126	
Estimated earnings	39,973	$174,099
Billings in excess of related costs and estimated earnings		$ 16,966

EXHIBIT 3

Metro Contractors *(continued)*

Note B: At February 28, 1971, gross profit from complete and incomplete contract work of $78,755 was computed as follows:

Notes to Financial Statements

	1	2	3	4	5
Description	*Percentage of Completion*	*Total Contract Price*	*Completed (2 x 1)*	*Estimated Contract Cost*	*Estimated Cost to Date (4 x 1)*
Eastview School	88	$ 163,452	$143,838	$ 138,252	$121,662
J. H. Brown School	73	307,200	224,256	266,400	194,472
Rockwood Stadium	71	142,780	101,373	118,780	84,333
Furlow School	40	325,440	130,176	281,520	112,608
The Food Mart	31	359,978	111,593	263,978	81,833
Rounder Restaurant	100	9,509	9,509	7,109	7,109
Totals		$1,308,359	$720,745	$1,076,039	$602,017

Total revenue (column 3)	$720,745	
Less: Revenue recognized at September 30, 1970, on incomplete contracts	193,379	
Revenue for five months ended February 28, 1971		$527,366
Total cost (column 5)	$602,017	
Less: Cost recognized at September 30, 1970, on incomplete contracts	153,406	
Cost for five months ended February 28, 1971		448,611
Estimated gross profit for five months ended February 28, 1971		$ 78,755

Costs and estimated earnings in excess of billings at February 28, 1971, are as follows:

Costs	$599,137	
Estimated earnings	118,728	$717,865
Less: Billings		696,672
Cost and estimated earnings in excess of billings		$ 21,193

EXHIBIT 3
Metro Contractors *(continued)*

Note C: At June 30, 1971, gross profit from complete and incomplete contract work of $109,418 was computed as follows:

Notes to Financial Statements

Description	1 Percentage of Completion	2 Total Contract Price	3 Completed (2 x 1)	4 Estimated Contract Cost	5 Estimated Cost to Date (4 x 1)
Eastview School	100	$ 164,588	$ 164,588	$ 146,954	$ 146,954
J. H. Brown School	98	306,773	300,637	278,400	272,832
Rockwood Stadium	100	142,778	142,778	132,433	132,433
Furlow School	78	325,440	253,843	289,440	225,763
The Food Mart	44	359,978	158,391	279,578	123,015
Rounder Restaurant	100	14,203	14,203	11,114	11,114
Hold Center	34	385,200	130,968	331,200	112,608
Triangle Court House	8	796,361	63,709	727,782	58,223
Jackson's Dept. Store	12	39,600	4,752	30,000	3,600
Riverdale Plaza	4	380,592	15,224	328,992	13,160
Totals		$2,915,513	$1,249,093	$2,555,893	$1,099,702

Total revenue (column 3)	$1,249,093	
Less: Revenue recognized at September 30, 1970, on incomplete contracts	193,379	
Revenue for nine months ended June 30, 1971		$1,055,714
Total cost (column 5)	$1,099,702	
Less: Cost recognized at September 30, 1970, on incomplete contracts	153,406	
Cost for nine months ended June 30, 1971		946,296
Estimated gross profit for nine months ended June 30, 1971		$ 109,418

Costs and estimated earnings in excess of billings at June 30, 1971, are as follows:

Costs	$1,099,702	
Estimated earnings	149,391	$1,249,093
Less: Billings		1,219,645
Costs and estimated earnings in excess of billings		$ 29,448

EXHIBIT 4
Metro Contractors
A Note on the Percentage-of-Completion Method of Accounting and the Completed-Contract Method of Accounting

The following statements on the percentage of completion method of accounting and the completed contract method of accounting are quoted from *Accounting Research Bulletin,* No. 45, issued by the Committee on Accounting Procedure, American Institute of Certified Public Accountants.

The percentage-of-completion method recognizes income as work on a contract progresses. The committee recommends that the recognized income be that percentage of estimated total income either:

(a) that incurred costs to date bear to estimated total costs after giving effect to estimates of costs to complete based upon most recent information, or

(b) that may be indicated by such other measure of progress toward completion as may be appropriate having due regard to work performed.

. . .

Under this method, current assets may include costs and recognized income not yet billed, with respect to certain contracts; and liabilities, in most cases current liabilities, may include billings in excess of costs and recognized income with respect to other contracts.

The principal advantages of the percentage-of-completion method are periodic recognition of income currently rather than irregularly as contracts are completed, and the reflection of the status of the uncompleted contracts provided through the current estimates of costs of completion.

The principal disadvantage of the percentage-of-completion method is that it is necessarily dependent upon estimates of ultimate costs and of currently accruing income, which are subject to the uncertainties frequently inherent in long-term contracts.

. . .

The completed-contract method recognizes income only when the contract is completed, or substantially so . . .

When the completed-contract method is used, an excess of accumulated costs over related billings should be shown in the balance sheet as a current asset, and an excess of accumulated billings over related costs should be shown among the liabilities, in most cases a current liability. If costs exceed billings on some contracts, and billings exceed costs on others, the contracts should ordinarily be segregated so that the figures on the asset side include only those contracts on which costs exceed billings, and those on the liability side include only those on which billings exceed costs.

EXHIBIT 5
Metro Contractors

Summary of Loans Outstanding
at Various Dates from CBH

Date	Amount of Loan Outstanding	Comments
September 1, 1970	$ 30,000	Due on November 30, 1970
November 15, 1970	$ 54,000	Replaces and increases loan of September 1, 1970. Due April 5, 1971.
March 18, 1971	——	Loans repaid.
April 2, 1971	$ 42,000	Due on June 1, 1971.
April 9, 1971	$ 42,000 $ 18,000	Same as April 2, 1971. Due on June 1, 1971.
April 30, 1977	$ 60,000 24,000 .	Total loan of $84,000 to be substantially reduced by June 1, 1971.
June 3, 1971	$ 84,000 20,000	Total loan of $104,000 to be substantially reduced by August 2, 1971.
July 8, 1971	$104,000 16,000	Total loan of $120,000 to be substantially reduced by August 2, 1971.

QUESTIONS

1. What have been the major developments in Metro Contractors since Mr. Robertson became president?
2. What risk does the bank face in granting the requested line of credit?
3. As Mr. Harris, what recommendation would you make to the loan committee?

Case 14
The Pacific Garment Company

On November 15, 1955, Mr. Roger Nash, Assistant Vice President of the Southwestern National Bank, was preparing a report for the loan committee regarding the Pacific Garment Company. Pacific Garment had requested: renewal of its account receivable line of credit for $240,000, 75% advance, 6¾% interest, to expire February 25, 1956; and renewal of its unsecured line for $60,000, expiring on the same date. These lines originally had been approved for 90 days, effective May 25, 1955, and subsequently renewed for another 90 days on August 25. The present request was the second application for extension of this accommodation.

The Pacific Garment Company, founded in 1901, manufactured men's pajamas, dress and sports shirts, and women's sportswear. The company also produced military uniforms under government contracts; however, after World War II this volume had declined and by 1954 amounted to approximately 10% of sales.

Pacific Garment had been a satisfactory customer of the Alhambra branch of Southwestern National for nearly 30 years, usually borrowing seasonally on a secured and unsecured basis. Mr. Nash had become personally familiar with the account while he was branch manager. Although he was now a member of the Loan Supervision Department at the bank's Los Angeles headquarters, Mr. Nash had

This case was prepared by Alan B. Coleman, Dean and Caruth Professor of Financial Management, School of Business Administration, Southern Methodist University and Leonard Marks, Jr., of Castle and Cooke, Inc., San Francisco, as a basis for classroom discussion and not to illustrate either effective or ineffective handling of an administrative situation.

Reprinted from *Standard Business Cases 1957,* with the permission of the Publishers, Stanford University Graduate School of Business,© 1957 by the Board of Trustees of the Leland Stanford Junior University.

remained in contact with the Pacific account, since many of its loan applications were referred to his department for review.

The company's management, in November, 1955, consisted of four officers: Bruce Perry, President; William G. Forbes, Vice President; Howard Olson, Secretary-Treasurer; and Michael Spaulding, Production Manager. Mr. Perry joined the company as a production worker after graduation from high school in 1928. He later transferred to the sales department and was promoted to sales manager in 1946. Perry was appointed president in March, 1955 after the death of the former president. Forbes and Olson were also veteran employees of the company, having been with Pacific for 16 and 22 years, respectively. Mr. Spaulding, the production manager, had recently been hired to replace George Knudsen, who had retired after nearly 40 years of service. The company maintained a sales force of eight men, who sold Pacific products directly to retailers throughout California. Most of these men had been with the company for many years; no new salesmen had been added since 1948.

Pacific Garment had been profitable in its early years; however, operating losses were sustained during the depression of the 1930's. The company finally earned a profit in 1937 and continued profitable from 1937 to 1941. At that time, sales and profits greatly expanded as a result of World War II.

After the war, the company's profits tapered off sharply, and in 1952 operating losses began. During that year, the management decided to embark upon an ambitious expansion program, increasing total plant investment $100,000 over a two-year period.

Early in 1953, the company began negotiating loans with the Southwestern Bank to finance the expansion of plant, the installation of new equipment, and additional inventory. The bank granted:

1. $90,000 in April, 1953 for eight years, secured by buildings appraised for $156,000, and a mortgage on production equipment appraised at $200,000; monthly repayments were $960 including interest.
2. $90,000 in March, 1954 for three years, secured by a mortgage on equipment appraised at $175,650; quarterly payments were $7,500, and interest was paid monthly.

Sales did not expand to utilize fully this added plant capacity; the company incurred a loss of $2,000 in 1953, $3,000 in 1954, and $44,000 for the first five months of 1955. Mr. Reed, president of the company for 22 years, died in March, 1955, and Mr. Perry was subsequently appointed president.

Borrowing History

On May 14, 1955, an analyst in the bank's credit department prepared the following routine report:

REVIEW REPORT

The Pacific Garment Company

Total Bank Debt—May 14, 1955 $283,735

Interest Rate: Unsecured loan   5%
                  Mortgage loan   4¾%
                  Real Estate loan   5%

Indebtedness to us increased $72,513 since review report of 10-4-54, principally in seasonal line. This borrower has not been out of debt for many years, with unsecured loan reaching a low of $12,000 in March 1954, and since has steadily increased to the $150,000 now outstanding. Debts appear disproportionate to net worth, operations unprofitable last three years. Seasonal liquidation of unsecured line appears highly desirable.

DETAILS OF PRESENT BORROWINGS

$150,000—Owing under a $175,000 unsecured line, which is to revert to a $150,000 line on 5-15-55 and is to expire on 3-1-56.

$60,000—Originated on 3-17-54 at $90,000, current quarterly repayment program of $7,500 plus interest monthly, with a maturity of 3-17-57. Secured by a mortgage on equipment appraised in January 1954 for an insurable value of $175,650.

$73,735—New at $90,000 on 4-12-53 with a repayment program of $960 monthly including interest and a maturity of 4-12-61. Secured by a light industrial building appraised in 1952 for $156,000, and a mortgage on equipment valued at $200,000.

$283,735

Outstandings are under various approvals of the headquarters loan committee, with the unsecured line subject to the following conditions:

Dividends are not to be paid except from profits.
If indebtedness is not paid by maturity, borrower will, if requested by bank, furnish satisfactory security.

Use of our credit facilities shows the following recent range of borrowings:

Year	High		Low	
1955 (to date)	April	$283,735	January	$240,000
1954	August	280,000	January	181,000
1953	April	239,000	January	120,000
1952	April	158,000	January	90,000
1951	November	90,000	October	NIL

On May 23, 1955, Mr. Perry visited the Alhambra branch of Southwestern National to discuss his financial problems with Mr. Peter Hayes, branch manager. Mr. Perry indicated that Pacific temporarily needed additional funds to increase working capital and to pay certain trade invoices which were maturing. Specifically, he requested an increase of $150,000 in the company's current credit line to cover maximum needs during the summer and fall selling season, thus extending the line to $300,000. Mr. Perry requested this accommodation for one year. He stated his willingness to place $240,000 on a secured basis, pledging accounts receivable for that purpose; the remaining $60,000 would be unsecured.

Since this credit request was beyond his authorized lending limit ($250,000), Mr. Hayes drew up the following loan application, which he forwarded to Mr. Nash in the Los Angeles office.

Memorandum to:

Loan Committee
Headquarters Office

Present Indebtedness (5-12-55):

Unsecured — under a $150,000 line	$150,000
Secured, Equipment, Mortgage	60,000
Secured, Real Estate	73,735
	$283,735

Average Deposit Balances — $21,000 (1954)

Application:

Cancel present unsecured line of —	$150,000

Approve — Accounts Receivable line of —   240,000
   with advances of 75%
Interest: 6¾%   Expiration: May 25, 1956

Approve — Unsecured line of —   60,000
Interest: 5%   Expiration: May 25, 1956

Financial:
Company prepared statement as of April 30, 1955 (000 omitted):

Current Assets	$590
Current Liabilities	359
Working Capital	231
Capital and Sur lus	289
Sales 4 months	800
Loss	(33)

Recommendation:

Recommended by Manager Peter Hayes

In preparing a recommendation for the Loan Committee, Mr. Nash reviewed the company's available operating statements, the credit analyst's report dated May 14, 1955 (on page 126), and the latest correspondence and memoranda in the company's file. After completing his analysis, Mr. Nash decided to recommend the $240,000 secured and the $60,000 unsecured lines; however, he stated that these lines should expire in 90 days—August 25, 1955. Mr. Nash realized the account was overextended, and he believed that immediate steps should be taken by company officials to reduce bank debt. He sent a memorandum to Peter Hayes, branch manager, advising that he was recommending approval of the loan request but asking Hayes to discuss reductions in outstanding bank debt with Mr. Perry as soon as possible.

On May 25, 1955, the loan committee reviewed and accepted Mr. Nash's recommendation. The following memorandum was dictated to record this decision:

EXCERPT FROM
Minutes of the Subcommittee on Loans of the Headquarters Loan Committee—May 25, 1955

ALHAMBRA BRANCH

" . . . On recommendation of Manager Peter Hayes, concurred in by Assistant Vice President Roger A. Nash, the committee approved an unsecured loan of $60,000 with interest at 5%, maturity August 25, 1955;

and, on recommendation of Manager Peter Hayes, concurred in by Assistant Vice President Roger Nash, the committee approved an accounts receivable line of credit of $240,000 with interest at prevailing rate but not less than 6¾%, expiration August 25, 1955. Advances will be at 75% . . ."

On August 15, 1955, Mr. Perry returned to the Alhambra branch to request his first extension of these credit lines, from August 25, 1955, to February 25, 1956. He explained to Mr. Hayes that Pacific's working capital position was still tight and the extension would be needed to maintain current production. Perry also indicated that operations continued unprofitable. However, the company had recently hired a firm of management consultants to conduct a comprehensive review. Mr. Hayes prepared the following loan application memorandum, which he forwarded to Mr. Nash, requesting approval.

Memorandum to:

Loan Committee
Headquarters

Present Indebtedness (8-16-55):

Accounts Receivable — Under a $240,000 line	$54,600
Unsecured — Under a $60,000 line	60,000
Secured — Chattel Mortgage	52,600
Real Estate	71,500

Average Deposit Balances — $25,200 (1955 to date)

Application:

Renew accounts receivable line of credit for — with advances at 75%	$240,000

Interest: 6¾%   Expiration: February 25, 1956

Renew unsecured line of credit for —   60,000
Interest: 5%   Expiration: February 25, 1956

Financial:
Company statement as of April 30, 1955
   (000 omitted):
      Current Assets $590
      Current Liabilities   359
      Working Capital   231
      Net Worth   289
      Sales   800
      Loss   (33)

Comments:
Receivable financing for this account originated in June, 1955, and our experience has been satisfactory. Turnover of accounts assigned has averaged 37 days.

Recommendation:

Recommended by Manager Peter Hayes.

In discussing this application two days later, before the loan committee, Mr. Nash pointed out the financial deterioration which had occurred in recent years. While he believed that the bank's interests probably were adequately protected at this time, Mr. Nash noted that Pacific's financial position was worsening steadily. He thought that additional or extended accommodation could not be justified from the bank's standpoint. The account had not been off the bank's books for five years, and total indebtedness had risen sharply. Mr. Nash recommended extension of the present lines for three months only, expiring November 25, 1955; however, he suggested that a formal understanding be reached at once with Mr. Perry concerning a plan for reduction of bank debt. He proposed that Perry be informed that only a considerable improvement in the company's financial condition would warrant further extension of credit. The loan committee accepted this recommendation, and extended the lines of credit for 90 days.

In early October, Mr. Perry came to the bank at Mr. Nash's request to discuss the company's financial problems and plans for the future. Mr. Nash pointed out that he reluctantly recommended the latest extension; he therefore questioned Perry regarding the possibility of immediate reductions in bank credit. Mr. Perry then revealed that the board of directors had decided during the past week to sell or merge the business, since they recognized that the company could not solve current sales and production problems without additional financing and new management. Mr. Perry said that the consultant's report had recommended any of these alternatives:

1. Sell the company.

2. Merge with a stronger company in which Pacific stockholders would retain an interest.

3. Contract out the production facilities to a major manufacturer.

Mr. Perry indicated that the directors favored selling the business on a going-concern basis rather than liquidating, since a forced sale of technical production equipment and specialized inventory would result in a lower realization on company assets. Pacific had already hired Frank Ross Associates, a firm which specialized in bringing together buyers and sellers of businesses, and Perry hoped that arrangements could be made to sell the company in the next three or four months. Mr. Nash asked about financial requirements during the time necessary to negotiate a sale, and Mr. Perry stated that Pacific would probably need to continue the present accommodation until a buyer was located or a merger arranged. He stressed the desire of Pacific's directors to sell or merge the firm as a going concern rather than liquidate. Mr. Perry believed, however, that no increase in the lines would be required and that if Ross Associates located a buyer in the next few weeks, the company could commence at once to reduce operations and liquidate bank loans. Perry gave Mr. Nash a copy of the management consultant's report together with a special auditor's report which the directors requested before reaching their decision to sell or merge the company. He promised to keep Mr. Nash closely informed regarding any prospective purchasers of the business.

After Mr. Perry had left the bank, Mr. Nash examined the auditor's report:

EXCERPTS FROM THE AUDITOR'S REPORT, SEPTEMBER 30, 1955

". . . A review of your statements indicates that not only does the company's financial position need strengthening but extreme measures are required to improve operating results. Net income for 1950 dropped to $37,624 from $62,287 in 1949, and in 1951 it dropped to $6,832. For the three years and nine months ended September 30, 1955, operating losses amounted to $54,584.

"In 1952, the company embarked upon an expansion program which increased total plant investment from $200,000 on December 31, 1951, to $300,000 on December 31, 1952. There was no appreciable increase in sales or output following the enlargement of plant capacity. The cost of this expansion program, the operating losses of recent years, and the continuance of dividends during unprofitable years have weakened the company. It is now clear the business cannot continue without additional financial aid and the reestablishment of profitable operations. . . .

". . . While we believe certain past actions of the directors and officers might be subject to criticism, we do not believe that an examination is required unless the directors have reason to question the integrity of the accounting. We believe one might fairly criticize the payment of high officers' salaries without the formal approval of the directors and the continuance of dividends during the loss years. However, the salaries and dividends have been paid. The company is now faced with conditions which require prompt remedial action. . . .

"We have reviewed the report of the management consultants and consider sound the alternatives they offer (sell, merge, or contract out your facilities). The rebuilding of the company from within would appear impossible without additional aid of a financial and management character. . . .

"While complete liquidation would cause the company to convert its assets into cash, pay off its liabilities, and distribute what remains to the stockholders, we believe it reasonable to consider the possibility of converting only current assets and equipment into cash so that the plant and real estate would remain for the shareholders in final liquidation. . . .

"The statements following show certain tentative estimated realizations from liquidation of current assets of the company. Comparative balance sheets and income statements are also shown. . . ." (See Exhibits 1, 2, 3, 4)

Mr. Nash questioned the liquidation value assigned to the inventory by the auditor. Therefore, he contacted a textile specialist in the Commodity Loan Section of the bank, asking him to estimate the worth of the stock in the event of a forced liquidation. Mr. Nash received the following reply:

". . . My original thinking was that this inventory might liquidate for approximately 50% of total collateral valuation, although the process might prove both tedious and expensive, involving sales in San Francisco and Los Angeles.

"However, friends in the trade uniformly feel that I was too optimistic. The consensus of their thinking is that a forced liquidation would do well to bring 40% of total collateral valuation. Sales would have to be predominantly in New York, as neither San Francisco nor Los Angeles could absorb any appreciable amounts of this inventory. Even with a fairly active New York sales program, it would take a year or more to liquidate such an inventory. The type of merchandise and the yardages involved complicate the picture. . . ."

Mr. Perry contacted Mr. Nash three times during the next 30 days, reporting that two large nationally known garment manufacturers had visited the plant and both showed interest. However, as of October 20, no firm offer had been received.

On October 24, Mr. Nash telephoned Frank Ross Associates to learn of any progress. Nash told Mr. Ross that in another two or three weeks Pacific would have to decide whether to continue in business, since the lines of credit would expire November 25 and continuing operations would require purchase of raw materials necessary to produce a spring line. Mr. Nash pointed out that the bank could no longer justify extension of interim credit on this account. Mr. Ross stated that a close-down of Pacific at this time would defeat any plan for selling the business at an attractive figure. He asked Mr. Nash to do whatever possible to "keep the doors open" for the next 60 days, since within that time Ross would have definite answers from the two concerns actively interested in buying or merging. He promised to telephone Mr. Nash immediately if he received a positive commitment from the prospective purchasers.

On November 15, Mr. Perry called on Mr. Nash to request the second 90-day extension of the $240,000 secured and $60,000 unsecured lines to finance raw material purchases and production for the spring line. Mr. Perry stated that Mr. Ross was still negotiating with the two garment manufacturers, both of whom had shown considerable interest in purchasing Pacific. Mr. Perry believed that a sale on satisfactory terms would soon be arranged.

EXHIBIT 1

The Pacific Garment Company

Comparative Balance Sheets

1949-1955

	Dec. 31, 1949	Dec. 31, 1950	Dec. 31, 1951	Dec. 31, 1952	Dec. 31, 1953	Dec. 31, 1954	Sept. 30, 1955
Cash	$ 9,856	$ 10,135	$ 9,788	$ 2,648	$ 3,655	$ 4,513	$ 15,660
Accounts receivable	126,774	109,919	97,084	103,372	85,810	106,051	171,023
Inventory	274,740	285,636	302,454	312,258	352,564	435,658	291,661
Prepaid expense	1,226	1,362	1,370	2,306	1,900	2,197	2,964
Cash value—life insurance	11,903	12,394	4,801	5,112	5,341	5,566	974
Total current assets	$424,499	$419,446	$415,497	$425,696	$449,270	$553,985	$482,282
Current liabilities*	154,426	126,112	128,249	244,241	186,937	239,153	230,736
Net current assets	$270,073	$293,334	$287,248	$181,455	$262,333	$314,832	$251,546
Building loan	—	—	$ 9,178	—	—	$ 76,020	$ 69,488
Chattel mortgage loan	—	—	—	—	—	67,500	45,000
Total long-term debt	—	—	$ 9,178	—	$ 83,533	$143,520	$114,488
Balance—current assets	$270,073	$293,334	$278,070	$181,455	$178,800	$171,312	$137,058
Land	6,498	6,498	6,498	6,498	1,225	1,225	1,225
Warehouse or leased land	—	—	—	2,566	2,566	2,566	2,566
Buildings	32,213	32,213	57,029	140,796	141,216	141,216	141,216
Machinery and fixtures	131,219	139,109	139,109	148,985	157,430	164,095	166,828
Autos	6,044	5,941	5,941	5,813	5,813	5,813	5,813
Total fixed assets	$175,974	$183,761	$208,577	$304,658	$308,250	$314,915	$317,648
Less depreciation	110,559	117,117	126,258	136,613	149,222	160,934	170,535
Net fixed investment	$ 65,415	$ 66,644	$ 82,319	$168,045	$159,028	$153,981	$147,113
Equity of stockholders	$335,488	$359,978	$360,389	$349,500	$337,828	$325,293	$284,171
Capital of stockholders	161,760	161,760	161,760	161,760	161,760	161,760	161,760
Earned Surplus	$173,728	$198,218	$198,629	$187,740	$176,068	$163,533	$122,411

*Current liabilities include outstanding short-term bank debt.

EXHIBIT 2

The Pacific Garment Company

Comparative Income Statements
Years Ending December 31, 1949-1954
9 months ending September 30, 1955

Income and Surplus	1949	1950	1951	1952	1953	1954	Jan. 1, 1955 to Sept. 30, 1955
Sales	$1,666,768	$1,513,428	$1,262,218	$1,243,374	$1,372,243	$1,432,826	$1,177,645
Cost of sales	1,258,989	1,166,134	982,516	965,752	1,070,555	1,109,057	958,309
Gross profit	$ 407,870	$ 347,294	$ 279,702	$ 277,622	$ 301,688	$ 323,769	$ 219,336
% of gross profit to sales	24.5%	23.0%	22.1%	22.3%	22.0%	22.6%	18.6%
Other income	2,609	2,086	—	1,284	8,693		
Total income	$ 410,479	$ 349,380	$ 279,702	$ 278,906	$ 310,381	$ 323,769	$ 219,336
Depreciation	$ 9,956	$ 10,590	$ 10,130	$ 12,892	$ 12,600	$ 11,984	$ 9,600
Compensation of officers	83,520	73,350	53,400	45,630	51,240	41,040	25,560
Other expenses	216,868	205,732	207,692	221,567	248,507	273,574	232,782
Total expenses	$ 310,344	$ 289,672	$ 271,222	$ 280,089	$ 312,347	$ 326,598	$ 267,942
% of expenses to sales	18.6%	19.1%	21.5%	22.5%	22.8%	22.8%	22.8%
Net income before taxes	$ 100,135	$ 59,708	$ 8,480	$ (1,183)	$ (1,966)	$ (2,829)	$ (48,606)
Taxes	37,848	22,084	1,648				
Net income after taxes	$ 62,287	$ 37,624	$ 6,832	$ (1,183)	$ (1,966)	$ (2,829)	$ (48,606)
Surplus at beginning of year	130,003	173,728	198,218	198,629	187,740	176,068	163,533
Life insurance proceeds	—		3,285				7,484
Balance—surplus	$ 192,290	$ 211,352	$ 208,335	$ 197,446	$ 185,774	$ 173,239	$ 122,411
Dividends	18,562	13,134	9,706	9,706	9,706	9,706	
Surplus at end of year	$ 173,728	$ 198,218	$ 198,629	$ 187,740	$ 176,068	$ 163,533	$ 122,411

EXHIBIT 3

The Pacific Garment Company

Estimated Liquidating Values
September 30, 1955

			Per Books	Estimated to Realize or Pay
Current Assets				
Cash			$ 15,660	$ 15,660
Accounts receivable			171,023	160,513
Inventory			291,661	240,752
Other			3,938	2,160
Total current assets			$482,282	$419,085
Liabilities			$345,224	$345,224
Trade accounts payable and accrued liabilities		$ 64,679		
Demand notes 3% dated July 31, 1955*		24,976		
Notes Payable, Bank		255,569		
Open account	$60,000			
Secured by acc. rec.	81,081			
Secured by real property	69,488			
Secured by equipment	45,000			
Balance—current assets			$137,058	$ 73,861
Estimated allowance for overhead and continuing expenses				(42,000)
Estimated expenses of liquidation (excluding commissions on sales of fixed assets)				(12,000)
Balance—cash available for distribution to stockholders				$ 19,861

*Demand notes owed to stockholders.

EXHIBIT 4

The Pacific Garment Company

Item	Physical Inventory Going Concern Value	Method of Disposition	Estimated % of Realization	Estimated Realization
Buttons and thread	$ 22,216	By bulk sale	50%	$ 11,108
Labels	3,816		—	—
Zippers, other sundries and supplies	13,475	Salable items totaling $10,054—by bulk sale— 50%	37.3%	5,027
Work in process	27,186	By completion and sale to trade	100%	27,186
Stock	117,694	By sale to trade at 90% of wholesale prices less shipping allowance of $1,350	116%	136,525
Piece goods and linings	92,738	By bulk sale	50%	46,369
Piece goods in transit and converters	14,537	By outright sales or open sales order	100%	14,537
	$291,662			$240,752

QUESTIONS

1. Evaluate the change in the financial condition of Pacific Garment Company over the past six years.
2. From the bank's point of view, analyze Pacific Garment's loan history.
3. As Mr. Nash, what recommendation would you make with respect to the requested loan extension?

Case 15
Tidewater Welding Supply Company

In December, 1965, J. D. Pearson was attempting to develop an appropriate response to a request for an increase in the size of term loan his bank had outstanding to the Tidewater Welding Supply Company. Mr. Pearson, a vice president and loan officer with Port City Bank & Trust Co., had "inherited" the Tidewater loan several months before from an officer who left the bank. Because of his relative lack of familiarity with the account, as well as the size of the loan and the importance of the existing bank-borrower relationship, Mr. Pearson intended to conduct an especially thorough analysis of the proposal.

The Company

Tidewater Welding Supply Company was a distributor of welding supplies and welding gases in the greater Charleston, South Carolina area. The company's offices, main warehouse, and acetylene generating plant were located in Charleston. Tidewater employed a number of driver-salesmen who periodically called on customers, taking orders and delivering welding supplies, and replacing empty welding-gas cylinders with full ones. Tidewater's owner, Mr. L. A. Reed, also owned three other welding supply companies in coastal South Carolina. Although these distributorships were nominally separate companies, they

This case was prepared by Professor Richard W. McEnally of the University of North Carolina at Chapel Hill with the cooperation of North Carolina National Bank, and under the auspices of a continuing program of business case research directed by Professor DeWitt C. Dearborn of the University of North Carolina. It is prepared as a basis for classroom discussion and not to illustrate either effective or ineffective handling of an administrative situation.

functioned much as branches—drawing most of their supplies from the Charleston company and providing office and loading facilities for driver-salesmen.

Mr. Reed was a somewhat colorful person. Born in 1917, he had dropped out of school at the age of seventeen and had held a number of jobs, none very successfully. At one time, he was employed by the Gas Products Company (GASCO), a major producer and distributor of industrial gases and welding supplies. However, this job terminated rather abruptly when Reed wrecked one of the company's gas-laden trucks. At the age of twenty-five, Mr. Reed obtained a job as a route salesman with a welding supply house based in the Charleston area.

In 1956, Mr. Reed left this employer. His oldest daughter wanted to enter nurses' training and needed $260 to pay for the program of her choice. Mr. Reed approached his employer for a loan, and possibly a wage increase, but received little sympathy. According to Mr. Reed, "He told me I was now forty years old and couldn't do much more for him, and that if I wanted to stay on the payroll I'd just better get back to my work." Instead, Mr. Reed persuaded GASCO, his former employer, to make him its distributor in the Charleston area. He borrowed $4,500 on his home to buy a truck, got a neighbor to teach him the rudiments of bookkeeping, and started selling welding supplies from shop to shop. Progress was spectacular; by 1964 the combined companies were selling well over a million dollars of welding supplies and gases annually. Exhibit A gives summary figures showing the growth of the companies from 1958, the year in which Tidewater Welding Supply Company was incorporated.

Bank Relations

Almost from the beginning, Mr. Reed and Tidewater Welding Supply Company maintained a close relationship with Port City Bank & Trust Co. Both Mr. Reed and the company kept their checking accounts with the bank. Beginning with a $5,000 ninety-day loan in 1959 to finance a temporary inventory increase, Tidewater was a frequent borrower from the bank's time and commercial loan departments, always with satisfactory repayment or renewal. Port City had been especially helpful in 1962 when GASCO was forced to give up the Thompson Products line of welding supplies under threat of antitrust action. Tidewater approached Thompson and was appointed regional distributor for Thompson Products. Mr. Reed estimated that volume would be increased 30% as a result—but an extra $12,000 inventory would be required. The bank promptly granted a loan for this amount. It was subsequently retired according to agreement. By the end of 1964, Tidewater Welding Supply Company's borrowings had been as high as $30,000 and $29,000 in the bank's commercial loan and time loan departments, respectively. Its average checking account balance ranged from $25,000 to $30,000. The bank's trust department administered Tidewater's profit-sharing plan and was named executor of Mr. Reed's will.

First Cylinder Loan

In April of 1965, Mr. Reed told the loan officer who supervised his account that Tidewater wanted to borrow $175,000 on a term basis. Mr. Reed explained that every customer who purchased welding gases from Tidewater had to be supplied with at least two steel storage cylinders at all times, and a number used gas in sufficient quantity to require additional cylinders. It was also necessary for Tidewater to have a number of cylinders on hand for refilling, transportation of gases, and so on. As the investment in cylinders would have been large relative to the company's size, Tidewater leased all the cylinders it needed from GASCO. Now, however, Mr. Reed said he was "having difficulties" in his relationship with GASCO and would like to purchase cylinders in place of those previously rented. He wanted Tidewater to buy 6,000 cylinders at a cost of $274,000. The cylinder manufacturer would finance the cost of 1,500 of the cylinders, but bank financing would be needed on the balance. Mr. Reed said that if Tidewater continued to lease the cylinders, the cost over the next ten years would total $409,000. He also indicated he could get all the gases he needed at a lower price than GASCO offered. The loan officer thought his source might be American Cryogenic, a subsidiary of Humble Oil, which was reputedly interested in entering the Charleston market.

The loan officer then prepared and submitted a loan request to his loan committee. A $175,000 loan, carrying a 5½% rate was approved, to be repaid at the rate of $17,500 per year for five years with a balloon repayment at the end of five years of $87,500. The loan was to be accompanied by a term loan agreement "with customary restrictive covenants" and an earnings recapture clause. In addition, Tidewater was to carry insurance on Mr. Reed's life in favor of the bank, with a maturity value equal to the amount of the loan.

Shortly thereafter, the loan officer left the bank, and Mr. Pearson acquired responsibility for the Tidewater Welding Supply account. He discovered that the $175,000 loan had not been taken down. Although the file on Tidewater was rather sketchy, Mr. Pearson did find an interesting letter from a Mr. Johns, a loan officer with the Pennsylvania National Bank of Philadelphia, written in response to an inquiry regarding Tidewater. According to Mr. Johns, his bank had been financing the GASCO cylinder-leasing operation. When a lease agreement was executed, Pennsylvania National would lend GASCO money against the cylinder purchase, taking a chattel mortgage on the cylinders and an assignment of the lease, with recourse to GASCO and with lessees remitting directly to the bank.

Mr. Johns said that for unspecified reasons GASCO had decided to encourage all dealers to own their own cylinders. In the event the dealers were not able to arrange their own financing, GASCO has arranged for a finance company to finance the cylinders. However, payments under the new plan would be considerably more than the old lease payments. Mr. Johns indicated that subsequently two dealers had applied to Pennsylvania National for credit to finance their cylinders; one request was accepted, a chattel mortgage being taken on the cylinders as security. In Mr. Johns' opinion, the cylinders were not very good collateral in terms of the control that could be exercised over them, as they were frequently exchanged very much like milk bottles. However, he did point out that the cylinders had a very long useful life; in fact, many of the leases Pennsylvania National handled for GASCO had been for twenty-five years, indicating the cylinders should be useful and retain some value for at least that period of time. Mr. Johns added that he routinely examined the financial statements of lessees, and those of Tidewater Welding Supply Company compared very favorably. (Financial statements of the company for 1962 through the first half of 1965 are presented in Exhibits B and C.)

In June, 1965, Mr. Reed indicated to Mr. Pearson that he had decided to buy 6,100 cylinders at a cost of $282,450, and wanted a loan of $225,000 against them. Following a request by Mr. Pearson, the loan committee approved a loan for this amount, to be repaid at the rate of $27,500 per year with a balloon payment of $87,500 at the end of five years. In the next several months, Tidewater actually drew down $220,000 of the loan approved, all for the purchase of cylinders. The loan carried a rate of 6%.

Subsequent Developments

In late August, two developments of some consequence occurred. On the 19th, Mr. Reed visited the bank and told Mr. Pearson that he had entered into the loan agreement with the impression that he would be able to borrow 100% of the value of the cylinders pledged. Mr. Pearson informed him that it had been the bank's understanding that the loan would not exceed 80% of the cylinders' value. Mr. Reed indicated that he had to have 100% financing, and he would have made other arrangements had he known the bank would not supply it.

On the 24th, a vice-president of sales for GASCO who lived in Charleston and was well known at Port City Bank & Trust Co. visited with one of the bank's officers. According to him, Tidewater was the only dealer not to go along with the new financing arrangement, and as a consequence GASCO was very disturbed. He suggested that it might be necessary for GASCO to terminate its relationship with Tidewater, in which case GASCO would have to obtain another dealer or enter the Charleston market directly. As a result, the coastal South Carolina market might then become "fiercely competitive"—with considerable reduction of prices and profits for all participants. The upshot of his visit was that it would be desirable for the officers of the bank to persuade Mr. Reed and Tidewater to accept the new GASCO financing plan.

In late 1965, Mr. Pearson was questioned by another officer of the bank as to why there was no restrictive term loan agreement or insurance of Mr. Reed's life in connection with the term loan to Tidewater. Mr. Pearson explained that after the request submitted to the loan committee was made up, he had asked for and received a chattel mortgage on the cylinders, plus Mr. Reed's personal endorsement (a personal financial statement filed with the bank indicated that Mr. Reed's outside net worth was approximately $145,000); in return, the loan agreement and insurance requirements had been deleted.

In December, 1965, Mr. Pearson learned that American Cryogenic was virtually certain to enter the Charleston market directly or via a large dealership. About the same time, Mr. Reed contacted Mr. Pearson, informing him that GASCO had approached him with an offer to buy Tidewater for a very substantial sum. However, he had declined the offer and was seriously considering severing his connection with GASCO. He also told Mr. Pearson rather pointedly that he wanted the term loan on the cylinders increased to $275,000. In light of these developments, Mr. Pearson decided to carefully review his bank's entire relationship with the Tidewater Welding Supply Company.

EXHIBIT A
Tidewater Welding Supply and Related Companies
Summary Data, 1958—1964
(in thousands)

| | Sales | | Net Income | | Total Assets | | Net Worth | |
	Charles-ton	Com-bined	Charles-ton	Com-bined	Charles-ton	Com-bined	Charles-ton	Com-bined
1958	$170	N.A.	$30*	N.A.	$ 51	N.A.	$ 37	N.A.
1959	315	N.A.	19	N.A.	95	N.A.	44	$ 45
1960	583	N.A.	32	$43	174	N.A.	78	91
1961	633	$709	14	28	216	N.A.	92	120
1962	840	950	17	26	259	$320	113	151
1963	970	1,124	23	39	301	377	138	194
1964	958	1,128	33	46	295	377	167	234

*Before federal income taxes.

EXHIBIT B
Tidewater Welding Supply and Related Companies
Statement of Financial Position
(in thousands)

	12/31/62		12/31/63		12/31/64		6/30/65	
	Charles-ton	Com-bined	Charles-Ton	Com-bined	Charles-ton	Com-bined	Charles-ton	Com-bined
Cash	$ 8.5	$ 21.0	$ 7.9	$ 12.3	$ 13.6	$ 34.1	$ 15.9	$ 35.5
Accounts Receivable	81.7	85.8	91.8	120.9	71.8	115.5	76.4	146.4
Inventory	83.6	102.7	91.8	122.2	111.6	135.1	133.0	189.3
Total Current Assets	$173.8	$209.6	$191.5	$255.4	$197.0	$280.7	$225.3	$371.2
Property, Plant, & Equipment	82.7	129.5	113.6	149.9	118.3	148.6	110.4	141.1
Less Accrued Depreciation	31.9	39.6	33.6	47.7	51.7	67.5	51.6	68.5
Net	$ 50.8	$ 89.9	$ 80.0	105.2	$ 66.6	$ 81.1	$ 58.8	$ 72.6
Other Assets*	34.0	20.4	29.0	16.2	31.4	15.1	48.6	44.1
Total Assets	$258.6	$319.9	$300.5	$376.8	$295.0	$376.9	$332.7	$487.9
Notes Payable—Bank	$ 17.1	$ 24.5	$ 21.3	$ 28.3	$ 19.6	$ 19.6	$ 20.8	$ 20.8
Accounts Payable	69.1	71.2	61.9	72.5	53.2	56.1	86.5	121.6
Due Officers	16.0	16.0	0	17.4	0	0	0	0
Income Taxes Payable	7.2	12.1	14.2	22.2	19.3	26.1	14.1	28.7
Accrued Expenses	10.5	12.1	16.1	17.2	22.2	27.1	20.3	23.9
Total Current Liabilities	$119.9	$135.9	$120.7	$157.6	$114.3	$128.9	$141.7	$195.0
Long-Term Debt	25.4	32.8	42.2	25.4	13.8	13.8	0	0
Total Liabilities	$145.3	$168.9	$162.9	$183.0	$128.1	$142.7	$141.7	$195.0
Owners' Equity	113.3	151.2	137.6	193.6	166.9	234.2	191.0	292.9
Total Liabilities & Equity	$258.6	$319.9	$300.5	$376.8	$295.0	$376.9	$332.7	$487.9

*Includes intracompany items, deferred charges, and amounts due from officers.

EXHIBIT C

Tidewater Welding Supply and Related Companies

Income Statement

(in thousands)

	1962		1963		1964	
	Charles-ton	Com-bined	Charles-ton	Com-bined	Charles-ton	Com-bined
Sales, Net	$840	$950	$970	$1,124	$958	$1,128
Cost of Goods Sold	634	634	N.A.	721	687	703
Gross Income	206	316	N.A.	403	271	425
Selling General & Administrative	193	277	N.A.	335	261	352
Net Operating Income	13	39	N.A.	68	10	73
Other Income (Exp.), Net	11	(1)	N.A.	(6)	39	(4)
Net Income Before Taxes	24	38	N.A.	62	49	69
Income Taxes	7	12	N.A.	23	16	23
Net Income	$ 17	$ 26	$ 23	$ 39	$ 33	$ 46
Depreciation Expense	$ 20	$ 28	N.A.	$ 29	$ 22	$ 29

QUESTIONS

1. Analyze carefully the financial statements of Tidewater Welding Supply Company and related companies.
2. Evaluate Mr. Reed's loan request from both the bank's and the company's points of view.
3. As Mr. Pearson, what response would you make to Mr. Reed?

*

PART THREE
FIXED ASSET MANAGEMENT: CAPITAL BUDGETING AND LEASING

*

Case 16
Jaxto Poultry Processing Company, Inc.

By early 1973, Jaxto Poultry Processing Company, Inc., had become the largest publicly traded poultry processor in Florida. Operations consisted primarily of purchasing live birds from outside suppliers, processing 9,600 birds an hour, and selling fresh ice-pack and frozen cut-up birds to large supermarket chains throughout Florida.

The company had a two-year prior history of funds shortage caused by an empty reservoir of funds at lending financial institutions and by low profits. The future for obtaining funds was bright, however, due to anticipated high broiler prices and to an increased supply of funds for corporate expansion caused by Federal efforts to stimulate the economy.

Three proposals to invest were before the president, Mr. Sam Rice. It was his job to evaluate the profitability of each one and to make a recommendation to the Board of Directors.

A. Cost Reduction Proposals

Mr. Rice was concerned that if the economy picked up during the summer months of 1972, labor would migrate to higher-paying jobs in other industries. He asked the plant superintendent, Mr. Jack Knox, to investigate the purchase of labor-saving equipment. Mr. Knox presented two alternative proposals for the installation of an automated eviscerating machine. Exhibit 1 summarizes the plant superintendent's report.

This case was prepared by Professor Jerome S. Osteryoung of the Florida State University as a basis for classroom discussion and not to illustrate either effective or ineffective handling of an administrative situation.

The Board of Directors had set an arbitrary payback period of four years in order to segregate prospective investments according to their speed of returning the original investment.

QUESTIONS

1. Calculate the payback period and accounting rate-of-return of each proposal. Assume a straight-line depreciation with no salvage value.
2. What are some deficiencies of this method?
3. If the cost of funds to the firm is 12%, what is the Net Present Value (NPV) of this investment?
4. What are some of the benefits of using Net Present Value?

EXHIBIT 1
Jaxto Poultry Processing
Cost Reduction Proposal

Item	Machine A	Machine B
1. Initial Cost	$112,000	$ 83,000
2. Annual Direct Labor Savings	36,000	24,000
3. Annual Depreciation on New Equipment	22,400	10,375
4. Annual Indirect Fixed Labor Expense Allocation	4,000	2,000
5. Tax Rate	48%	48%
6. Life of Equipment in Years	5	8

B. Product Line Expansion Proposals

Another proposal had been submitted by the sales manager, Mr. Fred Sells. Mr. Sells's proposal was prompted by several inquiries from customers asking Jaxto to produce a 5-pound box of pre-fried frozen chicken. In order to accommodate this type of product line increase, a new wing would have to be built on the plant and frying equipment purchased. A summary of Mr. Sells's proposal to expand the plant is presented in Exhibit 2.

Two things about this proposal bothered the president. First, he knew that inventory and accounts receivable necessary to support this new investment totaled $200,000 at cost. He did not know how to incorporate this cost into the evaluation of the proposal. The second problem he faced was the choice of a correct discount rate. The president felt that this proposal might help to revitalize the firm's earnings and therefore decrease the discount rate.

QUESTIONS

1. How should the additional investment in inventory and accounts receivable be treated?

2. Calculate the NPV of this investment. Assign a discount rate of 12%.
3. What effects will this investment have on the cost of funds?

EXHIBIT 2

Jaxto Poultry Processing
Product Line Expansion Proposal*

Item	
Construction Costs	$300,000
Equipment	100,000
Annual Revenue Increase	450,000
Annual Additional Direct Costs	300,000
Annual Depreciation Charges for Equipment and Plant Addition	40,000
Tax Rate	48%

*This proposal assumes both plant expansion and equipment have a life of only 10 years.

C. Diversification Proposal

Several major stockholders commented at the recent annual stockholders' meeting that the firm should diversify and thereby stabilize earnings. They estimated that the firm could improve its present price-earnings ratio of 10/1 to 15/1 with diversification. In order to appease the stockholders and stabilize earnings, the president was searching for additional products for the firm to manufacture.

After careful analysis, the president decided that plastic-injected molding products were a good prospect for stabilizing earnings. This decision was reached because of the following:

1. The caliber of labor would be the same in plastics and processing operations;
2. Long-term contracts in the plastics operation would stabilize the firm's earnings; and
3. Administration of the new venture could be handled by existing personnel.

A detailed analysis by Mr. Rice revealed that there were 7 chances out of 10 that this investment would fold during the first year. The company would thereby lose $1,000,000. If the new venture was still in existence after the first year, Mr. Rice forecasted it would generate an NPV of either $1,250,000, $2,000,000, or a negative $3,000,000. He estimated that there were 2 chances out of 10 that it would generate $1,250,000, 5 chances out of 10 that it would generate $2,000,000, and 3 chances out of 10 that the company would go in the hole $3,000,000.

QUESTIONS

1. Should this proposal be undertaken?
2. Is it realistic to have uncertainty in future projections?

Case 17
Tidewater Mobile Home Park

In January, 1973, the members of the Tidewater Real Estate Investment Partnership, a partnership organized for investing in local real estate, met to discuss the results of a survey made by a consulting service, University Associates.

The consultants had been hired to make a feasibility study on a piece of property which had been optioned several years earlier by the partnership. Specifically, the consultants were charged with determining the feasibility of building and profitably operating a mobile home park in Chesapeake, Virginia. Selected portions of the consultant's summary are presented here.

Summary
University Associates Report to the
Tidewater Real Estate Investment Partnership

According to Standard and Poor's Industry Surveys, nearly all homes sold for under $15,000 and about two-thirds of those sold for under $25,000 are mobile homes. In 1971, the mobile home industry shipped 496,570 units. In 1972, this figure rose over 19 percent to 592,665 units, to account for about 31 percent of all single-family housing produced. Production of around 640,000 units was estimated for 1973. With these dramatic increases in production and sales of mobile homes, demand for spaces on which to park them has also gone up.

A study of mobile home parks in Norfolk, Portsmouth, Chesapeake, and

This case was prepared by Professor Bernie J. Grablowsky of Old Dominion University as a basis for classroom discussion and not to illustrate either effective or ineffective handling of an administrative situation.

Virginia Beach revealed the area to contain 46 mobile home parks, with spaces for 4,108 units. Of these spaces, there were only 30 vacancies. Also, 30 parks reported extensive waiting lists. The remaining 16 did not maintain waiting lists, since they found no trouble filling empty spaces. Those parks using waiting lists indicated that up to one year could be spent waiting for a vacancy. It is noted in the report that the only definite plans for expansion were found in Chesapeake, where land shortages were not as critical as in the other, more populated areas.

Although the parks were generally found to be clean, there were some undesirable aspects associated with most. Five of the parks were located near undesirable environmental conditions, including fertilizer plant fumes, factory noise, and airport noise. Other factors causing the parks to be undesirable included the absence of sidewalks, drainage systems, recreational facilities, concrete pads, and street lighting. Even with the negative factors associated with most of the parks, we concluded that the mobile home park market is a "seller's market," because of the demand for space and the high occupancy rates.

Our study for the Tidewater Real Estate Investment Partnership is based on a site located near Highway 13 in Chesapeake, approximately six miles south of Military Circle. We found land values to be quite high in this area, with an average value of $10,000-$15,000 per acre. After talking to a representative of the Chesapeake Department of City Planning, we found that there has in the past been much opposition to the development of mobile home parks from adjoining land owners. In addition to getting the land rezoned, a developer also must obtain a use permit. The use permit is a controlling factor over uses of land which would have detrimental effects to the adjoining property. As with the cost of the land, it is assumed in our study that the land meets the proper zoning requirements and a use permit can be secured.

According to the city code of Chesapeake, there are several regulations which govern mobile home parks. These requirements appear to be somewhat stricter than conditions for the neighboring areas. Some of the most important requirements are as follows:

Off-drive parking.   Each mobile home space should be provided with at least one off-drive parking space located on or within 200 feet of the mobile home space it is to serve. If off-drive parking is not provided, all interior drives must have a paved width of 30 feet.

Recreation area and facilities.   Mobile home parks shall provide recreation space and equipment as determined by the department of recreation.
Street lights.   Street lights shall be installed as prescribed by the department of public works.

In our analysis, we feel we can reasonably expect the proposed home park to reach 100 percent occupancy within six months. There are several factors which lead us to this assumption. First is the high demand in the area. Demand is so great that several parks accept only homes purchased from a dealership associated with the park. The second factor is the location. This area is away from large commercial districts and is very attractive and quiet. The third major fact is that the park will be new. Although the developers should not expect to draw residents from other parks, we feel that the park would capture a large percentage of people moving into the area or buying new mobile homes.

Because of the demand for such a facility, we recommend that the entire park be developed as a single unit. In order to ensure proper drainage and thus a higher-quality court, we feel the land should be filled to a higher elevation. This would also add to the value of the land if, in later years, an alternative use of the land were more feasible. We feel that asphalt access roads would add to the beauty of the park and be less costly in the long run. Also, underground service wiring would be more attractive. Also, we have opted for underground street lighting. In keeping with the overall quality of the park, there are several other considerations which should be provided for the residents. These include the following:

1. Heavy-duty, coin-operated washers and dryers (Maytag) in the laundry room;
2. Large swimming pool and recreation equipment;
3. Off-street parking (two spaces per residence).

Because of the attractiveness of the area as a park site, we feel that there are several qualifications residents should meet for entrance. These are as follows:

1. No mobile homes over two years old; as homes get older they must be maintained according to management standards;
2. No outdoor or large pets allowed;
3. All vehicles kept within the park must be kept in running order, with proper licenses, etc., for street use;
4. All homes must have skirting which meets the approval of management;
5. A lease of one year must be signed initially for the site, with yearly renewals afterward. After the first year, two weeks' notice must be given before moving;
6. Rental should be $70 per month initially.

We feel that as a result of our marketing analysis, the proposed site would have sufficient appeal to attain a reputation as an attractive residential area, and would attract residents meeting the aforementioned qualifications. In our financial analysis, we have covered the overall profitability of such a venture.

Assumptions and Qualifications to Financial Statements

Exhibits 1 through 3 show the projected results and other data concerning the proposed development of the mobile home park. Before beginning the actual financial analysis, however, we would like to set forth some assumptions and clarifying information concerning some of the items that appear in the exhibits.

1. It was assumed that during the first six months of the first year of operations, the park would go from zero occupancy to 100% occupancy, resulting in an average occupancy rate of 75% for the first year of operations. Thereafter, the park was assumed to be operating at 100% occupancy.
2. Since the projections cover a period of three years, some allowance had to

be made for inflation. Rather than use one overall rate of inflation and assume that all prices increased in the same proportion, we chose to adjust certain costs in keeping with what we believed were representative increases. To offset this trend of rising costs, lot rentals have been set at $70 per lot per month and increase $5 per year in each of the succeeding years.

3. Laundry facilities consist of 20 washers and 10 dryers, or 1 washer for every 10.5 families. The washers cost $.25 to operate and the double capacity dryers also cost $.25 to operate.

4. The manager, in addition to his salary, receives the use of a lot for his trailer.

5. License fees are an annual city license and are computed at the rate of $50 per occupied lot.

6. Property tax is computed at the rate of $3.28 per $100 of assessed value. The assessed value is approximately 50% of the market value, and the market value has been established at $588,800.

7. Pool maintenance consists of a lifeguard's salary for four months at $350 per month and other related supplies.

8. Maintenance and repairs consist of the $600 annual maintenance on the roads, and approximately 2% of annual gross revenues for other necessary maintenance and repair items.

9. Water and sewage are paid by the park owners and are computed on an average usage of approximately 300 gallons per day per occupied lot.

10. The residents of the park pay their own electric bills; however, the park must provide electricity for all outdoor lighting and the laundry facility.

11. Insurance is a standard multi-perils policy for a mobile home park.

12. Since there are only four depreciable assets and their value is not significant, straight-line depreciation has been adopted. The laundry building is depreciated over 40 years, the swimming pool over 10 years, and the washers and dryers and playground equipment over 5 years.

13. All other development costs are capitalized into a land improvement account and are not amortized.

14. Since the venture is organized as a partnership, the net income from the operation is not taxed. Rather, each partner's share of the net income is considered as personal income and is taxed at the partner's particular tax rate.

15. Each partner has a one-third interest in the venture and shares in the profit and loss in that proportion.

16. The proposed site contains 30 acres which can be purchased for $8,500 per acre and the allowable density is seven mobile homes per acre.

17. The initial capital outlay required to develop the park is $598,700 as shown in Exhibit 2. The necessary financing was obtained from the following sources as provided to this consultant by the partnership.

   A. The U.S. government will provide an SBA loan for $1,200 per trailer site up to a maximum of $150,000 at 7%, due in 15 years. It can be an unsecured loan.

   B. The First National Bank will lend up to $200,000 at 12%, due in 10 years. The loan is to be secured by real assets of the proposed development.

C. The Second State Bank will lend up to $200,000 at 12%, due in 15 years. The loan must be secured by the land and trailer facilities.

D. The partnership will contribute $80,000.

Also of primary importance in our decision to recommend financing almost entirely with debt, was the availability of adequate bank and government-backed financing.

Exhibit 1 shows the pro forma income statements for the first three full years of operation. The project should be profitable from the very beginning, with first-year net income of $25,870 being achieved with a 75% occupancy rate. The net income in the following years will be even higher, as most of the costs are fixed costs, and the park should be operating at 100% occupancy in the succeeding years.

Exhibit 3 shows the pro forma balance sheets for the first three full years. The balance sheets were constructed assuming no withdrawals or additional investments of capital by the partners in order to show the growth of cash and partners' capital. Withdrawal could, of course, be made up to the limits shown in Exhibit 2.

EXHIBIT 1
Tidewater Mobile Home Park
Pro Forma Income Statements

	1975	1976	1977
Revenue:			
Lot Rental	$131,670	$188,100	$200,640
Laundry	15,000	15,000	15,000
Total Revenue	$146,670	$203,100	$215,100
Operating Expenses:			
Manager's Salary	$ 7,000	$ 7,490	$ 8,010
License Fees	7,875	10,500	10,500
Property Tax	9,665	10,630	11,700
Pool Maintenance	2,000	2,000	2,100
Maintenance & Repairs	4,680	4,680	4,680
Water & Sewage	18,450	24,600	24,600
Electricity	3,600	3,600	3,960
Telephone	480	480	520
Insurance	3,600	3,600	3,600
Advertising	450	450	475
Office Expense	600	600	625
Depreciation	3,900	3,900	3,900
Total Operating Expense	$ 62,300	$ 72,530	$ 74,670
Net Income From Operations	$ 84,370	$131,000	$140,430
Other Expense:			
Interest	58,500	56,070	53,371
Net Income	$ 25,870	$ 74,930	$ 87,059

EXHIBIT 2
Tidewater Mobile Home Park
Cash Flow Forecast

	1974	1975	1976	1977
Receipts:				
Loans	$550,000	—	—	—
Owner's Capital	80,000	—	—	—
Lot Rental	—	$131,670	$188,100	$200,640
Laundry	—	15,000	15,000	15,000
Total Receipts	$630,000	$146,670	$203,100	$215,640
Payments:				
Land	255,000	—	—	—
Land Fill	51,000	—	—	—
Sanitary Sewer	63,000	—	—	—
Asphalt Roads	21,900	—	—	—
Service Wiring	39,900	—	—	—
Street Lighting	20,300	—	—	—
Concrete	18,500	—	—	—
Potable Water	58,400	—	—	—
Natural Gas	27,700	—	—	—
Laundry Building	18,100	—	—	—
Swimming Pool	15,000	—	—	—
Washers & Dryers	9,300	—	—	—
Playground Equipment	500	—	—	—
Use Permit	100	—	—	—
Manager's Salary	—	7,000	7,490	8,010
License Fees	—	7,875	10,500	10,500
Property Tax	—	9,665	10,630	11,700
Pool Maintenance	—	2,000	2,000	2,100
Maintenance & Repairs	—	4,680	4,680	4,680
Water & Sewage	—	18,450	24,600	24,600
Electricity	—	3,600	3,600	3,960
Telephone	—	480	480	520
Insurance	—	3,600	3,600	3,600
Advertising	—	450	450	475
Office Expense	—	600	600	625
Loan Repayment	—	81,231	81,231	81,231
Total Payments	$598,700	$150,120	$149,420	$152,533
Net Gain or (Loss)	$ 31,300	$ (3,450)	$ 52,680	$ 62,107
Initial Cash Balance	—	31,300	27,850	81,530
Cumulative Cash Balance	$ 31,300	$ 27,850	$ 81,530	$144,637
Desired Level of Cash	30,000	30,000	30,000	30,000
Cash Available for Withdrawal	$ 1,300	$ (2,150)	$ 51,530	$114,637

EXHIBIT 3
Tidewater Mobile Home Park
Pro Forma Balance Sheets

	1974[1]	1975[2]	1976[2]	1977[2]
ASSETS				
Current Assets:				
Cash	$ 31,300	$ 24,849	$ 81,528	$144,637
Prepaid Insurance	3,600	3,600	3,600	3,600
Prepaid Advertising	450	450	475	475
Office Supplies	150	150	150	150
Total Current Assets	$ 35,500	$ 32,050	$ 85,765	$148,872
Plant Assets:				
Swimming Pool	15,000	15,000	15,000	15,000
Less Acc. Dep.	0	(1,500)	(3,000)	(4,500)
Playground Equipment	500	500	500	500
Less Acc. Dep.	0	(100)	(200)	(300)
Washers & Dryers	9,300	9,300	9,300	9,300
Less Acc. Dep.	0	(1,860)	(3,720)	(5,580)
Laundry Building	18,100	18,100	18,100	18,100
Less Acc. Dep.	0	(450)	(900)	(1,350)
Land	255,000	255,000	255,000	255,000
Land Improvements	300,700	300,700	300,700	300,700
Total Plant Assets	$598,600	$594,689	$590,778	$586,420
Intangible Assets				
Licenses	0	10,500	10,500	10,500
Use Permit	100	100	100	100
Total Assets	$634,200	$637,339	$687,143	$746,342
LIABILITIES				
Current Liabilities:				
Accounts Payable	$ 4,200	$ 4,200	$ 4,235	$ 4,235
Long-Term Liabilities:				
Small Business Administration Loan	150,000	144,031	137,644	130,810
First National Bank Loan	200,000	188,603	175,838	161,542
Second State Bank Loan	200,000	194,635	188,626	181,896
Total Liabilities	$554,200	$531,469	$506,343	$478,483
Contributed Capital[3]	80,000	80,000	80,000	80,000
Retained Earnings[3]	0	25,870	100,800	187,859
Total Liabilities and Net Worth	$634,200	$637,339	$687,143	$746,342

[1]Balance Sheet at start of operations.
[2]Balance Sheet at end of year.
[3]Assumes no withdrawals or additional investments of capital by the owners.

QUESTIONS

1. Comment on the assumptions the consultants have used in making their forecasts.
2. Would Tidewater Mobile Home Park provide a reasonable return to the partnership?

Case 18
Arizona Coal Mining

Background Information

Arizona Coal Mining, Inc., has been actively engaged in strip mining coal reserves in the Four Corners area of the Southwest for the past 15 years. Over the years, the company has become extremely profitable and has gained the reputation of being one of the best-managed coal companies in the country.

In March of 1975, the company's dynamic young president, Jim Charles, was approached by a representative of Dry Sky, Inc., a Navajo Indian cooperative, about the possibility of participating in a new coal mining venture in northeastern Arizona. The Indian group controls extensive coal reserves in that area but lacks the technical and managerial expertise to properly develop the coal.

After careful on-site inspection by Arizona Coal's top engineering and management people in April, Arizona Coal's top management team concluded that the deal might have merit and certainly warranted careful study. Paul Willeys, Arizona Coal's senior financial vice president, prepared a summary list of necessary capital expenditures that would be encountered during the 23-year life cycle of the job (Table 1). Due to the Environmental Protection Agency's new regulations on surface mining, it is anticipated that over $7 million must be spent in capital expenditures to backfill and contour the strip-mined areas during the last five years of the job. During that time, gross revenues would be essentially zero. During the first 18 years of the strip mining operation, however, Willeys projects that the annual net income before tax would total over $5 million. At the same time, Willeys

This case was prepared by Professor Dennis B. Fitzpatrick of Boise State University as a basis for classroom discussion and not to illustrate either effective or ineffective handling of an administrative situation.

also firmly believes that there is a 45% possibility that the state of Arizona will require the mine operators to fill in the mined-out overburden and create a state park in the area. Willeys predicts that the additional costs of refurbishing the mined area would increase operating expenses by almost $4 million per year (Table 2). When Willeys presented his revenue and costs estimate to the company's top strategy committee, Charles asked him whether he had adjusted his projections for future inflation in the operating expenses. Willeys responded that he had not adjusted for inflation since he believed that increasing coal prices should more than offset any inflation in operating expenses.

During further negotiations with the Indians, both parties agreed that the general structuring of the joint venture (if completed) should take the following general form:

1. A third corporation or partnership would be established;
2. The Indians would be paid a royalty fee by the new corporation for the coal of approximately $4.5 million per year;
3. Arizona Coal would receive $1.3 million per year for supplying the engineering and management expertise;
4. Although Arizona Coal would like to have an up-front equity investment of no more than 20%, while the Indians would like to see a more substantial initial investment from the coal company, both parties feel that this issue can be satisfactorily negotiated.

TABLE 1
Dry Sky Coal Project
Schedule of Capital Expenditures
(000's)

Year	Mobile Equipment	Other	Plant	Total
1975	$ 0		$ 650	$ 650
1976	8,997	$ 148	7,800	16,945
1977	5,908		325	6,233
1978—Start Production	0			0
1979	1,929	892		2,821
1980	200			200
1981	985	2,345		3,330
1982	560			560
1983	3,549			3,549
1984	3,458			3,458
1985	95			95
1986	1,082			1,082
1987	3,041			3,041
1988	3,276			3,276
1989	5,245			5,245
1990	183			183
1991	901			901
1992	734			734
1993—Cease Production	661			661
1994—Start Final Backfill	6,552			6,552
1995	735			735
1996	0			0
1997	0			0
1998	0			0
TOTAL	$47,591	$3,385	$8,775	$56,751

TABLE 2
Dry Sky Coal Project
Projection of Revenues and Expenses
(000's)

Revenues

2.25 Million Ton Coal Sales @ $12.00 per ton $27,000

Expenses

	Without Overburden Capital Adjustment	With Overburden Capital Adjustment
Contract Mining*	$12,180	$15,421
Coal Royalty Expenses	4,500	4,500
Coal Testing	42	42
Insurance	140	140
Environmental Expenditures	105	105
Production Taxes on Coal	2,100	2,457
Property Tax	280	280
Depreciation	1,750	1,750
Amortization Deferred Costs	630	630
General and Administrative	210	210
Total Expenses	$21,937	$25,535
Net Income Before Tax	$ 5,063	$ 1,465

*Includes Arizona Coal's $1.3 million management fee.

QUESTION

1. Assuming that Arizona Coal Mining, Inc., has a minimum "hurdle rate" of 30% for its proposed equity investment, determine whether the venture is an attractive investment for the company. Be sure to list your assumptions and be prepared to support your position.

Case 19
American Hotels, Inc. (A)

In May 1975, Mr. Andrew Schmit, the Vice President of Finance and Long Range Planning for American Hotels, Inc., chaired a meeting of his subordinates in order to review a report submitted by an outside consulting firm. Mr. Schmit had commissioned the firm to perform an eight-year market study that resulted in financial projections for ten of the corporation's wholly owned hotels located throughout the state of California. The specific aim of the meeting was to design recommendations for a future course of action for these assets.

Although a positive cash flow had been generated, the consolidated operations of the California Hotel Division had proved unprofitable over the past three years. As part of a critical examination of various facets of the total corporate structure, Mr. James Buckner, the President of American Hotels, had requested that Mr. Schmit and his department prepare a long-range corporate strategy for the California Hotel Division. The strategy designed by Mr. Schmit's division would be submitted for approval of the Board of Directors at their next monthly meeting.

The Company

American Hotels, Inc., evolved from a single hotel in Chicago in 1939 to a chain of over 100 hotels located throughout the United States, Canada, and Mexico by 1975. Total revenues in 1974 exceeded half a billion dollars (see Exhibits 1, 2, and 3 for recent financial results). The company was incorporated in 1954 with the founder, Mr. Gregory Caufield Crown III, receiving approximately 15% of the

This case was prepared by Mr. William Geiler and Professor David Springate of Southern Methodist University as a basis for classroom discussion and not to illustrate either effective or ineffective handling of an administrative situation.

company's common stock. Mr. Crown was Chairman of the Board, but had little involvement in actual operations. Aside from Mr. Crown, there were no shareholders who held more than 5% of the outstanding shares. The corporation's stock was actively traded on the American Stock Exchange. A recent history of its trading pattern is given in Exhibit 4. Exhibit 5 shows price/earnings ratios for some major hotel chains as of May 1975.

While the principal business activity of American Hotels, Inc., was hotel operations, the company did have some involvement in airline feeding and transportation. The corporation itself owned and operated 61 hotel properties. The remaining 43 hotels were franchised to various owners around the country.

American Hotels, Inc., received an initial franchise fee of $25,000 per hotel, plus yearly franchise income amounting to 2½% of gross sales for each of its franchised hotels. A franchise entitled its owner to use the chain name, its signs, and most important, its world-wide reservations system, which was one of the most active in the country and responsible for a major portion of total room bookings. All of the ten hotels within the corporation's California division were company-owned and not franchised.

American Hotels were principally downtown hotels located within the central business districts of most of the major metropolitan areas. They ranged in size from 150 to 800 rooms, and depending upon the size, usually contained several restaurants and cocktail lounges. Because of their excellent reputation and reservation system, they typically achieved a room occupancy rate several percentage points above city-wide averages.

The Consultant's Report

After talking with Mr. Buckner, Mr. Schmit had retained a Certified Public Accounting firm with a Management Advisory Services department experienced in the hospitality industry. In accordance with its charge, the consulting team first surveyed the operations of each of the ten hotels in California, with an aim of being able to better predict costs. It then carried out a detailed market study which included projections of supply and demand annually through 1983. Using a computerized risk analysis model which required as input certain projections about city economic activity and a number of associated probabilities, the consultants determined a room occupancy percentage which was estimated to be the average annual occupancy for each of the hotels for the eight-year period. The eight-year period was chosen at Mr. Schmit's request. He felt that each hotel was a real estate investment and that eight years was a reasonable maximum payback period to expect, given the relatively large depreciation and amortization considerations provided in the early life of the project.

In the report, the consultants attached a relatively high degree of confidence to the project occupancies and pro forma income statements for the first five years, 1976 through 1980. In 1981 through 1983, however, the report referenced the possibility of significant changes in hotel room supply. There could be additions or deletions in each market area, either of which would be expected to have a significant impact on the operating results of the various American Hotels.

Based upon the projected room occupancy percentages, pro forma statements of average annual income and cash flow were prepared by the consultants for each hotel (see Exhibit 6). These statements were in 1975 current dollars. The consultants estimated, however, that room rates, menu prices, and other revenue sources would increase by approximately 6% per year through 1983. They also estimated that the cost of the expenses associated with the operations would also increase by 6% per year. The resulting house profit (profit before fixed charges) was therefore expected to remain a constant percentage of total revenue. Exhibit 7 contains pro forma figures for gross sales and house profit by year for each hotel. The figures quoted are in current dollars and are not indexed to 1975.

Reactions to the Report

Mr. Schmit had specifically requested that the consulting firm not incorporate any financial recommendations in the report, but simply present projections of future market conditions and operating results. It was his intention to develop financial strategy within his own department.

Mr. Schmit distributed copies of this report, including the figures of Exhibit 6, to the members of his department and asked each of them to formulate his or her recommended strategy. A meeting was then scheduled one week prior to the board meeting at which Mr. Schmit was to present his department's recommendation for the long-range strategy concerning the ten California hotels.

At the departmental meeting, several divergent recommendations were made by the various members present.

Michael Hendel, Assistant Vice President of the department, urged that the ten hotels be sold as quickly as possible to realize immediate short-term cash flow. He reasoned that American Hotels, Inc., as a whole, was in a tenuous working capital position due to the significant economic recession that the country was experiencing at the time. Cash and cash equivalents on hand had dropped to approximately $15 million by May of 1975, and cash forecasts indicated that American would require a cash balance of $21 million for operations through the remainder of the year. Although other alternatives to raise cash existed, Mr. Hendel felt that the ten hotels might be sold as a package to one of the larger, more liquid hotel corporations at book value. This would relieve American Hotel's liquidity bind.

Frank Sikich, a junior analyst who was a recent MBA, disagreed with Hendel. He maintained that American Hotels, Inc., should be represented in each of the ten California locations. He pointed out that having no West Coast hotels would affect a significant portion of the company's steady executive traveling clientele. More important than West Coast representation, Sikich stressed the long-term positive cash flow aspects of keeping all of the properties. The consultants' report projected a sizable cash flow before tax in 1975 dollars for all years into the future for nine of the hotels. As the level of revenues increased through inflation, house profit would also increase, which would mean higher and higher cash flows through the years.

At this point, Susan Marshall, a senior analyst on the staff, reminded the group that while total cash flow for the corporation had increased over the past two years, earnings per share had actually decreased and were projected to decrease again for fiscal 1975. Stock prices had fallen from a high of $47.00 in 1973 to $24.00 in mid-1975. Ms. Marshall proposed that those five hotels which were estimated to show a net profit on the average over the next five years should be kept and the remaining five hotels should be sold to another company.

Donald Brennan, Head of the Real Estate Development section, informed Ms. Marshall that it would be extremely difficult at best to sell only the properties projected to be unprofitable to another company or even to private investors. He estimated that in order to dispose of all five hotels, he would have to sell them so as to net approximately two-thirds of the respective book values before consideration of tax effects. He added that any losses incurred in selling hotels would be used to offset gains elsewhere in American Hotels and would therefore serve to reduce taxes.

Brennan suggested an alternative course of action. He proposed that the ten hotels be packaged and sold to one major franchisee at perhaps 90% book value. He claimed that this would maximize the front-end cash flow through the proceeds from the sale, from reduction in taxes payable due to capital losses incurred in the sale, and from the ten franchise fees collected. In addition, it would eliminate any risk of future unprofitability for the ten hotels because American Hotels, Inc., would be guaranteed a percentage of gross revenue and annual income.

Robert Gray, the Assistant Vice President, agreed that Brennan's proposal would minimize risk and ensure profitability. But he noted that there were several hotels among the ten which were currently quite profitable and had excellent long-term potential for increased profitability. He pointed out that the net profit of two of these properties alone would be equal to the total franchise percentage income of all ten hotels. Gray went on to suggest that those hotels with a good profit potential over the next five years be kept and the remaining properties be sold to one or more franchisees. He maintained that even if American Hotels incurred a capital loss on the sale of the hotels to franchisees, the corporation would be maximizing its profit potential and, hopefully, its earnings per share in the future. Gray did admit, however, that the corporation might not desire any additional losses, capital or otherwise, in 1975, due to the impact that the recession was having on operating results of the year to date.

After considerable debate, Mr. Schmit rose to leave, informing the group that he had to go to an Executive Committee meeting. He summarized his feelings by stating that several worthwhile proposals had been aired. While he agreed that EPS, cash flow, and risk were probably valid considerations, he was concerned that choosing increased earnings might also imply the choice of a relatively poor return on investment. Yet earnings and stock prices did appear to be related. Pointing out that the company usually required that cash flow before taxes divided by the initial cost of any owned investment exceed 10% annually, Mr. Schmit went on to remind his subordinates this was not being achieved by the ten California properties. Stressing the importance of the matter and his desire to identify the best course of action for the California Hotel Division, Mr. Schmit asked the group to continue its meeting.

In May 1975, seasoned industrial bonds were trading to yield an average of approximately 9.2% per year if held to maturity.

EXHIBIT 1
American Hotels, Inc. (A)
Consolidated Balance Sheet
(000's)

	Year Ended	
	12/31/74	*12/31/73*
Current Assets		
Cash	$ 21,297	$ 23,918
A/R (net)	38,911	26,395
Inventories	20,815	18,444
Prepaid Expenses	8,019	7,679
Total Current Assets	$ 89,042	$ 76,436
Property and Equipment		
Land, Buildings & Equipment	$385,650	$358,347
Less Accumulated Depreciation	94,136	79,938
	291,514	298,409
Total Assets	$380,556	$354,845
Current Liabilities		
Current Portion of Long-Term Debt	$ 9,325	$ 8,637
Notes Payable—Banks	16,356	13,162
Accounts Payable	24,294	20,818
Total Current Liabilities	$ 49,975	$ 42,617
Long-Term Debt		
Long-Term Borrowings	$133,195	$134,131
Deferred Income Taxes	16,059	13,413
	$149,254	$147,544
Stockholders' Equity		
Common Stock (10,000,000 shares, $5 par)	$ 50,000	$ 50,000
Retained Earnings	131,327	114,484
Total Equity	$181,327	$164,684
Total Liabilities & Shareholders' Equity	$380,556	$354,845

EXHIBIT 2
American Hotels, Inc. (A)
Statement of Consolidated Income
(00's except per share figures)

	Year Ended	
	12/31/74	*12/31/73*
Revenues		
Hotel Division	$501,792	$465,400
Other Divisions	51,430	44,026
	$553,222	$509,426
Costs & Expenses	515,969	466,329
Net Income Before Taxes	$ 37,253	$ 43,097
Provision for Income Taxes	$ 13,411	$ 16,454
Net Income	$ 23,842	$ 26,643
Earnings per Common Share	$2.38	$2.66
Dividends Paid per Share	$ .65	$ .60

EXHIBIT 3
American Hotels, Inc. (A)
Earnings Record for Years 1970-1974
(000's except per share figures)

	1974	*1973*	*1972*	*1971*	*1970*
Consolidated Revenues	$553,222	$509,426	$475,619	$386,124	$339,172
Consolidated Net Income	$ 23,842	$ 26,643	$ 28,537	$ 25,092	$ 21,045
Earnings per Common Share	$2.38	$2.66	$2.85	$2.51	$2.10
Dividends Paid per Share	$ .65	$ .60	$ .55	$ .50	$ .45

EXHIBIT 4
American Hotels, Inc. (A)
Stock Price History

	Stock Price		
	Low	*Average*	*High*
1972			
1st Quarter	$28⅛	$30¼	$33½
2nd Quarter	32⅝	36⅛	37
3rd Quarter	31⅞	35⅛	38¼
4th Quarter	37⅜	39⅞	41¾
1973			
1st Quarter	40⅛	44½	46½
2nd Quarter	45	46¾	47
3rd Quarter	36⅞	40½	42½
4th Quarter	32¼	37⅜	39⅜
1974			
1st Quarter	30½	34¼	37
2nd Quarter	24⅛	29¾	32⅜
3rd Quarter	22⅝	26	29½
4th Quarter	19⅞	24	26⅜
1975			
1st Quarter	21	24¾	25½

EXHIBIT 5
American Hotels, Inc. (A)
P/E Ratios of Major Publicly Held Hotel Corporations

Chain	*P/E Ratio (May 1975)*
Hilton Hotels	5
Holiday Inns	11
Howard Johnson's	14
Marriott Inns	20
Ramada Inns	12
American Hotels	10

EXHIBIT 6

American Hotels, Inc. (A)

Pro Forma Statement of Average Annual Income and Cash Flow for California Hotels
for the Years 1976-1980 Expressed in 1975 Dollars (000s)

	Hotel 1	2	3	4	5	6	7	8	9	10
Sales										
Room Sales	723	2354	3285	3009	854	1369	1139	1506	1971	4170
Food Sales	362	1177	1643	1505	427	685	570	753	986	2085
Beverage Sales	241	785	1096	1004	285	457	380	502	658	1397
Other	72	235	329	301	85	137	114	151	197	417
Total Revenue	1398	4551	6353	5819	1651	2648	2203	2912	3812	8069
Operating Expenses	1118	3186	4765	3899	1156	2118	1652	2308	2859	5406
House Profit	280	1365	1588	1920	495	530	551	874	953	2663
Fixed Charges										
Real Estate Taxes	50	125	250	150	45	100	75	80	90	300
Interest on Mortgage	250	660	1300	970	312	500	380	400	240	920
Depreciation	225	430	700	485	156	300	210	250	270	560
Net Income Before Taxes	(245)	150	(662)	315	(18)	(370)	(114)	144	353	883
Add Back Depreciation	225	430	700	485	156	300	210	250	270	560
Cash Flow Before Income Tax and Principal Repayment	(20)	580	38	800	138	(70)	96	394	623	1443
Book Value	$2,500	4,600	8,000	5700	1,000	5,500	4,000	3,700	2,820	9,200
Number of Rooms	180	344	500	388	156	300	240	268	360	448
Occupancy %	55%	75%	60%	85%	75%	50%	65%	70%	60%	85%
1975 Average Room Rate	$20	$25	$30	$25	$20	$25	$20	$22	$25	$30

EXHIBIT 7

American Hotels, Inc. (A)

Sales and House Profit Projections for California Hotels for Years 1976-1983 (000s)
(In Current Dollars)

	1976		1977		1978		1979	
	Gross Sales	House Profit	Gross Sales	House Profit	Gross Sales	House Profit	Gross Sales	House Profit
Hotel 1	$ 1,482	$ 296	$ 1,571	$ 314	$ 1,665	$ 333	$ 1,765	$ 353
2	4,824	1,447	5,114	1,534	5,420	1,626	5,746	1,724
3	6,734	1,684	7,138	1,785	7,567	1,892	8,021	2,005
4	6,168	2,035	6,538	2,158	6,931	2,287	7,347	2,425
5	1,750	525	1,855	557	1,966	590	2,084	625
6	2,807	561	2,975	595	3,154	631	3,343	669
7	2,335	584	2,475	619	2,624	656	2,781	695
8	3,087	926	3,272	982	3,468	1,040	3,676	1,103
9	4,040	1,010	4,283	1,071	4,540	1,135	4,813	1,203
10	8,553	2,822	9,066	2,992	9,610	3,171	10,187	3,362
	$41,789	$11,890	$44,287	$12,607	$46,945	$13,361	$49,763	$14,164

EXHIBIT 7 ,

American Hotels, Inc. (A) **(continued)**

Sales and House Profit Projections for California Hotels for Years 1976-1983 (000s)
(In Current Dollars)

	1980		1981		1982		1983	
	Gross Sales	House Profit	Gross Sales	House Profit	Gross Sales	House Profit	Gross Sales	House Profit
Hotel 1	$ 1,871	$ 374	$ 1,983	$ 397	$ 2,102	$ 421	$ 2,228	$ 446
2	6,090	1,827	6,456	1,937	6,843	2,053	7,254	2,176
3	8,502	2,126	9,012	2,253	9,553	3,288	10,126	2,531
4	7,788	2,570	8,255	2,724	8,750	2,887	9,275	3,061
5	2,209	663	2,342	703	2,483	745	2,631	790
6	3,544	709	3,756	751	3,981	796	4,220	844
7	2,948	737	3,125	781	3,313	828	3,511	878
8	3,897	1,169	4,131	1,239	4,379	1,313	4,642	1,392
9	5,101	1,275	5,407	1,352	5,731	1,433	6,075	1,519
10	10,798	3,563	11,446	3,777	12,133	4,004	12,861	4,244
	$52,748	$15,013	$55,913	$15,914	$59,268	$16,868	$62,823	$17,881

QUESTIONS

1. Which criterion is more important for the decision-making process: project earnings or cash flows? Why?
2. What course of action should Mr. Schmit's division recommend for the California Hotel Division?

Case 20
National Guard Hangar Expansion

Historical Perspective

Durango International, Inc., a large construction firm based in Oklahoma City, specializes in the engineering, design, and construction of oil drilling facilities and pipelines throughout the world. Because of its far-reaching operations in remote parts of the world, the company has found it useful to acquire and maintain a large fleet of corporate aircraft since the 1940's. Originally, the company-owned airplanes were primarily small single-engine craft capable of flying equipment and key personnel into rough landing strips near remote job sites in South America, Canada, and Alaska. In 1970, the company started to reduce the number of small aircraft it maintained around the world and decided to consolidate its aircraft operations by purchasing five turbo props and two corporate-type jet aircraft. These planes are all based at the Oklahoma City airport.

Expansion of the Aviation Department

For years, the maintenance work on Durango's planes was contracted to local maintenance shops at airports throughout the world. With the acquisition of the turbo props and the jets, the Aviation Department was reorganized to provide its own maintenance and repair shops. George Chester, Durango's chief pilot since 1965, was named director of the Aviation Department in 1971. After two years of consolidating its own aircraft operations in Oklahoma City, Mr. Chester decided to

This case was prepared by Professor Dennis B. Fitzpatrick of Boise State University as a basis for classroom discussion and not to illustrate either effective or ineffective handling of an administrative situation.

expand his department's operations to the point where it could actively solicit outside work. In 1973, eight more full-time aircraft mechanics and four new avionics specialists were hired, and the maintenance facilities were opened to the general aviation public.

In 1974, a complete radio and avionics shop was established, and the department is now capable of radio overhaul, maintenance, and complete aircraft radio installation. New radio sales were also introduced as a result of the facility becoming an authorized dealer for several radio manufacturers. Additionally, Chester was able to obtain a Standard Oil fuel dealership and is currently negotiating to become a fully authorized service shop for Lear and Cessna Citation corporate jets. Chester firmly believes the expansion of his department from an internal maintenance shop to a full-fledged general aviation service center is healthy and in line with the company's policy to expand into profitable new ventures. Since approximately 75% of the department's work is still performed on Durango's own aircraft, the department remains a cash flow drain on the company. It is Chester's primary objective to expand rapidly enough to make a positive profit and cash flow contribution (in addition to servicing the company's aircraft) by 1976.

Chester worries, however, that his plans may well be stymied by lack of hangar and shop space. The Aviation Department currently operates from two large hangars and three smaller shops at the airport. In order to become a full aviation service station by late 1976, the company will need to double its hangar and shop space. Chester and his assistant, Art Paulson, have estimated that this type of expansion would cost between $1.5 million and $2.0 million. Two months ago, the local city council approached Chester and Paulson with a most interesting proposal that would sharply reduce these expansion costs. The city proposed to sell a 30-year-old National Guard hangar to Durango. The National Guard's hangar lease had expired, and the city planned to build an additional taxiway where the hangar was originally located. Chester estimated that the total cost of buying, moving, and remodeling the old hangar would be approximately $750,000 plus a $10,000 annual ground lease to the city for the next 35 years.

When Chester and Paulson approached top management with the National Guard hangar proposal, they were met with a mixed reaction. Jim Cheery, executive vice-president of operations, wondered if the general and business aviation market was an appropriate expansion area for an energy-related engineering firm. He was especially concerned that Durango might enter a very competitive new market without the necessary operating experience and capabilities. Carl Wickers, vice-president in charge of finance, also voiced skepticism and questioned whether the $750,000 investment could be justified on financial grounds. In addition, Wickers wondered if the total cost of renovating the old hangar might exceed Chester's estimate of $750,000.

Chester countered these comments by stating that pro forma income and cash flow analyses made by the Accounting Department indicate that the Aviation Department can be expected to earn between 25% and 30% on invested capital if the National Guard hangar is acquired (see Table 1). He also thought that the Accounting Department's assumptions (see Table 2) were ultra-conservative and stressed that more realistic assumptions would generate substantially better returns on invested capital (see Table 3).

Mr. Wickers and Mr. Cheery admitted that Chester's arguments appeared convincing but decided to hire an outside financial consultant to perform a completely independent investment analysis of the hangar proposal.

TABLE 1

National Guard Hangar Expansion

Aviation Department—Projected Income and Cash Flow Summary

($1,000)

	1974 actual	1975	1976	1977	1978	1979
Average Invested Capital	$ 558	$1,098	$1,494	$1,188	$ 792	$ 270
Projected Revenues						
Aircraft Inspection		108	216	270	324	360
Avionics		288	342	378	414	468
Maintenance & Repairs	468	684	828	900	954	1,044
Parts Sales	432	450	540	576	630	666
Fuel, Oil, Lube Sales	180	198	234	270	306	360
Hangar Rentals & Misc.	72	72	90	90	108	108
Total Revenues	$1,152	$1,800	$2,250	$2,484	$2,736	$3,006
Projected Expenses						
Direct Labor	$ 324	$ 666	$ 864	$ 936	$ 954	$ 990
Indirect labor		54	90	126	126	126
Parts	378	378	450	486	522	576
Fuel, Oil, Lube	126	144	180	198	234	270
Depreciation	36	108	108	108	108	108
Advertising		36	36	18	18	18
Liability Insurance Premiums		54	90	108	108	108
Operating Supplies	36	54	72	72	90	90
Equipment Repairs	18	18	18	18	18	18
General and Administrative	90	126	162	180	198	216
Total Expenses	$1,008	$1,638	$2,070	$2,250	$2,376	$2,520
Net Operating Income	$ 144	$ 162	$ 180	$ 234	$ 360	$ 486

TABLE 2
National Guard Hangar Expansion
Accounting Department's Assumptions

1. Additional Maintenance Revenues
    New hangar would allow enough room for six additional aircraft mechanics in 1976, seven more in 1977, two more in 1978, and one more in 1979 and 1980. Direct billing rate for mechanics is $15.00, while direct cost rate is $8.00. The mechanics are assumed to be kept busy 85% of the time.

2. Additional Avionics Equipment Sales
    Assume revenue of $13,000/month in 1976, $16,000/month in 1977, and a 10% inflation increase thereafter.

3. Additional Parts Sales
    Assume parts sales equal 65% of aircraft inspections.

4. Fuel, Oil, Lube Sales
    Assume these will increase by an additional 20% as a result of the additional hangar; also assume a 10% growth rate in succeeding years.

5. Hangar Rentals
    Assume additional hangar rentals will be zero.

6. Additional Indirect Labor
    Assume a total of two additional people for 1976 and 1977 and a total of three from 1978 on. Assume cost rate of $5.25 per hour.

7. Cost of Parts
    Assume parts cost 85% of sales.

8. Fuel, Oil, Lube Costs
    Assume a 25% mark-up.

9. Advertising & Liability Insurance
    As projected in Table 1.

10. Additional Cost of Operating Supplies
    Assume to be 3% of additional revenues.

11. Additional Equipment Repairs
    Assume 2% of additional maintenance repair revenues.

12. Additional General Expenses
    Assume 7% of revenues.

13. Avionics—New Equipment Jobs
    Assume 4% mark-up.

TABLE 3
National Guard Hangar Expansion
Aviation Department's Assumptions

1. Additional Mechanics:

4	in 1976
8 more	in 1977
8 more	in 1978
5 more	in 1979
3 more	in 1980

Total Additional
Mechanics   28

   Assume direct billing rate of $15.00 and direct cost rate of $8.00. Also assume 85% labor efficiency.

2. Avionics—New Equipment Sales
   1976 sales are estimated to be $300,000, with a 30% compounded growth rate for succeeding years.

3. Parts Sales
   Assumed to be 150% of repair shop revenues.

4. Fuel, Oil, Lube Sales
   Assume new hangar results in an increase in fuel, oil, lube sales of $100,000 and increases at a 25% compound rate for succeeding years. Also assume a 30% mark-up over cost.

5. Additional Hangar Rentals
   Assume $10,000/year in additional rentals, with a 10% compounded growth rate thereafter.

6. Additional Indirect Labor
   Assume two additional janitors and/or stockroom clerks during 1977 and a total of three additional personnel in 1978 and thereafter.

7. Advertising
   Assume to be $4,000 per year.

8. Additional Liability Insurance

$30,000	in 1976
$50,000	in 1977
$50,000	in 1978 and thereafter

9. Operating Supplies
   Assume to be 3% of gross revenues.

10. Equipment Repair
    Assume to be 1% of gross revenues.

QUESTIONS

1. How large is the expected profitability of the hangar investment?
2. What recommendation would you make to top management? Include in your recommendations comments on the nonfinancial aspects of the case.

Case 21
Tex-Tube, Incorporated (A)

During January 1960, the executive vice-president of Tex-Tube, Incoprorated, G. E. Cullen, Jr., was considering the proper course of action for his company to take regarding its need for additional capacity. In 1959, the firm's plant had operated at maximum capacity during the entire year, and the company had been forced to turn down sales orders. The future outlook for this increased demand appeared to be particularly bright. Because of the nature of its business, Tex-Tube could achieve expansion only through a major investment in a new mill, which would have a total installed cost of approximately $1 million. Since, at the end of 1959, the company's physical property, plant, and equipment had shown a net value of $1.7 million, this additional investment in a new mill would increase Tex-Tube's fixed assets approximately 60 percent. Currently, the company had two mills, a Yoder mill and a McKay mill.[1] Since a new mill would increase the plant's current

This case, which was made possible by the cooperation of Tex-Tube, Incorporated, was a project of Professor Richard L. Norgaard of the University of Connecticut, with Bowman Lee Wilbanks as research assistant. It was prepared as a basis for group discussion and not to illustrate either effective or ineffective handling of an administrative situation.

[1]The manufacture of pipe and other tubular products by the electric-resistance weld process uses coiled sheet steel as the starting material. The sheet steel, cut to the correct width, is drawn through a series of shaping rollers which form it into a tube or pipe. While the tubing continues to move through the mill, the open seam is electrically welded, the weld electronically inspected, and the pipe cut into desired lengths (usually 45 feet to 60 feet). The lengths of pipe then are placed on racks for further handling and processing. The entire manufacturing and handling processes are automated, and pipe is produced at an average of 125 feet per minute. Including the handling portion for the welded pipe, a mill is approximately 200 feet long. The two principal manufacturers of these mills are the Yoder Manufacturing Company (Yoder mill) and the McKay Machine Company (McKay mill).

capacity at least 50 percent, Mr. Cullen knew that the decision concerning whether or not to acquire a new mill would have far-reaching implications.

History of the Company

Tex-Tube was incorporated in Texas in 1946 for the purpose of manufacturing and selling shothole casing (i.e., expendable tubing used for seismic work in oil and gas exploration). In 1950, the company expanded its operations by entering the pipe-jobber field. As a jobber, the firm acted as a warehouser and distributor for all the major pipe mills.

Although Tex-Tube had become the largest pipe distributor in its locale, increasing competition had reduced the profit margin to such an extent that the company had sought diversification into other areas. In addition, the demand for shothole casing had been greatly decreased by the reduction of geophysical activity and the invention of the "knockoff" bit. In 1956, because of these inroads on its business operations, the company purchased a Yoder mill and began to manufacture and sell its own pipe in order to take advantage of the profit margin available to the manufacturer, as well as those for the warehouser and distributor. Since the pipe-manufacturing portion of the business had continued to expand, the company had purchased a McKay mill in 1957. Shortly thereafter, the company completed its first public offering of preferred and common stock.

During 1958 and 1959, the sales of pipe and tubular goods manufactured by the company increased in importance. By 1959, 55 percent of the firm's total net sales came from company-manufactured pipe and tubular goods, and 45 percent from goods manufactured by others. The product mix manufactured by the company during 1959 consisted of lightweight line pipe (used to transport oil and gas from the field to processing plants), oil-field casing and tubing, and shothole casing (which, by this time, was accounting for less than 5 percent of the firm's sales).

The management personnel of Tex-Tube consisted of the president, the vice-president of manufacturing, and the executive vice-president, Mr. Cullen. In addition to his executive duties, Mr. Cullen was also the financial manager for the firm. The four executives listed above made up the management group (i.e., executive committee) that guided the company's future. They met monthly to consider matters of company policy, overall coordination of efforts, and major capital expenditures.

Selection of Size and Type of New Mill

During the last three monthly executive meetings held in 1959, the management committee had discussed various alternatives for increasing the firm's plant capacity. Sales and manufacturing considerations had indicated that the purchase of a third pipe mill offered the most feasible solution. From the standpoint of demand for products to be produced by a new mill, the most promising areas were in small-diameter light-wall line pipe, small-diameter oil-well tubing and casing, and mechanical tubing.[2]

Tex-Tube's management committee believed that entry into the mechanical tubing field would encounter the least amount of competition, as compared to that for the company's products. Since the market for mechanical tubing consisted primarily of small orders of various sizes and shapes, it was too specialized to offer the volume required by the major steel producers. The committee believed a new mill could be operated initially to produce all four products, but with a gradual phasing out of the small-diameter line pipe, tubing, and casing. Then, in five to ten years, the major portion of the output would be in the areas of mechanical pipe and specialty tubing.

The current output from Tex-Tube's two mills was as follows: The Yoder mill produced pipe sizes of 1 inch to 3 inches in diameter, whereas the McKay mill pipe sizes were 3 inches to 6 inches. Pipe to be used as mechanical tubing would range from 1 inch to 5 inches, and, in addition, the company desired to produce oil-well casing with a 5-inch diameter. The design of the existing McKay mill was such that it produced the 6-inch pipe the most economically, becoming less efficient as the diameter of the pipe was reduced. The existing Yoder mill was limited not only by its capacity, which was one-third that of the McKay mill, but also by its inability to make the heavy-wall pipe necessary for small-diameter oil-well tubing (1¼ inches and 1½ inches). After studying the situation, the committee decided that a new mill should be intermediate in size as compared to the size of the two existing mills and that it should produce pipe of 1 inch to 5 inches in diameter, with the necessary wall thicknesses. In addition, it was decided that the mill should be able to produce pipe of the smaller diameters as economically as possible.

Having decided on the type and size of a new mill, the committee next wanted to consider the potential return from this investment in additional plant capacity. Mr. Cullen stated that he hoped he could have this information for the committee's next meeting in late January 1960. As a first step in securing the data needed, he talked with sales representatives for the manufacturers of both the Yoder and McKay mills. He found that each manufacturer could supply the mill desired and that not only was there essentially no difference in the cost of the mills or the accessory equipment, but also the cost of installation would be essentially the same. Based on this information, Mr. Cullen decided that the proper course of action would be for him to calculate the profitability of a new mill and then allow the selection of the particular make to be based on the preference of the Manufacturing Department.

Financial Aspects of a New Mill

The total installation of a new mill would include the mill proper, accessory equipment, foundations, and a building to house the operations. The installed cost of the mill and the accessory equipment would total $1,160,000, plus the cost of the

---

[2]Mechanical tubing is actually pipe which can be made in various types of cross-sectional shapes (circular, square, rectangular, elliptical, and oval); it is used for bridge railings, lightweight structural members, and fabricated products of various kinds.

erected building, which would be approximately $200,000. The cost breakdown would be as follows:

Item	Cost
Mill (excluding welder)	$ 550,000
Welder	150,000
Electrical, materials-handling, and other accessory equipment	410,000
Foundations	50,000
Total	$1,160,000

Depreciation for the entire investment (excluding the building) would be on an accelerated basis, using the double-declining-balance method. For depreciation purposes, the cost of the installed mill and equipment (excluding the building and the welder section of the mill) would have a life of twelve years and salvage value equal to 10 percent of the installed-cost value (see Exhibit 1). In referring to the company's previous experience with mills of this type, Mr. Cullen had discovered that the welder section of the mill should be treated separately from the rest of the mill. The welder would have an installed cost of $150,000, which was included in the above total cost of the mill. At the end of five years, the existing welder would be scrapped with no net salvage value. The first replacement welder should cost $150,000, but Mr. Cullen estimated that replacements after the first would cost an additional $50,000. Since the building was of the sheet metal variety, it would be depreciated over a twenty-year period on a straight-line basis with no net salvage value.

Mr. Cullen estimated that sales would reach 60 percent of capacity in the first year and 80 percent in the second. In looking beyond the second year, Mr. Cullen made the assumption that the mill would operate at nearly 100 percent of capacity, which appeared justified in view of the product mix possible from this mill. Although Mr. Cullen knew that a recession or the customary business cycle in steel pipe would cause sales to drop, he believed that the decreased production would be absorbed by the other two mills, since they were less efficient and produced a narrower range of products.

At 100 percent of capacity, output would be 3,000 tons per month of steel pipe and tubular goods[3] having an average selling price of $250 per ton. Since this new mill would allow Tex-Tube to shift its product mix to more profitable items, Mr. Cullen believed that a 25 percent gross margin would be realized throughout the life of this third mill. Administrative and general expenses would be $720,000 per year; selling expenses, 4 percent of sales; and miscellaneous expenses, 1.2 percent of sales.

[3]Mr. Cullen had estimated that, after the second year, the mill would operate as follows:

Level of operation (percent of capacity)	Output (tons per month)	Time at various levels (percent)	Weighted (tons per month)
100	3,000	20	600
90	2,700	50	1,350
80	2,400	30	720
Total		100	2,670

Mr. Cullen decided to use a tax rate of 50 percent in computing net income after taxes, because he believed this rate to be more indicative of long-range tax rates than the current 52 percent.

Working capital also would be needed to operate a new mill. Since the operation of the new mill was to be similar to that for the existing mills, current working capital requirements could be applied to the proposal under study. Mr. Cullen had found that working capital was directly related to production, and he had found also that sales and production were closely related over a yearly operating cycle so that the working capital could be related to sales as a good approximation of the investment required. Although in 1958 and 1959 (see Exhibits 2 and 3) working capital had averaged 24 percent of sales, Mr. Cullen believed that a slightly higher proportion (for example, 25 percent of sales) would be needed in the future.

Evaluation of the Investment

In order to evaluate the investment in a new mill, Mr. Cullen decided to use the payback and present-value methods. He further planned to calculate the payback, based on the investment in plant and equipment, less salvage and profits after taxes, plus depreciation. While the company preferred a payback of at least two to three years on capital investment projects, Mr. Cullen believed that a payback of five to ten years would be satisfactory for a major plant expansion.

In the application of the present-value approach, Mr. Cullen had decided to calculate the discounted rate of return.[4] After reviewing the necessary data, he realized that the overall cash inflow-outflow consisted of varous parts that should be discounted at different rates, in order to account for the varied risks involved. First, the current value of the investment, or certain cash outflow, would have to be calculated. The current value of a future outlay for the purchase of a replacement welder or for incremental working capital would have a much higher degree of certainty than would future income to be realized from the mill's operation. The current value of the investment should represent the amount needed today to assure having the required outlay at some time in the future. Since Tex-Tube could invest unneeded capital in treasury bonds yielding 4 percent, the after-tax discount rate should be 2 percent (for purposes of computing the present value of the investment outlay). The current value of the investment then would become the cash outflow to which the current value of net cash inflow would be compared.[5]

The second portion of the present-value calculation involved the cash inflow from operations and the return of working capital at the termination of the

[4]Also known as internal rate of return.

[5]In addition to the higher degree of certainty associated with the investment outlay, Mr. Cullen had noted that some fixed expenses (e.g., insurance) were more certain than others. These certain fixed expenses would be incurred even if the mill were shut down, whereas other fixed expenses would be terminated under such adverse conditions. Mr. Cullen reasoned that since less uncertainty would be associated with these cash outflows, they should be discounted at a low rate. A review of the fixed expenses showed that $170,000 of the total $720,000 would be in the "certain" category. He was of the opinion that discounting these certain expenses at 4 percent, and the resultant net cash flow from operations (excluding these certain expenses) at the discounted rate of return, would give a better representation of the risk of uncertainty involved.

evaluation period. The certainty of cash inflow from these two sources would not be the same. Mr. Cullen knew that the full value of the working capital could be obtained at the end of the period under consideration. Since these funds had been tied up in the operation of the new mill and had not been available for use in other operations of the firm, the current value should equal the amount returned discounted at the cost of capital. The most uncertain of all the cash flows would be those from operations. The discounted rate of return would be the rate necessary to discount the net cash inflows from operations such that the current value of the cash inflows from operations and of working capital return would equal the current value of the investment.

Establishment of a Cutoff Point

In evaluating the new mill proposal, Mr. Cullen knew he would also need to establish a cutoff point below which the proposal would not be acceptable. To establish this minimum rate, Mr. Cullen calculated Tex-Tube's cost of capital as 8 percent, book value. He realized that in setting a cutoff point for a project of this type (plant expansion or new plant), a risk factor was often added. Mr. Cullen believed that 4.0 percent would be an appropriate factor, setting the cutoff point for the new mill at 12 percent.

EXHIBIT 1

Tex-Tube, Incorporated

Depreciation Schedule for a Mill and Accessory Equipment
(Thousands of Dollars)

Installed cost

Mill	$ 550
Electrical, materials-handling, and other equipment	410
Foundations	50
Total installed cost	$1,010

Where:

Net salvage value, $101
Depreciable value, $909
Life, 12 years
Method, double-declining banace (D.D.B.)

Year	Depreciation base (at beginning of year)	Depreciation charge (D.D.B.)	Depreciation schedule
1	$1,010	$168	$168
2	842	140	140
3	702	117	117
4	585	98	98
5	487	81	81
6	406	68	68
7	338	56	56
8	282	47	47
9	235	39	39
10	196	33	33
11	163	27	31*
12	163*	—	31*
Total depreciation			$909

*Income tax rules permit a taxpayer to change from the double-declining-balance method to the straight-line method at any time. Such changes would occur when the amount of straight-line depreciation exceeded the amount available under the double-declining-balance method.

EXHIBIT 2
Tex-Tube, Incorporated
Condensed Balance Sheets
As of December 31
(Thousands of Dollars)

	1958	1959
Assets		
Current	$3,702	$5,665
Plant and equipment, net	1,280	1,652
Land	305	333
Other	153	292
Total assets	$5,440	$7,942
Liabilities and Equity		
Current	$1,243	$1,810
Deferred taxes	73	84
Bonds		
Nonconvertible, 6 percent	1,400	1,400
Convertible, 6 percent	—	300
Preferred stock, convertible, 6 percent	500	500
Common stock	400	500
Paid-in surplus	502	1,482
Retained earnings	1,322	1,866
Total liabilities and equity	$5,440	$7,942

EXHIBIT 3
Tex-Tube, Incorporated
Condensed Income Statements
Year Ending December 31
(Thousands of Dollars)

	— 1958 —		— 1959 —	
Net sales		$9,403		$18,119
Cost of sales	$7,873		$14,586	
Operating expenses	1,070		1,672	
Other expenses	165	9,108	246	16,504
Net Income Before Taxes		295		1,615
Income Taxes		157		829
Net Earnings		$ 138		$ 786

QUESTIONS

1. Comment on Mr. Cullen's approach to adjusting for risk. What other approaches for risk adjustment might be used?
2. Should the new mill be purchased? Why or why not?

Case 22
Tartan Corporation

The Tartan Corporation, a manufacturer of specialized equipment for over a quarter of a century, had experienced remarkable growth in the ten years from 1963 to 1972. During this period, sales increased nearly 400%, while profits and investments in property, plant, and equipment increased 500%. The sales outlook for the specialized equipment produced at their Midwest plant (one of eight plants located across the United States) prompted the company to expand that plant by 75,000 square feet in 1972. In April 1973, an additional expansion was under way involving 160,000 square feet of plant space plus engineering, manufacturing, and administrative offices. Tartan's surge in growth was also reflected by the anticipated $3,000,000 expenditures in 1973 for new plant equipment.

After a series of informal discussions in early 1973, the Industrial Engineering Manager, Milt Sears, and the Fabrication Shop General Foreman, Dayton Cline, agreed that additional steel-shearing equipment would be needed in the Fabrication Shop if the company expected to meet 1974 sales demands.

Most of the steel used in the Fabrication Shop was purchased in various rectangular sheet sizes varying in thickness. Presently, the shop has seven conventional steel-shearing machines and one light-gauge coil steel-shearing machine, which were used to cut the steel into specified shapes and sizes for subsequent manufacturing processes. The shearing function performed in the Fabrication Shop is divided into three types of cuts: (1) cut-to-length, (2) cut-to-width, (3) miscellaneous specialized cuts as illustrated below. For example, if a 6′ x 4½′ sheet is needed for production, a 7′ x 5′ sheet of steel will be cut to these

This case was prepared by Professors Leo A. Poland of Wichita State University and Joseph A. DeFatta of Northeast Louisiana University as a basis for classroom discussion and not to illustrate either effective or ineffective handling of an administrative situation.

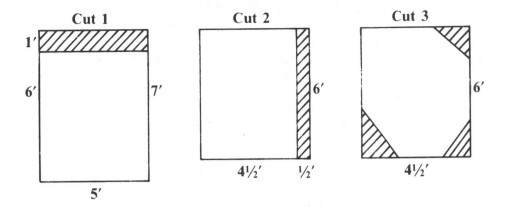

specifications as follows: (1) the first cut is made at a 6' interval leaving a 1' end dropoff, (2) the 6' x 5' is removed from the shear machine and transferred to a second shear machine, where it is cut to a 4½' width, leaving a ½' side dropoff as shown by the shaded area in the second illustration, (3) the 6' x 4½' sheet is then given specialized irregular cuts if necessary.

All three shear functions as described above can be achieved with conventional shears; however, only the first cut can be performed by a coil shear machine. The coil-cutting process is similar to cutting paper off a roll.

Cline and Sears determined that the additional shearing capacity could be obtained by purchasing one ¼" x 60" coil steel-shearing machine or two ¼" x 12' conventional shears. As early as 1969, the company had considered the possibility of replacing one of their present conventional shear machines with a new coil-shear machine. A coil-shear machine purchase justification study was first prepared in January 1970, and was later revised and updated in May and August 1970, and again in April 1971.

In April 1973, Richard Webb, an industrial engineer in charge of Special Projects, was assigned the task of preparing a recommendation as to which type of equipment should be purchased (coil shears or conventional shears). He was informed by Sears that his report must be completed by the end of May since the machine was needed for production starting in January 1974, and a long lead time was required from the time the machine was ordered and actual production was started. The justification report would be submitted for action to the Corporate Executive Committee in June in order to receive special approval prior to the submission of the regular 1974 capital budget requests.

Webb first set out to ascertain what action had been taken in preparation of the earlier justifications and what decisions, if any, had been reached. He learned that the Industrial Engineering Department had initiated the consideration of the heavy-gauge coil-shear machine in 1969. The Fabrication Shop General Foreman, Dayton Cline, raised several objections to such a purchase. It was his contention that the coil shear was more complicated to operate than a conventional shear and it would be difficult to train men to operate it. He argued that the maintenance costs would be greater with a coil-shear machine versus a regular shear since the coil machine had more motors to malfunction and more electronic parts to fail than regular shears. Cline also stated that if the one coil machine were down, it would affect production schedules much more seriously than if one of the two conventional shears were down. In addition, the Quality Control Manager, Bob Lynch, was concerned about the quality of the steel parts cut by a coil shear; he wanted to know whether the coil steel would be flattened sufficiently during the shearing process to meet their manufacturing standards.

In 1970, a Task Force was given the assignment of selecting the type of shearing machine and the manufacturer that would best meet the company's needs. The Task Force was composed of Dayton Cline, Bob Lynch, Jack Peck, and Paul Winter. Peck was the Manufacturing Engineering Manager and Winter was an Industrial Engineering Supervisor. The Task Force met with steel suppliers to discuss the coil-shear operation versus the conventional shear operation and to get their comments on buying material, equipment needs, etc. Visits were also made to several plants in the area to observe heavy-gauge coil-shear lines in operation. Several coil-shear suppliers were consulted regarding options available on the machine, replacement parts availability, service provided after purchase, ability to add additional components, ability of the machine to remove the coil set, amount of space required, equipment needed for loading and unloading the coils, and set-up time.

After the observation of heavy-gauge steel coil shears in operation and the discussion with the equipment manufacturers, Lynch was satisfied that the coil-shear operation could flatten the steel coil sufficiently to meet Tartan's quality control standards. Part of Cline's objections to the coil shear were satisfied when the manufacturers agreed to provide in-plant training for the coil-shear operators at no cost to Tartan.

At the conclusion of their study in November 1970, the Task Force unanimously agreed to transfer to the Manufacturing Committee a recommendation for the purchase of a coil shear. Exhibit 1 is a payoff chart which was part of the justification submitted by the Task Force. The Manufacturing Committee, consisting of the Vice-President of Manufacturing, the Quality Control Manager, Manufacturing Engineering Manager, and the Director of Purchasing and Materials, unanimously concurred with the Task Force's recommendation and passed it on to the Finance Department. The Finance Department was not fully satisfied with the justification and requested further study of the proposal before sending it to the Corporate Executive Committee. This delayed the decision beyond the deadline for inclusion in the 1971 budget, and no further action was taken in 1970.

Webb found a report dated July 6, 1971, which had been prepared to update and revise costs and savings figures of the November 1970 coil-shear justification study. The report included an estimation of the rate of return on the proposed investment as shown in Exhibit 2. The updated justification study was approved by the Manufacturing Committee. The Corporate Executive Committee agreed that the proposal indicated an adequate rate of return, but because currently available funds were limited and profits had been down in 1970, they were reluctant to spend $142,000 for one machine replacement.

After reviewing all the previous reports, Webb ascertained that two major cost savings will occur if the coil shear is purchased. The labor cost of operating the one coil-shear machine is anticipated to be lower than the labor cost associated with the two conventional shear machines. A conventional shear can be operated by one worker for small steel pieces but will require as many as four workers when large steel sheets are being cut. A coil shear will require only two men, one will be used on a part-time basis to load the coil initially and to remove any unused portion of the coil at the end of the operation, and another worker will monitor the semiautomatic machine during its operation. Using data supplied by three coil-shear equipment suppliers and the Tartan Company's expected volume in 1974, Webb estimates that the annual differential savings in labor cost on the coil versus the conventional shear machines will be approximately $19,200 over the life of the coil machine.[1]

In addition to a labor savings, the coil machine is expected to produce substantial direct material cost savings. As shown in the illustration on page 185, the conventional shearing process produces an end dropoff in the length-cutting process. There is no end dropoff when a coil shear is used, because the coil (a continuous roll of steel) can be cut to the exact length as required in the manufacturing specifications. There is, however, a slight amount of waste at the beginning and end of the coil.

In order to determine the savings associated with better materials utilization, Webb examined a study made by Charles Tobin, a former Industrial Engineering Technician, dated November 25, 1971, and accepted his conclusion that the company could achieve a 3% steel materials savings if a new coil shear were used instead of a conventional shear.[2] Webb next examined data on 1972 steel usage as shown in Exhibit 3. In addition to this information, Webb also ascertained from his discussion with Fred Reynolds, Production Manager, that a 40% volume change in material usage is predicted for the 1974 production run over the 1972 actual usage figures.

The coil shear being considered for purchase in April 1973 was more sophisticated than the machine under consideration earlier and was priced at $199,395. The current price of a conventional shear was $27,500.
Both types of shears were assumed to have a life of ten years. Webb assembled the

---

[1]Cycle time data supplied by three different coil-shear equipment suppliers were averaged and standards set for 52 random parts and compared to present company standards (based on 50% performance for both methods). The average difference was then applied against the total square footage estimated to be used to arrive at the labor-savings figure.

[2]Tobin's conclusion was based on a sample he took of actual end dropoff amounts for various sizes of sheet steel used in 1970. He computed an average percentage of end dropoff loss from that usage and compared it with the expected average percentage of loss resulting from the end scrap on each coil. The amount of linear feet of steel in each coil varied from 87 to 200 depending on the width and thickness of the steel.

following additional data related to the alternative machines:

	One Coil Shear	One Conven- tional Shear
Annual maintenance	$ 9,000	$2,000
Freight and installation	10,605	1,000
Annual electrical power and supplies	2,000	200
Purchase of initial replacement parts package	8,000	0
Planning changes required by Materials Control and Industrial Engineering Departments to convert to the use of coil steel	2,000	0
Average price per ton of: Sheet steel		174
Coil steel	167	
Salvage value	25,000	1,000

On the last Friday afternoon in May, Sears asked a group of men who had an interest in the acquisition of additional steel-shearing equipment to meet for an informal discussion with Webb. Sears and Webb felt that such discussion would assure them that Webb was giving consideration to all the relevant factors before he prepared his final report. Webb started the discussion by asking a question.

Webb: How will the choice of equipment affect floor space requirements?

Cline (Fabrication Shop General Foreman): We will have sufficient space for either type of equipment, but arranging the equipment layout will be more complicated if the coil shear is purchased. It will require a space 14′ x 85′, while each conventional shear will require a space 14′ x 30′. The physical arrangement of the two conventional shears would be more flexible because they could be placed side by side or end to end.

Sid Fenner (Materials Manager): We will need less floor space to store coil steel than sheet steel. We anticipate that less steel inventory will be required because, unlike coil, the sheets must be stocked in a variety of different lengths. Also, a larger quantity of steel can be safely stacked in a given square footage of space when in coils than in sheets.

Webb: Dave Hall (Purchasing Agent) told me that the use of steel coils would simplify their procurement problem due to this reduction in variety of sheet sizes and also because more and more steel manufacturers prefer to produce the steel coils.

Fenner: At the present, we don't anticipate storing steel outside, but in the event this became necessary, there would be less deterioration from rust in the case of coil steel. Only the outside of the coil is subject to rust damage.

Fred Reynolds (Production Manager): I think it is significant to note that the coil shear could do the work of two conventional shears in four to six hours per day. This will provide us extra capacity for any future increase in production.

Art Williams (Assistant Treasurer): Are we giving any consideration to disposing of our light-gauge coil line? It is apparent that the new coil shear has the capacity available to handle the work now done on the present coil line.

Bob Lynch (Quality Control Manager): No. We aren't convinced that the heavy-gauge coil shear will handle the light-gauge steel coil without roughing it up.

Webb: One of our earlier studies indicated that the projected material quantity saving if a coil shear is purchased would be only 75% as much the first year as thereafter. Is that still what is expected, Sid?

Fenner: Not quite. Except for the few rarely used gauges which we will continue to stock in sheet-steel form, we expect to use up our stock of sheet steel by the end of March next year. The tons saved in the first year will probably be about 85% of what it will be after the first year.

Paul Winter (Industrial Engineering Supervisor): One advantage of the coil shear will be the automatic oiling of the steel just before it goes through the cutter. The oiling is important because it eliminates or reduces the rusting of steel parts and lubricates the dies, making them last longer.

Cline: The automatic oiling will also assure a more uniform application and reduce the amount of oil used.

Fenner: The use of a coil shear will complicate scheduling of the shear operation. We now schedule the various parts by due date. If we use coil steel, we will have to anticipate needs in advance, and when at all possible, cut all of a given coil before changing to a different gauge or width.

Sears: I don't think that will pose a serious problem after the first few weeks. Some parts will need to be stocked farther in advance, but it will be possible to have a computer program written which will adequately coordinate daily runs of like coils.

Webb: Mr. Reynolds, is the previous estimate that the 1974 volume of steel used will be 40% over the 1972 actual usage still valid?

Reynolds: Yes.

Webb: Thank you, gentlemen. My notes from this discussion will be a real help. I plan to review them tomorrow and will start writing my final report Monday morning.

On Monday morning, Webb called Dave Hall to get the latest quoted price on steel. Hall stated that coil steel was still $167 per ton and sheet steel was still $174 per ton. He called Art Williams to be sure of the firm's average cost of capital. Williams gave him a rate of 8% and reminded him that the company was using straight-line depreciation on the books but double-declining-balance depreciation on the tax returns.

Webb secluded himself in his office and started preparing his report.

EXHIBIT 1
Tartan Corporation
Payoff Chart

Prepared November 5, 1972

Year	Investment	Gross Savings[1]	Depreciation & Maint.	Savings After Depr. & Main.	Net Profit[2]	ROI
1	$136,700	$72,000[3]	$22,288	$49,712	$18,891	14%
2	$119,612	$96,000	$31,903	$64,097	$24,357	20%
3	$ 89,709	$96,000	$24,428	$71,572	$27,197	30%
4	$ 67,281	$96,000	$18,820	$77,178	$29,328	44%
5	$ 50,461	$96,000	$14,616	$81,384	$30,926	61%
6	$ 37,848	$96,000	$11,462	$84,538	$32,124	85%
7	$ 28,386	$96,000	$ 9,097	$86,903	$33,023	116%
8	$ 21,289	$96,000	$ 7,322	$88,678	$33,698	158%
9	$ 18,628	$96,000	$ 4,661	$91,339	$34,709	186%

[1]Material price differential (coil vs. sheet), reduction in scrap material, and labor savings.

[2]Savings after depreciation and maintenance less taxes and profit sharing. The company has a retirement profit sharing plan for both salaried and hourly employees. The plan is administered by the trust department of a bank and provides for annual contributions of from 10% to 20% of consolidated income before profit-sharing contributions, charitable contributions, and income taxes and after deducting 10% of consolidated stockholders' equity at the beginning of the year. No contributions are required to be made by employees. Allocation of contributions to the eligible employees is based upon annual salary.

[3]The first-year gross savings will be only 75% of expected annual savings.

EXHIBIT 2
Tartan Corporation
New Machine Annual Projected
Net Income and Cash Flow
Prepared June 28, 1971

Cost Savings:		
Direct Material	$ 64,000	
Material Utilization	40,000	
Labor	10,000	
Total Savings		$114,000
Additional Costs:		
Maintenance Yearly	9,000	
Electrical Power and Supplies (4 hrs/day)	2,000	
Insurance, Supplies, Etc.	1,000	
Total		12,000
Net Income Before Depreciation		$102,000
Depreciation ($142,800 Over 10 Years)		14,280
Net Income Before Tax and Profit Sharing		$ 87,720
Income Tax and Profit Sharing 67%		
(See Note 2, Exhibit 1)		58,772
Net Income		$ 28,948
Net Cash Inflow		
Net Income Before Depreciation	102,000	
Less Income Tax	58,772	
		$ 43,228

Payback Period:

142,800/43,228 = 3.3 years

Rate of Cash Return

Total Cash Inflow[1] (43,228 x 10 + 26,000)	458,280	
Average Cash Inflow 458,280/10	45,828	
Factor 142,800/45,828	3.12	
Rate of Return		32%

[1]Salvage value estimated at $26,000.

EXHIBIT 3
Tartan Corporation
1972 Steel Usage

Material No.	Description	Sheet Size W" x L"	Tons Used
R 186	12ga HR P&O	36 x 144	108
R 180	12ga HR P&O	40 x 150	400
S 499	12ga HR	56 x 84	85
R 648	11ga HR P&O	25 x 112	250
R 671	11ga HR P&O	39 x 146	184
S 185	11ga HR	47 x 72	350
Q 184	11ga Drawing Qual.	31 x 125	88
S 309	11ga HR	48 x 96	10
S 377	11ga HR	44 x 140	515
R 808	11ga HR P&O	58 x 120	403
R 721	10ga HR P&O	43 x 100	150
S 810	10ga HR	32 x 100	145
R 827	3/16 HR P&O	29 x 79	502
S 186	3/16 HR	39 x 105	393
S 836	3/16 HR	40 x 90	670
S 119	3/16 HR	58 x 96	950
			5,203

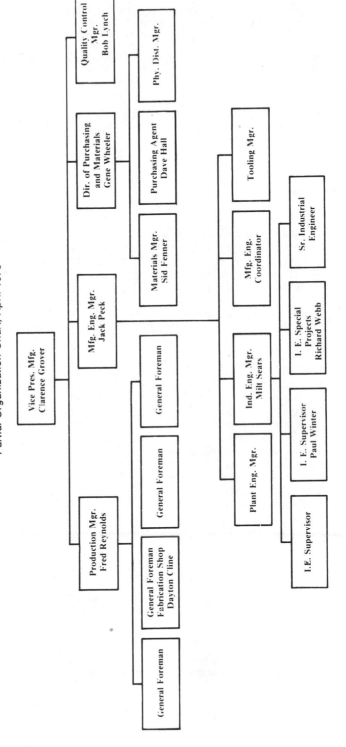

APPENDIX A
Tartan Corporation
Manufacturing Department
Partial Organization Chart, April 1973

Vice Pres. Mfg.
Clarence Grover

Production Mgr.
Fred Reynolds

Mfg. Eng. Mgr.
Jack Peck

Dir. of Purchasing
and Materials
Gene Wheeler

Quality Control
Mgr.
Bob Lynch

General Foreman

General Foreman
Fabrication Shop
Dayton Cline

General Foreman

General Foreman

Materials Mgr.
Sid Fenner

Mfg. Eng.
Coordinator

Purchasing Agent
Dave Hall

Tooling Mgr.

Phy. Dist. Mgr.

Plant Eng. Mgr.

Ind. Eng. Mgr.
Milt Sears

I. E. Special
Projects
Richard Webb

Sr. Industrial
Engineer

I.E. Supervisor

I. E. Supervisor
Paul Winter

Tartan Corporation

Consolidated Balance Sheet
December 31, 1972 and 1971

	1972	1971
ASSETS		
Current Assets:		
Cash	$ 2,056,800	$ 989,400
Marketable securities at cost which approximates market	900,000	—
Accounts receivable	9,449,700	7,003,200
Inventories at lower of cost (first-in, first-out) or market	15,894,900	14,667,900
Prepaid expenses	232,800	258,900
Total current assets	$28,534,200	$22,919,400
Other Assets	1,036,200	542,600
Property, plant, and equipment, at cost:		
Land	442,300	289,300
Buildings	8,745,100	6,542,500
Machinery and equipment	8,170,700	6,772,500
Office furniture and fixtures	1,216,200	972,800
	18,574,300	14,577,100
Less accumulated depreciation	7,955,600	6,882,900
Net property, plant, and equipment	$10,618,700	$ 7,694,200
Total Assets	$40,189,100	$31,156,200
LIABILITIES		
Current Liabilities:		
Accounts payable	$ 2,772,300	$ 2,048,000
Notes payable to banks	1,129,300	—
Accrued sales discounts	2,289,900	1,567,800
Accrued income taxes	1,152,800	829,400
Accrued payroll and profit-sharing contributions	2,937,800	1,718,400
Other accrued liabilities	1,060,000	811,400
Long-term debt payable within one year	997,900	513,000
Total current liabilities	$12,340,000	$ 7,488,000
Long-term debt payable after one year:		
Notes payable to insurance company	8,916,000	7,800,000
7½% subordinated debentures, payable through 1984	264,000	265,800
First mortgage notes, 4½-8½% payable in varying amounts to 1992	342,500	120,000
Total long-term debt	$ 9,522,500	$ 8,185,800
Deferred federal income tax	183,300	168,800
Stockholders' equity:		
Common stock, $1 par value, 5,000,000 shares authorized, 1,250,000 shares issued	1,250,000	1,250,000
Contributed capital in excess of par	4,026,500	4,026,500
Retained earnings	12,866,800	10,037,100
Total stockholders' equity	$18,143,300	$15,313,600
Total Equities	$40,189,100	$31,156,200

APPENDIX C
Tartan Corporation
Combined Consolidated Statement of Income
and Retained Earnings
Years Ended December 31, 1972 and 1971

	1972	1971
Net Sales	$68,215,000	$50,169,400
Cost of sales	42,107,000	30,467,000
Gross profit	$26,108,000	$19,702,400
Operating expenses:		
Marketing and selling	7,925,400	6,225,200
General and administrative	6,403,300	4,747,400
Research and development	2,074,800	1,564,000
	$16,403,500	$12,536,600
Operating profit	$ 9,704,500	$ 7,165,800
Other (income) deductions:		
Interest and finance charges	3,256,800	3,207,000
Other income	(27,000)	(70,300)
	$ 3,229,800	$ 3,136,700
Income before income taxes	$ 6,474,700	$ 4,029,100
Provision for income taxes:		
Current	3,310,800	2,207,000
Deferred	(165,800)	(193,300)
	$ 3,145,000	$ 2,013,700
Net income	$ 3,329,700	$ 2,015,400
Retained earnings, beginning of year	10,037,100	8,521,700
	$13,366,800	$10,537,100
Dividends ($.40 per share)	(500,000)	(500,000)
Retained earnings, end of year	$12,866,800	$10,037,100
Earnings per share	$2.66	$1.61

QUESTIONS

1. Comment on the justification studies presented in Exhibits 1 and 2 of the case.
2. What nonquantitative factors should be evaluated before deciding which type of shear to purchase?
3. What type of shear should be purchased and why?

Case 23
Snow Clear, Inc.

In May 1973, Mr. Ray Farley, the President of Snow Clear, Inc., was reviewing a meeting just held with his top subordinate managers (see organization chart in Exhibit 1), considering the acquisition of a computer system for improved production control. A proposal for such a move had recently been submitted to Snow Clear management by the local branch of a large firm specializing in computer manufacture, service, and sales. Since the managers of Snow Clear had expressed considerably different views on the merit of proceeding with the proposal, Mr. Farley wanted to consider his next step carefully.

The Company

Snow Clear, Inc., had been organized in 1963 by its Canadian parent to manufacture snow clearance and control machinery for the eastern United States market. The product line manufactured in the wholly owned American subsidiary had been gradually expanded during the ten years and in 1973 included nine models of combination graders/ploughs, street cleaner/ploughs, and snow blowers. In the near future, it was expected that serious consideration would be given to starting the manufacture of further caterpillar treaded equipment.

      Company operations were centered in a new factory situated in an industrial suburb of a large upstate New York city. The site had been chosen because it was near the center of the intended market, because labor was readily available in the area, and because it was within a day's drive of the Canadian parent's head office.

This case was prepared by Professor David J. Springate of Southern Methodist University as a basis for classroom discussion and not to illustrate either effective or ineffective handling of an administrative situation.

Of the 300 people employed by the company, 210 were production employees and the remainder were mainly clerical.

Sales of Snow Clear equipment were made throughout the Northeastern United States and had been gradually extended westward into the American Midwest. The company did not sell direct to dealers but sold all production through 11 strategically located distributors. Since Snow Clear relied on the sales efforts of these distributors in order to move its finished inventory, it employed only four people in its sales department. Total company sales in 1972 had been about $24 million. This figure represented a rapid increase in sales. In 1970, for example, sales had been about $12 million.

Although in reality a division of the parent company, Snow Clear, Inc., operated, to a large degree, independently of the Canadian company. In large measure the president of the U.S. subsidiary was held responsible for results only and not the methods which he used to obtain these results. Thus Mr. Farley would not have to clear his final decision with the Canadian head office before implementing it unless a computer was purchased. In the latter case, the purchase price would exceed his $70,000 personal authorization ceiling.

Production Control System

The existing system of production control had grown out of the need to control the 11,000 kinds of parts used by the company in producing its product line. The system was a manual one that used the sales forecasts of three sales editors as input data. The editors, one assigned to each major product line grouping, used past sales histories, field visits, and knowledge of current distributor inventory levels to help them come up each month with a forecast of company sales by product for the next eight months. This forecast of demand was then sent to the Internal Control Manager.

The Internal Control Manager, with seven clerks to help him, was responsible for two basic jobs. The first requirement was to calculate the number and type of parts that had to be ordered or put into production in each of the next eight months, while the second was to identify items that would be out of stock within two months at expected usage rates unless a replenishment order arrived at the plant. In order to carry out his function, the Internal Control Manager was supplied with the following:

1. The sales forecasts as determined monthly for the next eight months. These were the forecasts supplied by the sales editors.
2. A bill of materials for each product sold. A current copy was supplied by the Engineering Department and showed exactly how many parts of each type were required to produce each product.
3. The parts inventory position as of the end of the last month. A ledger card was kept for each of the 11,000 parts used in production. This card was updated monthly to reflect the actual inventory position. Once a year, a physical inventory count was carried out to validate the numbers shown on the inventory cards.
4. The number of machines completed in the plant during the month just finished.

5. The number of parts of each type received by the plant during the last month. This information was collected on cards by the clerks during the month as shipments arrived.

The clerks processed the 11,000 inventory ledger cards or so each month in two passes, with each clerk assigned approximately 1,700 cards. On the first pass, the clerks were able to use the above information to determine for each part in turn what month different quantities should be ordered from an outside supplier or from one of the four Snow Clear plants situated in Canada. The resulting lists of purchase requirements were then passed on to the two company buyers for action. About 5,500 of the items used at Snow Clear were purchased from outside suppliers, while another 1,500 items came from other Snow Clear plants. In the purchase requirement calculations, clerks used a fixed figure of five months' lead time for all parts. The figure had been fixed because management felt that it would be nearly impossible to maintain an accurate list of lead time by item. Furthermore, a standard figure made the clerk's job easier.

During the first pass, the clerks also figured out what quantities of internally produced parts should be put into production in each of the coming months in order to allow sub-assemblies to be ready when required. The lead times used here were different for each part but were independent of plant production level. They were known to the clerks by experience. The information about required inside order scheduling that resulted from the clerk's work was passed on to the expediters for detailed production scheduling. About 4,000 of the inventory items were produced internally in the plant.

The clerks then processed the 11,000 ledger cards a second time and determined which parts would be needed within two months but would be out of stock unless replenishment orders from suppliers arrived. The results were passed on to three expediters who attempted to secure delivery of the required orders before an out-of-stock position occurred. Each expediter was assigned a certain number of regular plant suppliers as his contacts.

Although requests were sometimes made by the Sales Department for rush production orders, it was not always possible to accommodate these requests. Sometimes delivery of parts that were needed from an outside supplier to finish the rush order could not be speeded up. Extra work for the internal control clerks was caused by rush orders, since it was necessary to go through all the 11,000 inventory ledger cards in order to locate those cards for which order-quantity determinations had to be made.

The internal control clerks took about six working days to make the required two passes through the 11,000 inventory ledger cards. Approximately four days were required to determine when purchases and internally produced parts should be made, and about two days were required to determine shortages for the action of the expediters. During the other working days of the month, clerks made up various operating reports for management, for example, reports on scrap and on material usage, and updated the cards which kept track of the receipts of parts from suppliers. As time allowed, they also did some production scheduling, which was part of the job normally assigned to the expediters. In doing this, the clerks refined the monthly schedules they had drawn up into weekly schedules showing when parts should be started into production.

The Proposal of the Computer Manufacturer

Although Snow Clear's existing control systems worked well, Mr. Farley was anxious to keep up with advancing technology as it applied to business decisions and business methods. Accordingly, in March 1973, he invited a large computer manufacturer to investigate the firm's operations and determine whether data processing equipment could be profitably used by the company. In May, the manufacturer submitted its recommendation, which called for the installation of an annually leased random access computer system (see Exhibit 2). The main purpose of this system would be to reduce Snow Clear's investment in raw material and parts inventories. In place of the internal control clerks who used fixed lead times in calculating order dates, the computer would be supplied with different lead times for each part purchased. Using the order dates that the computer determined, Snow Clear would be able to avoid purchasing material until it was really required. The computer company estimated that inventories could be cut by perhaps 8 percent or $300,000 if automation took place. At an inventory carrying cost of 18 percent a year, which was a figure suggested by the selling firm as appropriate, an annual saving of about $54,000 or $4,500 a month could be realized.

Another purpose of the suggested computer system would be to schedule parts that were produced in the plant. When supplied with lead times necessary for production, the computer would be able to tell management when certain assemblies and sub-assemblies had to be ready in order to have machines available to meet the sales forecasts. It would thus simplify the job of the expediters considerably. The computer would also ease the clerical workload involved in rush production orders. In place of the manual search through 11,000 ledger cards in order to find those cards representing parts needed for the rush order, the computer would be able to quickly scan the inventory on hand and determine what shortages of parts would be encountered.

During talks with the sales representative of the computer company, Snow Clear management had been told that a computer could complete a monthly run for production control, inventory updating, and parts ordering in a single morning. In the proposal submitted to Snow Clear, it was suggested that the time left over be used for accounting applications such as payroll and the updating of accounts receivable and accounts payable, for routine applications such as aggregating the parts requirements of the Service Department with the forecasts of the Sales Department, and for any other desired management reports.

The initial costs of a computer installation were estimated by the manufacturer to be $64,000. Of this, $16,000 would be required to prepare the computer room for the installation, while $48,000 would be required to pay for installation assistance and the salaries of Snow Clear's data processing staff before they became productive. The monthly outlays once the system was in operation were predicted to be $3,600 for computer staff salaries and $6,300 for rental if the proposed equipment was leased. The monthly inflows or savings expected totaled $12,400. Of this, $4,500 would be saved in inventory carrying costs, and $7,300 would be saved due to a reduction of the clerical staff by 15 people. Savings of $600 represented money Snow Clear had always paid for outside computer services. Thus the net savings to be produced by renting the proposed equipment was estimated by the manufacturer to be approximately $2,500 a month.

While Mr. Farley was not inclined to purchase the suggested equipment and had therefore deemphasized this option in his discussion with his top subordinates, he was aware he could purchase the entire computer package for a cash price of $360,000. Initial costs would remain at an additional $64,000. The clear necessity to seek head office approval, with its resultant time delay, and the feeling that the firm would be effectively locked into a given system configuration if purchase was ultimately approved, weighed heavily in his thinking. Mr. Farley felt his company could arrange for an 8.4% loan of $360,000 to be repaid in ten equal installments of $55,000 if it attempted to do so.

Reactions of Top Management

After he received the sales proposal, Mr. Farley had copies distributed to his five top managers. Subsequently, he had asked them to attend a meeting where individual views were sought. It was the views expressed at this meeting that Mr. Farley was now actively reviewing.

Mr. Frank Larsen, the Plant Manager, was of the opinion that the proposed system would cut inventory carrying costs by $3,000 a month. Feeling that the need for programmers and key punch operators would probably exceed the estimates of the computer manufacturer, he did not think that the total number of people in the Production Department would decrease even though the internal control clerks would no longer be required. He did think, however, that the addition of more people would not be necessary in order to handle the higher sales levels expected in future. If it was decided to obtain a computer, Mr. Larsen felt that Mike Leblanc, the present Internal Control Manager, should be made the manager of the new installation. He believed that Leblanc's job in charge of the seven materials clerks fitted him admirably for the job.

One further advantage of automating the system that occurred to Mr. Larsen was that it would probably mean fewer errors in the calculations of what parts should be ordered. The work of the girls was sometimes erroneous since the people hired for the job were not well qualified and turnover was rapid. These conditions arose due to the relative low pay of the clerk's positions and the apparent lack of advancement opportunities. Although mistakes were not frequent, they could be quite costly. For instance, if there was a discrepancy between the actual and recorded inventory position of a critical part and it was discovered only when parts were being picked for production, several machines might not be able to meet scheduled completion dates and sales would be lost. When this happened, it was usually because the critical components could not be obtained from a supplier on short notice.

Mr. Gordon Robertson, the Director of Engineering, saw the computer system mainly as a potential source of management reports on all kinds of things. It could be used to generate scrap reports, material usage reports, and the receipt reports, for instance. It could also be used to calculate economic order quantities, parts availability, and excess inventory positions, which were currently unknown. After the more obvious applications had been carried out, he felt that people could start working on fully automated scheduling of production through the shop, including the loading of machines.

The Sales Manager, Mr. Dwight Smith, felt that if the sales increase of the last two years was to be kept going, the company should start to find out exactly what made Snow Clear products sell. He thought that with a computer, sales trends to show the effects on sales of various factors such as tariffs, population levels, and size of product line could quickly be calculated. He also suspected that there were many accounting applications for the proposed system.

The Controller, for his part, felt that although the computer could be used to automate the payroll and keep accounts receivable and accounts payable up to date, an acceptance should not be based on these reasons. Some time ago, Mr. Ron Cartwith had been associated with a system that was authorized on the grounds of expected clerical savings in accounting. The savings never did materialize, since the number of clerks stayed about the same, while the computer remained in use for accounting purposes only. Mr. Cartwith felt that it would be better to base any acceptance on the grounds that the computer could help the company in production scheduling and parts control where the applications could be imaginative and lead to great cost saving. Accounting applications, he felt, tended to be rather limited. Mr. Cartwith held that the $7,300 figure quoted by the computer manufacturer as a saving to be expected from clerical staff reduction was debatable. He felt the company would not be able to release 15 people right away; in fact, he wondered if any would be released. However, it did seem quite possible to him that Snow Clear would not have to hire more clerical workers in the future as the plant expanded. Within a couple of years, the savings thus achieved might easily add up to $7,300 a month.

The sixth member of top management, Mr. Ian Bundy, the Purchasing Agent, thought the computer manufacturer's report was much too optimistic. He did not believe that savings of anywhere near $2,500 a month could be squeezed out of the company. As he put it, "I think that any savings will be a lot less than $2,500; in fact, they may not materialize. And how do we put a value on what the company may save due to improved management decisions? There's just no way. No, I think that the savings resulting from computer installation would be a lot less than most people think. The best that can be said is that the savings to be obtained are somewhat indefinite."

As a final consideration, Mr. Farley wondered how to take into account the fact that the parent company had recently turned down a project concerned with manufacturing components for snowmobiles, although the project was expected to return 20 percent per year. The reasons cited were that returns seemed low for the associated risks and that the total corporate financial resources were too strained at the moment.

Recent financial statements for Snow Clear, Inc., are found in Exhibits 3 and 4.

EXHIBIT 1
Snow Clear, Inc.

Organization Chart

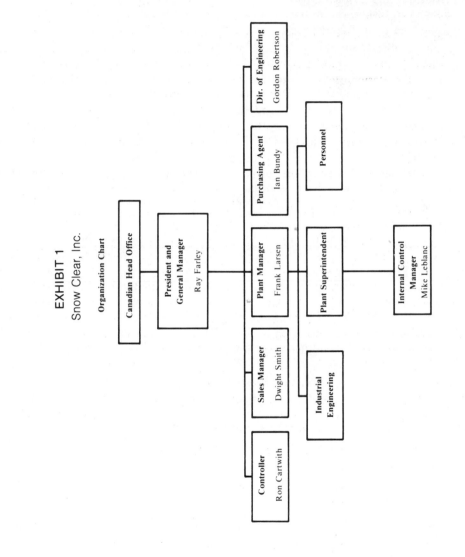

EXHIBIT 2
Snow Clear, Inc.

Proposal Submitted to Company

May 3, 1973

Mr. R. Farley
President and General Manager
Snow Clear, Inc.

Dear Sir:

We are pleased to submit our recommendations for an advanced random access computer system. Our recommendations are based on our knowledge of your Bill of Materials explosion, Job Costing, Production Inventory Control, Service Parts Billing and Service Parts Inventory, Accounts Receivable, Accounts Payable, Customs Drawback, Payroll and Sales Statistics.

The suggested procedures will form a firm foundation from which to build and develop detailed operating procedures. They will also give you the following advantages.

1. Complete flexibility in the preparation of management reports through the use of a random access system.
2. Handling of all your data processing requirements with an economic system.
3. Provision of a basis for growth leading to more applications without changing the basic approach.

We believe that this recommendation indicates that we have an appreciation of your business and have the abilities, equipment, and resources to enable you to best utilize the advantages of mechanization. Our company's equipment has proven its capabilities in manufacturing industries. The Rochester office is now ready to help apply these capabilities to your operation. Furthermore, you will have the benefit of our company's proven leadership in engineering research and new developments.

We have listed the features of our proposed system below. Confident that our proposal will meet Snow Clear's requirements, we request your early approval as the initial step toward the successful installation of the random access computer system.

Yours very truly,

S. O. Morton,
Sales Representative

EXHIBIT 2 *(continued)*

Features of the Random Access System

General Advantages

Information recorded on disk files can be processed entirely by machine. The elimination of manual operations and the high speed of the data processing machines will result in the rapid preparation of any required report. This will mean that information required for managerial action will be available promptly and that the periodic peak workloads will be substantially reduced.

The elimination of manual operations avoids the possibility of manual error.

Specific Advantages

Bill of Materials Explosion

1. The ability to consolidate requirements quickly and accurately into a usable form for planning.
2. Ease of entering engineering changes on Bills of Material.
3. Reduction of time required for planning cycle resulting in better service to customers.
4. Automatic triggering of orders for those parts or subassemblies which are below minimum or are out-of-stock.
5. Updating of inventory ledger cards by manual methods is eliminated.

Job Costing

1. Excellent for analysis of estimated vs. actual production costs. Accurate and rapid.
2. New applications could be readily innovated, e.g., job cards could be used as input for payroll application.
3. Will provide the ability to forecast job costs. Can see the effect of an engineering change on production costs.

Production Inventory Control

Inventory is automatically updated by the Bill of Materials explosion, with stock status reports being produced and automatic triggering of orders for the parts or subassemblies which must be purchased.

Service Parts Billing and Inventory Control

Since all of the constant information regarding an item is stored on a disc file, the writing of this invoice line from a disc pack ensures that:

1. The item is correctly coded, priced, and costed.
2. The inventory, accounts receivable, and sales analysis are automatically updated.

Customs Drawback

Drawback claims can be produced more frequently and more accurately.

EXHIBIT 2 *(continued)*

Sales Statistics

1. Ability to obtain varied Sales Reports quickly as a by-product of the billing operation. No manual posting required.
2. All year-to-date information available for reporting.

Payroll

1. Payroll is prepared from the labor cards returned from the factory.
2. W-2 slips, payroll deduction registers and checks are printed automatically.

Accounts Receivable

1. Accounts Receivable is automatically updated at the same time as the billing operation is performed. Manual posting is eliminated.
2. Statements are automatically printed and checked to a control figure on the system.
3. Information necessary to produce an Aged Trial Balance is stored on the disc pack.

Accounts Payable

1. Elimination of hand posting. Printing of checks done by machine.
2. All the information necessary for budget analysis of any department is contained on the disc pack.
3. Each week the files can be scanned to search out the invoices that should be paid in order to obtain the discount.
4. Cash requirements report is easily obtainable.

Staff Requirements

We recommend that a capable person from your existing staff be appointed Data Processing Manager of this installation, not only to coordinate and develop the present conversion, but also to develop additional applications. In addition, we suggest that two female key punch operators be trained from your existing staff, and that a machine operator and a programmer be either trained or hired. It has been estimated from the study that was made that Snow Clear can reasonably expect clerical savings of approximately 15 people if the recommended computer system is installed.

EXHIBIT 3
Snow Clear, Inc.

Condensed Balance Sheet as of March 31, 1973
for Snow Clear, Inc., and Finance Subsidiary
(Dollars in thousands)

Current Assets
Cash	$ 361
Accounts and Notes Receivable	879
Inventories	3,718
Prepaid expenses	136
Total current assets	$5,094

Rental Equipment, at cost less accumulated depreciation of $254,992	402
Investment in finance subsidiary at equity in underlying net assets	672
Property Plant and Equipment, net	2,514
Total Assets	$8,682

Current Liabilities
Notes payable to banks	$ 110
Accounts payable	1,715
Current installments on long-term debt	63
Total Current Liabilities	$1,888

Long-Term Debt
Long-term borrowings	$1,463
Rental Equipment installment obligations to finance subsidiary	1,517
Accrued items	125
Deferred gross equipment rentals	289
Deferred income taxes	162

Stockholders' equity
Capital Stock (100,000 shares, no par value)	$2,100
Income retained in the business	1,138
Total Equity	$3,238
Total Liabilities and Shareholders' Equity	$8,682

EXHIBIT 4

Snow Clear, Inc.

Condensed Statement of Income for the year ending March 31, 1973,
for Snow Clear, Inc., and Finance Subsidiary
(Dollars in thousands)

Sales and other revenues	
Net Sales	$23,718
Pretax income of finance subsidiary not consolidated	348
Other income	101
	$24,167
Cost and Expenses	
Cost of goods sold	$18,628
Selling, general and administrative expenses	2,361
License fees paid to parent	154
Interest paid on outside borrowings	321
Interest and service charges paid to finance subsidiary	558
	$22,022
Income before taxes	$ 2,145
Provision for income taxes	
Snow Clear, Inc.	742
Finance Subsidiary	194
	$ 936
Net income for the year	$ 1,209
Net income per share	$ 12.09

QUESTIONS

1. What alternative courses of action are available to Mr. Farley?
2. Determine the least costly alternative of choosing between purchasing and leasing the computer system.
3. As Mr. Farley, what course of action should be taken?

Case 24
Davis Financial Services

In early January 1971, Mr. Harry P. Davis, Jr., President of Davis Financial Services, was considering the desirability of establishing an on-line computer terminal system at each of his nine branch offices, located in seven different communities in Ohio. The on-line system, with the acronym ACTIVO, was proposed by ICN Data Services to Mr. Davis as an automated data processing service to reduce and modernize the workload at all levels of operation.

Historical Development

Davis Financial Services (DFS) originated as a sales finance business in Columbus, Ohio, in 1935 by Mr. Davis's father, Mr. Harry P. Davis, Sr., as a sideline to a new-car dealership business. The following year, Mr. Davis, Sr., sold his car dealership to devote full time to his new venture. In 1940, DFS was incorporated and obtained a license from the state of Ohio to make direct cash loans.

DFS remained primarily a sales finance company throughout the 1940's. At this time, there were relatively few banks and captive sales finance companies, like General Motors Acceptance Corporation, buying auto paper, and DFS could buy all the business it wanted. However, by the early 1950's, direct cash loans comprised 60% of the DFS portfolio of receivables. The shift to consumer loans was due in part to the state small-loan act, which provided more profitable returns on direct loans. Second, after 1950, DFS no longer engaged in new-car financing, because it was unable to offer terms comparable with banks, captive sales finance companies, and credit unions to the more creditworthy clientele. In addition, DFS was severely

This case was prepared by Professor Robert W. Johnson of Purdue University as a basis for classroom discussion and not to illustrate either effective or ineffective handling of an administrative situation.

limited in its capital; its first sale of investment certificates to the public had not occurred until 1949, and building investor confidence in DFS was a slow process.

In 1961, DFS also withdrew from the used-car sales business. In the late 1950's, the demand for new cars slackened, and to maintain their sales levels, new-car dealers began to handle the retailing of their trade-ins. As a result, small used-car dealers doing business with DFS found it difficult both to obtain good used cars and to attract customers. As conditions deteriorated for the used-car dealers, they became desperate for sales and, as a result, passed on deceptive information to DFS and other finance companies about the quality of both their customers and their cars. Also, these dealers were able to attract only the marginal customers, since the larger used-car dealers were buying their cars from new-car dealers, who in turn provided customer financing through banks or a captive finance company supplying floor plan accommodations. Mr. Harry P. Davis, Jr., who took over active leadership of DFS in 1960, observed that as the quality of merchandise decreased, so did the quality of the merchant and the customer.

Two major changes occurred in the Ohio small-loan law in the 1960's. In 1960, the maximum loan size was increased from $1,000 to $2,000, the maximum maturity expanded from 25 months to 37½ months, maximum rates were increased, and use of the add-on method of computation was permitted, as is shown below:

Maximum rates before 1960 law (unpaid balance)	Maximum rates after 1960 law (add-on)
3% / month on first $150	$16/$100 loan/year on first $500
2% / month on second $150	$9/$100 loan/year on second $500
2/3% / month above $300 up to $1,000	$7/$100 loan/year on second $1,000
(Effective rate on a $1,000 loan, with a 24-month maturity: 19.0%)	(Effective rate on a $1,000 loan, with a 24-month maturity: 22.41%)

In 1965, Ohio law granted consumer finance companies the right to obtain the "403" second mortgage loan license, which permitted direct loans with maximum size of $15,000, 60-month maturities, 8% add-on interest ceiling, and a fee of 5% of the principal balance or $200, whatever is greater.

Mr. Davis, Jr., was quite reluctant to move into the larger size of loans in the sixties. Working capital was limited, and he was afraid the high bad-debt losses experienced with present customers would carry over to the larger loans. After-tax profits seemed to be very sensitive to changes in losses (see Table 1, page 212, for selected financial data). Since the permitted gross yields on large loans were not nearly as attractive as small-loan yields, he feared that the narrowed margin would make these loans unprofitable. While he anticipated that many of his current customers would obtain large, long-term loans elsewhere, he still expected to retain their future business for smaller, shorter-term loans. This did not occur; DFS lost numerous accounts to firms that supplied larger loans. As a result, as better customers left, the DFS portfolio of loans shifted to a larger percentage of less creditworthy customers who could only carry the smaller loan sizes.

TABLE 1

Davis Financial Services
Selected Financial Data

	1960		1961		1962		1963	
	Amount	% of TLO	Amount	% of TLO	Amount	% of TLO	Amount	% of TLO
Direct cash loans outstanding	$1,812,696	57.00	$2,254,611	69.00	$2,890,309	86.30	$3,092,741	87.00
Sales finance loans outstanding	1,369,156	43.00	966,741	31.00	463,062	13.70	463,667	13.00
Total loans outstanding (TLO)	$3,181,852	100.00	$3,121,352	100.00	$3,353,371	100.00	$3,556,408	100.00
Earnings after taxes	15,805	0.49	9,304	0.30	(5,513)	—	51,684	1.45
Charge-offs, net	44,504	1.40	96,757	3.10	124,336	3.70	75,940	2.13

	1964		1965		1966		1967	
	Amount	% of TLO	Amount	% of TLO	Amount	% of TLO	Amount	% of TLO
Direct cash loans outstanding	$4,415,496	89.10	$4,355,892	92.20	$4,754,646	94.10	$4,884,021	93.5
Sales finance loans outstanding	542,286	8.90	368,104	7.80	302,427	5.90	336,814	6.50
Total loans outstanding (TLO)	$4,957,772	100.00	$4,723,936	100.00	$5,057,073	100.00	$5,220,835	100.00
Earnings after taxes	33,094	0.68	(31,493)	—	42,665	0.84	47,176	0.90
Charge-offs, net	80,864	1.53	108,328	2.30	98,772	1.96	72,393	1.39

	1968		1969		1970	
	Amount	% of TLO	Amount	% of TLO	Amount	% of TLO
Direct cash loans outstanding	$4,866,858	91.60	$5,144,236	91.60	$5,511,038	92.20
Sales finance loans outstanding	441,859	8.40	483,985	8.40	466,374	7.80
Total loans outstanding (TLO)	$5,308,717	100.00	$5,628,248	100.00	$5,977,412	100.00
Earnings after taxes	42,191	0.79	75,468	1.34	52,257	0.87
Charge-offs, net	101,913	1.92	76,711	1.36	97,642	1.64

Although DFS had not followed the trend to larger loan sizes, Mr. Davis, Jr., was swept into the wave of diversification that was occurring in the consumer finance industry since 1950. DFS decided to finance $35,000 in receivables of a large landscaping contractor in 1966, and lent $50,000 to a local asphalt manufacturing and paving company the same year. Both ventures proved unwise. Each firm developed financial difficulties, and DFS found itself the reluctant owner of the asphalt company. Unable to find a buyer, Mr. Davis, Jr., operated the firm for two seasons, and in the summer of 1968, with himself as manager. In 1969, the asphalt firm was leased to a new manager with an option to buy, and DFS expected eventually to obtain the return of its initial investment in both companies. The landscaping contractor underwent a reorganization and has been paying DFS on schedule. The major effect on DFS was from the drain of managerial talent, as Mr. Davis, Jr., spent much of his time involved with the asphalt business and away from the consumer-loan segment of company business.

Reevaluation of Strategy

Returning to full-time emphasis on the finance business in 1970, Mr. Davis, Jr., sought to reevaluate the strategy that had carried DFS through the sixties. He was cognizant of several forces which were reshaping the consumer finance industry and the role played by consumer finance companies. Competition was becoming more intense as the various financial institutions that provided consumer installment credit pushed aggressively for increased business. These institutions were principally commercial banks, sales finance companies, credit unions, and consumer finance companies. In the Columbus area, Mr. Davis, Jr., estimated there were 75 to 80 licensed small-loan offices, 5 major banks with 50 offices, 5 to 10 captive sales finance companies, and about 100 credit unions. Intense competition characterized all credit markets, including the small-size, high-gross-yield segment of the direct loan market in which DFS specialized.

A second major force was increased costs of operations, especially in the area of payrolls. This is illustrated by the recent profit trend of consumer finance companies in Ohio:

Year	Profits after taxes[1]
1967	$14,000,000
1968	$12,000,000
1969	$10,000,000
1970	$ 3,000,000

[1]Note: These figures apply to small-loan (maximum of $2,000) licensees only.

In early January 1971, DFS' services consisted primarily of making direct installment loans secured by automobiles, household goods, and other chattels, and also unsecured loans. Operations also included some purchases of consumer installment contracts from selected dealers in carpeting, soft goods, and appliances. At the end of 1971, the company's consumer receivables were as follows:

	Number of Accounts	Dollars Outstanding
Direct installment loans	7,555	$5,511,038
Sales finance installment notes	554	466,374
Total	8,109	$5,978,412

The major source of direct loan business was from current customers. Important secondary sources included walk-in business and referrals from new-car dealers for their customers for down-payment borrowing, and conversion of sales finance customers to direct loans. The latter sources frequently generated larger consolidation loans.

Mr. Davis's recent evaluation of the status of DFS directed him to the conclusion that the loan portfolio was not growing and that the firm was losing many of its better customers because they were not being provided desired services. To combat this and the cost increases, he knew DFS would have to increase the ratio of accounts per employee, the average size of account balances, and the quality of the customers served. This he felt could be accomplished by taking a new direction, that of applying for the 403 license and entering into the larger-loan market. Yet he was still apprehensive about making larger loans without closer controls of branch offices. (He was currently quite dissatisfied with the failure of branch personnel to follow all company procedures on a timely and uniform basis.)

Action Proposal

In October 1970, representatives of International Computer Network (ICN) provided DFS with a preliminary study of the feasibility of installing the ACTIVO (A Computerized Terminal Instantaneous Visible Output) system at DFS. This was brought about by contact between Mr. Davis, Jr., and Mr. Robert Tuttle, Marketing Manager for ICN Data Services Division, at an industry convention earlier in the year. The preliminary study appeared promising and both firms decided a comprehensive study would be of value.

The ACTIVO system had been developed by ICN Data Services initially for ICN Finance Corporation (more than 280 offices). The system, located in St. Louis, Missouri, included an IBM 360/40 central processing unit (CPU) and external on-line storage devices to provide on-line,[1] time-sharing,[2] data processing services to

---

[1]"On-line processing permits transaction data to be fed under CPU control directly into secondary on-line storage devices from the point of origin without first being sorted. These data may be keyed in by the use of a typewriter-like terminal. . . . Appropriate records . . . may therefore be quickly updated. Information contained in any record is accessible to managers without the necessity of a sequential search of the file and within a fraction of a second after the inquiry message has been transmitted. Thus, on-line processing systems may feature random and rapid input of transactions and immediate and direct access to records as needed." From Sanders, Donald H., Ph.D., *Computers and Management,* New York: McGraw-Hill, 1970, p. 74.

[2]"Time-sharing is a term used to describe a processing system with a number of independent, relatively low-speed, on-line simultaneously usable stations. Each station provides direct access to the central processor to switch from one using station to another and to do a part of each job in the allocated 'time-slice' until the work is completed. The speed is frequently such that the user has the illusion that he alone is using the computer." (Ibid., pp. 76-77.)

consumer finance companies. Developed in 1966-67, the ACTIVO system was the first fully implemented on-line data processing system used by and designed expressly for consumer finance.

The system operated at a typical branch office of ICN Atlas in the following way. Each branch office had a computer terminal connected directly to the ICN Data Services computer in St. Louis. Major branch-office functions (e.g., processing loans, making disbursements, postpayment transactions, making inquiries into customer account status) were typed into the terminal and thus fed into the computer. The computer updated, filed, and relayed responses to inquiries. Related monthly management reports were prepared by ACTIVO off-line and mailed to the respective offices and headquarters. The system also provided for interoffice communications on the terminal.

The proposal made by ICN Data Services to Mr. Davis, Jr., promised numerous tangible benefits that could be reaped by DFS with the ACTIVO system. These are listed in part in Table 4 in the Appendix. The most significant tangible advantage claimed for ACTIVO was the simplification and reduction of record keeping at the branch offices. This would permit a significant reduction in loan-office clerical personnel. With ACTIVO, the remaining personnel should be capable of handling up to 350 accounts per employee. At the time the system was proposed, the firm's office personnel was handling about 225 accounts per employee.

The major cost reductions predicted by the ICN proposal are shown in Table 2.

TABLE 2

Estimated Cost Reductions or Revenue Increases

	Annual Amount
Salary reductions from reduced personnel:[1] Branch office employees: 1 @ $595/month 6 @ $357/month	$32,844
Reduced training time: ($100 per office per year)	900
Telephone cost reduction: ($1.00 per office per day)	2,376
Mail cost reduction: (50¢ per office per day)	1,188
Increase in late charges and first payment extensions	2,028
Reduction in rebate and interest errors, form changes, technical and administrative cost	840
Total anticipated cost reduction and revenue increases	$40,876

[1]See Table 5, Appendix, for a personnel reduction breakdown by branch office.

The ACTIVO system also promised numerous intangible benefits. Foremost was an improvement in personnel morale and job attitude. Mr. Tuttle pointed out that branch personnel would think the idea modern and view the company as a leader in the finance industry. With easier and simpler workloads, employees could produce higher-quality work. A terminal operator position was considered more important and prestigious than being merely a "cashier" or "bookkeeper." Thus branch personnel working with ACTIVO would not be interested in leaving the company—especially if it meant going to work for a competitor and reverting to the old method of bookkeeping and reporting. (Additional intangible advantages are listed in Table 5, Appendix.)

The basic ACTIVO system requirements and expenditures included the terminal equipment on either a direct purchase or a purchase leaseback agreement with a third party, an annual basic service charge, and an activity or usage charge payable to ICN Data Services, annual form and report expenses for standard and optional reports, and initial start-up costs. Based on leaseback agreement and inclusion of optional reports, the first-year costs are summarized in Table 3. These costs are itemized in Tables 7 through 10, in the Appendix.

TABLE 3
Summary of Estimated Costs

Lease, service, and usage costs	$45,252
Estimated cost of forms	4,620
Summary of estimated start-up costs	5,040[1]
Optional reports expense	2,698
Total estimated expenditure first year	$57,610

[1]Note: Start-up costs will not recur.

ICN Data Services estimated that a contract signing by January 15, 1971, would permit pilot operations to begin by March 1, 1971, as basic training sessions and installation of equipment would have been completed. Conversion to the ACTIVO system of current accounts and a "catch-up" on new loans and payment transactions would require two months of dual operations at each office. This parallel operating method would also ensure that all new procedures were adequate and that the interface between the ACTIVO system and current operations was functioning as expected. All branch offices could be expected to be in normal operations with ACTIVO by July 1971.

ACTIVO currently served ten firms, including ICN Atlas, ranging in size from 9 offices to over 475 offices. A comment by the president of one such firm was, "We now definitely know that the on-line program is a must for all consumer finance offices in the very near, 'inflated cost of doing business,' future." Mr. Davis, Jr., knew of other programs that were similar to ACTIVO, such as one called SUPER. He had not looked closely at these programs, although he did know the SUPER system had a much slower transmission time than did ACTIVO, and he felt quick response was an important factor for customer service.

Mr. Davis, Jr., was favorably impressed with the proposals of ICN Data Services, although he was unsure that DFS could afford it currently. With the ACTIVO system, DFS would be emulating the large companies in the industry, which should have favorable effects on the attitudes of both employees and customers. Second, he believed that the efficiency of branch offices would be increased through the elimination or reduction of nonproductive detail work, and the managers would have more time to devote toward collections and the acquisition of new business. The use of the terminals might also permit using cashiers with no bookkeeping experience.

Perhaps the most important attribute that Mr. Davis, Jr., saw in the ACTIVO system was the increased control he would have over the operations. With more reliable, accurate, and timely reports, through computer preparation, Mr. Davis, Jr., thought he would be in a better position to incorporate the changes in the business he wanted. This was of particular importance, since he had a strong desire to retain complete control of the business (i.e., family ownership of common stock). He felt that ACTIVO offered greater opportunities for success, and if failures and mistakes did occur, as in the sixties, he could still avoid fear of being replaced with a new management. ACTIVO also offered possibilities of additional uses in the future. These included on-line credit scoring, check writing, sale of investment certificates to the public, and off-line bank reconciliation, audit confirmation, and posting of noncash ledger accounts.

Before deciding whether or not to adopt ACTIVO, Mr. Davis, Jr., believed that he had to resolve some basic policy issues concerning the future operations of the firm. First, there still remained questions about the future course for DFS to take. The company could attempt to move exclusively into the larger-loan segment and abandon its present role of serving the small-loan customer, or it could attempt to serve both sets of clientele. Second, if the company should curtial its small-loan activity in favor of making larger loans, there would be a strong likelihood that initially the number of accounts would drop, since larger-loan customers were more scarce than other types of customers. Such being the case, would a system permitting more accounts per employee warrant the additional cost? And, finally, there was an important question of timing. Would it be advisable for management to change both the operating philosophy and the entire control system of the firm simultaneously? If not, which move should precede the other?

Other important variables that hindered the decision were the value to DFS of the intangible benefits that should result with ACTIVO and, if the proposal were accepted, the question of whether it should be on a lease or purchase basis. The aid the decision process, Mr. Davis, Jr., decided to start by evaluating the relative merits of lease or purchase and, second, to determine the minimum required value of the intangible benefits that would be necessary to enable the proposal to meet the DFS standards of return.[3] As he started this task, he was interrupted by a visitor, Mr. Howard Allyn, the vice president of a national consumer finance company. Mr. Allyn's visit was to propose an offer to buy DFS. His offer was at a price of 10% over the current book value of $5,600,000. In addition, he hoped Mr. Davis, Jr., would remain to manage the nine branch offices with a position of vice president at an increased salary.

---

[3]Although DFS has currently been paying interest on investment certificates to the public at a 7% rate (before tax), Mr. Davis, Jr., expected a somewhat greater return than this for new investment opportunities; typically, 10% (after tax), which he estimated was the firm's cost of capital. The applicable tax rate for DFS has been 50% on ordinary income and 25% for capital gains income.

Appendix
TABLE 4
Tangible Benefits Claimed for ACTIVO

The system increases operational control of the Home Office through prompt management reports. Accurate, complete month-end reports, generated on the first working day each month, are in management's hands within three days.

ACTIVO provides for future expansion, growth, and productivity without increasing present staffing.

ACTIVO maintains excellent records for both internal and external auditing.

The system reduces time and cost involved in training personnel necessary for bookkeeping operations.

ACTIVO supplies complete and instantaneous information on all accounts.

ACTIVO eliminates duplicate record keeping, at either the branch or Home Office level.

ACTIVO automatically performs accurate computations for such items as interest-bearing loans, refunds, rebates, late charges, etc.

ACTIVO relieves branch personnel of time formerly spent in double-checking manual calculations.

The system eliminates potential branch discrepancies in rate and charge application. All computer calculations follow specifications of state parameter records designed in accordance with legal requirements and company policy.

The system can provide centralized mailing of receipts for all mail payments.

Statistics generated by the system allow a basis for establishing better dealer relations.

ACTIVO can permit reduction of bank balances maintained for branch offices through daily control of cash funds. Freeing unnecessary money from branch accounts assumes great importance in today's costly money market.

ACTIVO controls and balances all types of disbursements.

Readily accessible, correct figures yield more accurate federal, state, and city tax reports.

The computer calculates all interest and insurance premiums, assuring accurate records for loan and sales finance transactions.

Generating statistics for market penetration analysis, ACTIVO encourages control of advertising.

The system facilitates accurate and timely monitoring of group performances by Home Office management.

TABLE 4

Tangible Benefits Claimed for ACTIVO *(continued)*

ACTIVO insures top security measures at the branch level.

With pertinent statistics generated by the system, management can exercise better control of profit and loss accounts.

ACTIVO has complete built-in compliance with the Consumer Credit Protection Act.

The ability to transmit messages among branch offices, as well as between the branch and Home Office, allows ACTIVO to reduce telephone costs in most phases of daily operation.

Terminal typing of all legal documents prevents spoilage of forms due to typing errors.

ACTIVO assures your firm will have the latest legal changes affecting the consumer finance industry. ICN Data Services will research any changes affecting your particular operation and upgrade the system accordingly.

TABLE 5

Personnel Reductions Expected with ACTIVO

Office	No. of Accounts	Personnel before ACTIVO	Accts. per Employee	Personnel after ACTIVO	Accts. per Employee	Dollar Savings
1	2,040	9[1]	226	6	340	$15,708
2	1,016	4[2]	254	3	338	4,284
3	1,040	4[2]	260	3	346	4,284
4	967	4[2]	242	3	322	4,284
5	1,060	4[2]	265	3	353	4,284
6	726	3[3]	242	3	242	—
7	890	3[3]	296	3	296	—
8	200	3[3]	67	3	67	—
9	170	2[4]	85	2	85	—
Total	8,109	36	225	29	279	$32,844

[1]Includes three cashiers, two bookkeepers, a secretary, controller, branch supervisor, president—two cashiers, one bookkeeper to be eliminated with ACTIVO.

[2]Includes branch manager, assistant manager, two cashiers—one cashier to be eliminated with ACTIVO.

[3]Includes branch manager, assistant branch manager, one cashier.

[4]Includes branch manager, one cashier.

TABLE 6

Intangible Benefits Claimed for ACTIVO

Eliminates purchase of additional equipment — Performing the largest part of calculations in the branch, ACTIVO eliminates or greatly decreases the need for calculators and adding and posting machines. Growth of an operation does not require purchase of additional equipment of this type.

Eliminates forms — ACTIVO eliminates all but seven basic forms for making and reporting loans and payments.

Promotes prestige within the industry — Companies using the ACTIVO on-line system are considered industry leaders.

Total customer service — Relieving branch personnel of routine clerical functions provides additional time to devote to a higher caliber of customer service.

Counter solicitation — Easing the pressures of manual bookkeeping and reporting enables staff members to more effectively make personal offers of additional money.

Cash security — By keeping accurate records of all loans made and cash received, the system prevents misapplication of company funds.

Legibility of records — Preparing all records by ACTIVO results in clear, concise, and legible reports and ledgers.

Customers' impression — Companies having the ACTIVO system impress customers with their modern business techniques.

Accuracy of mailing list — The ACTIVO system changes addresses in a matter of seconds, insuring correct files, and thus reducing return mail.

Promotes uniform operation — The ACTIVO system promotes uniform branch operations by predefining office procedures.

Merger or sale of operation — A company's incorporation of ACTIVO increases its total market value.

Controls solicitation of accounts — ACTIVO has the ability to make an account "solicitable" or "not solicitable" instantaneously, preventing Home Office solicitation of ineligible present customers.

Management meetings — ACTIVO reduces the need for regional management meetings to discuss the incorporation of legal changes into bookkeeping procedures. All law changes are programmed and ready for use by the effective date.

TABLE 7

Basic ACTIVO System Cost—IBM 1971-1980 Terminal Purchase/Lease,
Service, and Usage Costs

RPQ	Description	Purchase Price per Unit	Monthly Maintenance
M22276	1971 Model 30 Control Unit	$4,120.00	$12.00
M39842	150 Baud Adapter	300.00	2.00
833383	1980 Model 9 I/O Writer	1,600.00	12.50
833386	Split Platen	60.00	
833560	Finance Keyboard	15.00	
M38359	Document Insertion Device	—	
	Terminal Purchase Price	$6,095.00[1]	$26.50

Terminal Cost 9 x $131/mo. x 12 mos., incl. Maint. and based on 8-Yr. Leaseback	$14,148.00
Basic Service Cost Based on 9 terminals @ $135.00/Mo. x 12 mos.	14,580.00
Transaction Cost[2] Based on 9,000 accts. x 1.7 activities per month per acct. x $ .09 x 12 mos.	16,524.00
	$ 45,252.00

Notes:

[1] If the terminals were purchased, they would be depreciated on a straight-line basis for 15 years to zero net book value. The estimated salvage value at that time would be 5% of cost.

[2] A transaction is defined as the activation of the system from the terminal by depressing the send key. The charge for each transaction is $0.09 for the year 1971, with a $.005 increase each succeeding calendar year. DFS estimates 1.7 activities per account per month, which is within the ACTIVO experience range.

TABLE 8
Basic ACTIVO System Cost—Estimated Forms Cost

Category	Form	Quantity	Cost
Loans	Loan Sets (10-part)	10/M	
	Continuation Cards (1-part)	1/M	
	Conversion Sets (2-part)	10/M	$2,200.00
Sales Finance	Loan Sets (5-part)	500	
	Continuation Cards (1-part)	500	
	Conversion Sets (2-part)	500	400.00
Transaction Journal	Regular (1-part)	25/M	
	Conversion (1-part)	10/M	750.00
Counter Receipts	Receipts (1-part)	20/M	150.00
Mail Receipts	Receipts (1-part)	49/M	360.00
Reports	Daily Cash Summary (2-part)	2½/M	
	Branch Month End (4-part)	250	325.00
	Daily Operations Summary	250	25.00
Flat Forms	Message Report Blanks	5/M	50.00
	Loan Application Coding Sheets	5/M	50.00
	Downtime Logs	1/M	25.00
Postage for Mailing Receipts @ $ .06 each		49/M	295.00
	Total Estimated Cost		$4,620.00

TABLE 9
Basic ACTIVO System Cost—Summary of Estimated Start-Up Costs

Conversion Expense

9,000 active accounts @ $ .020 account	$1,800.00
9,000 Tabbies @ $20.00/M	180.00
20 Ledger Card Trays @ $8.80/ea.	176.00
Customerize Flip Chart pages	300.00
Total	$2,456.00

Installation Expense

Electrical Modifications @ $75.00/office	$ 675.00
Terminal Freight @ $26.00 terminal	234.00
Binders for specified documents	108.00
Western Union Hook-Up Charge @ $10.00/office	90.00
Counter preparation	225.00
Total	$1,332.00

Training Expense

Room rent in motel for 9 days	$ 162.00
Lunches for 5 days	120.00
Hook-up and miscellaneous expense	70.00
Total	$ 352.00

Programming Modification Charges

Monthly Check Register Report	$ 250.00
Miscellaneous Receipts and Disbursement Accounting Codes	400.00
Monthly Accounting Data Report	250.00
Total	$ 900.00
TOTAL ESTIMATED START-UP COST	$5,040.00

TABLE 10

Basic ACTIVO System Cost—Optional Report Expense

Generalized Detail Delinquence Report
     700 Accounts x $ .005/account x 12 months $ 42.00
     Basic report charge—$18.00/mo. x 12 months   <u>216.00</u> $ 258.00

Consolidated Month-End Report
     Basic report charge—$20.00/month x 12 months   240.00

Fire Insurance Premium and Refund Report
     Basic report charge—$20.00/month x 12 months   240.00

Life/A&H Premium/Refund Report
     Basic report charge—$20.00/month x 12 months   240.00

Direct Cash Lending Questionnaire
     Basic report charge—$20.00/month x 12 months   240.00

Loan Register
     Basic report charge—$20.00/month x 12 months   240.00

Check Register
     Basic report charge—$6.40/office x 9 offices
     x 12 mos.   691.00

Gummed Label Solicitation List
     Solicitable open accounts 4,500 x $11.00/M x 4 mos.   198.00

Payment Receipts
30% of 9/M accts. — 27,000 basic service x 12 mos. = 32,400
49,000 Est. Annual Usage — 32,400 Basic Service = 16,600
     @ .01   166.00

Postage for mailing reports to Davis Financial Services
Home Office estimated at $15.00/month x 12 months   185.00

Total Estimated Annual Charge   <u>$2,698.00</u>

QUESTIONS

1. Review the alternative courses of action available to Mr. Davis, Jr.
2. Determine the least costly alternative, choosing between purchasing and leasing the terminals.
3. How large must the minimum value of the intangible benefits be in order for Mr. Davis, Jr., to undertake the ACTIVO system?
4. What action would you recommend for Mr. Davis, Jr.?

PART FOUR
SOURCES OF LONG-TERM FINANCING

*

Case 25
Superior Air Conditioners, Inc.

In late February, 1971, Mr. Gerald Kirksey, commercial loan officer of the Gator National Bank (henceforth known as GNB) of Jacksonville, Florida, was discussing with a bank vice president, the loan of Superior Air Conditioners, Inc., prior to meeting in two days with the president, Mr. Arthur Horridge, and the treasurer, Mr. Lewis Lapham. The purpose of the meeting was to convey the bank's decision concerning a request to increase GNB's term loan commitment by $150,000. Mr. Kirksey was responsible for formulating the basis for the bank's decision on the loan request, since he had been in charge of the account for the past years.

Superior Air Conditioners, Inc., was the exclusive metropolitan Jacksonville area distributor for Cool King Air Conditioners, a large national producer. Superior installed only in commercial buildings, with about 80% of the installations being Cool King. About three-quarters of the company's contracts to install new equipment were negotiated, and the remainder were on a bid basis. Most of the firm's jobs were in the $150,000 to $225,000 range. The greater share of the firm's contracts were on a fixed contract basis, but some of the smaller jobs were on a cost plus basis. In addition, Superior serviced all types of commercial air conditioning installations. The company had about 200 employees, all non-union except for those who worked in construction and in the sheet metal shop.

As measured by total assets, GNB was the second largest bank in the metropolitan Jacksonville area. It was organized into four divisions: trust, operations, control and planning, and banking. The banking division was further subdivided

This case was prepared by Professor Harry R. Kuniansky of the College of Charleston as a basis for classroom discussion and not to illustrate either effective or ineffective handling of an administrative situation. The material for this case was provided by an anonymous donor.

into two branches: metropolitan and national. Mr. Kirksey's position was in the metropolitan subdivision. Each loan officer was assigned a number of commercial accounts to service, all located within the metropolitan Jacksonville area. Each officer administered a broad spectrum of business accounts, although over time some degree of specialization developed. For example, Mr. Kirksey was considered the resident expert on contracting firms.

Before attempting to write a report and recommendation on the company's loan request, Mr. Kirksey decided to review information taken from the firm's credit file, which contained financial statements, credit reports, and periodic activity reports. The last summarized the firm's activities for up to a year at a time. They were written by the loan officers who serviced the account, usually after a visit to the company. Mr. Kirksey believed they provided a valuable source of data concerning the firm's progress. Excerpts from various summary reports are shown below.

Report of April 24, 1964

Mr. Alton Hall of Superior Air Conditioning acquired 100% of the firm in February, 1961. Still owing from the purchase was a $37,500 note to the former owner. In order to retire this note, Mr. Hall requested $37,500 from GNB, to be liquidated with a $7,500 payoff every six months. GNB requested that Mr. Hall personally endorse the notes, but he refused to do so because borrowings from his major banking connection, the Bank of Duval County (known henceforth as BDC), did not require such an endorsement. GNB decided to make the loan without the endorsement, but insurance was required on the loan. GNB told Mr. Hall they expected him to shift his main account to them within the next few months. At present, Superior had only a $7,500 payroll account with GNB. Hall stated that he intended to do this, as he had no great love for BDC, but they did provide him with business.

Prepared by C. S. Gillen

Report of May 11, 1965

The company borrowed $15,000 unsecured, needed as a result of the purchase of equipment. The note was payable in $3,750 installments every ninety (90) days. The company's recent average balances with GNB were $13,000. GNB continued to solicit the main account, which was still located at BDC. Hall said that he would not remove the account completely from that bank, but he would favor GNB with larger balances. At present, Superior did not borrow from BDC.

Prepared by C. S. Gillen

Report of January 10, 1966

Sales in 1965 were $2,200,000 with profits of $49,150, which was more than double 1963 profit. As of the end of 1965, the firm had $1,400,000 worth of contracts outstanding, against which costs of $660,000 had been incurred. An increase in receivables was the result of a decline in receivables turnover. The worth to debt ratio declined slightly from 1.0 in 1963 to .9 in 1965.

The firm appears to be operating profitable, and its balance sheet position was generally favorable. The company was out of debt on GNB, and payroll deposit balances have averaged about $15,600.

Prepared by C. S. Gillen

Report of November 16, 1966

In October, Mr. Alton Hall retired, and the firm named George Bennett as its new president. Mr. Bennett had been with the firm seven years, and his most recent position was vice president—construction. He was in charge of all construction projects, and he was responsible for insuring that projects progressed according to plan and that budgeted profitability was attained. Mr. Bennett asked the GNB to discount a customer's note in order to pay off the balance of a note owing to GNB. Mr. Gilligan, senior vice president of GNB, used this opportunity to press for an increased share of Superior's business, pointing out that most of the officers did their banking business with GNB. Mr. Bennett stated that BDC employed the firm to service all its branches' air conditioning units, and for that reason, Superior felt an obligation to use BDC to some extent. Mr. Gilligan pointed out that the firm did similar work for GNB's branches. GNB discounted the note.

The operation statement of September 30, 1966, disclosed sales in excess of $3,050,000, a 44% increase over 1965. Gross margin declined from 31% to 29% while profit was up 115% over 1965, due mainly to a 3% drop in operating expenses as a percentage of sales.

Superior Air Conditioners was both highly liquid and well capitalized and at the same time was producing a better than average return on investment. Both the current and debt to worth ratios improved in 1966. In fiscal 1966, one-fourth of the company's gross revenue originated from servicing and three-fourths from sales of air conditioning equipment.

The firm's payroll account averaged $18,000 for the last six months. As of this report's date, the firm has unsecured credit of $52,500 with GNB.

Prepared by R. T. Saxonby

Report of March 23, 1967

Currently, Superior owed GNB $40,000 from $52,000 lent in 1966. The company planned to use the proceeds from a customer's note to retire the loan, but these proceeds were employed for working capital purposes because of a large increase in work-in-process inventories and slow collections. Mr. Lewis Lapham asked GNB to lend an additional $33,000 to pay trade bills pending the collection of certain outstanding accounts. Mr. Lapham estimated these accounts would be collected within thirty days. He stated that the receivables in question were from two large firms, but based on past experience Superior was confident of payment. The company had $100,000 worth of commercial paper that it could liquidate if tight financial conditions continued, but they preferred not to do this at present. GNB granted the loan at 6½%.

For the five months ending February 28, 1967, the firm showed a loss of $69,000. Mr. Lapham indicated that certain contracts would be completed in the next few months and credited into sales and profits. This would eliminate the five months' loss, and the company would show a good operating profit.

Again, the representative of GNB mentioned to Mr. Lapham the status of the firm's principal bank account, which was still located at BDC. Mr. Lapham again reiterated that they were reluctant to move the account due to the servicing volume furnished by the BDC. The GNB representative again pointed out that Superior has service contracts on all their branches and that three new branches would open soon. Mr. Lapham responded that the firm is no longer close to BDC and they would likely move the account.

Hopefully, in a short while, all banking business would be transferred to GNB.

Prepared by H. L. Hensing

Report of October 31, 1968

Superior decided to purchase seven acres of land in the St. John's Industrial District in order to erect a 64,000-square-foot facility which would house office space, warehouse, and workshop. They had been renting, but due to steady growth, existing facilities are totally inadequate. In order to purchase this parcel of land, the company requested and was granted a $115,000, 7¼% ninety-day loan. The loan was secured by the real estate described above and was 100% of the purchase price. GNB's commitment was based on the financial strength of the company and not the real estate taken as security. The reason for taking the deed to secure debt was to perfect a first lien on an open-end deed in anticipation of a $525,000 construction loan, which GNB believed they would lose in thirty days.

Superior switched for financial reporting purposes its accounting method (see Exhibit 4) from completed contract to percentage of completion. The firm anticipated it would continue to pay income tax based on the completed-contract method. The effect of the accounting change was to increase net income before taxes $53,500 and to also increase the current asset, excess cost over billing, by approximately $220,000. There may have been some overstatement of income, but it did not appear to be excessive.

Superior continued to be in an adequate working capital and equity position. The current ratio had been in excess of 2 to 1 for the last three years, although it did drop from 2.87 in 1967 to 2.15 in 1968. The worth to debt ratio did decline in 1968 to 1.33, but nevertheless the firm seemed to have a solid equity cushion.

Service revenue continued to play an important role in gross revenues.

Service revenue as a percentage of net sales:

1966	27.5
1967	27.9
1968	27.7

It contributed an even greater proportion to net profit, averaging 42% for the years 1966-1968. As of September 30, 1968, a schedule of work on hand revealed that Superior had a long list of respected customers and thus high-quality receivables.

Prepared by L. C. Harbin

Report of January 6, 1969

Superior requested a $100,000 unsecured loan in addition to the $115,000 loan granted earlier and the $525,000 construction loan negotiated in November, 1968. Funds from the latter loan would be drawn as construction progressed. The firm expected to repay the new loan within thirty (30) days as collection of some large outstanding receivables was imminent.

GNB had solicited the firm's main checking account for a number of years as Superior maintained only a small unprofitable payroll account. Credit reports indicated that cash balances averaged in the moderate six figures; however, the company had reported only $60,000, $152,000, and $25,000 on its last three audits. Sales were between $3,100,000 and $3,800,000 the last three years, so it was likely that the company's account at the BDC had an average balance between $150,000 and $225,000 due to the float on checks written by the company.

The solicitations paid off to some degree when Superior gave GNB the opportunity to handle the construction loan. Mr. Bennett told Mr. Lyman Akins, a senior vice president of GNB, that he held a number of GNB officers in high regard. The company finally opened a checking account and indicated they planned to split their business between GNB and BDC.

GNB agreed to the loan at a rate of ¾% above prime, as long as the firm maintained substantial collected balances with GNB. Substantial was meant to encompass collected balances in the $75,000 to $90,000 neighborhood, given the Company's present financial condition. As Superior's sales grew, the bank would expect larger collected balances.

Prepared by T. N. Hendricksen

Report of March 3, 1969

Superior Air Conditioners requested and was granted a short-term loan of $245,000 at ¾% above prime and a term loan of $200,000 at 1¼% above prime. The short-term loan was needed to finance receivables and start-up costs on new jobs. The term loan, to be repaid in thirty-six (36) monthly principal installments, was necessary to cover a surplus of expenditures for the new plant over and above the funds provided by permanent financing. The construction loan with GNB was terminated because, as a requirement for a permanent loan, the lender, Markham Jones and Company, required that the construction loan be placed with them.

GNB's representative talked with Mr. Lapham, the treasurer, for over two hours. Mr. Lapham said that in the first four months of 1969 as compared to 1968, contract income was up from $750,000 to $1,585,000, service income increased from $265,000 to $300,000, and net profit before taxes jumped fourfold ($27,000 to $108,000). Mr. Lapham presented a progress report of the firm's largest jobs:

Company	Job Size (000's)	Percent Completion	Gross Profit (000's)
1	$338	55	$ 87
2	250	80	33
3	220	95	27
4	336	5	53
5	375	95	56
6	985	50	213

The company's checking account had average collected balances of $51,000 during the last two months, with the account providing an average monthly profit of $120 (see Exhibit 7). In addition, the company president carried a balance of $13,500 in his personal checking account. The firm's balance at the BDC averaged about $98,000, and the GNB representative believed a switch of $30,000 to $45,000 was possible. Superior presently owed GNB $230,000 on a short-term basis. No funds were owed to BDC, and there was no contemplation of borrowing any in the future.

Prepared by T. N. Hendricksen

The ten-month statement of Superior revealed a firm quite different from the eight-month statement:

	8 months	10 months
Revenue	$4,019,000	$4,700,000
Net Income	82,000	(75,000)

Mr. Lapham stated that the decline in net income was caused by a slowdown of sheet metal workers which occurred between March and May, but the results did not have significance until June-July because of the company's bookkeeping practices. Income was reported by approximating the percentage of completion on each job. If a job was expected to produce a profit of $30,000 and total estimated labor on the job was $75,000, the company will have recorded net income of $15,000 when $37,000 worth of labor is expended. Income realized was directly variable with labor expenses. The method works reasonably well so long as the amount spent for labor does not exceed the original estimate. Superior's problem proceeded from the slowdown of March-May, which resulted in actual labor cost exceeding estimated labor cost on several big jobs. This situation was not recognized until June-July.

As of July 31, 1969, the company had a backlog of about $900,000, three months' work at the current rate. They expected that profit would equal overhead for August and September, so that the firm would probably report a loss of $70,000 to $75,000 for the year. The firm hoped that greater plant efficiencies could be obtained in the new facility, which was to be occupied within the next two months. A return to profitability was forecast for 1970.

Prepared by G. M. Snizer

Report of October 28, 1969

The company had approximately $1,000,000 worth of jobs on hand representing four (4) months of work at the current rate. This amount of work represented a backlog of jobs that was slightly less than the company desired. The following is a list of the firm's jobs in progress:

Job	Adjusted Contract Amount (000)	Percent Complete 10/3/69	Estimated Total Profit (000)	Profit Through 8/30/69 (000)
1	$294	98	$53	$44
2	81	100	12	11
3	67	100	26	20
4	84	99	15	10
5	194	95	30	18
6	318	85	97	60
7	181	85	32	0
8	56	55	17	0
9	34	0	7	0
10	216	0	49	0

Although Superior was experiencing difficulties in generating its estimated profits, GNB continued to have confidence in the management of the firm. The firm's activity was closely monitored by a GNB representative.

Report of March 23, 1970

Two weeks ago, the firm applied for an additional short-term loan of $100,000, which was to be repaid in sixty days. GNB agreed to make the loan but wanted the personal endorsement of Mr. Hall, the owner. Mr. Bennett was upset over this condition, and he withdrew the loan request. He said that he would get along by stretching his payables and increasing the pressure on customers for payment.

Superior was operating at a deficit for the year. The interim statements for four months ending January 31, 1970, showed a $76,000 pretax loss. Mr. Bennett expected March and April to be profitable.

The GNB representative believed the new building was larger than necessary, producing a short-term excess capacity, and had consumed a large amount of working capital. However, its increased efficiency over the old quarters should provide a satisfactory long-term return on investment. Based on pro forma projections of profits and capital requirements at various levels of contract and service volume, the bank representative agreed with company management that limits should be placed on contract volume in 1970.

Expansion of the servicing funciton and direct sales from the sheet metal shop should be encouraged.

The reasons for this policy were:

1. The amount of capital required for servicing was much less than that for construction work.
2. The service area was more profitable than construction.
3. There was less risk of large loss on servicing since each job tended to be smaller than each construction job.
4. There was a tremendous amount of excess capacity in the machine shop.

GNB has practically all of the firm's checking account balances. The account still is not profitable, however, because collected balances have averaged only $36,000 during the past five months, with analysis profit about $70 a month. When GNB was lending last winter, rates for the company were ¾% above prime on short-term and 1¼% above prime on term loans. Although it had developed that the relationship was not profitable at these prices, because Superior was not able to carry the bank balances expected and the risk element was greater than anticipated, GNB's only action at present was to raise the premium on short-term loans to 1%. In addition, if the firm was not profitable by April 1, GNB considered securing a second mortgage on all buildings and land. The second mortgage would provide GNB about $185,000 worth of extra collateral. GNB hoped the firm would be profitable by April 1 and the relationship would be profitable for the bank within six months.

Prepared by G. Kirksey

Report of February 4, 1971

Superior Air Conditioners, Inc., owed GNB as of January 31, 1971, $78,000 on its term commitment plus $125,000 extended under short-term arrangements. Due to adverse circumstances outlined in the paragraph below, the short-term loan has reverted to an unamortized long-term loan. Both loans were still unsecured.

The company reported a before-tax loss of $113,000 for the first three months of the current fiscal year. The firm's poor showing stemmed basically from losses on jobs with which it had poor experience, excessive overhead due in part to construction and ownership of facilities far in excess of current and future needs, and excessive and wasteful spending.

Accordingly, the balance sheet position deteriorated, and as of December 31, 1970, reflected the following:

Current Assets	$ 720,000
Current Liabilities	$ 810,000
Total Assets	$1,730,000
Total Liabilities	$1,380,000
Working Capital	$ (90,000)
Net Worth	$ 350,000

As a result of the aforementioned situation, the presendent, Mr. George Bennett, was dismissed. Appointed in his place was Mr. Arthur Horridge, who had been with the company for three years as general manager.

GNB was in the process of collateralizing all of its loans, using most of Superior's assets; second mortgage on land and building $240,000, service contract receivables $40,000, inventory $120,000, machinery and equipment $200,000, and furniture and fixtures. GNB does not intend to take contract receivables as collateral, as the bank believes this action might cause alarm among Superior's suppliers and could possibly impair the firm's ability to obtain bonds on future contracts. The total situation has been discussed with GNB's attorneys, and they have advised the bank to proceed like any other tenuous loan situation.

Upon the recommendation of GNB, Superior has hired Mr. Larry Higby,

CPA, to act as a consultant to the firm. Mr. Higby prepared a forecast which indicated the firm needed an immediate injection of $150,000 for working capital if it was to survive. He was optimistic about the company's future prospects if it could get the necessary working capital to meet critical short-term needs. The forecast underlined the urgency of the need because it projected a company loss of an additional $60,000 through March. These losses must be financed from sources other than working capital and trade suppliers. Superior owed 125 suppliers approximately $400,000. The smaller ones were expressing impatience and demanded to be paid immediately. Large suppliers assumed a wait-and-see attitude, but at present they were not willing to expose themselves further by shipping on open account.

Prepared by G. Kirksey

EXHIBIT 1

Superior Air Conditioners, Inc.

Selected Financial Data 1961-1963

(000's)

	9/30/61	9/30/62	9/30/63
Current Assets	$ 417	$ 423	$ 516
Current Liabilities	141	129	206
Working Capital	$ 276	$ 294	$ 310
Total Assets	$ 458	$ 456	$ 548
Total Debt	228	207	276
Net Worth	$ 230	$ 249	$ 272
Net Sales	$1,653	$1,766	$2,000
Net Profit	24	18	23
Dividends	0	0	0

EXHIBIT 2
Superior Air Conditioners, Inc.
Comparative Balance Sheets 1966-1970
(000's)

	9/30/66	9/30/67	9/30/68	9/30/69	9/30/70
ASSETS					
Cash	$ 60	$ 152	$ 25	$ 15	$ 38
Marketable Securities	395	149	89	0	0
Receivables (Net)	438	539	590	985	681
Inventory	93	92	125	114	115
Excess Cost Over Billing	83	62	336	126	62
Other	0	5	39	16	66
Total Current Assets	$1,069	$ 999	$1,204	$1,256	$ 962
Fixed Assets (Net)	$ 20	$ 42	$ 75	$ 642	$ 977
Deferred Charges	0	2	2	18	12
Officers and Employees Loans	5	6	25	17	16
Total Assets	$1,094	$1,049	$1,306	$1,933	$1,967
LIABILITIES					
Accounts Payable	$ 143	$ 136	$ 321	$ 436	$ 431
Notes Payable, Banks	0	0	0	245	125
Miscellaneous Accruals	163	180	186	93	61
Excess Billing Over Cost	45	0	0	0	53
Deferred Income Taxes	0	0	53	19	18
Long-Term Debt Current	0	0	0	0	85
Income Tax Accrued	98	32	0	0	0
Total Current Liabilities	$ 449	$ 348	$ 560	$ 793	$ 773
Long-Term Liabilities					
Term Loan—Gator National Bank	$ 0	$ 0	$ 0	$ 167	$ 100
Construction Loan—Markham Jones	0	0	0	250	525
Total Long-Term Liabilities	$ 0	$ 0	$ 0	$ 417	$ 625
Total Liabilities	$ 449	$ 348	$ 560	$1,210	$1,398
NET WORTH					
Common Stock	$ 24	$ 24	$ 24	$ 24	$ 24
Retained Earnings	621	677	722	699	545
Total Net Worth	$ 645	$ 701	$ 746	$ 723	$ 569
Total Liabilities and Net Worth	$1,094	$1,046	$1,306	$1,933	$1,967

EXHIBIT 3
Superior Air Conditioners, Inc.
Comparative Income Statements as of 9/30, 1966-1970
(000's)

	9/30/66	9/30/67	9/30/68[1]	9/30/69	9/30/70
Net Sales	$3,165	$3,245	$3,837	$5,878	$4,106
Cost of Goods Sold	2,235	2,283	2,762	4,833	3,027
Gross Profit	$ 930	$ 962	$1,075	$1,045	$1,079
Operating Expenses					
Not Including Noncash Charges	726	872	1,004	1,065	1,189
Other Income	11	18	13	0	2
Other Expenses	0	0	0	15	83
Profit Before Noncash Charges					
and Income Taxes	$ 215	$ 108	$ 84	$ (35)	$ (191)
Noncash Charges	5	10	15	18	26
Profit Before Income Taxes	$ 210	$ 98	$ 69	$ (53)	$ (217)
Income Taxes	102	42	24	(30)[2]	(63)[2]
Net Profit	$ 108	$ 56	$ 45	$ (23)	$ (154)
Dividends or Withdrawals	$ 0	$ 0	$ 0	$ 0	$ 0

[1]Beginning in 1968, the accounting procedure has been changed from the completed-contract method to the percentage-of-completion method. As a result, net profit before taxes for the year was increased by $53,500 in the conversion.

[2]Represents an income tax refund as net loss results in applying carryback provisions of income tax law.

EXHIBIT 4

Superior Air Conditioners, Inc.
*A Note on the Percentage-of-Completion Method of
Accounting and the Completed-Contract Method of Accounting*

The following statements on the percentage-of-completion method of accounting and the completed-contract method of accounting are quoted from *Accounting Research Bulletin,* No. 45, issued by the Committee on Accounting Procedure, American Institute of Certified Public Accountants.

The percentage-of-completion method recognizes income as work on a contract progresses. The committee recommends that the recognized income be that percentage of estimated total income either:

(a) that incurred costs to date bear to estimated total costs after giving effect to estimates of costs to complete based upon most recent information, or

(b) that may be indicated by such other measure of progress toward completion as may be appropriate having due regard to work performed   ...

Under this method current assets include costs and recognized income not yet billed, with respect to certain contracts; and liabilities, in most cases current liabilities, may include billings in excess of costs and recognized income with respect to other contracts.

The principal advantages of the percentage-of-completion method are periodic recognition of income currently rather than irregularly as contracts are completed, and the reflection of the status of the uncompleted contracts provided through the current estimates of costs of completion.

The principal disadvantage of the percentage-of-completion method is that it is necessarily dependent upon estimates of ultimate costs and of currently accruing income, which are subject to the uncertainties frequently inherent in long-term contracts.

The completed-contract method recognizes income only when the contract is completed, or substantially so. . . .

When the completed-contract method is used, an excess of accumulated costs over related billings should be shown in the balance sheet as a current asset, and an excess of accumulated billings over related costs should be shown among the liabilities, in most cases a current liability. If costs exceed billings on some contracts, and billings exceed costs on others, the contracts should ordinarily be segregated so that the figures on the asset side include only those contracts on which costs exceed billings, and those on the liability side include only those on which billings exceed costs.

EXHIBIT 5
Superior Air Conditioners, Inc.
Selected Ratios Prepared by Various
Bank Officers of the Gator National Bank
1966-1970

	1966	1967	1968	1969	1970
Current Ratio	2.38	2.87	2.15	1.58	1.24
Worth/Debt	1.43	2.01	1.33	.60	.41
Worth/Fixed Assets	32.25	16.69	9.63	1.13	.58
Sales/Ending Receivables	7.19	6.02	6.50	5.97	6.02
Cost of Sales/Inventory	24.03	24.82	22.09	42.39	26.32
Gross Profit/Net Sales	29.38	29.64	28.01	17.77	26.28
Operating Expenses/Net Sales	22.93	26.87	26.16	18.11	28.96
Profit Before Noncash Charges and Income Taxes/Net Sales	6.79	3.32	2.18	(.59)	(4.65)
Profit Before Income Taxes/ Net Sales	6.63	3.02	1.79	(.90)	(5.28)
Income Taxes/Pretax Income	48.57	42.85	34.78	NA	NA
Net Profit/Net Sales	3.41	1.73	1.17	(.39)	(3.75)
Net Profit/Ending Net Worth	16.74	7.98	6.03	(3.18)	(27.06)

EXHIBIT 6
Superior Air Conditioners, Inc.
Reconciliation of Working Capital Changes
Prepared by Gator National Bank Officers
1966-1970

	1966	1967	1968	1969	1970
Increase (Decrease) in Net Worth	$108	$56	$45	$(23)	$(154)
Add:					
Noncash Depreciation and Other	5	10	15	18	26
Sale of Fixed Assets					
Sale of Investments					
Decrease Other Noncurrent Assets	10				7
Increase Term Loan					
Sale of Debt Securities					
Increase Other Noncurrent Liabilities				250	275
Less:					
Purchase of Fixed Assets	1	32	48	585	361
Additional Investments					
Increase Other Noncurrent Assets		3	19	8	
Repayment of Term Loan					
Retirement Other Long-Term Debt					
Decrease Other Noncurrent Liabilities					
Net Increase (Decrease) Working Capital	$122	$31	$(7)	$(348)	$(207)

EXHIBIT 7
Superior Air Conditioners, Inc.
Analysis of Commercial Checking
Accounts at Gator National Bank

MEMO TO: All Commercial Loan Officers

FROM: Account Analysis

SUBJECT: Procedure for Analyzing Commercial
                   Accounts and an Illustration

Each account is analyzed to determine the actual cost of handling. To determine the credit (or value) of the account balance, the average collected balance less $17\frac{1}{2}\%$[1] of the required reserve equals the balance available for investment. The value of the investment balance (determined at the rate of $4\frac{1}{4}\%$[1] per annum) equals the amount of credit applied to either offset or eliminate the service charge fee which is debited to the account.

The activity charges on a monthly basis are as follows:

Items paid	1-1,000	7¢ each
Items paid	1,001-3,000	6¢ each
Items paid	over 3,000	5¢ each
Items deposited	1-1,000	3¢ each
Items deposited	1,001-2,000	2½¢ each
Items deposited	over 2,000	2¢ each

Items deposited—encoded 1½¢ each

Monthly maintenance fee is $2.00 if there is any account activity.

Miscellaneous Charges: Drafts 4¢ each. Transfers 75¢ each.

The following is an example of the above procedures:

Assume a Collected Balance of $33,000
Reserve Requirement   .175
                                      $ 5,775

Loanable Funds	$ 27,225
Applicable Interest Rate	.0425
Allowable Credit	$1,157.06
Monthly Profit Before Charges	$\dfrac{1,157.06}{12}$ = $96.42

Assume 27 checks deposited x 3¢	=	$ .81
30 checks paid x 7¢	=	5.60
		$ 6.41
Maintenance charges		2.00
Total activity cost		$ 8.41

$96.42
  8.41
$88.01   monthly profit from
              account

Realizing that this is only one of the many variables that will determine the interest rate charged to your customers, we believe this information will help to clarify your thinking on the profits from their accounts.

[1]These figures are subject to change.

EXHIBIT 8
Superior Air Conditioners, Inc.
Guidelines for Determining Interest
Rates on Loans of Gator National Bank

GNB's desired minimum profitability on loans was 2½% above prime, unadjusted for risk and for credits received for maintaining a deposit balance at the bank. The following examples will illustrate this policy.

Assume a prime rate of 5% and that a prime corporate borrower requests a loan. If this borrowing firm had no deposit balances, then the rate would be 7½%. If this borrower's deposit balance earned him a credit (see Exhibit 7) of $100 or $1,200 a year and he had an average loan balance of $120,000, then the borrower's cost would be reduced by $1,200/$120,000 or 1%. His rate would then be 6½%. No borrower would ever be charged less than prime, regardless of the credits earned. If the borrower were something other than a prime risk, then the rate would be scaled upward, depending on the amount of risk perceived by the bank.

The rate could be further adjusted for other variables such as tax account balances carried by the customer or the future potential of the borrowing firm. Normally, however, the prime rate, adjusted for earned credits from deposit balances and perceived risk exposure of the bank, will play the greater part in determining the interest rate charged the customer.

EXHIBIT 9
Superior Air Conditioners, Inc.
Summary of Loans Outstanding at Various Report Dates

Date of Report	Amount of Loans Outstanding	Comments
April 24, 1964	$ 37,500	6-month installment
May 11, 1965	$ 15,000	1-year installment
January 10, 1966	$ 0	
November 16, 1966	$ 52,500	1-year installment
March 23, 1967	$ 37,500	Part of Nov. 1966 loan still outstanding
	$ 33,000	
October 31, 1968	$115,000	30-day
January 6, 1969	$115,000	
	$100,000	90-day
March 3, 1969	$245,000	
		Same as Oct. 31, 1968, loan
	$200,000	90-day
August 27, 1969	$245,000	Replaces and increases loans of Oct. 31, 1968, and Jan. 6, 1969, 90-day
	$178,000	
October 28, 1969	$200,000	
	$167,000	3-year term loan repaid 36 equal principal installments
March 23, 1970	$125,000	
	$139,000	Same as Mar. 3, 1969, loan
February 4, 1971	$125,000	Balance due on term loan of Mar. 3, 1969
	$ 78,000	
		Balance due on loan of Mar. 3, 1969
		Balance due on term loan of Mar. 3, 1969
		Balance due on loan of Mar. 3, 1969
		Balance due on term loan of Mar. 3, 1969
		Balance due on loan of Mar. 3, 1969
		Balance due on term loan of Mar. 3, 1969

EXHIBIT 10
Superior Air Conditioners, Inc.
Data on Nonresidential Construction, Jacksonville, Florida
1951-1970
(in millions)

1951	$14,910	1961	$45,898
1952	13,832	1962	35,502
1953	24,264	1963	41,035
1954	41,890	1964	44,795
1955	31,575	1965	75,768
1956	27,479	1966	46,306
1957	31,590	1967	68,668
1958	42,234	1968	81,095
1959	38,137	1969	77,922
1960	49,807	1970	70,135

average 1951-1960 = $31,590
average 1961-1970 = $58,712

Source: Jacksonville Area Chamber of Commerce, Research Department, January 1971.

QUESTIONS

1. Outline the major factors affecting Gator National Bank's relationship to Superior Air Conditioners, Inc., from 1964 to 1971.
2. What responsibility, if any, does GNB have toward Superior?
3. What profitability should GNB expect from the Superior account? What are the risks in either accepting or rejecting the requested loan?
4. As Mr. Kirksey, write a report on the loan proposal of Superior. In the report, outline the various alternatives available to the bank. Choose an alternative course of action and provide support for your choice.

Case 26
Advanced Computer Systems, Inc.

In May 1976, Messrs. John Fitzpatrick, Walter Bernstein, and William Gibbons were reviewing the current status of Advanced Computer Systems, Inc. (Adcomp), in contemplation of an important new financing step. The three men were the principal officers and owners of Adcomp. They had before them the latest financial statements and a commitment letter outlining the terms of the financing proposal.

Fitzpatrick finally put the papers aside, gazed at the picture of various computer-related products which adorned his well-appointed office, and remarked, "With a $2 million order backlog—more than the $1.8 million sales all of last year—this should be the best year in our history, although you sure can't tell it from the latest financials. The way our orders have been bunched, shipments have been slow and cash is awfully tight again. Lots of hard work went into the large contracts we closed earlier in the year, but it's been mostly engineering. We haven't built much of the hardware yet where the big dollars are in terms of billings.

"In addition, we agreed to the five-year plan involving diversification into several sophisticated product lines. We're adding expensive people, facilities, and overhead."

Bernstein chimed in, "Yes, and if we are to achieve that plan we must commit more dollars to the development work. There are a couple of good technical people available if we have the money to hire them."

Gibbons interrupted with, "I don't see how we can hire more high-priced engineers when I'm having all I can do to meet the payroll now. We've got our suppliers all stretched out and they're screaming for payment. Pretty soon, they'll

This case was prepared by Professor Jack D. Ferner of Babcock Graduate School of Management, Wake Forest University, Winston-Salem, North Carolina, as a basis for classroom discussion and not to illustrate either effective or ineffective handling of an administrative situation.

stop shipping, and then see what happens to the five-year plan. John, we really need that financing."

Fitzpatrick fidgeted for a moment before replying, "I agree we need the cash from the financing, but we already have a lot of debt to service and I'm nervous about taking on more. Do you think we can—safely?"

Advanced Computer Systems, Inc., is a high-technology company engaged in the design and manufacture of minicomputer systems and related peripheral products for sale to industry, science, and medicine.

Company History

Adcomp was founded in October 1967 as an 80% subsidiary of Tennessee Electronic Corporation, a nuclear instrumentation company in Oak Ridge, Tennessee. There were four other founding stockholders of the company: John Fitzpatrick; Dr. Walter Bernstein, who became President and Technical Director; Dr. William Gibbons, Vice President and General Manager; and Mr. Norman Hall, another scientist who never took an active role.

For several years prior to the formation of the company, Drs. Bernstein and Gibbons had worked with nuclear instrumentation systems at the Oak Ridge National Laboratory where they were experimental physicists. They participated in the rapid growth of small computer systems in scientific instrumentation. It was evident to the founders that the rapidly falling price and versatility of the storage program logic of the small computer made it ideally suited to many applications. At the time of Adcomp's founding, there was no commercial source for a complete computer-oriented analytical instrumentation system, although an increasing number of such systems are being constructed on a "do it yourself" basis. The founders thought that the time was ripe for offering a modular system which would take advantage of their accumulated experience. With this background, Adcomp was formed in 1967.

The company's first product was a nuclear pulse height analysis system used in nuclear research and industrial applications. Most of the company's first year was spent designing and testing the company's first minicomputer system, the TP-1000, and associated peripheral devices and software to support the system.

The peripheral components that were developed included a small cartridge-type magnetic tape recorder, an operator-oriented control panel, an automatic loading and starting device, a light pen, several display systems, and interfaces with various other instrumentation. The company's first sales were to universities and governmental agencies.

In 1968-69, the Vietnam buildup had depressed nuclear research, and as a result, Tennessee Electronics began to experience falling sales and mounting operating losses. Thus the parent company could not supply Adcomp with the management time, sales support, and services that were originally envisioned. Divestment was agreed to by all parties, and as a result, Mr. Fitzpatrick's offer to buy out Tennessee Electronic's 80% interest in Adcomp for $80,000 in installment notes was accepted.

Free of Tennessee Electronic's marketing organization, which was entirely in the nuclear field, Adcomp was able to seek wider markets. Rapid growth followed as industrial and medical markets were opened up, until these segments of the business became 75%-80% of total sales. The company has seen rising sales and profits in all years except one, 1972, when the electronics industry in general, and computer firms specifically, suffered a recession, and there was a drastic shake-out of marginal firms. (See Exhibits 1 and 2 for historical financial statements.)

Investment and Growth Philosophy

The company's 1967 "Corporate Mission" was stated:

"To invest in any area of suitable profit and growth potential in which Adcomp Systems has or can acquire the technical and marketing capabilities and which involves customers solving problems through the use of dedicated minicomputers and related peripheral equipment."

The owners of Adcomp believe strongly in the potential that exists for their product line as well as their technical abilities. In approaching the market, they chose a strategy of diversification rather than specialization. This strategy is intended to protect against overreliance on a single customer, changing economic conditions and government priorities, and product obsolescence.

In carrying out this mission, the owners have tended to avoid large amounts of equity funds, and thus suffer substantial dilution. Their opinion is that reckless growth and investment can be risky and are what produced the inevitable disaster in 1972 when hundreds of electronics and computer-related firms failed or were assimilated by other companies.

Nonetheless, at the end of 1975, management viewed the prospects for the company to be excellent. After a careful evaluation of their technical capabilities, the needs in the marketplace and the competitive factors, they adopted an ambitious five-year plan which would require additional financing. Exhibit 3 is a summary of this plan, showing sales and profit projections.

Company's Product Lines

1. **Nuclear Systems**
   Management states that Adcomp is recognized as a pioneer in this field and enjoys a growing position of leadership as physicists become aware of the advanced system hardware and software programming the company offers.

2. **Peripheral Products**
   Adcomp developed a line of low-cost peripheral devices to support its original TP-1000 system, and these products represent a significant portion of the company's total sales. The most widely sold item in this line has been a magnetic tape unit used for data input/output and data storage.

3. **Special Systems**
   These systems are designed to fit a customer's specific data handling problems. The design and manufacture of these systems represents a substantial part of the company's business volume, and although this

product line involves committing resources to "one of a kind" efforts, it can lead to solutions of more universal problems and is looked upon as a feeder in establishing "standard systems" for much wider markets. The most recent example was a $732,000 sale to TVA for a reactor safety control system, which may ultimately become a standard system for sale to the entire utility industry.

4. **Medical Systems**

   Adcomp designed and constructed the first data acquisition/analysis systems for the Body Fluids Analysis System developed at Oak Ridge National Laboratory. Adcomp was approached by most of the large pharmaceutical and instrument manufacturing firms interested in this field and ultimately signed a long-term manufacturing agreement with American Instrument Company. Adcomp has delivered over 75 of these "Rotochem" systems, which are marketed throughout the world by AMINCO.

5. **Environmental Systems**

   Monitoring air and water quality on a continuous basis has become a required activity in many industries. The most stringent quality requirements relate to the nuclear power industry. Adcomp developed an Isotopic Indentification System and supporting software programs. Important sales have been made to Radiation Management, Inc., Utah State Division of Health, and Allied General Nuclear Services.

6. **Fiber Optics System**

   This system employs glass fibers developed by Corning Glass to communicate mass amounts of computer data optically rather than by present conductive wire transmissions. Adcomp has developed a pilot system which communicates 500 feet over a varied environment. This has already led to two contracts to develop larger systems, one with Arnold Research Center for a 7,000-foot underground data link between two computer facilities.

Operations

Adcomp's operations include engineering capabilities and a development laboratory containing a sizable amount of electronic and computer gear. R&D is budgeted for $150,000 in 1976.

In addition, there are facilities for light fabrication and assembly of components. Much of the work, however, is subcontracted. Buyouts (the company's term for purchased components) are estimated to account for 60% of the cost of goods sold.

The company has historically grown in a series of leased quarters and occupies space in two buildings approximately one-half mile apart, both in Oak Ridge, Tennessee. Recognizing the inefficiency of cramped and spread-out quarters, the Board decided to construct a new building which would provide for more orderly expansion and bring all employees under one roof.

Sales of standardized products are made through an international network of manufacturers' representatives who are paid on a commission basis. The company's product managers, however, deal extensively with customers when custom designs or special problems are involved.

Management

The company has grown for seven years with its original management, although introduction of a new professional manager-chief executive has been under consideration for some time by the Board. Dr. Bernstein served as President since the founding of the company and managed its day-to-day affairs until 1972. At that time, Dr. Gibbons, Vice President, was given the additional duties of General Manager, responsible for day-to-day operations, in order to free Dr. Bernstein for product development and sale of special systems. In May 1969, when Mr. Fitzpatrick acquired the major interest in Adcomp, he became Chairman of the Board and Treasurer. Mr. Fitzpatrick's role is only part-time, his main occupation being President of another corporation in Oak Ridge. Nevertheless, he spends many evening and weekend hours on Adcomp business. Together, Messrs. Bernstein, Gibbons, and Fitzpatrick own over 90% of the outstanding stock in the company.

Adcomp management prides itself in discriminating selection of technically qualified people. The company presently employs 50 people, half of whom hold college degrees; four are Ph.D.s; and five hold Masters' degrees in technical or business fields.

Financial Performance

The company's audited balance sheets and income statements for the past seven years are summarized in Exhibits 1 and 2. Pro forma financial statements for the next five years (1976-1980) are summarized in Exhibit 3. Internal, unaudited statements for the four months ending April 30 are shown in Exhibits 4 and 5.

With the exception of 1972, the performance trends are upward. Net worth advanced from $50,000 to $465,000 by December 31, 1975. The company's return on net worth ranged between 20% and 40%, and return on sales has been between 5% and 10%. The current ratio has been between 1.35 and 2.64 over five years and was 1.95 at December 31, 1975.

The company's growth has been financed principally from retention of earnings, short-term bank loans, SBA-guaranteed term loans, a mortgage loan, and progress payments from customers:

1. **Equity**

   The company was originally financed through a $100,000 issue of common capital stock with subsequent additions to common stock and paid-in capital accounts totaling $67,000.

   Early development costs resulted in a retained earnings deficit that was not erased until 1971. The recession and resulting loss in 1972 pushed the retained earnings into a deficit position again, but recent profits have been retained in the business and the stockholders' equity has grown to approximately $465,000.

2. **Short-Term Loans**

The company borrows short-term funds from banks to finance temporary working capital needs. For example, in the spring of 1976, the company was enjoying a backlog of about $2 million. Most of the initial work, however, was engineering, with little equipment being shipped. Thus revenue recognized was low (the company recognizes revenue on large contracts on a percentage-of-completion method), and an interim loss occurred. The company currently has $38,000 in notes payable to a local bank.

3. **SBA Guaranteed Loans**

In 1971, the company secured a $260,000 five-year 7% term loan from a local participating bank with a 90% guarantee by the U.S. Small Business Administration (SBA). Payments of $5,149 per month will continue until November 1976, when the loan will be retired. In December 1975, a new loan was negotiated in the principal amount of $370,000, interest 10%, term seven years, equal monthly installments of $6,143 beginning January 31, 1976. The note was secured by the accounts receivable, inventories, and equipment which existed on December 31, 1975, plus the personal guarantees of the officers and their wives.

4. **Mortgage Loan**

Early in May 1976, an arrangement was finalized with a bank and a local development company, Ridge Development Corporation, for the financing of a 15,000-square-foot building. This move will consolidate operations and provide much-needed space for development.

The total cost of the project is estimated at $310,000; the term is for 20 years. The financing was done under the 503 SBA program, which involved 50% bank participation on a first mortgage, 40% SBA participation (second mortgage), and 10% participation by Ridge Development. The average interest rate on the loans is 8¾%, and the monthly payment $3,100. Other than the land, which had been previously acquired, this project and the financing are not reflected on the current financial statements. The design has been completed, foundations started, and the company expects to move into the new premises and begin mortgage payments shortly after the first of 1977.

5. **Proposed Debentures**

In his search for additional financing, Fitzpatrick approached Chadwick Associates, financial consultants, and subsequently the following agreement was entered into:

Dear Mr. Fitzpatrick:
    This letter is to set forth our understanding whereby Chadwick Associates is authorized to act as Adcomp Systems, Inc.'s nonexclusive agent in approaching venture capital firms, investment bankers, and other sophisticated investors for the purpose of securing capital for Adcomp Systems, Inc., along the following lines:

A seven-year $500,000 subordinated debenture; interest only payable quarterly for the first two years at 8%; interest at 10% on the unpaid balance and principal repayments in 20 equal quarterly installments for the next five years. The debenture will have warrants to purchase from 15% to 25% of the company's stock at a nominal cost (15% with $200,000 of after-tax profits in 1976 and 25% with $50,000 of after-tax profits)."

In conversation with the principal, Mr. Cecil Chadwick, Fitzpatrick had been assured that Chadwick had commitments for the funds as outlined. Also, when asked about the possibility of a straight equity issue, Chadwick responded, "Possible, but harder to do in today's market, and if we did, you would have to take a lot more dilution, maybe 50%." Fitzpatrick had been unable to secure a firm commitment for straight equity although he had talked to several parties.

John Fitzpatrick's Background

Fitzpatrick was in his mid-forties. He had been raised in a middle-class family in a small industrial town in Massachusetts. After college, he entered an MBA program. His schooling was interrupted by a two-year stint in the Air Force, where he served as a procurement officer. After receiving his MBA, Fitzpatrick joined a three-man consulting firm which became heavily involved with the shoe industry. He participated in the development of a patented shoe manufacturing system which was marketed in Europe as well as the United States.

He stated that he left this job mostly because his employer refused to let him participate in the ownership of the new process. He then accepted a position as President of a small company in the irradiation business in Oak Ridge, Tennessee. He became active in the community, being appointed Director of the Chamber of Commerce, Director of a venture-capital group, and Director of companies in the electronics and chemical process industries. He was elected "Young Man of the Year" in Oak Ridge and the state of Tennessee. He participated with a small group of businessmen who acquired and then expanded a local bank. Later, the bank was sought after by a large bank in the area, and the group sold out for a handsome profit.

In 1968, Fitzpatrick changed jobs, moving to another company in Oak Ridge. He became President of the company in 1971, and the company prospered under his direction. He invested $50,000 in stock in that company, borrowing the funds. Fitzpatrick acquired his 80% ownership in Adcomp during this period, through an installment purchase.

The Fitzpatrick family had expanded to five children, a dog, a couple of resort properties, a country club membership, a Winnebago, and an antique fire truck. Fitzpatrick was intent on achieving business and financial success. Further, he expressed willingness to assume personal risks and make sacrifices as necessary.

EXHIBIT 1
Adcomp, Inc.
Comparative Balance Sheets (Audited)

	11/30/69 $	11/30/70 $	12/13/71 $	12/31/72 $	12/31/73 $	12/31/74 $	12/31/75 $
ASSETS							
Current Assets:							
Cash	17,509	52,590	225,452	122,143	78,877	88,266	385,323
Accounts Receivable—Net	14,200	68,127	68,784	134,536	337,931	420,583	373,802
Inventories (Note a)	26,006	33,365	46,359	60,387	109,787	153,470	205,190
Prepaid Expenses/Tax Refunds	573	937	—	—	—	—	45,479
Revenues in excess of billings on incompleted contracts (b)	—	43,648	83,708	11,677	115,128	167,462	420,510
Total Current Assets	58,288	198,667	424,303	328,733	641,723	829,781	1,430,304
Equipment/Leaseholds: Net (c)	3,340	9,178	21,342	20,652	18,269	34,677	52,193
Land:	—	—	—	—	—	—	38,350
Deferred Charges:							
Systems Development Costs (d)	35,486	76,091	124,795	124,452	106,262	—	—
Organizational Expense	4,315	2,744	1,043	79	—	—	—
Total Assets	101,429	286,680	571,483	473,916	766,254	864,458	1,520,847

See accompanying Notes to Financial Statements.

(Balance Sheet continues on following page)

EXHIBIT 1
Adcomp, Inc. (continued)
Comparative Balance Sheets (Audited)

	11/30/69 $	11/30/70 $	12/31/71 $	12/31/72 $	12/31/73 $	12/31/74 $	12/31/75 $
LIABILITIES AND STOCKHOLDERS' EQUITY							
Current Liabilities:							
Notes Payable—Current (e)	14,135	73,157	45,277	48,550	56,236	55,823	231,717
Accounts Payable	9,448	25,746	38,713	77,434	241,654	226,003	338,718
Advance Customer Payments	—	—	30,475	—	—	—	—
Accrued Expense	11,474	38,714	27,451	15,836	9,623	28,821	23,389
Income Taxes Payable	—	250	13,200	—	69,470	125,402	—
Deferred Income Taxes (b)	—	9,700	5,800	—	1,090	15,815	141,402
Total Current Liabilities	35,057	147,567	161,006	141,820	378,073	451,864	735,226
Long-Term Debt (f)	—	—	211,091	162,542	110,482	54,659	320,620
Deferred Income Taxes	15,810	39,760	53,460	53,760	53,760	—	—
Stockholders' Equity:							
Common Capital Stock	119,602	120,802	128,312	147,176	151,616	161,061	167,221
Retained Earnings (deficit)	(69,040)	(21,449)	17,614	(31,382)	72,323	196,874	297,780
Total Stockholders' Equity	50,562	99,353	145,926	115,794	223,939	357,935	465,001
Total Liabilities and Stockholders' Equity	101,429	286,680	571,483	473,916	766,254	864,458	1,520,847

See accompanying Notes to Financial Statements.

EXHIBIT 2
Adcomp, Inc.
Comparative Income Statements (Audited)

	8 Mos. Ending 11/30/69 $	12 Mos. Ending 11/30/70 $	13 Mos. Ending 12/31/71 $	12 Mos. Ending 12/31/72 $	12 Mos. Ending 12/31/73 $	12 Mos. Ending 12/31/74 $	12 Mos. Ending 12/31/75 $
Sales—Net (a)	73,791	407,701	712,361	531,465	1,025,248	1,548,527	1,804,097
Cost of Goods Sold	19,613	188,323	347,542	199,983	537,562	831,385	1,054,893
Gross Profit	54,178	219,378	364,819	331,482	487,686	717,142	749,204
Systems Development Expense	—	16,159	66,731	104,365	72,348	62,387	126,963
Marketing Expense	18,589	61,738	118,128	137,014	122,765	162,403	239,046
Gen. & Admin. Expense	28,419	59,990	117,897	143,318	118,308	147,350	197,932
Total Expense	47,008	137,887	302,756	384,697	313,421	372,140	563,941
Income Before Tax & Extraordinary Items	7,170	81,491	62,063	(53,215)	174,265	345,002	185,263
Provision for Income Tax	3,786	40,200	24,300	(15,258)	81,870	167,949	84,357
Income Before Extraordinary Income	3,384	41,291	37,763	(37,957)	92,395	177,053	100,906
Extraordinary Items	—	6,300	1,300	—	11,310	—	—
Net Income (Loss)	3,384	47,591	39,063	(37,957)	103,705	177,053	100,906

See accompanying Notes to Financial Statements

Notes to Financial Statements

(Exhibits 1 and 2)

a. **Inventories**

Inventories are stated at the lower of cost or market. Cost of raw materials used in systems development is determined by the first-in, first-out method. cost of finished goods and work in process is determined by the standard cost method and is substantially actual cost.

Inventories, priced on the basis described above, are summarized as follows:

	1975	1974
Finished goods	$ 69,023	$ 34,707
Work in process	47,672	67,311
Raw materials	88,495	51,452
	$205,190	$153,470

b. **Incompleted Contracts**

Income from incompleted contracts is accounted for using the percentage-of-completion method. Accordingly, revenues are included in sales in the amount of $420,510 for 1975 ($167,462 for 1974) and related costs in the amounts of $224,434 for 1975 ($90,642 for 1974) are included in cost of sales which are applicable to incompleted contacts. For income tax purposes, income is accounted for using the completed-contract method. Deferred income taxes (those contained in current liabilities) are provided for the timing difference.

c. **Equipment and Leaseholds**

Depreciation and amortization are determined principally using the straight-line method and are based on the following estimated useful lives: equipment 3 to 10 years; leasehold improvements 2 years.

d. **Research and Development Costs**

Research and development costs are expensed in the year incurred. In 1975, these costs amounted to $88,172 ($35,005 in 1974).

In prior years, the company's policy was to capitalize research and development costs which were deemed to have continuing value and amortize such costs to income of subsequent years. As required by Statement No. 2 of the Financial Accounting Standards Board, the company has changed its accounting to expense such costs as incurred, and the financial statements of prior years have been restated to apply the new method retroactively. The effect of the accounting change was to reduce net income for 1975 by $26,772 ($.10 per share) and to increase net income for 1974 by $15,499 ($.06 per share).

The balances of retained earnings for 1974 and 1975 have been adjusted for the effect (net of income taxes) of applying retroactively the new method of accounting.

The deferred income taxes in the long-term liability account prior to 1974 account for the timing differences between reporting income incorporating the deferred systems development cost method and tax reporting which does not allow the deferment of such costs (must be expensed in the current year).

e. **Notes Payable—Current**

	1975	1974
Short-term bank loans	$122,875	$ —
Current maturities of long-term debt	108,842	55,823

f. **Long-Term Debt**

Long-term debt consists of the following:

	1975	1974
7% and 10% SBA guaranteed bank loans, due in monthly installments of $5,149 and $6,143, respectively, including interest, through May 1976 and July 1982, collateralized by pledge of accounts receivable, inventories, and equipment having a net cost of $631,185 at June 30, 1975	$429,462	$110,482
Less: Current maturities	108,842	55,823
	$320,620	$ 54,659

EXHIBIT 3

Adcomp, Inc.
Five-Year Corporate Plan
Summary of Sales and Net Income

Pro Forma Income Statements
(000 Omitted)
Year Ending December 31

	Actual	Projections				
	1975 $	1976 $	1977 $	1978 $	1979 $	1980 $
Sales:						
Systems	1,709	2,340	3,040	3,990	4,940	5,890
Peripherals	90	350	450	500	550	600
Other	5	10	10	10	10	10
Total Sales	1,804	2,700	3,500	4,500	5,500	6,500
Cost of Goods Sold:						
Systems	1,005	1,440	1,850	2,410	2,970	3,530
Peripherals	50	135	180	200	220	240
Total COGS	1,055	1,575	2,030	2,610	3,190	3,770
Gross Margin	749	1,125	1,470	1,890	2,310	2,730
Expenses:						
Systems Development Expense	127	150	175	200	225	250
Marketing	239	330	450	630	825	975
G & A	198	300	400	500	600	700
Total Expenses	564	780	1,025	1,330	1,650	1,925
Income Before Taxes	185	345	445	560	660	805
Taxes	84	155	220	260	310	380
Income After Taxes	101	190	225	300	350	425

Note: The complete Five-Year Corporate Plan included a detailed analysis of technical capabilities of Adcomp, the market needs, competitive factors, and sales forecasts and cost estimates by product line.

EXHIBIT 4
Adcomp, Inc.
Balance Sheet
(Unaudited)
April 30, 1976

ASSETS
Current Assets:

Cash		$ 19,537
Accounts Receivable—Net		309,513
Inventories:		
Parts & Materials	$116,093	
Work in progress—systems	49,196	
Work in progress—peripherals	41,384	
Completed systems for resale	69,046	$ 275,719
Prepaid Expenses/Tax Refunds		—
Revenues in excess of billings on incompleted contracts		340,672
Total Current Assets		$ 945,431
Equipment & Leasehold Improvements:		
Manufacturing & test	$ 75,087	
Office furniture & fixtures	14,834	
Less: Accumulated depreciation and amortization	(38,571)	$ 51,350
Land		$ 38,350
Deferred Charges		—
Total Assets		$1,035,131

LIABILITIES & STOCKHOLDERS' EQUITY
Current Liabilities:

Notes Payable—Current	$ 38,000	
Current maturities of long-term debt	52,857	
Accounts Payable	161,123	
Advance Customer Payments	—	
Accrued expense	(5)	
Sales commissions payable	13,479	
Income Taxes Payable	(45,479)	
Deferred Income Taxes	141,402	
Total Current Liabilities		$ 361,377
Long-Term Debt		307,887
Deferred Income Taxes		—
Stockholders' Equity:		
Common Capital Stock	$167,221	
Retained Earnings—prior years	297,780	
—current year (loss)	(99,134)	$ 365,867
Total Liabilities and Stockholders' Equity		$1,035,131

EXHIBIT 5

Adcomp, Inc.
Statement of Income
(Unaudited)
Four Months Ending April 30, 1976

Revenues:			
Sales:			
Systems	$264,084		
Peripherals	20,518		
Less: Discounts & Allowances	(13,943)		
Net Sales	$270,659		
Other income	1,402		$272,061
Cost of Sales:			
Systems:			
Materials	$ 93,644		
Production Labor	16,721		
Engineering Labor	21,172		
Quality Control	4,271		
Other Direct Costs	8,438		
Direct Overhead	16,498	$160,744	
Peripherals:			
Materials	$ 5,228		
Direct Labor	2,311		
Other Direct Costs	—		
Direct Overhead	920	$ 8,459	
Other Costs & Expenses:			
Manufacturing:			
Indirect and Nonchargeable labor	$ 12,119		
Consultants	—		
Payroll Taxes	2,667		
Group Insurance	1,072		
Travel	—		
Rent	2,517		
Instruction Manuals	—		
Equipment Lease & Rental	—		
Expendable Tools & Equipment	388		
Supplies & Expense	3,544		
Freight In	1,632		
Product Support	1,146		
Depreciation & Amortization	2,525		
Under (Over) Absorbed Labor	(134)		
Overhead Applied	(26,635)	$ 1,109	$170,302
Gross Profit on Sales			$101,759
Other Expenses:			
Research & Development	$ 32,470		
Marketing Expense	92,424		
General & Administrative	76,223		$201,117
Net Income (Loss) Before Income Taxes			$(99,358)
Income Tax Expense			—
Net Income (Loss)			$(99,358)

QUESTIONS

1. Why is Adcomp short of cash despite its profitable operations over the past several years?
2. If Adcomp were to achieve its five-year projections, what additional capital needs would it have?
3. Is the debt position of Adcomp too high? What is the optimal level?
4. Should Fitzpatrick go ahead with the issue of debentures? If not, what alternatives would you suggest?

Case 27
Truss Joist Corporation

I. Introduction—Company History

Harold Thomas and Art Troutner organized Truss Joist Corporation in 1960 with $8,000 in cash plus some homemade machinery and a small amount of lumber. Troutner, an architect and builder, had invented a new roof and floor joist consisting of 2″ x 4″ lumber chords supported by tubular steel webs. Thomas and Troutner called the invention an "L joist" and felt that the joist was structurally superior to other joists then available. Additionally, Thomas was a lumber distributor and salesman and predicted that there was a potentially large market for the new joist.

This prediction has proven to be accurate as Truss Joist's sales volume grew rapidly from $49,000 in 1960 to $11.8 million in 1969. During the 1960's, the company developed and successfully marketed a medium and a heavy series of open web joists and in 1969 introduced a solid plywood web joist (called the I joist) that also was well received by the light construction industry. In 1970, Troutner invented a new process (called MICRO-LAM) designed to convert thin layers of lower-quality veneers into a high-quality billet, 1½″ thick. In 1973, the total output of the MICRO-LAM production was utilized by the company in the manufacture of the I joist, but management believes that MICRO-LAM lumber could be eventually marketed by the company as a final product.

The development of the I joist and the MICRO-LAM process further strengthened the company's market position and annual sales expanded to over $40

This case was prepared by Professor Dennis B. Fitzpatrick of Boise State University as a basis for classroom discussion and not to illustrate either effective or ineffective handling of an administrative situation.

million in 1973 (see Table 1). Although the company's sales are directly dependent on the underlying economic strength of the light construction industry, annual sales have declined only once since Truss Joist was organized in 1960. The company has relied heavily on its ability to continually increase its market share in order to offset the cyclical nature of the building industry.

TABLE 1
Truss Joist Corporation
Annual Sales (1968-1973)

Year	Net Sales *(continuing operations)*	Percent Change from *Preceding Year*
1968	$ 7,922,410	
1969	11,760,967	48.45
1970	11,292,959	-3.98
1971	17,684,101	56.59
1972	26,988,696	52.62
1973	40,928,782	51.65

II. Marketing Strategy and Competitive Forces

Truss Joist products are proprietary and consequently not produced or sold by competitors.[1] However, the company's joists compete directly with other types of roof and floor structural components. Consequently, Truss Joist's competitors number in the thousands, the great majority of which are relatively small. If all manufacturers of floor and roof structural systems utilized in light construction were to be considered as competitors, the company's sales would represent a very small fraction of the combined sales of its competitors. Additionally, many of these competitors have sales volume that substantially exceeds Truss Joist's 1973 net sales.

Consequently, management believes that the potential market for the company's products is still largely untapped. For example, as much as 25% of all buildings in the light construction class in certain areas of the western United States utilize Truss Joist products, while market penetration in the eastern United States for the most part is less than 1%.

The management of the company decided several years ago that promotion and sales efforts should be directed principally to architects and structural engineers. Peter T. Johnson, Truss Joist President, is convinced that the company's joists are superior in quality to alternative structural components available, and the architects and structural engineers have a great deal of discretion concerning building materials used in light construction projects. As a result, Johnson feels that the basic objective of the company's marketing efforts should be the education of architects and structural engineers concerning the increased quality and cost savings inherent in Truss Joist products. To achieve this goal, the company employs 90 salesmen, 35 independent sales agents, and 65 distributor employees. These

[1]The company has several patents on the design of its joists, manufacturing processes, and some of the machinery used in the manufacture of its products.

people operate from 80 offices located throughout the continental United States and western Canada.

In addition to the large potential domestic market for Truss Joist products, Johnson and Thomas are convinced that the international markets in Great Britain, Europe, and possibly Asia should be carefully appraised for possible penetration. Thomas has made several exploratory trips to these areas and is confident that the British and the European market for structural joists may be profitably exploited at some future time.

III. Sales Forecast and Capital Expenditure Plans: 1974-1978

During December, 1973, Peter Johnson and Walt Wadman, Treasurer, decided jointly that a decision must be made concerning the appropriate mix of financing the company should employ over the next five years. Johnson felt that although the company's marketing strategy had enabled Truss Joist to grow rapidly, the company's future ability to tap external sources of financing would be critical to future expansion plans.

Wadman felt that forecasts of the company's long-range financial requirements must be based on sales projections and the company's capital expenditure plans. Wadman anticipated that sales were likely to increase from approximately $45 million in 1974 to $120 million by 1978, a 67 percent increase (see Table 2). He also felt that income (after taxes) as a percent of net sales should increase gradually from approximately 4.1 percent in 1973 to 5.0 percent in 1978, due primarily to increasing production efficiencies.

In order to achieve this increase in revenues by 1978, Wadman predicted that the company would have to embark on a capital expenditure program totaling over $21 million from 1974 to 1978 (see Table 3). This money would be spent principally in the construction of new manufacturing plants in California, Texas, Pennsylvania, and at an undetermined eastern Canada location. (In 1973, Truss Joist operated ten manufacturing plants located throughout the United States and one in Alberta, Canada.) Johnson was in fundamental agreement with Wadman's sales projections and capital expenditure plans but was concerned that a severe economic slump in the light construction industry in 1974 and 1975 might exert negative pressure on the company's sales volume. Johnson also noted that the company was highly dependent on a limited number of suppliers of machine stress rated lumber. The demand for this type of lumber was beginning to outpace the supply by late 1973, and Johnson felt that serious consideration should be given to vertically integrating their operations to include the production of high-quality lumber employed in the production of the company's joists.

IV. Availability and Costs of External Financing

Wadman felt that financing costs associated with expanding the company's operations, although uncertain, would continue to be relatively high. By early 1974, Truss Joist's common stock was not actively traded on either an exchange or in the over-the-counter market, and management felt that most of these transactions were consummated at a price per share of 15 to 20 times current earnings. The price of the

TABLE 2
Subjective Probability Distribution of Sales Projections*
1974-1978

Year	Probability (Pi)	Net Sales (in millions of $)
1974	.10	35.0
	.20	40.0
	.40	45.0
	.20	50.0
	.10	55.0
1975	.10	40.0
	.20	50.0
	.40	60.0
	.20	65.0
	.10	70.0
1976	.10	65.0
	.20	74.0
	.40	78.0
	.20	80.0
	.10	85.0
1977	.10	85.0
	.20	95.0
	.40	100.0
	.20	110.0
	.10	130.0
1978	.10	100.0
	.20	110.0
	.40	120.0
	.20	135.0
	.10	150.0

*These sales projections are hypothetical.

TABLE 3
Five-Year Capital Expenditure Plan*
1974-1978

(in thousands of $)

Expenditures on:

Year	Land	Buildings	Machinery	Office Equipment	Total
1974	285	1,614	1,399	44	3,342
1975	450	2,887	1,461	62	4,860
1976	150	1,700	1,975	75	3,900
1977	350	2,250	1,275	60	3,935
1978	500	2,600	1,800	100	5,000

*Company's buildings are depreciated on a straight-line basis for 30 years; other depreciable assets are depreciated on a double-declining basis for 8 years.

common stock was determined to be trading at: bid $14½, ask $15½. In 1972, Wadman had arranged an 8⅝ percent loan for $3 million directly from a large insurance company. Truss Joist was obligated to repay the loan in equal $200,000 annual installments from 1975 to 1987, with a balloon payment of $400,000 in 1988. The company also has approximately $1.5 million in intermediate and long-term notes outstanding, with an average interest cost of 7½ percent (see Tables 4 and 5 for 1971-1973 financial statements).

Some consideration had been given to a public offering of common stock, but Wadman felt that the stock should be sold at a price of at least 20 times current earnings. Floating stock at a lower price would unduly dilute the equity position of present stockholders. Wadman knew, however, that the sale of new common stock at a P/E multiple of as much as 15 did not appear likely in view of the depressed stock market conditions of early 1974. He also felt that Truss Joist could secure an additional $1 million from short-term bank loans. Any additional capital could be raised in privately placed insurance company loans with maturities of 5 and 15 years and with sales/leaseback agreements. Wadman predicted that long-term interest rates were likely to range between 9 percent and 11 percent during the next five years.

TABLE 4
Truss Joist Corporation
Balance Sheets
1971-1973

	1971	*1972*	*1973*
ASSETS			
Current Assets:			
Cash	$ 52,089	$ 476,368	$ 809,168
Marketable securities, at cost	—	299,765	—
Receivables, less reserves of $36,178, $54,400 and $100,000	1,820,478	2,506,498	3,707,497
Inventories, at lower of cost or market	1,470,652	2,473,440	3,249,475
Prepaid expenses	56,385	174,695	24,663
	$3,399,604	$ 5,930,766	$ 7,790,803
Property, Plant and Equipment:			
Land	$ 198,533	$ 267,559	$ 473,524
Machinery and equipment	1,931,000	2,888,046	4,020,252
Autos and trucks	92,650	134,910	151,509
Buildings and leasehold improvements	2,064,415	3,521,031	4,185,251
Office equipment	207,542	266,038	800,956
	$4,494,140	$ 7,077,584	$ 9,631,492
Less—Accumulated depreciation	1,142,784	1,661,062	2,501,817
	$3,351,356	$ 5,416,522	$ 7,129,675
Other Assets:			
Goodwill	$ 158,802	$ 146,604	—
Other	107,637	141,139	244,545
	$ 266,439	$ 287,743	$ 244,545
	$7,017,399	$11,635,031	$15,165,023
LIABILITIES AND STOCKHOLDERS' EQUITY			
Current Liabilities:			
Notes payable	$ 302,378	$ —	$ 275,000
Current portion of long-term debt	213,589	135,182	231,107
Accounts payable	939,353	1,505,825	1,893,561
Accrued liabilities	459,899	747,358	1,313,881
Income taxes payable	243,491	526,189	777,984
	$2,158,710	$ 2,914,554	$ 4,491,533
Long-Term Debt, net of current portion shown above	$1,516,039	$ 4,319,550	$ 4,282,444
Stockholders' Equity:			
Common stock, par value $1.00, authorized 10,000,000 shares, outstanding 315,086, 317,512, and 1,691,785*	$ 315,086	$ 317,512	$ 1,691,785
Paid-in capital	956,128	975,862	9,029
Retained earnings	2,096,186	3,132,303	4,690,232
	$3,367,400	$ 4,425,677	$ 6,391,046
Less—Treasury stock, at cost, 1,320 shares	24,750	24,750	—
	$3,342,650	$ 4,400,927	$ 6,391,046
	$7,017,399	$11,635,031	$15,165,023

*After 5 for 1 split in June, 1973.

TABLE 5
Truss Joist Corporation
Income Statements
1971-1973

	1971	1972	1973
Net Sales	$17,775,240	$26,988,696	$40,928,782
Cost of Sales	$11,838,286	$18,292,315	$28,075,659
Selling Expenses	2,407,887	3,677,531	5,452,779
General and Administrative Expenses	2,123,350	2,856,611	3,784,116
Interest	124,528	187,122	438,920
Total costs and expenses	$16,494,051	$25,013,579	$37,751,474
Income before provision for income taxes and extraordinary item	$ 1,281,189	$ 1,975,117	$ 3,177,308
Provision for Income Taxes:			
Federal	$ 578,814	$ 907,000	$ 1,476,000
State	68,268	112,000	127,000
Investment tax credit	(24,146)	(80,000)	(115,000)
	$ 622,936	$ 939,000	$ 1,488,000
Net income before extraordinary item	$ 658,253	$ 1,036,117	$ 1,689,308
Extraordinary Item	(102,519)	—	—
Net income	$ 555,734	$ 1,036,117	$ 1,689,308
Earnings Per Share, restated for 5 for 1 stock split in 1973:			
Income before extraordinary item	$ .40	$ .61	$ .96
Extraordinary item	(.06)	—	—
Net income per share	$ .34	$ .61	$ .96

QUESTIONS

1. What are the long-term financial requirements of Truss Joist Corporation?
2. Evaluate the various sources of capital for the company, giving consideration to the effect of these sources on the firm's capital structure.
3. As Mr. Wadman, what course of action would you recommend? Support your recommendation.

Case 28
Phoenix Aircraft Company

In May, 1966, Mr. John Larson, president of Phoenix Aircraft Company, was preparing a proposal to present at the June meeting of the board of directors concerning how to finance $40 million in long-term funds needed for working capital, plant expansion, and other purposes over the next several years. After conferring with his senior vice president of finance, he had narrowed the possible sources of funds down to debt instruments, but the questions of what form this debt should take and the date of issue were yet to be decided.

The past three years had brought spectacular growth to Phoenix, with dollar sales doubling in the period from 1963 to 1966 (estimated), thereby creating pressing new needs for additional funds. A larger pool of long-term money was needed to support rising working capital requirements. This would allow the retirement of substantial short-term bank borrowing. Outstanding short-term bank loans had risen to $8.4 million as of the fiscal year ended September 30, 1965, and the combination of short-term bank loans and commercial paper had risen to $16 million by March 31, 1966 (Exhibit 1). The company was also engaged in an expansion program to enlarge the plant and equipment needed to meet increased sales demands and to introduce new production models. Expansion plan commitments for 1966 and 1967 alone entailed the addition of nearly one million square feet of plant space to existing facilities in Columbus at a cost of $11 million,

This case was prepared by Professor George Robert Sanderson of San Jose State University and Alan B. Coleman, Dean and Caruth Professor of Financial Management, School of Business Administration, Southern Methodist University as a basis for classroom discussion and not to illustrate either effective or ineffective handling of an administrative situation. Reprinted from *Stanford Business Cases, 1969* with the permission of the Publishers, Stanford University Graduate School of Business © 1969, by the Board of Trustees for the Leland Stanford Junior University.

in addition to new machinery and equipment costing about $12 million. Part of these funds would be provided from profits (profits had nearly tripled in four years, going from $5.1 million in 1963 to an estimated $14 million in 1966, as shown in Exhibits 2 to 4), but outside sources were needed to supplement flows into retained earnings. In his latest evaluation of these needs, Mr. Larson had decided that a total of $40 million of long-term capital within two years would be adequate to finance this growth.

Management believed that the company's outlook for the future was bright. The company's main thrust was in the general aviation market, which included all civil flying except that of public air carriers. The total time accumulated in general aviation flying in the United States had grown very rapidly in the postwar years, to the point that general aviation averaged nearly four times the total scheduled flying time each year of domestic airline transports. Total industry sales of general aircraft had spurted in recent years, rising from $125 million in 1961 to nearly $320 million in 1965, with projections pointed steadily upward. Phoenix officers foresaw in the future a continued strong economy, with rising discretionary incomes and increased leisure time, all of which would contribute to expanding demands for business and pleasure flying.

In 1966, Phoenix was one of the top three manufacturers of general aviation aircraft for the 21st consecutive year. Out of all the light aircraft flying in the United States in 1966, Phoenix claimed nearly one-fourth of the total small aircraft. Phoenix had first been incorporated in Ohio in the 1920's. Prior to World War II, the company had manufactured several types of small aircraft, principally the Skychief, a single-engine, four-place, cantilever-wing plane. During World War II, the company produced twin-engine trainer aircraft for the United States government. After the war, Phoenix reentered the private and business aircraft fields, retaining some government business while at the same time starting to diversify.

The company's marketing strategy was to maintain a balanced mix of commercial and military business to hedge against any downturn in defense expenditures. The company had also been able to diversify through acquisitions of existing companies. For example, Phoenix had acquired manufacturers of aircraft accessories, airborne communication and navigation equipment, and fluid power components for industrial equipment. By 1965, two-thirds of sales resulted from commercial aircraft, 15% were in government business, and the rest came from other lines of manufacture.

In looking at its future business mix, the Phoenix management foresaw a continued rapid increase in government orders due to the war in Vietnam. The company's policy in the past with respect to government contracts had been to bid only on work that could be performed with existing engineering and manufacturing facilities. As a result, sales to the United States government and to foreign governments over the past few years, which had been substantial, were regular commercial aircraft models. By May, 1966, the backlog on government work had grown to $21 million and was rising rapidly, with approximately 75% of this backlog in prime contracts and 25% in subcontracts.

Phoenix maintained a centralized manufacturing center, producing all its aircraft in company plants near Columbus, Ohio. Most component parts of the aircraft were fabricated by Phoenix. Those components that were not company-produced were purchased from independent sources.

Phoenix maintained a separate marketing division for commercial aircraft. Made up of 300 employees, the division conducted marketing research and established sales promotion and advertising programs for the network of distributors and dealers. Generally, sales were made directly to franchised distributors who had developed some 460 dealers in the United States and 110 in foreign countries. These dealers sold aircraft as well as providing flight instruction, servicing, and other ground support services. The company's capable marketing organization, which had conducted such successful promotional campaigns as the $5 first flight lesson, helped Phoenix meet active competition in the production and sale of general aviation aircraft. In addition to this strong network of distributors and dealers, the company had developed a reputation for producing quality products, with good engineering and design, all of which contributed to maintaining its prominent position in the industry.

From 1962 to 1966, Phoenix produced about one-third of the industry's total unit output and dollar value. The other two large competitors together accounted for one-half of unit output and one-half of dollar volume for the industry. Phoenix also encountered strong competition in government business, where many of its competitors were corporations with total sales and resources far in excess of those of Phoenix. These competitors were at the same time customers buying various Phoenix products.

In order to assist dealers in financing its inventory and to provide retail financing, Phoenix established in 1957 a wholly owned unconsolidated finance subsidiary, Phoenix Finance Company, Inc. (P.F.C.) which contributed greatly to Phoenix's aircraft sales and was growing rapidly. At fiscal year-end 1965, P.F.C.'s net notes receivable were $14.9 million, up 45% from the prior year (Exhibit 5). By the spring of 1966, these notes receivable had risen to about $25 million. Phoenix's investment in P.F.C., stated at cost plus undistributed earnings, totaled $3.3 million on September 30, 1965, and was expected to rise by more than $2 million by September 30, 1966, to support P.F.C.'s rapid rate of growth. In late 1965, after the close of the 1965 fiscal year, P.F.C. had negotiated with two insurance companies a 12-year $5.5 million unsecured loan, which was not guaranteed by Phoenix. In 1965, P.F.C.'s net earnings rose by 40% to $180,000.

P.F.C.'s earnings growth in 1966 was expected to be interrupted because of a temporary lag in realizing the benefits from increased rates charged by P.F.C. and from the higher level of receivables as compared with the more immediate effect of recent high money costs to P.F.C. and greater acquisition costs.

In the examination of alternative methods of financing the $40 million long-term capital needs, a new issue of common stock was considered, but it was generally agreed that at existing stock prices the dilution of earnings per share would be prohibitively high. The two most promising alternatives remaining were some form of long-term debt, either straight debt or convertible debt.

After discussion of these issues with Kidder, Peabody & Co., Incorporated, the investment bankers with whom the Phoenix management had built up a close relationship over the years, the following possibilities stood out as the best alternatives for the board of directors to consider:

A. The sale in 1966 of either:
   1. A straight debt issue of $20 million taking the form of:
      a) A private placement with a New York insurance company, or
      b) A public issue underwritten by a syndicate headed by Kidder, Peabody & Co.
   2. A $20 million public issue of convertible debt, convertible into common stock at a price 20% above the common price at the time of the offering, to be sold by the syndicate.
B. An issue next year for $20 million in the form of the instrument not used this year.

Members of the Phoenix management appreciated the possible advantages of these different financial methods, and it was planned to present the alternatives to the board of directors for their consideration. Several persons who had studied this problem and discussed the alternatives with Kidder, Peabody & Co. felt that a $20 million straight debt issue should be sold immediately, to be followed by a $20 million convertible issue to be sold approximately one year later. Other company officers, backed by the opinion of a different investment banking house, believed the company should reverse the order. That is, Phoenix should sell the convertible debt now and wait one year before issuing the $20 million of straight debt. Another possibility raised was to issue the entire $40 million package in one bundle, either immediately or in one year.

Several points of speculation about future conditions concerned Mr. Larson as he grappled with these strategic timing questions. Sales and earnings had grown rapidly over the past few years, with profits after taxes projected to increase more than 250% over 1963 profits. In projecting these sales and earnings into the future, Mr. Larson was trying to determine whether the slope of the earnings line would be a straight extension of the trend, would increase faster than the recent past performance, or would increase less rapidly. As president of the company, his outlook for the future was generally very optimistic, with continued increases foreseen in sales demand. But Phoenix would encounter several special operating problems in the near future. The company was planning to introduce three new small aircraft models over the next two years, possibly involving high start-up production and marketing costs. Capacity production levels were being approached in nearly every facility, causing increases in overtime hours and shortages in strategic components. Moreover, the completion of the new Columbus plant was slated for the coming year, possibly involving high moving expenses and initial costs. On the other hand, aggregate disposable income within the economy had continued to post strong gains in the past few months, which normally would mean higher demand for Phoenix airplanes. Government orders due to the Vietnam War were also being stepped up, thus expanding Phoenix's sales of trainers and light observation aircraft.

Exhibit 4 presents management's projected increase in sales through 1968. In this exhibit, earnings were projected to expand in proportion to sales. As a first approximation, changes in current assets and liabilities were also projected to increase proportionately to sales. The other items shown seemed reasonable in the light of management plans. For the reasons indicated in the preceding paragraph, there was considerably more uncertainty with respect to the earnings estimates than to the anticipated increase in sales and consequent changes in current assets and current liabilities.

Mr. Larson was also concerned about whether the price of the company's common stock would increase in proportion to the anticipated rise in earnings. He did not know the degree to which the current stock price already reflected the outlook for improved earnings. Recent stock prices and price-earnings ratios are given in Exhibit 6. In any event, Mr. Larson knew that continued increases in stock prices would be essential to the success of a convertible issue. A higher market price for the common stock at the time the convertible was issued would mean less dilution when the bonds were ultimately exchanged for stock, as is illustrated by Exhibit 7. Moreover, a further increase in the common stock price after the convertible issue would permit early retirement of the outstanding debt, thereby reducing interest payments by Phoenix and, more importantly, lowering the relatively high debt ratio. Mr. Larson tried to consider all these factors and their implications in determining the timing and sequence in which to issue the straight and the convertible debt.

Phoenix's debt policy had been discussed many times before by the board of directors, and Mr. Larson knew that several questions concerning the new capital proposal would be raised at the coming meeting. The outstanding long-term debt had never exceeded $10 million. The projected $10 million in new debt issues would therefore represent a major shift in capital structure policy. As additional information, Kidder, Peabody & Co. had provided the ratios of similar companies that had recently sold new debt issues (Exhibit 8). The high debt position of the unconsolidated finance subsidiary, P.F.C., made the burden of the proposed $40 million of new debt financing seem even heavier. As of September 30, 1965, P.F.C. had $11 million of bank debt and commercial paper outstanding (Exhibit 5). These obligations had grown somewhat during 1966; and in addition, P.F.C. had negotiated the $5.5 million term loan, previously described, in late 1965.

In the light of these facts, Mr. Larson knew that he would be called upon to demonstrate the need for the planned large increase in external capital and to justify the reasons for raising it in the form of debt. He planned to emphasize the rapid past and projected increase in sales, which would have the effect of raising the sales-to-debt ratio and of diminishing the relative burden of the proposed debt issues in comparison with historical figures. Mr. Larson could see no other means of meeting the financial needs created by expanding sales without a very large dilution of earnings per share. More plant and equipment and a greater working capital base clearly were required. Mr. Larson also knew that the stockholders would expect dividends on the common stock to be maintained at their present level of $1.15 per share and to be increased if earnings rose as projected.

The additional leverage provided by debt in raising future earnings per share seemed attractive to Mr. Larson. Nonetheless, he remained concerned about the question of excessive risk due to high debt obligations and the burden of mandatory interest and sinking fund payments. This risk was further compounded by the possibility of a "frozen convertible" if the stock price failed to perform as hoped.

The crucial nature of timing the company's entry into the bond market brought up the question of future interest rates. The total dollar interest cost of the proposed debt over the next 20 to 25 years would vary depending upon the rate demanded in the money markets at time of issue. (See Exhibit 9.) Interest rates on a convertible debenture normally ran about 1% less than the rate paid on straight debt. Since interest costs would affect company earnings up until conversion, thereby affecting the company's stock price, the Phoenix management was attempting to anticipate the direction and movement of interest rates in the relatively near term future. Corporate bond yields were rising steadily in the months preceding May, 1966, and were approaching record levels. Whether interest rates would continue to climb or had already reached their peak seemed uncertain. A survey of capital spending plans reported in *The Monthly Economic Letter* of the First National City Bank of New York showed that business outlays were slated to increase on new plant and equipment in the near future and that backlogs of unfilled orders for durable goods were lengthening. These pressures had tended to reverse the decline in interest rates that occurred in mid-March of 1966, causing rates to climb during April. Mr. Larson was well aware that the current rate of about 5.8% on corporate bonds of a quality similar to the prospective Phoenix issue was the highest he had encountered in the last 35 years, but the prospect of still higher rates in the future made the postponement of the debt issue seem even less attractive.   ·

In addressing himself to the remaining question of whether the straight debt issue should be publicly or privately placed. Mr. Larson outlined the differences in terms of the two debt issues. Since the analysts at Kidder, Peabody & Co. were most familiar with the acceptable design of debt instruments under the latest market conditions, Mr. Larson asked for an appraisal of the most important differing features between a public offering of senior debentures and a private placement of senior notes. Assuming that both these debt issues would be for the same amount, i.e, $20 million, the maturity of the private placement would probably be 20 years, whereas the maturity date of the public offering of senior debentures would be 25 years. The coupon interest rates would be nearly the same, about 5¾%, plus or minus ⅛%-¼%, depending on the immediate market conditions, with the slight possibility that the public offering might be somewhat less than the private placement. The spread by the investment banker would be ⅜% on the private placement and 1¼% on the public issue. The length of nonrefundability at a lower interest cost on the debentures would be 5 years, whereas the privately placed notes would be nonrefundable for 10 years. The private issue with a financial institution might involve some restrictions on the amount of subordinated debt and on working capital balances, whereas the public issue would not carry such restrictions.

Several other relevant considerations were raised by Mr. Larson in deciding between the private placement and the public debt. Since the company was considering two separate issues of $20 million each, the prospectus covering an initial public offering of debt would be made available to analysts, allowing them to become familiar with the company's current situation and thereby helping to prepare the investment community for a later security offering. Sinking fund payments on the debentures would be set at $800,000 per year starting at the end of the fifth year. Debt retirement on the private placement would be at the rate of $1.2 million per year beginning at the end of the fourth year. Credit against mandatory sinking fund requirements for debentures acquired by the company on the open market in advance of the specified date would be permitted under the public issue, but this same flexibility would not be available under the private placement. In the case of the public issue, Phoenix would probably be able to buy its own debentures on the open market at less than par if interest rates continued to rise, thereby realizing savings on its debt retirement. The timing of the issue was extremely important since the period was one of rapidly changing interest rates. In this respect, the private placement had the advantage in that it could be consummated one month sooner than the public issue.

The debt retirement provisions of the convertible debentures would be considerably more lenient than those of either form of straight debt. Under the convertible issue, it was proposed that debt retirement start at the end of the 11th year at the rate of 5.9% of the amount of the issue, or $1,180,000 annually. Credit would be given for converted debentures or for debentures acquired on the open market.

With these data before him, Mr. Larson was preparing to present his conclusions to the board of directors, recommending a specific course of action and asking for prompt board ratification so that the financing decision could be promptly implemented.

The following quotation summarized key economic trends at this time:

> The economy continues to push ahead into high ground with undiminished vigor. While the physical volume of goods and services produced and consumed has expanded—and will no doubt continue to expand—this expansion has been accompanied increasingly by price advantages, as pressures on the economy's resources have mounted. . . . The rate of growth in spending for business fixed investment continued to exceed the rate of increase in over-all GNP in the first quarter. The latest survey of business plans by McGraw-Hill clearly supports earlier indications that the remainder of this year will see further strong advances in outlays for new plant and equipment.

EXHIBIT 1

Phoenix Aircraft Company

Comparative Statements of Financial Position

As of September 30, 1961-65, and March 31, 1966

(In millions of dollars)

	September 30					March 31
	1961	1962	1963	1964	1965	1966
ASSETS						
Cash	$ 2.6	$ 1.7	$ 1.9	$ 2.4	$ 2.1	$ 4.5
Notes and accounts receivable	8.2	7.9	9.2	10.6	12.6	17.8
Inventories	26.6	28.0	30.4	36.8	53.7	55.1
Prepaid expenses	0.2	0.2	0.3	0.2	0.2	0.4
Total current assets	$37.6	$37.8	$41.8	$50.0	$68.6	$ 77.8
Investments and other assets	$ 5.7	$ 6.1	$ 5.4	$ 4.9	$ 5.4	$ 5.5
Property, plant, and equipment	$30.1	$29.3	$31.5	$33.2	$37.1	$ 40.8
Less: Accumulated depreciation	17.8	18.0	19.2	20.6	22.9	24.0
Net fixed assets	$12.3	$11.3	$12.3	$12.6	$14.2	$ 16.8
Deferred charges	3.5	4.1	3.4	4.0	3.5	3.4
Total assets	$59.1	$59.3	$62.9	$71.5	$91.7	$103.5
LIABILITIES						
Accounts payable	$ 3.8	$ 3.2	$ 4.4	$ 5.3	$ 7.7	$ 6.2
Federal income taxes	3.4	3.1	2.9	5.3	6.7	7.0
Other taxes	0.6	0.6	0.7	0.8	1.1	0.8
Accrued and other liabilities	1.7	1.5	1.9	3.1	4.0	4.5
Bank notes payable	4.1	5.1	—	0.5	8.4	16.0*
Long-term debt — current portion	0.5	0.5	0.4	0.4	0.4	—
Total current liabilities	$14.1	$14.0	$10.3	$15.4	$28.3	$ 34.5
Long-term debt	4.3	3.3	9.6	8.8	8.4	8.4
Stockholders' equity	40.7	42.0	43.0	47.3	55.0	60.6
Total liabilities and net worth	$59.1	$59.3	$62.9	$71.5	$91.7	$103.5

*Includes $5 million of commercial paper outstanding.

EXHIBIT 2

Phoenix Aircraft Company

Comparative Statements of Operations for Years Ended September 30,
1961-65

(Dollar figures in millions)

	1961	1962	1963	1964	1965
Sales	$87.7	$89.8	$96.4	$122.9	$148.4
Other income	0.5	0.5	0.6	0.6	0.7
	$88.2	$90.3	$97.0	$123.5	$149.1
Manufacturing and engineering costs	$67.1	$69.8	$75.4	$ 94.4	$110.5
Depreciation	2.1	1.8	1.6	1.6	2.4
Sales and administrative expenses	6.4	6.8	6.9	9.2	11.2
Taxes other than federal income	1.6	1.8	2.1	2.6	2.9
Interest	0.3	0.5	0.5	0.5	0.6
	$77.5	$80.7	$86.5	$108.3	$127.6
Earnings before taxes	$10.7	$ 9.6	$10.5*	$ 15.2	$ 21.5
Provision for federal taxes	5.5	4.9	5.4	7.7	10.5
Earnings after taxes	$ 5.2	$ 4.7	$ 5.1*	$ 7.5	$ 11.0

(As percentage of net sales)

	1961	1962	1963	1964	1965
Sales	100.0%	100.0%	100.0%	100.0%	100.0%
Other income	0.6	0.5	0.5	0.4	0.4
	100.6%	100.5%	100.5%	100.4%	100.4%
Manufacturing and engineering costs	76.5%	77.7%	78.2%	76.8%	74.5%
Depreciation	2.4	2.0	1.6	1.3	1.7
Sales and administrative expenses	7.3	7.6	7.2	7.5	7.5
Taxes other than federal income	1.8	2.0	2.2	2.1	1.9
Interest	0.4	0.5	0.5	0.4	0.4
	88.4%	89.8%	89.7%	88.1%	86.0%
Earnings before taxes	12.2%	10.7%	10.8%	12.3%	14.4%
Provision for federal taxes	6.2	5.5	5.5	6.2	7.0
Earnings after taxes	6.0%	5.2%	5.3%*	6.1%	7.4%

*Before special charge of $900,000 (after taxes) from discontinuance of helicopter program in 1963.

Note: Figures may not add due to rounding.

EXHIBIT 3
Phoenix Aircraft Company
Comparative Statement of Operations for the Six Months
Ended March 31, 1965 and 1966
(In millions of dollars)

	1965	1966
Sales	$70.5	$99.4
Other income	0.5	0.7
	$71.0	$100.1
Manufacturing and engineering costs	$53.9	$ 76.9
Depreciation	0.8	1.2
Sales and administrative expenses	5.3	6.9
Interest	0.3	0.5
	$60.3	$ 85.5
Earnings before taxes	$10.7	$ 14.6
Provision for income taxes	5.4	7.1
Earnings after taxes	$ 5.3	$ 7.5

EXHIBIT 4
Phoenix Aircraft Company
Projections as of May, 1966, of Selected Financial Accounts
For Years Ended September 30
(In millions of dollars)

| | Actual | | Projected | | |
	1964	1965	1966	1967	1968
Sales	$122.9	$148.4	$189.0	$225.0	$252.0
Depreciation	1.6	2.4	2.5	3.6	3.9
Net profit after taxes*	7.5	11.0	14.0	16.7	18.6
Dividends	3.3	3.8	4.9	5.8	6.5
Retained earnings	4.2	7.2	9.1	10.9	12.1
Increase in current assets			19.2	16.7	12.5
Increase in investments and other assets†			5.7	3.5	0
Outlays on fixed assets			11.5	11.5	6.0
Increase in current liabilities‡			5.9	4.8	3.6
Reduction of long-term debt			0.4	0.7	0.7

*In this projection, allowance is made for interest payments on the outstanding bank loans, estimated at $8.4 million (the September 30, 1965, level) and for the existing long-term debt of $8.4 million, less the scheduled reduction of the existing long-term debt. As a crude approximation, these interest payments on existing indebtedness are estimated at $1.0 million a year. No allowance is made for any new borrowing that may be needed to finance the projected expansion during the years 1966-68.

†This item consists primarily of an allowance for anticipated investments in Phoenix Finance Company and in unconsolidated foreign subsidiaries.

‡Increases in current liabilities as shown here are for all current liabilities *except* short-term bank loans. One of the decisions confronting the Phoenix management was whether to replace its short-term bank loans with long-term debt.

EXHIBIT 5
Phoenix Finance Company, Inc.
Financial Statements, 1964-65
(In thousands of dollars)

Statement of Financial Position
(As of September 30)

	1964	1965
ASSETS		
Cash	$ 319	$ 1,018
Notes and contracts receivable	10,272	14,889
Accrued interest and other receivables	129	203
Repossessed aircraft, at estimated realizable		
value	0	4
Prepaid expenses	37	83
Depreciable assets — net	44	29
Total assets	$10,801	$16,226
LIABILITIES		
Short-term notes payable:		
Banks and commercial paper	$ 6,400	$11,000
Phoenix Aircraft Company	900	750
Accounts payable:		
Phoenix Aircraft Company	49	675
Other	107	186
Federal income tax	100	148
Other	144	187
Total liabilities	$ 7,700	$12,946
Stockholders' equity	3,101	3,280
Total liabilities and net worth	$10,801	$16,226

Statement of Operations and Earnings Reinvested in Business
(Years ended September 30)

	1964	1965
Income:		
Interest	$ 765	$ 1,072
Service	23	31
	$ 788	$ 1,103
Expenses:		
Interest	$ 318	$ 458
General and administrative	170	211
Provision for doubtful items	34	83
Depreciation	10	10
Other	3	2
	$ 535	$ 764
Earnings before federal income tax	$ 253	$ 339
Provision for federal income tax	125	159
Net earnings	$ 128	$ 180
Earnings reinvested in business at		
beginning of year	722	850
Earnings reinvested in business at end of year	$ 850	$ 1,030

EXHIBIT 6

Phoenix Aircraft Company
*Prices of Common Stock, Earnings per Share,
and Price-Earnings Ratios, 1959-66*

September 30	Stock Prices*			Earnings per Share	Price-Earnings Earnings Ratio†
	High	Low	Close		
1959	$30	$13	$26	$2.47	10.5
1960	35	28	29	2.24	12.9
1961	46	26	37	1.58	23.4
1962	38	16	18	1.41	12.7
1963	26	16	21	1.55	13.5
1964	31	21	29	2.27	12.8
Period Indicated					
October-December, 1964	32	28	32		14.1
January-March, 1965	35	31	32		14.1
April-June, 1965	36	29	32		14.1
July-September, 1965	43	31	41	3.30‡	18.1
October-December, 1965	51	37	50		15.2
January-March, 1966	57	44	49		14.8
April, 1966	58	49	53		16.1
May, 1966	54	42	49		14.8

*Stock prices are rounded to the nearest dollar.
†Price-earnings ratios for annual data are computed on the basis of closing prices and earnings per share for the current year. Price-earnings ratios for quarterly and monthly intervals are computed on the basis of the earnings per share of the preceding fiscal year.
‡Earnings per share for the year ended September 30, 1965.

EXHIBIT 7

Phoenix Aircraft Company
*Potential Effect of Delayed Convertible Offering
On Number of Shares of Common Stock Issued*

Price of Common Stock	Price-Earnings Ratio*	Conversion Price†	Total Common Shares Issuable‡ (In 000's)	Net Savings in Number Of Shares Issuable § Number (In 000's)	Percentage
May, 1966:					
$46	13.9	$55.20	362		
May, 1967:					
$42	10.0	50.40	397	-35	-9.7%
46	11.0	55.20	362	0	0.0
50	12.0	60.00	333	29	8.0
54	12.9	64.80	309	53	14.6
58	13.9	69.60	287	75	20.7
66	15.8	79.20	253	109	30.1
74	17.7	88.80	225	137	37.8
82	19.6	98.40	203	159	43.9

*The price-earnings ratio in May, 1966, was computed on the basis of the earnings per share of $3.30 for the year ended September 30, 1965. The price-earnings ratio for May, 1967, was based on earnings per share of $4.18, computed from the figure for net profit after taxes projected in Exhibit 4 for the year ended September 30, 1966.

†Computed at a 20% premium over the price of the common stock.

‡$20 million divided by the conversion price.

§Amount by which the total number of shares issuable if the convertible was offered in 1967 at indicated prices differs from the 362,000 shares issuable if the convertible was issued immediately.

EXHIBIT 8
Phoenix Aircraft Company
Comparative Capitalization Ratios

	Senior Debt	Subordinated Debt	Preferred Stock	Minority Interest	Common & Surplus
Certain companies recently offering convertible debentures by rights offerings:*					
Stauffer Chemical	18.3%	11.4%	1.1%	—	69.2%
R. H. Macy	10.7	12.6	13.4	—	63.3
American Airlines	49.0	16.9	0.5	—	33.6
International Silver	8.2	18.5	2.3	—	71.0
Celanese Corporation	37.1	8.9	10.9	—	43.1
United Air Lines	41.2	12.9	2.7	—	43.2
W. R. Grace	34.5	13.4	1.6	2.4%	48.1
Cluett, Peabody	27.0	11.7	2.1	—	59.2
Certain companies recently offering convertible debentures directly to the public:*					
Great Northern Paper	38.8%	5.6%	9.4%	—	46.2%
Reynolds Metals	41.5	7.2	8.7	—	42.6
Chicago Musical Instrument	10.0	29.5	—	1.2%	59.3
Rockwell-Standard	17.4	16.7	—	1.0	64.9
Reeves Brothers	17.3	20.6	—	—	62.1
International Minerals & Chem.	37.0	15.0	3.0	—	45.0
General Instrument	1.5	25.5	—	—	73.0
United Merchants & Mfrs.	20.9	14.4	—	—	64.7
Beaunit	27.5†	18.1	—	—	54.4
W. T. Grant	15.0	15.0	6.4	—	63.6
J. P. Stevens	24.3	7.6	—	—	68.1
Certain companies recently offering senior debentures publicly:*					
Weyerhaeuser	23.8%	—	—	0.3%	75.9%
Allied Chemical	35.6	—	—	—	64.4
Anheuser-Busch	35.1	—	—	—	64.9
Rockwell-Standard	17.4	16.7%	—	1.0	64.9
Hooker Chemical	29.5	—	3.8%	—	66.7
Sun Oil	15.3	1.2	—	0.4	83.1
Texas Instruments	29.3	—	—	—	70.7
Magnavox	28.5	—	—	—	71.5
General Mills	35.8	—	—	—	64.2
Lone Star Cement	31.9	—	—	—	68.1
Burlington Industries	33.2	3.5	—	0.9	62.4
Champion Papers	27.4	7.5	3.8	—	61.3
Times Mirror	37.7	—	—	—	62.3
Deere	21.7	8.4	—	—	69.9
Ralston Purina	22.6	0.9	—	—	76.5
Honeywell	27.0	—	—	—	65.8
Firestone Tire & Rubber	17.8	—	—	0.3	81.9

*Based on pro forma capitalization in prospectus.
†Includes commitment.

EXHIBIT 9
Phoenix Aircraft Company
Effect of Decline in Interest Rate
(Based on Projected Net Income for 1968)
(In thousands except for per share data)

	Financing Alternative	
	No. 1	No. 2
Net income	$18,600	$18,600
Less: After-tax interest cost	575	475
	$18,025	$18,125
Common shares now outstanding	3,350	3,350
Plus: Common shares issued in conversion	315	378
Pro forma common shares	3,665	3,728
Pro forma earnings per share	$4.92	$4.87

Financing Alternative No. 1:
   Direct offering of $20 million of senior debentures at 5¾% now, and $20 million of subordinated debentures convertible at $63.40 (120% x $52.90—projected 1967 common price) in one year.
Financing Alternative No. 2:
   Rights offering of $20 million of subordinated debentures convertible at $52.90 (115% x $46—approximate current price) now and $20 million of senior debt at 4¾% in one year.

QUESTIONS

1. Comment on the projected earnings (Exhibit 4) in light of the facts presented in the case.
2. What are the advantages and disadvantages of placing the straight debt issue privately as opposed to placing it publicly?
3. Analyze, in detail, the alternative methods available for raising the $40 million.
4. What specific course of action should Mr. Larson recommend? Why?

Case 29
Western Kentucky Steel Company

Mr. Irv Hastings, treasurer of Western Kentucky Steel Company, was examining the various sources of funds available to finance the first phase of the Company's capital expansion. The president of Western Kentucky Steel, Mr. Lloyd Hodges, wanted a report on the advantages and disadvantages of each type of financing and Mr. Hastings's recommendation. Mr. Hodges wished to have the report by late February, 1971, or within approximately three weeks.

The Company

Western Kentucky Steel Company was located in Paducah, Kentucky, which was situated in the far western portion of the state, approximately equidistant from St. Louis and Memphis. The Company was founded in 1913 as Paducah Steel and in 1937 changed its name to Western Kentucky Steel. The firm produced steel with open hearth furnaces until the mid-fifties, when it converted to the electric furnace due to superior operating efficiencies associated with the latter and the declining cost of scrap. Most of the firm's output was composed of low-carbon steel, although some high-carbon items were manufactured. For the most part, the Company marketed its output in Kentucky, Illinois, Indiana, Missouri, and Tennessee.

The Company produced a varied combination of products, mostly falling into two groupings. Hot rolled products comprised approximately 60 percent of

This was was prepared by Professor Harry R. Kuniansky of the College of Charleston as a basis for classroom discussion and not to illustrate either effective or ineffective handling of an administrative situation.

Western Kentucky's dollar output and 75 percent as measured by tonnage. Among the most important goods in this grouping were reinforcing bar, structural shapes, flats, and angles, with structural shapes showing the most rapid growth during the last five years. The other grouping consisted of wire products, which accounted for 35 percent of the firm's dollar output and 20 percent tonnage-wise. Among the more important products in this grouping were nails, bright wire, welded reinforcing mesh, and high-carbon spring wire. The latter two items had shown extraordinary growth over the last two years. The remaining 5 percent of the Company's dollar sales and tonnage consisted of various miscellaneous items.

The Industrial Environment

Historically, the steel industry was oligopolistic in nature. There were a few major producers such as United States Steel and Bethlehem, and the major producers tended to initiate price changes. Generally, Western Kentucky followed the price movements of the large firms. Only in very rare instances did it deviate from this pattern, and the price variance was usually achieved through freight absorption. However, in the last five years, the company faced a new source of competition, the so-called mini-mills. The mini-mills produced a limited number of products in only the most popular sizes. Very often they utilized non-union labor, and the greater majority of them used a new steel-making process called continuous casting.* For the above reasons, the mini-mills were able to produce steel at a lower cost than Western Kentucky. These mills' average price was between 15 percent and 25 percent below that of the Company. Western Kentucky's policy was to price its products in line with those of the large steel companies, and generally to ignore the prices of the mini-mills. At present, the Company believed it could compete with the mini-mills by emphasizing its ability to assure continuity of supply for its customers and by offering a wide range of sizes in all products. Whether this nonprice type of competition would be successful or whether the firm would have to cut prices to meet those of the mini-mills was uncertain.

In addition to competition from the mini-mills, foreign steel, notably from Japan and West Germany, posed a competitive challenge to all the steel industry. The industry was attempting to gain some relief from Congress in the forms of quotas and higher tariffs, but had met with little success. The foreign pressure had been especially intense on several of the firm's products, notably reinforcing bar and wire goods. However, there was a possibility of some relief from Japanese imports as a result of the voluntary quota system imposed by Japan. Since this quota was based on tonnage and not dollars, it was possible that imports would shift to steel products with a higher dollar mark-up, such as special alloy and stainless steel goods. Such a shift would benefit Western Kentucky, as the Company produced very few of these goods. Regardless of the import situation, the Company's management believed that modernization of its facilities and aggressive marketing procedures would enable it to meet foreign competition.

---

*Continuous casting—the casting of semi-finished shapes that eliminates the ingot and primary mill stages of rolled steel production, with the expectation of reducing production costs.

The Investment Decision

Western Kentucky's first phase expansion was estimated to require about $20,000,000 in external funds. Most of the expenditures were for an electric furnace and supplementary equipment. Vigorous debate had ensued as to what project the Company should invest in. Some production executives preferred to install a continous casting system. They believed this type of installation was necessary if the Company was to compete effectively with the mini-mills. On the other hand, some marketing officers argued that the new funds should be expended toward the development of a plastics operation in order to diversify somewhat the firm's activities. They pointed out that the firm was highly cyclical and that the plastics operation could lend more stability to the firm's sales. However, the debate was resolved in favor of the electric furnace, but the idea of diversification was received quite enthusiastically by all of top management. The consensus among top management was that some sort of diversification should be effectuated within the next three years and that external financing funds would be necessary. Estimates of outside requirements from the diversification project ranged from $10,000,000 to $15,000,000.

The addition of the electric furnace was estimated to increase earnings before interest and taxes an additional $1,750,000 to $2,250,000 in 1972. The new equipment would generate very little earnings in 1971 as the furnace was not expected to become operative until the latter part of the year. Exhibit 3A provides an estimate of the range of future EBITs from 1971 through 1976 and, except for 1971, assumes the installation of the new furnace and excludes any diversification projects.

The Financing Decision

Mr. Hastings believed three financing alternatives feasible for the Company: 1) finance with common stock, 2) sell debenture bonds, and 3) issue a convertible preferred stock. Accordingly, Mr. Hastings had been exploring each of the three alternatives. From preliminary discussions with an underwriting firm in St. Louis, Mr. Hastings had determined that a common stock offering would net the Company $50 a share. The common was currently selling in the over-the-counter market at $54. Mr. Hastings believed the figure of $50 per share to be a reasonable one, in light of the overall weakness in the new issues market. Of course, he realized that stock market conditions might change during the next three months and this would cause the offering price to vary accordingly. Although a common stock sale would increase the number of outstanding shares approximately 45 percent, the underwriters assured management that this would not pose a control problem for the Company.

The debenture bond issue would be for $21,240,000, the additional $1,240,000 being necessary to cover underwriting fees. The bonds would mature in twenty years and be callable after five years. A sinking fund provision required no payments for the first two years, with annual installments of $1,180,000 beginning in December, 1973, and continuing for the following eighteen years. The interest rate would be in the neighborhood of 8 percent, and the bonds would sell at par.

The following restrictive covenants would likely be imposed on Western Kentucky Steel Company:

1. Maintenance of a current ratio of at least 2.5 to 1.
2. Prohibition of any additional senior long-term debt including long-term bank notes payable.
3. Restriction of cash dividends to 50 percent of cumulative earnings per share, unless approval is received from the trustee.

The preferred stock issue would carry a 7 percent rate and would sell for $100 par. It would be cumulative, nonparticipating, and convertible to 1.5 shares of common stock. The convertible feature would become operative in 1973. Underwriting fees were estimated at $1,500,000. The issue was callable in 1976 at $102.

The board of directors believed that the target pay-out ratio should be between 35 percent and 45 percent of earnings. Although the board wished to avoid cutting dividends per share, they realized the difficulties of this policy in a cyclical company such as Western Kentucky. Accordingly, they were more likely to stress a target pay-out ratio rather than a stable dividend per share.

EXHIBIT 1

Western Kentucky Steel Company
Comparative Balance Sheets

	1968	1969	1970
Current Assets			
Cash	$ 4,071	$ 4,543	$ 3,732
Accounts Receivable, Net	16,100	17,516	19,936
Inventory	37,499	38,533	38,766
Prepayments	704	911	491
Total Current Assets	$ 58,374	$ 61,503	$ 62,925
Long-Term Assets			
Land	$ 1,820	$ 1,820	$ 1,820
Buildings	37,517	37,615	38,223
Machinery and Equipment	117,751	121,275	128,006
Less Accumulated Depreciation	(55,888)	(61,905)	(68,285)
Note Receivable	1,355	1,316	1,138
Total Long-Term Assets	$102,555	$100,121	$100,902
Total Assets	$160,929	$161,624	$163,827
Current Liabilities			
Accounts Payable	$ 12,747	$ 8,425	$ 10,038
Accruals Except Taxes	3,378	2,142	3,066
Taxes Payable	871	1,390	1,219
Current Maturity of Long-Term Debt[1]	2,356	2,293	3,200
Total Current Liabilities	$ 19,352	$ 14,250	$ 17,523
Long-Term Debt[2]	30,191	34,822	31,622
Stockholders Investment			
Common Stock (par value $3, authorized 4,000,000 shares, issued 860,000 shares)	$ 2,580	$ 2,580	$ 2,580
Paid-in Capital	23,898	23,898	23,898
Retained Earnings	84,908	86,074	88,204
Total Capital	$111,386	$112,552	$114,682
Total Liabilities and Capital	$160,929	$161,624	$163,827

[1]Principal payments on the current maturities of the notes are made on the first day of the following year.

[2]The Company's long-term debt at December 31, 1970, is presented below:

6½% Notes due in 1980 minimum of $2,200,000 payable annually. Prepayments not to exceed $1,100,000 in any one year	$21,622
6¾% Notes maturing 1981, payment of $1,000,000 per year, first payment 1971	10,000
Long-Term Debt	$31,622
Current Maturities of Long-Term Debt	3,200
Total Long-Term Debt	$34,822

EXHIBIT 2
Western Kentucky Steel Company
Comparative Income Statements
(in 000's)

	1968	1969	1970
Net Sales	$165,218	$164,931	$173,554
Less: Cost of Goods Sold (excluding depreciation)	137,648	137,959	142,979
Less: Selling and Administrative Expenses	12,928	12,603	13,556
Less: Depreciation	5,093	6,017	6,380
Less: Other (Income) Expense	(317)	211	(108)
Net Income Before Interest and Taxes	$ 9,866	$ 8,141	$ 10,747
Less: Interest	2,144	2,391	2,291
Less: Federal Income Taxes*	4,077	3,036	4,262
Net Income	$ 3,645	$ 2,714	$ 4,194
Earnings per Share	$4.24	$3.16	$4.88
Cash Dividends per Share	$1.80	$1.80	$2.40

*In the future, the firm expects its effective tax rate to be 48 percent.

EXHIBIT 3
Western Kentucky Steel Company
Selected Operating Data
(in 000's)

	Net Sales	Earnings Before Interest and Taxes	Depreciation Charges	Interest Charges
1961	$ 80,617	$ 3,967	$2,422	$ 900
1962	91,393	5,986	2,520	945
1963	96,582	6,529	2,569	1,800
1964*	90,043	3,010	3,378	1,800
1965	135,065	10,235	3,479	1,800
1966	150,910	11,771	3,819	1,873
1967	180,586	13,543	4,498	2,018
1968	165,218	9,866	5,093	2,144
1969*	164,931	8,141	6,017	2,391
1970	173,554	10,747	6,380	2,291

*Strike for two months.

EXHIBIT 3A
Western Kentucky Steel Company
Estimated Future EBIT
(in 000's)

	Average High	Average Low	Median of Expected EBITs
1971	$12,400	$11,600	$11,900
1972	14,600	12,300	13,000
1973	16,400	12,400	15,000
1974	17,000	11,500	14,000
1975	18,600	14,000	16.000
1976	19,400	14,600	16,900

*Estimates made by seven members of the Board of Directors and eight operating officers. The estimations assume no steel strike.

EXHIBIT 4
Capital Structures of Selected Steel Companies
Between 1963-1969
(in 000,000's)

Steel Company	Type of Capital	1963	1965	1967	1969
United States	Long-Term Debt*	$ 770	$ 705	$1,200	$1,434
	Preferred Stock	360	360	0	0
	Common Equity	3,379	3,624	3,220	3,432
		$4,509	$4,689	$4,420	$4,866
Bethlehem	Long-Term Debt	$ 128	$ 240	$ 370	$ 418
	Preferred Stock	93	0	0	0
	Common Equity	1,667	2,609	1,857	2,024
		$1,888	$2,849	$2,227	$2,442
Inland	Long-Term Debt	$ 186	$ 169	$ 202	$ 240
	Common Equity	578	658	708	774
		$ 764	$ 827	$ 910	$1,014
C F & I	Long-Term Debt	$ 64	$ 49	$ 37	$ 51
	Preferred Stock	7	5	0	0
	Common Equity	112	130	141	161
		$ 183	$ 184	$ 178	$ 212
Granite City	Long-Term Debt	$ 63	$ 90	$ 148	$ 137
	Common Equity	107	·117	121	112
		$ 170	$ 207	$ 269	$ 249

*Represented by funded debt and excluding deferred credits and other long-term liabilities.

EXHIBIT 5
Western Kentucky Steel Company
Selected Financial Data

	Common Stock Price Range		Number of Shares Traded	Earnings	Dividends
	High	Low	(in 000's)	per Share	per Share
1961	$47¾	$37⅝	155	$5.17	$2.60
1962	42½	37⅛	255	4.24	2.60
1963	44⅛	33½	305	5.50	2.60
1964	54½	39	300	2.37*	1.60
1965	88⅝	41⅞	190	6.83	3.00
1966	73¾	51⅜	180	6.10	3.00
1967	73½	48¼	217	6.78	3.40
1968	57½	30⅝	225	4.24	2.80
1969	47⅞	33⅛	205	3.16*	1.80
1970	55½	34	262	4.88	2.40

*Strike for two months.

EXHIBIT 6
Western Kentucky Steel Company
Industrial Production of Ingots and Steel for Casting
1950-1969
(tons in thousands)

1950	96,836	1960	99,282
1951	105,200	1961	98,014
1952	93,168	1962	98,328
1953	111,610	1963	109,261
1954	88,312	1964	127,076
1955	117,036	1965	131,462
1956	115,216	1966	134,101
1957	112,715	1967	127,213
1958	85,255	1968	131,462
1959	93,446	1969	141,262

QUESTIONS

1. Comment on the reasonableness of the EBIT projections (Exhibit 3A) in light of the facts presented in the case.
2. Using either the median of expected EBITs in Exhibit 3A or your own EBIT projections, calculate earnings per share for each plan for 1972 and 1973. Prepare an EBIT chart for 1973, both with and without conversion of the preferred stock.
3. Compare each plan in light of income, risk, flexibility, and control.
4. Which financing alternative should Mr. Hastings select? Why?

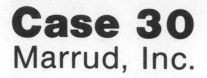

Case 30
Marrud, Inc.

In late October 1964, Mr. Saul Margolis, Financial Vice President of Marrud, Inc., was preparing for the November meeting of the board of directors. Mr. Margolis planned to propose adoption of regular semiannual cash dividends as a policy, and that the initial dividend be 20 cents per share to be paid in January 1965.

During the last several years, Marrud had experienced extremely rapid growth of both sales and earnings. Although the company had never paid a cash dividend, Mr. Margolis had felt for some time that a policy of regular dividend payments would benefit both the company and its shareholders. Recent financial statements presented in Exhibits 1 and 2 indicate the magnitude of Marrud's growth.

Even though the board of directors was responsible for dividend policy, it relied to a large extent on Mr. Margolis's recommendations concerning financial matters.

Company Background

Marrud, Inc., was organized in 1953, and its executive offices and central warehouse were located in Norwood, Massachusetts, a suburb of Boston. The principal business of the company consisted of the retail sale in a highly competitive market of a wide variety of drug sundries, health and beauty aids, costume jewelry, and other relatively low-priced items, through 362 leased departments operated in

This case was made possible by the cooperation of Marrud, Inc. It was prepared by Charles W. Young of the University of North Florida as a basis for classroom discussion and not to indicate either effective or ineffective handling of administrative situations.

discount department stores. The company believed that it operated more leased departments in the health and beauty aids field than any other similar firm.

Marrud had achieved its rapid growth through leasing departments in new stores and by purchase of departments in established stores. The following table indicates how the number of retail units had expanded in recent years.

July 31	Number of Units in Operation
1960	49
1961	79
1962	148
1963	196
1964	345

The company had also followed a policy of expansion and diversification through acquisition. Acquisition of 80% of D. W. Jewelry, Inc., in December 1963 extended Marrud into the costume jewelry field and added approximately 97 leased jewelry departments. Control of D. W. Jewelry was acquired by the exchange of 106,852 shares of Marrud common stock for 80% of the stock of D. W. Jewelry and an option to purchase the remaining 20% from the former owners at any time during 1969. The option price was indeterminate because it was based on a growth and profitability arrangement designed to motivate the management and former owners. However, the agreed price would be no less than $300,000 and probably no more than $2 million payable in cash.

To reduce its dependence on the operation of leased departments, Marrud had initiated a diversification policy with the acquisition in February 1964 of a modern plant, fully equipped for the manufacture and packaging of cosmetics and drugs. This acquisition was made for approximately $1.6 million in cash and notes and was operated as Clifton Private Brands, Inc., an 80%-owned subsidiary. Clifton manufactured a number of cosmetic and drug products sold by the company in its retail departments. In addition, Clifton packaged cosmetics, drugs, and other products sold by the company under its private labels. Management estimated that 25% of Clifton's sales volume was taken by Marrud and the remainder by outside   stomers. Clifton had sales revenue of $400,000 for the quarter ended October 26, 1964. However, it was operating on a breakeven basis and was not expected to reach a profitable volume until early 1965. Sales for fiscal year 1965 were estimated by management to be approximately $2 million.

Future Expansion

In carrying its program of rapid expansion into 1965, Marrud had firm plans to open 53 new leased departments between November 1, 1964, and May 1, 1965. The capital required to establish a new unit varied widely, but experience indicated that $30,000 was the average amount needed for retail inventory, and $4,500 was required for fixtures. The average department employed four people. Although there were no firm plans for opening additional units after May 1965, it was the company's policy to accept every attractive opportunity to open a new department, and it was expected that new units would continue to be opened at the rate of 50 to 75 per year.

To further reduce its dependence on leased departments, the company was planning to open a number of small retail stores located in central or "downtown" shopping areas. These stores would sell basically the same products as were sold through the leased health and beauty aid, and jewelry departments. Initial stocking of each of these stores was estimated to require approximately $75,000, and $10,000 would be needed for fixtures. Plans called for opening 9 stores of this type by the end of fiscal year 1965. Each of these stores was expected to generate sales revenue of $350,000 to $400,000 per year after one year of operation. In addition, the company hoped to open about 25 of these stores each year starting with fiscal year 1966.

Management was also negotiating for the purchase of a chain of 42 drug stores and franchise contracts relating to an additional 39 drug stores affiliated with the same chain. If this acquisition was successful, it would add $20 million of profitable sales volume during the first year of operations and another $5 million by the end of the second year. Mr. Margolis estimated that this acquisition would require an initial cash payment of $1 million during fiscal year 1965 and payment of an additional $3 million in 60 monthly installments. An additional $1.5 million would be needed during 1965 to provide working capital for the new operation.

Financing Operations

Marrud common stock was closely held until 1961. At that time, the company sold 100,000 shares to the public at $20.50 per share. In April 1962, the company declared a 100% stock dividend to increase the number of outstanding shares from 500,000 to 1,000,000 and to effectively split the stock 2 for 1. In October 1964, there were 1,136,517 shares issued, of which 6,818 shares were held in the treasury. The stock was widely held by approximately 2,600 investors. The 450,000 shares owned by Marrud's President, Mr. J. E. Margolis, was the only block of any size held by one individual.

Although Marrud had never paid a cash dividend and all earnings had been retained, the company's rapid growth and its constant need for additional working capital had required it to rely heavily on debt financing. In December 1962, the company borrowed $3 million from the Prudential Life Insurance Company. The loan agreement called for interest of $5\frac{7}{8}\%$ and for warrants to purchase 25,000 shares of common stock at $10.50 per share until December 1, 1972. This loan was repaid in April 1964, with part of the proceeds of a new borrowing of $5.5 million from the same lender. The new loan was due May 1, 1979, and required interest payments of $5\frac{3}{4}\%$ on the unpaid balance. Warrants to purchase an additional 5,000 shares of common stock at $14 until May 1979 were also issued. Annual sinking fund payments of $300,000 were required on May 1, 1965 through 1969, and $400,000 from 1970 through 1978. In addition to retiring the principal and accrued interest on the old note, the net proceeds of $5,483,000 from this borrowing were applied to discharge the unpaid balance and accrued interest on a first mortgage note in the amount of $514,000, which was assumed as part of the purchase price of the recently acquired packaging plant; to replenish funds in the amount of

$580,000, which were previously utilized to discharge a second mortgage note on the same property; and to provide additional working capital.

On February 1, 1963, Marrud had issued an aggregate of $750,000 principal amount of 6% convertible subordinated notes, due February 1, 1976, to two insurance companies and an employees' retirement fund. Sinking fund payments were deferred until February 1967 when they would require an annual payment equal to 10% of the principal amount of the notes outstanding on January 31, 1967. The notes were convertible into common shares at $11.85 per share until February 1, 1965, at $12.37 until February 1, 1967, and at $13.40 until maturity. In April 1964, one lender had converted $50,000 of these notes into 4,219 shares of common stock.

Restrictions on Dividends

The April 1964 loan agreement between Marrud and Prudential restricted the payment of dividends (other than stock dividends) on the common stock to 70% of consolidated net earnings after July 28, 1963, less the sum of all dividends paid, the net amount of funds committed to repurchase of stock, and all payments of principal on outstanding term debt. In addition, the agreement relating to the 6% convertible notes prevented the payment of dividends if, after giving effect to the dividend payment, consolidated tangible net worth would be less than the principal amount of all the then outstanding debt. Both loan agreements also prohibited the company from permitting consolidated working capital to be less than $6.75 million.

The effect of all the above restrictions was to limit retained earnings available for dividends on July 26, 1964 to approximately $1.1 million.

Lease Commitments

The majority of the company's departments were operated under lease agreements with store owners. The typical lease provided for a percentage rental of approximately 10% of net sales revenue of the applicable unit and specified a minimum annual rental. In October 1964, Marrud had leases with original terms of more than one year with an aggregate minimum annual rental of approximately $2.5 million. The company would normally be held liable for the minimum rental during the unexpired term of the lease in the event the company vacated the lease prior to its expiration.

Dividend Policy and Market Valuation

Since 1961, Marrud's stock had been traded over the counter and its price had fluctuated considerably. Monthly high and low bid prices from June 1961 to October 1964 are presented in Exhibit 3. Exhibit 4 compares the price of Marrud common stock with Moody's 200 common stock average, Barron's retail merchandise group stock average, and the National Quotation Bureau's over-the-counter index for the same period. Financial data and stock prices for a few roughly comparable companies are presented in Exhibit 5. In an effort to enhance the investment quality of the stock by increasing its marketability and reducing its susceptibility to speculative influences, Marrud had submitted an application for listing to the American Stock Exchange. This application was pending, but Mr. Margolis anticipated that it would be approved and that the stock would be listed by early December 1964.

Mr. Margolis also thought that a regular cash dividend would enhance the investment quality of the stock. He was certain that if institutional investors became interested in the stock, their buying would stabilize the price and reduce its volatility. Although Mr. Margolis did not feel that the 40-cent-per-year dividend he was considering would have any immediate effect on the stock's price, he did feel that it would support the price over the longer term. In addition, Mr. Margolis felt that it was appropriate to distribute some part of the company's rapidly growing earnings to its stockholders. Approximately 60% of the individuals who purchased shares in 1961 still held at least the number of shares which they had bought initially.

To sustain the rate of growth which the company envisaged would require large amounts of new capital during the next few years. Debt financing would supply most, but Mr. Margolis anticipated that the company would also sell equity securities. If the dividend stabilized and raised the market price of the common stock, future equity issues would be less costly and less subject to speculative pressures.

Marrud's relations with its primary lender were very good, and so long as earnings and cash flow provided adequate coverage of debt service, additional debt would be available. However, Prudential followed the practice of capitalizing annual lease obligations at 10% when evaluating the company's debt position, and it was not certain what effect further increases in lease obligations would have on Prudential's willingness to provide additional amounts of funded debt.

Marrud had very little excess liquidity, and if earnings should drop sharply, particularly without a commensurate reduction in sales and working capital, it would be impossible to maintain the dividend. The discount store business was steadily becoming more competitive and, in addition, the company's diversification plans would require larger investments per retail outlet and would also change the nature of the risks to which the company was exposed.

As part of his presentation for the board of directors, Mr. Margolis had prepared cash budgets for the next five years, which are shown in Exhibit 6.

EXHIBIT 1

Marrud, Inc., and Subsidiaries
Consolidated Balance Sheet
(000 omitted)

	July 31, 1961	July 29, 1962	July 28, 1963	July 26, 1964	*(unaudited)* Oct. 25, 1964
ASSETS					
Current Assets:					
Cash	$ 1,121	$ 629	$ 1,024	$ 1,230	$ 501
Accts. receivable	458	1,459	1,555	2,028	2,670
Inv.: Retail units	$ 1,325	$ 3,784	$ 5,803	$ 8,548	$10,435
Warehouse	1,119	2,695	2,793	3,168	4,256
	$ 2,444	$ 6,479	$ 8,596	$11,716	$14,691
Prepaid expenses	25	106	205	253	251
Total current assets	$ 4,048	$ 8,673	$11,380	$15,227	$18,113
Other assets	$ 75	$ 89	$ 282	$ 364	$ 361
Property and equipment:					
Land	$ 0	$ 0	$ 0	$ 155	$ 155
Building	0	0	0	1,058	1,058
Fixtures and equipment	210	634	1,182	2,404	2,490
Leasehold improvements	14	29	50	68	81
	$ 224	$ 633	$ 1,232	$ 3,685	$ 3,784
Less: Accum. depr.	78	195	320	513	590
	$ 146	$ 468	$ 912	$ 3,172	$ 3,194
Intangibles	0	292	187	408	407
Total assets	$ 4,269	$ 9,522	$12,761	$19,171	$22,075

EXHIBIT 1
Marrud, Inc., and Subsidiaries *(continued)*
Consolidated Balance Sheet
(000 omitted)

	July 31, 1961	July 29, 1962	July 28, 1963	July 26, 1964	(unaudited) Oct. 25, 1964
LIABILITIES AND CAPITAL					
Current Liabilities:					
Notes payable	$ 0	$ 2,022	$ 837	$ 1,197	$ 1,000
Current portion LTD	0	0	0	300	300
Accounts payable	804	3,037	2,932	4,085	6,792
Accruals	175	218	325	517	493
Income tax payable	405	363	411	790	801
Total current liabilities	$ 1,384	$ 5,640	$ 4,505	$ 6,889	$ 9,386
Long-term Debt (LTD):					
5¾% notes, due 1979	0	0	0	5,200	5,200
5⅞% notes, due 1974	0	0	3,000	0	0
6% conv. sub. debentures, due 1976	0	0	750	700	700
Minority interests	0	0	0	83	89
	$ 1,384	$ 5,640	$ 8,255	$12,872	$15,375
Capital:					
Common stock, $2 par	1,000	2,051	2,051	2,273	2,273
Paid-in capital	1,673	905	905	731	731
Retained earnings	212	926	1,765	3,394	3,795
	$ 2,885	$ 3,882	$ 4,721	$ 6,398	$ 6,799
Less: Treas. stock			215	99	99
Total capital	$ 2,885	$ 3,882	$ 4,506	$ 6,299	$ 6,700
Total liabilities and capital	$ 4,269	$ 9,522	$12,761	$19,171	$22,075
Number of shares issued	500,000	1,025,446	1,025,446	1,136,517	1,136,517
Number of shares in treasury	0	0	20,081	6,818	6,818
Number of leases with terms in excess of one year	48	144	116	250	270
Annual lease obligation, in thousands	$ 515	$ 1,200	$ 1,560	$ 2,300	$ 2,500

EXHIBIT 2

Marrud, Inc., and Subsidiaries
Consolidated Statement of Earnings
(000 omitted)

	52 Weeks Ended					13 Weeks Ended (unaudited)	
	July 31, 1960	July 31, 1961	July 29, 1962	July 28, 1963	July 26, 1964*	Oct. 25, 1964*	Oct. 27, 1963*
Sales	$6,608	$10,618	$20,676	$32,773	$45,832	$12,573	$10,078
Cost of goods sold	4,364	6,941	13,891	22,349	31,023	8,373	6,703
Gross margin	$2,244	$3,677	$6,785	$10,424	$14,809	$4,200	$3,375
Selling, general, and administrative expenses	1,729	2,821	5,643	8,550	12,180	3,444	2,791
Interest and amortization of debt expense	27	40	38	190	317	140	71
Net income applicable to minority interests	0	0	0	0	47	11	6
Other (income) deductions	2	(4)	(9)	(15)	(37)	(10)	(8)
Earnings before taxes	$ 486	$ 820	$ 1,113	$ 1,699	$ 2,302	$ 651	$ 515
Provision for federal taxes on income**	210	400	400	646	766	250	225
Write-off of nonrecurring loss – net of taxes	—	—	—	214	—	—	—
Net earnings	$ 276	$ 420	$ 713	$ 839	$ 1,536	$ 401	$ 290
Depreciation	NA	NA	$ 144	$ 157	$ 206	$ 77	NA
Net earnings per share*** (as reported)	$ .69	$ .84	$ .71	$ .83	$1.37	$ .36	$ .26
Net earnings per share**** (adjusted)	$ .34	$ .42	$ .71	$ .83	$1.37	$ .36	$ .26

*Includes D. W. Jewelry, Inc., for entire period as a pooling of interest.

**The company and its subsidiaries file individual tax returns, and the provision for federal income taxes has been computed at the separate rates applicable to each of the companies.

***Based on the number of shares outstanding on the last day of the period.

****Adjusted to reflect the 100% stock dividend declared in April 1962.

EXHIBIT 3
Marrud, Inc.
*Common Stock Prices, 1961-1964**

Marrud, Inc. common stock was traded over the counter. Prices shown are the monthly high and low bid prices as reported by the National Quotation Bureau. The monthly closing price is the bid price reported for the last trading day of the month.

	High	Low	Close
June 1961	12⅞	10⅞	12¼
July	13⅝	13	13½
August	15⅜	13⅞	15¼
September	16⅝	14¼	16⅜
October	20⅝	17¾	19⅞
November	21½	18⅞	21½
December	21⅜	16½	17¾
January 1962	19	16½	18¼
February	19¾	18⅜	18¾
March	21⅜	18¾	21⅜
April	20	19½	19½
May	18¼	11¼	11¼
June	13¼	10¼	10½
July	13½	10¾	13½
August	13¼	11¼	11¼
September	12⅝	10	10
October	9¾	8	8
November	9⅞	7⅝	9⅞
December	9⅝	8	8
January 1963	11¼	8¼	10½
February	10¼	9⅛	9⅜
March	9¼	8⅜	8½
April	10⅜	9¼	9¼
May	9⅜	7½	7⅝
June	9⅜	7	7⅝
July	10½	7⅝	10⅜
August	10	9¼	9¼
September	9	7⅞	7⅞
October	9½	8¾	8⅞
November	9	8⅝	9
December	10⅜	8⅞	10⅜
January 1964	13	9⅞	11¼
February	12¾	10	12½
March	15¼	12⅜	14⅝
April	14⅝	12½	12¾
May	13⅜	12	12
June	14⅜	12¾	14⅜
July	14⅛	13¼	13½
August	13½	12¾	12⅞
September	14¾	12⅞	14⅛
October	16¼	12	16

*Prices have been adjusted to reflect the 2:1 stock split in April 1962. The offering price of the first public offering, in June 1961, was $20.50.

EXHIBIT 3
Marrud, Inc. *(continued)*

Quarterly high and low bid prices for Marrud, Inc., common stock and four quarter cumulative earnings per share for fiscal years 1961-1964. Quarters correspond to the company's reporting practice, i.e., August-October, November-January, February-April, and May-July.

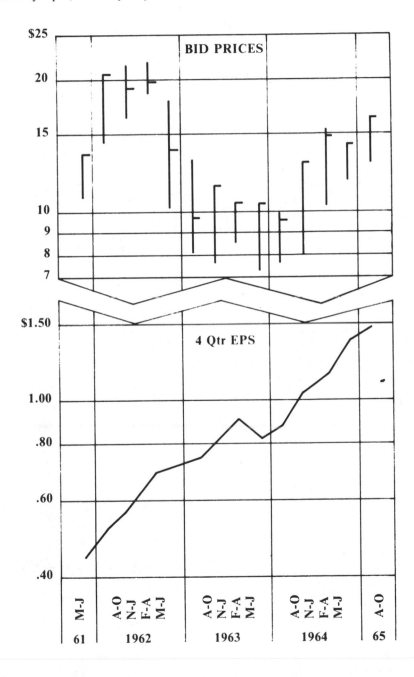

EXHIBIT 4
Marrud, Inc.

Range of Market Prices of Marrud, Inc. Common Stock, Barron's Retail Merchandise Group Stock Average, Moody's Price Index of 200 Common Stocks, and National Quotation Bureau's Over-the-Counter Stock Index, June 1961 through October 1964.

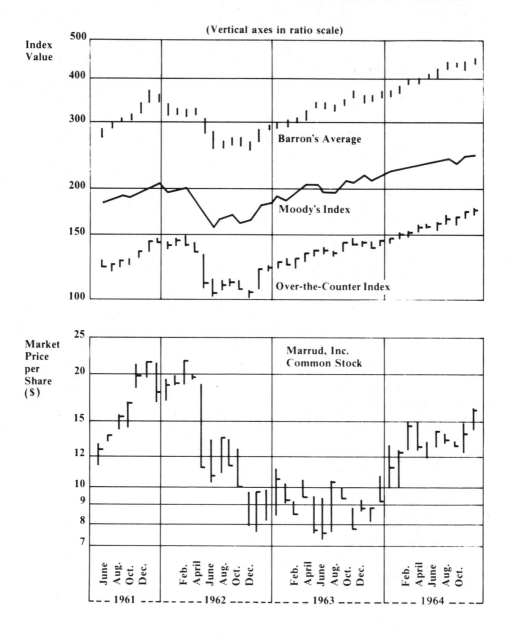

EXHIBIT 5

Marrud, Inc.
Financial Data for Selected Companies

Cunningham Drug Stores, Inc.

Operates directly or through stores wholly-owned subsidiaries conventional and discount drug and variety stores, including leased drug departments in discount department stores. The common stock is listed on the New York Stock Exchange.

	12 Months Ended September 30				
	1960	1961	1962	1963	1964
Sales (000 omitted)	$ 54,700	$ 52,488	$ 53,189	$ 53,920	$ 57,616
Earnings after taxes (000 omitted)	1,122	755	193	407	925
Net earnings per share	$ 2.91	$ 1.96	$ .50	$ 1.06	$ 2.40
Dividends per share	1.50	1.90	1.90	.80	.80
Number of shares	385,119	385,119	385,119	385,119	385,119
Number of operating units	211	206	216	211	227
Total assets	$ 26,096	$ 26,025	$ 25,649	$ 25,457	$ 26,889
Net working capital	11,418	12,224	11,442	11,239	12,032
Long-term debt	0	0	0	0	0
Net worth	20,102	20,306	19,767	18,975	19,592
Annual lease obligations	2,100	2,050	1,800	1,875	1,875

Gateway Sporting Goods Company, Inc.

Sells at retail and wholesale, sporting goods, photographic equipment, toys, luggage, etc., through ten conventional sporting goods stores and licensed departments in discount department stores and mail order, school, and wholesale divisions. An initial offering of the common stock was made to the public in August 1960 at $10 per share. The stock was split 2:1 in February 1962 and listed on the American Stock Exchange in June 1963.

	12 Months Ended December 31			
	1960	1961	1962	1963
Sales (000 omitted)	$ 7,709	$ 10,785	$ 15,307	$ 23,115
Earnings after taxes (000 omitted)	$ 201	$ 340	$ 496	$ 615
Net earnings per share*	$ .53	$ .71	$ 1.03	$ 1.16
Dividends per share*	$ .15†	$ .30	$ .32	$ .32
Number of shares*	379,150	479,406	479,986	528,786
Number of leased units	NA	NA	103	145
Total assets	NA	$ 6,076	$ 9,819	$ 11,838
Net working capital	NA	3,326	5,563	6,124
Long-term debt	NA	700	3,000	3,052
Net worth	NA	3,128	3,544	4,352
Annual lease obligations	NA	NA	NA	671

*Adjusted to reflect 2:1 stock split in February 1962.
†Six months only.

EXHIBIT 5
Marrud, Inc. *(continued)*
Financial Data for Selected Companies

Peoples Drug Stores, Inc.

Operates directly or through wholly-owned subsidiaries conventional and self-service discount drug stores. The common stock is listed on the New York Stock Exchange.

| | 12 Months Ended December 31 | | | | 9 mos. to |
	1960	1961	1962	1963	9/30/1964*
Sales (000 omitted)	$93,185	$98,667	$108,439	$117,654	$92,728
Earnings after taxes					
(000 omitted)	1,312	1,986	1,517	2,032	1,179
Net earnings per share	$ 2.39	$ 3.6	$ 2.63	$ 3.51	$ 1.96†
Dividends per share	2.00	2.00	2.00‡	2.00	2.00#
Number of shares	550,000	550,000	577,709	578,495	601,723
Number of operating units	196	205	221	225	NA
Total assets	$32,022	$35,103	$ 39,913	$ 42,825	$45,700
Net working capital	12,438	12,359	16,459	17,074	17,861
Long-term debt	0	0	5,700	5,400	5,250
Net worth	23,815	24,701	25,054	25,960	27,199
Annual lease obligations	3,065	3,575	3,986	4,020	NA

*Unaudited.
†$1.19 for 9 months to 9/30/1963.
‡Plus 5% stock dividend.
#Annual rate.

Unishops, Inc.

Sells men's and boys' clothing at retail through leased departments in discount department stores. An initial offering of common stock was made on April 17, 1962, at $14 per share. The common stock was listed on the American Stock Exchange in October 1963.

| | 12 Months Ended December 31 | | | | 9 mos. to |
	1960	1961	1962	1963	9/30/1964*
Sales (000 omitted)	$8,419	$15,627	$23,630	$27,384	$22,080
Earnings after taxes					
(000 omitted)	424	702	891	1,198	517
Net earnings per share	$ .42	$ .70	$ .85	$ 1.14	$ .49†
Dividends per share	0	0	0	0	0
Number of shares (1,000's)	1,000	1,000	1,050	1,050	1,060
Number of operating units	33	69	91	104	137
Total assets	NA	$ 6,302	$ 7,374	$ 9,388	NA
Net working capital	NA	811	1,915	4,623	NA
Long-term debt	NA	0	0	1,500	NA
Net worth	NA	1,655	3,103	4,301	NA

*Unaudited.
†$.25 for 9 months to 9/30/1963.

EXHIBIT 5
Marrud, Inc. *(continued)*

Quarterly High and Low Common Stock Prices and Four Quarter Cumulative Earnings Per Share for Cunningham Drug Stores, Inc., Gateway Sporting Goods Company, Inc., Peoples Drug Stores, Inc., and Unishops, Inc. Range of market prices shown for second quarter 1961 are for the month of June only.

(Ratio Scale)

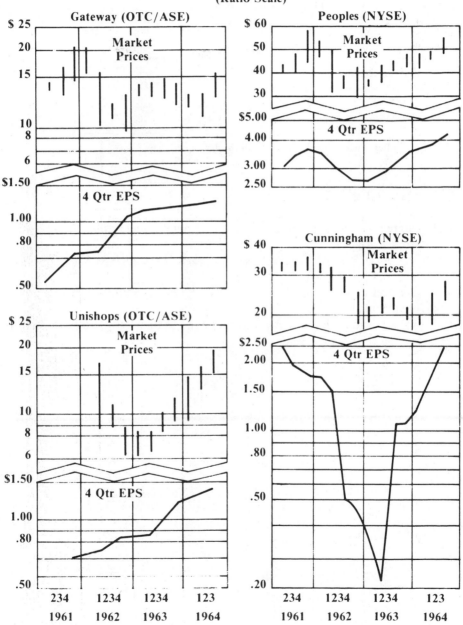

EXHIBIT 6

Marrud, Inc.

*Cash Budget, Fiscal Years 1965-1969**

(000 omitted)

	1965	1966	1967	1968	1969
Estimated expenditures:					
Capital expenditures	$ 400	$ 400	$ 400	$ 400	$ 400
Net addition to working capital	1,750	2,500	1,740	2,290	2,960
Sinking fund payments	300	300	370	370	370
Dividend requirements	450	450	450	450	450
Total	$2,900	$3,650	$2,960	$3,510	$4,180
Estimated receipts					
Net earnings	$1,760	$2,000	$2,400	$2,840	$3,400
Depreciation	340	450	560	670	780
Total	$2,100	$2,450	$2,960	$3,510	$4,180
Net need	$ 800	$1,200	$ 0	$ 0	$ 0

*Does not include the proposed acquisition of the drug store chain.

QUESTIONS

1. Evaluate and discuss Marrud, Inc.'s growth achievements and strategy over the past few years.
2. Do you agree with Mr. Margolis's cash forecasts for the next few years given in Exhibit 6?
3. Assess and comment on Mr. Margolis's proposal with respect to the firm's dividend policy.
4. What dividend policy would you recommend in light of the firm's growth and financing objectives?

Case 31
Hammond Publishing Company

In June 1967, Mr. George Hammond, president and principal owner of Hammond Publishing Company, considered several financing alternatives affecting the company's capital structure and possibly its shareholder composition. Hammond Publishing Company had grown rapidly in the several preceding years, and its need for funds now outstripped the company's internal supplies. Specifically, Mr. Hammond weighed issuing stock against issuing additional long-term debt. At the same time, he wondered whether he should continue to hold the majority of the shares of the company or, indeed, any shares at all.

Company Description

Although Hammond Publishing Company was relatively small by industry standards, it carried out the complete range of activities associated with publishing, including the search for and selection of authors, evaluation and editing of manuscripts, design and illustration of publications, and promotion, sale, and distribution of books. Published books fell into four general classes: fiction, nonfiction, school and college texts, and professional books. Company activities were carried out from a modern one-store combined office and warehouse building located in San Mateo, California. Since the company had recently completed a staff and warehouse expansion program, management felt Hammond Publishing could easily handle a higher level of sales than it was then experiencing. Hammond did

This case was prepared by Professor David J. Springate of Southern Methodist University as a basis for classroom discussion and not to indicate either effective or ineffective handling of an administrative situation.

not own printing or binding facilities. While no long-term agreements for printing or binding services were in effect, it was clear that through careful advance scheduling, the company could arrange for the provision of adequate services.

The company employed about 310 people. Of these, 21 were executives and department heads; approximately 30 were engaged in editorial work; about 50 were in sales, promotion, and publicity; approximately 130 were in clerical and office work; and approximately 80 were engaged in shipping and warehousing activities. The company was governed by no collective bargaining agreements. On the whole, the company's employee relations were good. Authors were compensated by royalties at various rates on books sold. In accordance with standard industry practice, the company extended royalty advances to authors while manuscripts were being prepared or revised.

Hammond Publishing Company was established by Mr. Hammond's father late in the 1800's. Growth was slow through its early years, most occurring after World War II. For many years, Hammond's publications consisted primarily of fiction and nonfiction works of broad interest for both adults and children that reached the public through retail book stores and libraries. In the late 1950s, the company expanded into the elementary, high school, and college market, primarily through the development of supplemental information books for use with standard high school and college textbooks.

The greater part of the company's works of fiction and nonfiction and a portion of its children's books were sold directly through the company's retail sales force or through wholesalers to retail book stores and department stores throughout the country. Sales to local school boards and libraries were made by a second segment of the company's sales force and also by an independent sales agency. The third part of the company's sales force was composed of "travelers." These men were responsible for the selling of both college textbooks and college supplementary books. As a large part of the job, they also solicited manuscripts and maintained relationships with college book authors.

Expected Growth

Hammond Publishing Company expected to continue growing faster than the industry, and expected sales to increase by over 30 percent in 1967. This sales growth would be due to both the capture of sales of other firms and to the broadly based rise in book sales. No reason for future slackening in company growth was foreseeable, although a 30 percent annual rise could not be sustained indefinitely.

Between 1965 and 1966, total book sales in the nation rose 15 percent to $2.3 billion. A similar jump was expected for 1966-1967, with a large part of this growth expected to come in textbooks, the most important segment of the industry. Since the rise in school and college enrollments was expected to continue for at least the next ten years (see Exhibit 1), with the trend of the future toward more general and larger educational exposure per person, and since per capita annual book expenditures in 1966 were $5.92 in grammar school, $10.16 in high school, and $36.49 in college, it was easy to conclude that textbook sales would increase faster than the 20 percent figure attained in 1965-1966.

The public mood encouraged such feelings. In 1966, federal expenditures for educational purposes reached unprecedented levels. Sales of books other than textbooks were also on the upswing, benefiting from libraries and schools having new buying power from federal funds. Sales were also stimulated by population growth, upgraded reading tastes, and higher disposable incomes.

The Need for External Funds

The company's need for funds derived from sales growth. (See Exhibit 2 for income statements for 1964-1966 and Exhibit 3 for balance sheets for the years 1964-1966.) Between the years 1964 and 1965, sales grew by over 30 percent. In 1966, sales growth was 35 percent. Mr. Hammond was convinced that growth in the neighborhood of this rate would continue. The principal need for funds was to finance growth of accounts receivable and inventory supporting increasing sales, but funds were also used for printing plates and royalty advances. (Exhibit 4 shows sources and uses of funds for 1964-1965 and 1965-1966.) Year-end figures in the exhibits do not reflect seasonal influences. Accounts receivable and inventory were higher in the summer and autumn, due to the larger percentage of sales made at this time of year. Sixty-two percent of company sales took place in the months of June, July, August, and September. Traditionally, the seasonal need for funds had been met through short-term borrowing.

A large part of the additional funds requirements in 1965 and 1966 were financed by deferral of royalty payments. Under the provisions of federal income tax law, it was to the advantage of authors to spread the income received from a publication over a period of years. The maximum period permissible was three years. When such deferrals were made, the company was enabled, in essence, to finance a portion of its requirements thereby. If the allowable period of deferral were ever reduced, or if for some reason a substantial number of authors demanded their royalty payments at one time, fund outflows would be occasioned, possibly in large amounts.

During 1966, funds supplied by deferral of royalties dropped from the preceding year's level, and partly in consequence, the company was forced to borrow over $1.5 million in short-term loans from the Valley Trust Company. These notes were due on September 1, 1967. Although the loans could possibly be renewed, this was not a permanent answer. It seemed unlikely that internal sources could provide the needed funds. Inventories were as low as could be comfortably tolerated. Amounts receivable had been increased relative to sales as a competitive necessity. Profit margins in the industry would not change appreciably in the foreseeable future, and at a level of about 35 days' purchases, the company's accounts payable were extended about as far as could be expected. Thus, it seemed that it would be necessary to tap external sources of permanent funds.

Possibilities of Additional Equity

One possible means of raising equity was through an underwritten public stock flotation. In recent stock flotations of other publishing firms (see Exhibit 5), the total of the underwriter's spread (the difference between the amount raised by the underwriter of an issue and the amount remitted to the issuing company) and the "out-of-pocket" costs involved in the flotation varied between 5.3 percent and 8.3

percent of the total issue. Most of this total, perhaps 80 percent, was made up of the underwriter's spread. The remaining direct costs involved in an issue, such as printing, registration, and legal fees were partially variable and might well total $40,000 on a $4 million public issue. Market price per share at issue in the publishing flotations shown in Exhibit 5 ranged between $15 and $34. Price/earnings ratios at issue varied between 14 and 26.

Some preliminary discussions took place with Mr. Harry Cameron, a senior partner in the underwriting and brokerage firm of Riley and Liggett. From these discussions, it was apparent that a number of warrants equal to 20 percent of the number of shares in an initial public offering would almost certainly be required by the underwriter in return for his support of the "after-market." The warrants would be exercisable for five years at the offering price of the first issue. Support for the after-market would be desirable in the case of Hammond Publishing shares since the company would almost certainly have its shares traded over the counter. In the first few months of such trading, the market might prove to be a "thin" one, and it is here that the underwriter could help maintain the market by being willing to buy and sell for his own account. In supporting the after-market, an underwriter, in effect, becomes an active participant in stock trading in order to preserve an active market in the stock being supported. Through his actions, drastic swings in stock prices are avoided in the period immediately following the stock issue.

Several months would be required for preparation of the issue by the underwriter and registration of the issue with the Securities and Exchange Commission.

A second alternative in raising equity was to use an underwriter's help in finding a private party or parties able to supply a suitable amount of funds, for example a pension fund. In this case, the company would remain closely held. Such an alternative had several advantages. A private issue could be carried out faster and would be cheaper than a public issue. There would be an underwriter's fee of perhaps a half point. Potential dilution of the warrants would be eliminated. Also, private placement might reduce subsequent problems of stockholder relations since there would be fewer stockholders involved.

Mr. Hammond owned 15,000 of the 25,000 outstanding shares of the company. With most of his personal estate invested in Hammond Publishing, he could not invest any further sizable sum in the company. The remaining 10,000 shares were held among Mr. Hammond's relatives. These holdings represented a large part of the wealth of the various individuals in most instances.

The most compelling argument for public sale involved Mr. Hammond's personal estate. Since he was nearing 60 years of age, such matters were of increasing importance to him. In addition to providing for his wife in the event of his death, Mr. Hammond was desirous of establishing a trust fund for his grandchildren. From tax data (see Exhibit 6), he concluded that a public market in Hammond Publishing shares would almost certainly reduce the Internal Revenue Service valuation of his estate by a substantial amount. A lower valuation would reduce estate taxes.

A public market would also provide Mr. Hammond with liquidity for his holdings. At the present time, there was no established value for Hammond Publishing shares and no trading in its shares. By long-standing agreement, shareholders sold to the company when divesting themselves of holdings of Hammond stock. The price involved in such transactions was the book value per share. The book value of Mr. Hammond's shares was about $2.5 million.

In the past, the company declared dividends at irregular intervals. A declaration was usually made when one or more of the shareholders had large fund needs. Hammond's management felt that if a public market in Hammond Publishing shares were made, the company would establish some consistent dividend policy and could not be as arbitrary as heretofore.

An alternative that combined the advantages of a public offering for the company and provided liquidity directly for present shareholders was to combine the sale of new shares and currently outstanding shares in a public sale. If some of the shares now closely held were added to new ones in a public flotation, the size of the public market would be increased. The sale of some of his shares would provide funds for Mr. Hammond's retirement or, in the event of his death, for the payment of estate taxes that would then fall due.

Other Possibilities

Floating long-term debt was a practicable alternative to raising new equity. From informal conversations with executives of other publishing firms of approximately the same size, Mr. Hammond was certain that he could negotiate a loan of about $2 million, assuming the bank notes had been paid off, without additional equity funds being added. Such loans were often made by the small loan departments of life insurance companies and other institutional lenders. A loan larger than $2 million would be improbable without the sale of new company stock and certianly would be much more expensive if it could be raised at all. Apparently, most lenders would insist that about $2 of equity be added for each $1 of long-term debt above the $2 million level. A total long-term debt ceiling of about $4 million would apply. Likely provisions in connection with a loan in the region of $2 million would be an annual amortization of about $300,000 starting within one year, an interest rate of about 7.5 percent, reflecting the high interest rates still in effect following the 1966 "credit crunch," a net working capital restriction requiring the maintenance of $1 million minimum, and a partial restriction on dividends. The condition most likely to be imposed was a restriction that dividends would be paid on only 35 percent of the net earnings subsequent to the date of the loan.

Yet another alternative was the merger of Hammond Publishing into a larger concern. Mr. Hammond had been approached about a corporate merger several times during the preceding five years, but he resisted each effort, feeling that he wanted to "run his own show." However, the increasing premiums being paid for publishing companies gave him pause. During the past few years, many publishing companies merged into electronic giants, and some of the latter were known to be still actively searching for publishing acquisitions. Two recent examples of such acquisitions (see Exhibit 7) were RCA's purchase of Random House in which $2 was paid for each $1 of assets, and International Telephone and Telegraph's payment of $50 a share for Howard Sams, although at that time Sams sold for $30 on the open market. Other merger possibilities were with larger publishers. One offer still open to him was made by the publisher of a large national weekly news magazine. In exchange for all outstanding shares of Hammond, the larger company offered to provide an amount of its common stock with a market value of approximately $24.2 million.

Merger offered several advantages. First, the transaction would be tax-free if carried out by means of an exchange of shares. Second, since the exchange would presumably be made with a large company whose shares were listed on a national exchange, valuation and liquidity problems connected with Mr. Hammond's estate would be eliminated. Finally, a merger would solve the problem of management succession and a buyer for Hammond Publishing Company in one transaction and at a time favorable to Mr. Hammond. Other owners of the company were willing to participate in a merger if the price was satisfactory.

On the other hand, there were several disadvantages to a merger. The plans might miscarry after the expenditure of much time and effort. Mr. Hammond remembered the comments he had read concerning the cancellation of a merger, agreed to two months before, between a publisher of business and economics texts and a very large periodical publisher. The president of the larger concern said, ". . . [The smaller company's officials] ran into some difficulties in trying to agree on how their operations would be carried on as a division of [the larger company]. I think this is understandable in a company which has been developed largely by one man and has been run as a privately operating organization for most of its history." The chairman of the board of the smaller company, on the other hand, said in his letter to the stockholders that the merger was called off as "not being in the best interest of [the] employees or stockholders." Also, he said, contrary to some reports regarding the proposed merger, "the . . . firm is not a family-owned corporation operated by just one individual. . . ."

Merger would mean the loss of control of the company by its present owners. A merger might not be successful and might result in the subsequent resale of Hammond Publishing to a second buyer. Whether successful or not, a merger might well result in a restructuring of the company and the release of long-term loyal employees.

EXHIBIT 1
Hammond Publishing Company
Projected Educational Enrollment in U.S. 1966-1975

Year	Projected Fall Enrollment in Grades K-12 of Regular Day Schools (thousands)	Projected Fall Degree Credit Enrollment in All Institutions of Higher Education (thousands)
1966	49,700	6,055
1967	50,700	6,541
1968	51,500	6,923
1969	52,000	7,050
1970	52,300	7,299
1971	52,600	7,604
1972	52,600	7,976
1973	52,800	8,335
1974	53,100	8,684
1975	53,600	8,995

Source: *Projections of Educational Statistics to 1975-76,* U.S. Dept. of Health, Education and Welfare, 1966.

EXHIBIT 2
Hammond Publishing Company
Income Statements for Years Ended Dec. 31, 1964-1966
(dollar figures in thousands)

	1964		1965		1966	
Sales		$8,562		$11,437		$15,648
Less returns and discounts		945		1,257		1,425
Net sales		$7,617		$10,180		$14,223
Cost of Sales:						
Royalties	$1,363		$1,775		$2,585	
Other	2,374	3,742	3,343	5,118	4,346	6,931
Gross profit		$3,875		$ 5,062		$ 7,292
Expenses:						
Selling	$ 862		$1,141		$1,402	
Administrative	1,683		1,938		2,299	
Other	836	3,381	1,222	4,301	1,908	5,609
Operating profit		$ 494		$ 761		$ 1,683
Interest expense		12		14		62
Income before taxes		$ 482		$ 747		$ 1,621
Federal income taxes		181		304		803
Net income		$ 301		$ 443		$ 818

EXHIBIT 3

Hammond Publishing Company
Balance Sheets as of Dec. 31, 1964-1966
(dollar figures in thousands)

	1964	1965	1966
ASSETS			
Cash	$ 596	$ 627	$ 846
Accounts receivable, net	841	1,854	3,427
Inventory	2,190	2,820	3,774
Prepaid expenses	74	91	157
Total current assets	$3,701	$5,392	$ 8,204
Plant and equipment	$2,183	$2,370	$ 2,637
Less: Reserve for depreciation	371	435	515
Net plant and equipment	$1,812	$1,935	$ 2,122
Plates at amortized cost	$ 395	$ 532	$ 718
Royalty advances	678	894	1,239
Miscellaneous assets	680	757	754
Total other assets	$1,753	$2,183	$ 2,711
Total assets	$7,266	$9,510	$13,037
LIABILITIES AND STOCKHOLDERS' EQUITY			
Notes payable	$ 30	$ 35	$ 1,575
Accounts payable	317	478	671
Other accruals	215	363	868
Royalties due in current year	1,059	1,644	2,189
Total current liabilities	$1,621	$2,520	$ 5,303
Mortgage notes less current portion	$1,099	$1,047	$ 995
Royalties due after one year	1,562	2,504	2,463
Deferred taxes	42	54	73
Total long-term liabilities	$2,703	$3,605	$ 3,531
Common stock, $15 par value, auth. 25,000 sh., issued and outstanding 25,000 shares	375	375	375
Retained earnings	2,567	3,010	3,828
Stockholders' equity	$2,942	$3,385	$ 4,203
Total liabilities and stockholders' equity	$7,266	$9,510	$13,037

EXHIBIT 4

Hammond Publishing Company
Funds Flow Statements for Years Ended Dec. 31, 1965-1966
(dollar figures in thousands)

	SOURCES		USES	
1965	Nonoperating flows		Cash	$ 31
	Notes payable	$ 5	Accounts receivable	1,013
	Accounts payable	161	Inventory	630
	Other accruals	148	Royalty advances	216
	Deferred royalties	1,527	Other assets	418
	Deferred taxes	12	Liabilities	52
	Depreciation	64		
		$1,917		
	Funds provided by operations	443		
		$2,360		$2,360
1966	Nonoperating flows		Cash	$ 219
	Notes payable	$1,540	Accounts receivable	1,573
	Accounts payable	193	Inventory	954
	Other accruals	505	Royalty advances	345
	Deferred royalties	504	Other assets	519
	Deferred taxes	19	Liabilities	52
	Miscellaneous assets	3		
	Depreciation	80		
		$2,844		
	Funds provided by operations	818		
		$3,662		$3,662

EXHIBIT 5

Hammond Publishing Company

Selected Equity Flotations of Publishing Firms 1960-1967

Company Name	Issue Date	Size of Issue ($000)	Number of Shares Involved	Underwriting Cost ($000) (Underwriter's spread and "out of pocket" costs)	Total Underwriting Cost per Share as a Percent of Total Issue Cost	Market Price at Issue ($)	Price/Earnings at Issue	Proportion of Issue Representing New Financing (Percent)
Harper & Row*	Feb. 1960	2,470	157,346	217	8.3	15.00	14.3	10
Richard D. Irwin	Aug. 1961	2,560	160,000	204	8.0	16.00	25	20
Addison Wesley	Mar. 1965	2,010	60,000	129	6.4	33.50	14	0
John Wiley	Apr. 1962	2,625	150,000	164	6.25	17.50	21	0
	Apr. 1967	3,400	100,000	200	5.9	34.00	26	50
G. P. Putnam's Sons	May 1967	8,047	309,126	447	5.6	26.00	20.7	0
Houghton Mifflin	May 1967	19,873	662,440	1,060	5.3	30.00	25.9	40

*Incorporated as Row, Peterson and Company. Present title adopted May 1, 1962, on merger of Harper and Brothers.

EXHIBIT 6

Hammond Publishing Company
Tax Provisions Relevant to Estates and Closely Held Stock

Para. 120,011 (Excerpts from) Table for Computation of Gross Estate Tax

(A) Taxable Estate Equal to or More Than ($)	(B) Taxable Estate Less Than ($)	(C) Tax on Amount in Col. (A) ($)	(D) Rate of Tax on Excess Over Amount in Col. (A) (Percent)
100,000	250,000	20,700	30
250,000	500,000	65,700	32
500,000	750,000	145,700	35
1,000,000	1,250,000	325,700	39
1,500,000	2,000,000	528,200	45
2,000,000	2,500,000	753,200	49
3,000,000	3,500,000	1,263,200	56
5,000,000	6,000,000	2,468,000	67
8,000,000	10,000,000	4,568,000	76

Para 120.311 Valuation of Unlisted Stocks

If there have been bona fide sales, much the same procedure is followed in the case of unlisted stock as is followed with listed stocks (i.e., the fair market value is used). If there have been no sales some of the factors to be considered in arriving at the fair market value are the following: the bid and asked prices for the unlisted stock; the company's net worth; the dividend capacity of the company, and its earning power; value of securities of a like corporation engaged in a similar business whose securities are listed on an exchange.

Para 120,312.1 Basis of Valuation of Stock of Close Corporations

It is obvious that where an estate owns the stock of a close corporation, it is taxed ordinarily on a much higher basis than that of an estate owning listed securities. In the latter case the value is definitely established by actual quotations, and experience has shown that sales of such stock are usually made at a much lower price than the theoretical fair market value determined as in the case of closely held stock by an examination of financial data and the application of the usual methods of valuation.

Source: Prentice-Hall Federal Taxes. *Estate and Gift Taxes Volume.* By permission.

EXHIBIT 7

Hammond Publishing Company
Selected Mergers of Publishing Firms 1964-1967

Year	Purchasing Company	Sales Level ($000)	Earnings after tax last complete year ($000)	Publishing Firm Merged	Sales Level ($000)	Earnings after tax last complete year ($000)	Price*
1964	Encyclopedia Britannica	125,000	NA	G & C Merriam Company	NA	NA	$18.0 million cash
1966	Radio Corporation of America	2,042,001	101,161	Random House	32,000	973	Common stock of RCA worth $37.7 million
1966	International Telephone & Telegraph Corp.	1,639,143	76,110	Howard Sams	17,241	1,179	Convertible preferred and common stock of ITT worth $33.8 million
1966	Scott, Foresman	47,817	11,730	Wm. Morrow and Company	5,400	NA	Convertible preferred stock of Scott, Foresman worth $7.0 million
1966	Encyclopedia Britannica	140,000	NA	Frederick A. Praeger	2,975	NA	$2.5 million
1966	McGraw-Hill	216,198	18,151	Standard and Poor's	NA	2,700	Convertible preferred stock of McGraw-Hill worth $50.0 million
1966	International Publishing Corporation	366,735	30,618	Cahners Publishing Corporation (40% of shares)	20,000	NA	$12.5 million cash
1967	McGraw-Hill	307,606	28,579	Ipma Publishing Company	1,946	141	Common stock of McGraw-Hill worth $2.0 million

*Stock values quoted at announcement-day values.
NA—not available

QUESTIONS

1. What will be Hammond Publishing Company's need for funds over the next three years?
2. Describe the characteristics of a new equity issue.
3. Compare the new equity issue with an issue of debt.
4. What are the pros and cons of the merger option?
5. Which alternative should Mr. Hammond select?

Case 32
Mountain Bell

Mountain Bell, a large telephone company based in Denver, Colorado, is a member of the Bell System and is 87 percent owned by AT&T. The company is presently engaged in providing communications in seven rapidly growing mountain states, one county in Texas (El Paso), and one county in Oregon (via a subsidiary, Malheur Telephone Company). The company's gross operating revenues have expanded relatively rapidly during the last decade. Similarly, total long-term invested capital[1] has more than doubled since 1963 (see Tables 1, 2, 3, and 4 for 1963-1973 summary of Mountain Bell's financial statistics).

The company's enormous investment in long-term assets (exceeding $2.7 billion in 1973) reflects the basic capital-intensive nature of the public communications industry. Being a regulated company, the timing of Mountain Bell's long-term capital expenditures is largely uncontrollable because of required commitment to continued service, and profitability on investment is only partially controllable through extensive cost-saving programs.

Capital Expenditure Plans

Mountain Bell has been forced by unrelenting demand pressures to increase its capital expenditure by over 100 percent in the four years since 1969. In addition,

This case was prepared by Professor Dennis B. Fitzpatrick of Boise State University as a basis for classroom discussion and not to illustrate either effective or ineffective handling of an administrative situation. Although some actual company data were used, conversations between company officials are hypothetical.

[1]Exclusive of current liabilities and deferred credits.

severe inflationary pressures in the national economy in 1973 and 1974[2] resulted in management's upward revision of the company's future dollar investment in plant and equipment. The company's secretary and treasurer, George Brown, has conservatively forecasted that capital expenditures will average between $600 million and $700 million per year during the next five years. In spite of this large investment in plant, Mr. Brown feels that Mountain Bell's spare service capacity may be severely restricted.

Mr. Brown has also forecasted that internal cash generation (from retained earnings, depreciation, and tax deferrals) will provide only about half the money needed for the company's capital budgeting program—external sources of financing must be relied on for the rest (see Table 5).

Earnings History

Rates of return on rate base are set by regulatory commissions (see Table 1). The company must deal directly or indirectly with ten such bodies: seven state regulatory commissions on intrastate rates and through AT&T, with the Federal Communications Commission (FCC), on interstate rates. The company is actively engaged in rate requests in those jurisdictions where earnings are inadequate; however, delays inherent in the regulatory process limit the effectiveness of such increases. Additionally, the FCC has embarked fairly recently on a policy of encouraging competition in communications services. Management feels that this policy shift may have an adverse impact on Mountain Bell's gross revenues in the long run.

The company's earnings per share have grown by approximately 13 percent during 1973 over 1972 largely due to earlier-than-anticipated rate case decisions, but management does not expect to sustain such growth in 1974.

Financial Structure

After huge demands for service immediately following the Second World War, Mountain Bell reduced its debt-to-total capital ratio to 25-35 percent during the 1950's. By the mid-1960's, management felt that the economy was less susceptible to boom-and-bust swings that had characterized the pre-WWII economy. Consequently, the company began to increase its debt ratio toward 45 percent (the current objective of the Bell System). By the end of 1973, depressed stock market conditions coupled with nondeferrable demand for construction funds had pushed the debt ratio to 48 percent.

Long-Range Financing Alternatives[3]

On April 15, 1974, Mountain Bell's president, Robert Hay, requested George Brown to prepare a detailed report relating to the appropriate external financing

[2]The GNP price deflator, which includes construction costs, increased by more than 10 percent for the year ending in March, 1974.

[3]This section contains hypothetical conversations and individuals and does *not* represent actual conversations of Mountain Bell officials.

that should be tapped by the company during the next five years. The report is to be presented to the Board of Directors on May 15, 1974. In order to receive a broad range of input prior to finalizing the report, Mr. Brown arranged for a meeting with Steve Smith, assistant treasurer, Tom Brady, and Dick French. Mr. Brady is employed by a large investment banking house in New York, and Mr. French specializes in utility financing for a regional investment banking firm headquartered in Denver.

Mr. Brown opened the meeting by expressing concern over the financing options presently available to Mountain Bell. The market price of the company's common stock had remained relatively static for years (see Table 1), while the firm's earnings per share have increased substantially. These conditions have resulted in a rapid decline of the company's price-earnings multiple from twenty-four in 1961 to less than nine in 1973. This compares to relatively higher price multiples for other industrial and utility firms in recent years (see Table 6). Mr. Brown noted that the common stock was presently trading on the New York Stock Exchange at approximately $21 per share.

Mr. Brady commented that the recent escalation of AAA utility bond and preferred stock yields[4] to well over 8 percent preclude the desirability of issuing bonds or preferred stock for the rest of 1974. Consequently, Brady suggested that the only option open to Brown is to issue at least $350 million of common stock during the next twelve months.

Mr. French strongly disagreed with Brady's recommendations and urged Brown to consider issuing at least $200 million in long-term bonds in 1974, thereby maintaining the company's present capital structure posture. French argued that although bond rates appeared to be extremely high currently, the present cost of debt may well be cheap in a historical sense. French indicated that in an era of extreme inflationary pressures in the American economy, combined with severe raw material shortages, higher long-term interest rates were likely to occur for the next several years. In addition, French noted that issuing more common stock at the present time would unduly dilute the earnings of the present stockholders. In support of this contention, French showed Brown a chart (see Table 7) indicating that the market price of the stock was currently less than book value per share and was likely to decline further if new common stock severely diluted the earnings.

Mr. Brady reacted rather strongly to Mr. French's line of argument and suggested that although relatively high long-term interest rates may persist, there is convincing evidence that utility interest rates may well peak in 1974. Consequently, Brady urged Brown to defer issuing debt issues until 1975. Brady also argued that issuance of more debt in 1974 would result in unacceptable interest coverage ratios of less than three times earnings (for a recent history of the firm's interest coverage ratio, see Figure 1). Brady also suggested that coverage ratios of less than three times may result in a downgrading of the firm's bonds and preferred stock by Standard & Poor's and Moody's. Brady noted that three Bell System companies have recently been downgraded by Standard & Poor's from AAA to AA. Such a downgrading is undesirable for the following reasons: (1) top credit rating will be most important during capital shortages expected over the next decade; (2) the

[4]Mountain Bell's bonds and preferred stock are presently rated AAA by the major rating agencies.

AAA rating is the most sought after investment by institutional investors, and would insure a market; (3) a downgrading would advertise the company's increased riskiness, further reducing the chance of a successful equity issue; (4) since the company relies on commercial paper and notes for short-term financing (in addition to advances from AT&T), a strong credit rating is important during credit crunches such as the one experienced in 1970; (5) a downgrading of the company's bonds would reduce the value of all bonds now outstanding and would mean higher interest costs for all future debt.

Finally, Brady told Brown that issuing common stock in 1974 would not unduly dilute stockholder earnings since AT&T can be expected to exercise its pre-emptive right to purchase 87 percent of any new common stock issued by Mountain Bell at a subscription price of between 5 percent and 15 percent less than the current market price.

TABLE 1

Mountain Bell—Financial Statistics

	1973	*1972*	*1971*	*1970**	*1969**	*1963**
Operating Results *years ended Dec. 31*						
Operating Revenues	$1,062,138,000	$ 904,434,000	$ 800,599,000	$ 714,949,000	$ 660,788,000	$ 406,747,000
Operating Expenses	$ 649,015,000	$ 561,335,000	$ 495,943,000	$ 432,845,000	$ 383,246,000	$ 228,510,000
Operating Taxes	$ 202,157,000	$ 173,140,000	$ 156,260,000	$ 149,445,000	$ 158,078,000	$ 105,255,000
Net Income	$ 145,024,000	$ 118,017,000	$ 105,300,000	$ 100,097,000	$ 95,986,000	$ 62,318,000
Operating Taxes Per Share	$3.45	$3.21	$3.17	$3.03	$3.20	$2.48
Earnings Per Share	$2.48	$2.19	$2.13	$2.03	$1.95	$1.47
Dividends Declared Per Share	$1.44	$1.36	$1.36	$1.36	$1.27	$0.95
Average Equity Per Share	$22.37	$21.61	$21.01	$20.27	$19.59	$15.82
Percent Return on Average Equity	11.08	10.13	10.16	10.01	9.93	9.28
Ownership And Capital *end of year*						
Number of Share Owners	28,438	28,234	26,965	26,954	25,959	19,970
Average Shares Outstanding†	58,528,865	53,935,819	49,342,772	49,342,772	49,342,772	42,392,198
Total Capital	$2,577,881,000	$2,248,461,000	$2,012,434,000	$1,773,238,000	$1,534,963,000	$ 978,053,000
Percent of Debt in Total Capital	47.98	43.06	47.56	42.66	35.91	25.18
Market Performance of Stock *(N.Y.S.E.) years ended Dec. 31*						
Market Price High and Low	23½-19⅞	23¾-19⅝	24⅞-20⅝	23½-19⅝	24⅞-20¾	31⅞-26¼**
Average Yearly Price#	$21.47	$21.51	$22.87	$21.50	$22.95	$29.46
Price-Earnings Ratio	8.7	9.8	10.7	10.6	11.8	20.0

TABLE 1
Mountain Bell—Financial Statistics (continued)

	1973	1972	1971	1970*	1969*	1963*
Telephone Plant, *at cost, end of year*	$3,442,513,000	$3,006,936,000	$2,642,669,000	$2,330,656,000	$2,027,500,000	$1,217,407,000
Plant Per Telephone	$661	$620	$590	$561	$521	$434
Telephones *end of year*						
Company—Total	5,208,140	4,853,243	4,476,579	4,156,072	3,893,541	2,805,316
Business	1,494,635	1,396,832	1,304,409	1,227,648	1,161,035	854,937
Residence	3,713,505	3,456,411	3,172,170	2,928,424	2,732,506	1,950,379
Percent Extensions to Main	52.2	50.0	48.0	46.0	44.2	31.9
Increase in Company Telephones†	354,897	376,664	320,507	262,531	234,519	130,289
Service and Private Line	88,685	82,652	81,470	79,522	81,330	59,557
Independent Company	284,641	262,286	244,891	229,646	219,717	161,890
Long Distance Messages†† *years ended Dec. 31*	339,040,000	294,396,000	257,158,000	227,063,000	200,798,000	109,265,000
Employees *end of year*	40,065	35,860	34,233	32,598	29,470	26,046

*Figures for years prior to 1971 do not reflect the consolidation of the company and its two wholly owned subsidiaries. These figures have not been restated.
†For years ended Dec. 31.
#Average of daily high and low quotations on days of trading.
**American Stock Exchange.
††Not adjusted for reclassifications from toll to local.

TABLE 2
Mountain Bell—Income Statements (1972-1973)

	Thousands of Dollars Year	
	1973	1972
Operating Revenues		
Local service	$ 511,919	$444,810
Toll service	505,563	420,702
Directory advertising and other	51,407	44,548
Less Provision for uncollectibles	6,751	5,626
Total operating revenues	$1,062,138	$904,434
Operating Expenses		
Maintenance	$ 194,090	$159,586
Depreciation	150,609	142,460
Traffic—Primarily costs of handling messages	87,636	72,775
Commercial—Primarily costs of local business office operations	46,977	41,445
Marketing	44,826	37,678
Accounting	28,019	24,184
Provision for pensions and other employee benefits	69,676	60,709
Services received from parent under license contract	9,901	8,392
Other operating expenses	17,281	14,106
Total operating expenses	$ 649,015	$561,335
Net operating revenues	$ 413,123	$343,099
Operating Taxes		
Federal income taxes—Current	$ 49,565	$ 46,986
—Deferred	38,941	26,406
—Investment tax credit—net	14,086	12,422
State income taxes—Current	7,443	5,076
—Deferred	4,035	2,510
Property taxes and other	88,087	79,740
Total operating taxes	$ 202,157	$173,140
Operating income	$ 210,966	$169,959
Other Income		
Interest charged construction	$ 8,822	$ 9,040
Other miscellaneous income and deductions—net	(689)	(524)
Income before interest deductions	$ 219,099	$178,475
Interest Deductions	74,075	60,458
Net Income	$ 145,024	$118,017
Earnings Per share	$2.48	$2.19
Based on average shares outstanding: 58,528,865 in 1973 and 53,935,819 in 1972		
Reinvested Earnings		
At beginning of year	$ 385,601	$341,068
Add—Net income	145,024	118,017
	$ 530,625	$459,085
Deduct—Dividends declared per share: $1.44 in 1973, $1.36 in 1972	84,280	73,353
Other—Principally cost of issuance of common shares	—	131
	$ 84,280	$ 73,353
Reinvested Earnings at End of Year	$ 446,345	$385,601

TABLE 3
Mountain Bell—Balance Sheets (1972-1973)

	Thousands of Dollars Year	
	1973	1972

Assets

Telephone Plant—at cost

In Service	$3,293,952	$2,885,984
Under construction	146,946	118,032
Held for future use	1,615	2,920
	3,442,513	3,006,936
Less: Accumulated depreciation	672,822	619,598
	$2,769,691	$2,387,338

Current Assets

Cash	$ 7,344	$ 6,115
Receivables—less allowance for uncollectibles:		
1973. $799,000		
1972. $721,000	128,497	110,760
Materials and supplies	24,450	22,072
Prepaid expenses	1,359	1,300
Deferred Charges	$ 38,186	$ 27,795
Total Assets	$2,969,527	$2,555,380

Liabilities and Capital

Equity

Common shares—par value $12.50 per share	$ 731,611	$ 731,611
Authorized 76,000,000 shares		
Outstanding 58,528,865 shares		
Proceeds in excess of par value	163,067	163,067
Reinvested earnings	446,345	385,601
	$1,341,023	$1,280,279
Long- and Intermediate-Term Debt	$1,065,000	$ 815,000
Interim Debt (due within one year but intended to be refinanced)	$ 171,858	$ 153,182

Other Current Liabilities—(excluding interim debt)

Accounts payable	$ 110,182	$ 111,115
Taxes accrued	61,146	44,887
Advance billing and customers' deposits	27,414	24,660
Dividend payable	22,241	19,900
Interest and rents accrued	15,864	13,174
	$ 236,847	$ 213,736

Deferred Credits

Deferred income taxes	$ 92,770	$ 49,794
Unamortized investment tax credit	52,533	38,447
Other	9,496	4,942
	$ 154,799	$ 93,183

Lease Commitments

Total Liabilities and Capital	$2,969,527	$2,555,380

TABLE 4
Mountain Bell—Changes in Financial Position

	Thousands of Dollars Year (1972-1973)	
Source of Funds:		
From Operations		
Net income	$145,024	$118,017
Add Expenses not requiring funds:		
Depreciation	150,609	142,460
Deferred income taxes	42,976	28,916
Investment tax credit—net	14,086	12,422
	$352,695	$301,815
Less Income not providing funds		
Interest charged construction	8,822	9,040
Total funds from operations	$343,873	$292,775
From Financing		
Issuance of common shares	—	$180,508
Issuance of long-term debt	$250,000	—
Change in interim debt—net	18,676	10,986
Decrease in working capital	1,708	19,330
	$614,257	$503,599
Application of Funds:		
Telephone plant	$524,140	$429,788
Dividends	84,280	73,353
Other—net	5,837	458
	$614,257	$503,599
The decrease in working capital is accounted for by:		
Increase (decrease) in current assets:		
Cash	$ 1,229	$ 1,586
Receivables	17,737	21,030
Material and supplies	2,378	4,292
Prepaid expenses	59	(24)
	$ 21,403	$ 26,884
Increase (decrease) in other current liabilities (excluding interim debt):		
Accounts payable	$ (933)	$ 40,562
Advance billing and customers' deposits	2,754	2,161
Dividend payable	2,341	3,123
Taxes accrued	16,259	82
Interest and rents accrued	2,690	286
	$ 23,111	$ 46,214
Decrease in working capital (excluding interim debt)	$ 1,708	$ 19,330

TABLE 5
Mountain Bell—Sources of Financing

Year	Internal	External	Total
1969	63.4%	36.6%	100%
1970	43.7%	56.3%	100%
1971	47.5%	52.5%	100%
1972	57.0%	43.0%	100%
Est. 1973	50.4%	49.6%	100%

TABLE 6
Price-Earnings Ratio Comparisons

| | Standard & Poor's | | Moody's | | |
	425 industrials	55 Utilities	Aaa Electrics	AT&T	MST&T
1960	19.1	18.02	17.9	16.26	17.37
1961	22.7	21.63	23.0	21.93	24.08
1962	18.4	18.85	19.5	20.37	20.07
1963	17.7	20.20	21.5	20.66	20.03
1964	16.6	20.02	21.2	21.55	19.29
1965	16.6	19.36	20.3	19.61	17.39
1966	15.3	16.08	16.9	15.15	14.15
1967	18.3	15.39	15.6	14.47	14.56
1968	20.6	15.19	15.5	13.83	13.93
1969	20.1	13.69	13.8	13.23	11.77
1970	18.1	11.87	12.4	11.72	10.59
1971	20.5	12.43	13.4	11.74	10.74
1972	18.8	NA	12.0	10.43	9.82
1973	NA	NA	NA	9.99	8.66

TABLE 7

Ratios of Market Price to Book Value

Various Groups and Mountain Bell

	Industrials			Electric Utilities		
	DJ 30*	Moody's 125	S&P 425	Moody's 24	S&P 87	Mountain Bell
1960	2.22	2.28	2.37	1.95	2.06	1.67
1961	2.37	2.46	2.66	2.46	2.55	2.11
1962	2.07	2.04	2.24	2.22	2.29	1.86
1963	2.20	2.22	2.29	2.45	2.50	1.79
1964	2.40	2.29	2.33	2.51	2.60	1.70
1965	2.49	2.52	2.50	2.55	2.63	1.52
1966	2.21	2.32	2.43	2.17	2.19	1.24
1967	2.07	2.50	2.76	2.02	2.02	1.28
1968	2.03	2.51	3.06	1.89	1.93	1.19
1969	1.87	2.27	2.73	1.69	1.72	1.15
1970	1.67	1.82	2.21	1.41	1.44	1.04
1971	1.91	2.07	2.40	1.44	1.46	1.07
1972	1.84	2.03	2.54	1.31	1.34	.98
1973	NA	NA	NA	NA	NA	.96

*Excludes AT&T.

FIGURE 1
Mountain Bell After-Tax
Interest Coverage
(1965-1973 est.)

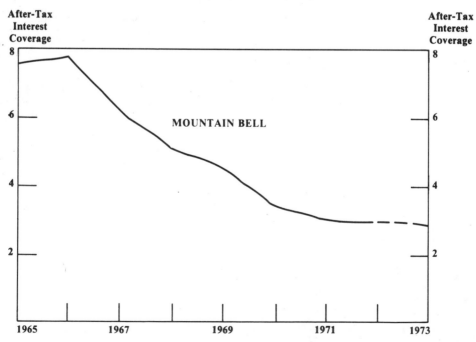

MOUNTAIN BELL

QUESTIONS

1. Comment on the suggestions made by Mr. Brady and Mr. French.
2. Analyze, in detail, the probable impact of a rights offering on the market price of Mountain Bell's common stock.
3. Giving particular attention to the firm's financing needs over the next 12 months, what financing strategy would you suggest for Mountain Bell?

Case 33
Crawford & Company

In early October 1968, Mr. Carlton Caster, an underwriting partner of Courts & Co., an Atlanta-based investment banking firm, neared a decision on the offering price of Crawford & Company stock. Crawford & Company, also located in Atlanta, Georgia was the largest independent insurance claims adjusting firm in the world. Ninety-six percent of the stock was held by the Trust Company of Georgia as trustee for the family of the company founder, James H. Crawford, and 4 percent was held by one of Mr. Crawford's sons (see Exhibit 7). The entire proceeds of the offering would accrue to the stockholders for their personal use. The proposed offering was 225,00 shares or 25 percent of the total number outstanding.

Mr. Caster's responsibility was to determine the price at which his firm would underwrite the issue. Courts & Co.'s reputation rested on bringing to the market issues of sound and growing firms. At this time, Courts & Co.'s facilities were available to investors through 2 offices in Atlanta, 16 other offices in six southeastern states, and an eastern office in New York. The firm engaged in the full range of investment banking activities.

The Company

Crawford & Company was founded in 1941 and operated as an individual proprietorship until 1943, when it was incorporated. The company provided claims adjusting services mainly to casualty-property insurance companies. It specialized in all casualty, automobile physical damage, and inland marine lines.

This case was prepared by Professor Harry R. Kuniansky of the College of Charleston as a basis for classroom discussion and not to illustrate either effective or ineffective handling of an administrative situation.

In certain locations, the company provided service for straight fire and extended coverage claims. The company had no contract or other arrangement with any insurance company, but depended on its abilities to supply satisfactory service to the various insurance companies.

The service rendered by Crawford & Company involved diverse elements. Its customers assigned claims to the company, either because they relied exclusively upon independent adjusters and maintained no force of field adjusters of their own, or possessed such a force that was overburdened at the time, or Crawford & Company's location made the company's service less costly. The company's adjusters then investigated to ascertain the obligation of the client to a third party or to its policyholder. After the client's liability was determined, the adjuster attempted to settle the claim by negotiation with the damaged party. If negotiations were not successful and litigation ensued, the adjuster supplied information required to defend the action.

Exhibit 9 discloses the approximate number of claims assigned to Crawford & Company in the period 1957-1966. The largest single account was 8 percent of the number of claims. From 1960 to 1967, 50 to 75 insurance companies were the source of at least 50 percent of the claims assigned to the company. Crawford & Company also received some claims from certain self-insurers, but these contributed only slightly to volume.

Crawford & Company charged its customers on the basis of individual claims assigned. The charge for each case was calculated by the application of hourly rates for time worked by adjusters and clerical personnel. The company billed for expenses directly traceable to the case and charged a fixed amount per mile for automobile usage. Rates varied geographically. Periodically, the company made adjustments in hourly rates. The most recent rate adjustment was implemented in July 1968, and represented an increase of approximately 14%.

The independent casualty property claims adjusting industry was composed of a large number of companies of different size. The company faced competition from small firms competing only locally. Also, there were several independent adjusting firms operating branches, and competing with the company over wider geographical areas. However, there was no independent adjusting company competing with Crawford & Company nationally. Certain stock companies owned an adjustment bureau, larger than Crawford & Company, which adjusted property-casualty claims. This bureau in the past functioned mostly in the property field, but in recent years had moved into the casualty area. It was possible that the bureau would become an increasing source of competition.

The executive staff located at headquarters in Atlanta consisted of principal corporate officers, a supervisory claims and management staff, and an educational staff. The company had 357 field offices, located in every state, employing 1,500 adjusters. It also had field offices in Puerto Rico, the Virgin Islands, Vancouver, Toronto, and Montreal, Canada, and London, England. A significant part of the company's growth arose from expansion of field offices into new geographical areas. Generally, each field office covered an area 50 miles in radius. Periodic trips were made to service routine claims, but any bodily injury case or one requiring immediate attention was handled by a special trip.

The company owned none of the premises on which its offices were located. It leased 189 office locations, including that of the home office, with leases extending for an average of 2.7 years. Annual aggregate rentals of this type were approximately $633,000. The remaining 168 locations were rented on a short-term basis. The company's 1,400 automobiles used by the field adjusters and certain management personnel were also leased.

The corporate officers included the following:

A. R. Robertson	President
G. R. Dunagan	Executive Vice President
R. T. Moreland	Vice President and Controller
Virginia C. Crawford	Vice President, Treasurer
C. M. Freeman	Secretary

There were seven other vice presidents. Thirteen regional vice presidents were located in branch field offices in major cities. They had responsibility for their own branch offices and supervisory responsibility for each of their geographical areas.

Crawford & Company carried on extensive recruiting activities on college campuses, through professional employment agencies, and advertisements in various media. The company employed some adjusters who had finished two years of college, but these comprised only about 25 percent of the trainees. The remainder were college graduates. The company brought each new adjuster to the home office for a thorough training program, which emphasized technical aspects of adjustment work. The company also conducted a continuing education program for adjusters in the field. Participation was required for a period of 2.5 years. Management training correspondence courses were undertaken to continue training field and home office management personnel. The company believed the educational program was vital to its success, and stressed its importance at all levels of employment.

Since Crawford & Company was an organization selling, in essence, its reputation for uncompromising honesty, the company placed strict emphasis on employee integrity. The company put forth maximum effort to insure that this integrity was maintained. In the company's formal educational program, a portion of the adjuster's time was devoted to ethics and how it related to company policy. It was impressed upon the adjuster the importance of impartial investigation and accuracy in the recording of time charges. Adjusters found in violation were subject to dismissal.

Managers were similarly indoctrinated. For example, branch managers reviewed all bills before they were sent to the customer. The branch manager had the responsibility to reduce the charges, if he deemed it necessary. He could not increase the bill under any circumstance and would be discharged for so doing. In addition, the records in any branch office were open to inspection by any company man, at any time, without notice. The company believed very strongly this emphasis on employee integrity was a major reason it grew into a successful nationwide organization.

The Proposed Offering

Since there were no considerations as to the number of shares and the type of security to be issued, all of Mr. Caster's energies were devoted to pricing the stock offering. He considered several factors important in establishing a price.

Mr. Caster believed that the average stock price of a company's first public issue was somewhere between 10 and 20 times recent earnings. However, it was difficult to ascertain the appropriate earnings base in this instance because of the recency of the last rate change. Although the rate change affected earnings favorably, Mr. Caster was unsure of its long-range effect. Whether this change would produce a permanent reversal of the preceding decline in company earnings was difficult to determine.

Mr. Caster weighed the fact that Crawford & Company was a service organization, entirely. Service industries had grown at a higher than average rate. Due to this growth feature, the company stock would probably be priced toward the higher end of the price-earnings range. However, Crawford & Company had grown in business volume substantially through geographical expansion. Since the company was now well located in all states, this could no longer be a major source of growth.

A perplexing factor was the uniqueness of Crawford & Company. Because competition existed in the form of locally based or regional claims adjusting firms, there were no authoritative industry-wide statistics available. In most underwriting situations, the underwriter has available data referring to companies in the same type of industry that can guide the pricing decision. In this instance, Mr. Caster was forced because of Crawford's singular character to use as a general guide the financial data of service industries, realizing their variety of differences from Crawford & Company. Financial and descriptive data were compiled as an aid to the pricing decision (Exhibits 5 and 6).

Mr. Caster believed that the new issue market would be receptive to this issue at this time. Other offerings by Courts & Co. had been well received (Exhibit 10). Most underwriters prefer to price in a market where the stock would rise in the immediate future about 10 percent above the offering price.

EXHIBIT 1
Crawford & Company
Condensed Consolidated Balance Sheets

	December 31, 1967	(unaudited) June 30, 1968
ASSETS		
Current Assets		
Cash	$ 465,973	$ 510,825
U.S. Govt. securities, approx. market	199,748	199,703
Accounts and other receivables, net	7,277,895	7,297,959
Other current assets	103,582	114,713
Total Current Assets	$8,047,198	$8,123,200
Fixed assets, at cost		
Furniture fixtures and equipment	$2,722,560	$2,817,068
Leasehold improvements	11,974	11,974
Total Fixed Assets	$2,734,534	$2,829,042
Less: Accumulated depreciation and amortization	1,399,151	1,493,768
Net Fixed Assets	$1,335,383	$1,335,274
Other assets	226,234	199,687
Total Assets	$9,608,815	$9,658,161
LIABILITIES		
Current liabilities		
Accounts payable	$ 397,915	$ 415,665
Accrued liabilities	756,647	694,406
Accrued income taxes	3,698,063	3,560,353
Dividends payable	57,457	57,457
Total Current Liabilities	$4,910,082	$4,727,881
Stockholders' equity		
Common stock (see Notes 2, 4, Exhibit 2)	$ 28,075	$ 28,075
Retained earnings	4,670,658	4,902,205
Total Stockholders' Equity	$4,698,733	$4,930,280
Total Liabilities	$9,608,815	$9,658,161

Source: Crawford & Company, Prospectus for offering of common stock, October 31, 1968.

EXHIBIT 2
Crawford & Company
Selected Notes to Balance Sheet

Note 1—Lease Obligations

The company conducts its branch and home office operations from leased office space. Annual rentals and total obligations under leases with terms of 36 months or longer and extending through 1974 were approximately $263,000 and $1,014,000, respectively, at December 31, 1967, and $262,135 and $1,368,330 at June 30, 1968.

The remaining obligation under a fleet leasing arrangement amounted to approximately $1,385,000 at December 31, 1967, and $688,791 at June 30, 1968, of which approximately $1,368,000 and $674,060 are payable within 12 months of those dates.

Note 2—Capital Stock

See Note 4 regarding subsequent recapitalization of the company's common stock.

At December 31, 1967, the company had 5,000 authorized shares of 6% nonvoting, cumulative preferred stock which had a par value of $100 per share. All shares of this issue previously outstanding were redeemed as of June 30, 1967.

In 1963, the company entered into an agreement with the Estate of James H. Crawford (former president of the company) which provided for the purchase of a sufficient number of shares of the Class A common stock from the Estate to pay estate taxes, etc., in accordance with Section 303 of the Internal Revenue Code of 1954.

During 1966, a final determination was made as to the total estate liability. Accordingly, the company redeemed and retired 46,781 shares of Class A common stock from the Estate at a total cost of $1,356,649.

Note 3—Supplementary Profit and Loss Information

The following items are included as deductions in the statement of consolidated income:

	For the Year Ended December 31			6 months Ended 6/30/68
	1965	1966	1967	(Unaudited)
Charged directly to the income account:				
Maintenance and Repairs	$ 52,350	$ 68,312	$ 269,115	$ 227,147
Depreciation and Amortization	240,502	304,118	306,965	143,362
Taxes other than income taxes:				
Payroll	432,740	590,633	650,441	412,490
General	101,083	97,810	143,353	81,476
Rents	822,112	877,276	2,177,476	1,242,560

There were no management or service contract fees paid during the periods under review.

Because of the accounting practices followed, involving the allocation of branch office and other departmental costs, it is not practicable to provide the details of the expense classifications charged. The majority of the amounts are included in cost of services rendered.

The amounts reflected for rentals above do not include costs associated with the rental of photo copy equipment; such expenses are not separately classified in the company's accounts and, therefore, it is not practicable to determine the specific amounts of such costs. Management estimates that these will approximate $75,000 per year.

EXHIBIT 2
Crawford & Company *(continued)*
Selected Notes to Balance Sheet

Note 4—Subsequent Recapitalization

On October 25, 1968, the company effected a recapitalization whereby the 133,219 shares of Class A, nonvoting stock and the 20,000 shares of Class B, voting stock, outstanding at December 31, 1967, and June 30, 1968, were exchanged for 900,000 shares of a new class of voting common stock. Since this recapitalization was not effected at June 30, 1968, it is not reflected in the accompanying balance sheets. However, the per share amounts included in the statement of consolidated income have been adjusted to reflect this recapitalization.

Source: Crawford & Company, Prospectus for offering of common stock, October 31, 1968.

EXHIBIT 3

Crawford & Company
Statements of Income for the Periods Indicated

	Year Ended December 31					(Unaudited) 6 months ended June 30	
	1963	1964	1965	1966	1967	1967	1968
Revenue for services	$15,889,733	$18,646,778	$20,856,438	$23,977,921	$25,708,026	$12,954,045	$13,215,732
Costs and expenses							
Cost of services rendered	$12,819,434	$15,074,456	$17,095,875	$19,500,898	$21,429,920	$10,766,100	$11,346,695
Selling, general, and administrative expenses	1,744,791	1,762,186	1,959,159	2,132,088	2,369,196	1,077,508	1,134,102
Operating income	$ 1,325,508	$ 1,810,136	$ 1,801,404	$ 2,344,935	$ 1,908,910	$ 1,110,437	$ 734,935
Other income (expense)—net	(5,083)	(29,898)	(3,246)	(2,298)	(2,114)	569	3,740
Income before provision for income taxes	$ 1,320,425	$ 1,780,238	$ 1,798,158	$ 2,342,637	$ 1,906,796	$ 1,111,006	$ 738,675
Provision for income taxes (Note B)	764,000	915,000	865,000	1,159,000	905,000	553,284	392,214
Income before extraordinary items	$ 556,425	$ 865,238	$ 933,158	$ 1,183,637	$ 956,796	$ 557,722	$ 346,461
Extraordinary (charges) credits	361,604	—					
Less income tax reduction							
Extraordinary (charges) credits, net of tax reduction	$ 361,604	$ —	$ —	$ —	$ —	$ —	$ —
Net income	$ 918,029	$ 865,238	$ 933,158	$ 1,183,637	$ 956,796	$ 567,722	$ 346,461
Dividends on preferred stock (Note C)	26,313	26,256	26,110	26,028	13,014	13,014	—
Net income applicable to common stock	$ 891,716	$ 838,982	$ 907,048	$ 1,157,609	$ 943,782	$ 544,708	$ 346,461
Per share of common stock (Note A):							
Income before extraordinary items, after preferred dividends	$ .59	$ .93	$1.01	$1.29	$1.05	$ .61	$ .38
Extraordinary (charges) credits, Net of tax reduction	.40	—					
Net income	$ .99	$ .93	$1.01	$1.29	$1.05	$ .61	$ .38
Cash dividends			$ .07	$ .18	$ .26	$ .26	$ .13

Source: Crawford & Company, Prespectus for offering of common stock, October 31, 1968.

EXHIBIT 4
Crawford & Company
Notes to Income Statements

Note A

Net income and dividends per share of common stock have been computed for each year based on the shares outstanding (900,000 shares) after giving retroactive effect to the recapitalization referred to in Note 4, Exhibit 2.

On July 23, 1968, and October 23, 1968, the Board of Directors declared dividends on common stock of $.10 per share each, based on the shares outstanding after the recapitalization referred to above. The dividends per share based on these declarations are not reflected in the per share data shown above.

Note B

The provisions for federal income taxes for 1964, 1965, 1966, 1967, and the six months ended June 30, 1967, and June 30, 1968, have been reduced by investment tax credits of $21,398, $49,576, $23,346, $23,499, $4,512, and $6,418, respectively. The investment tax credits deferred in 1962 and 1963 (total of $43,600) were credited to the tax liability account and, through December 31, 1967, and June 30, 1968, remain in the tax liability account as an additional reserve for income taxes. The provision for income taxes for the six months ended June 30, 1968, includes provision for the 10 percent Federal income tax surcharge effective as of January 1, 1968.

Note C

All preferred stock previously outstanding was redeemed by the company as of June 30, 1967.

Note D

During 1959 and 1960, retained earnings was charged with a total of approximately $48,000 for discounts associated with preferred stock transactions.

Source: Crawford & Company, Prospectus for offering of common stock, October 31, 1968.

EXHIBIT 5

Crawford & Company

Comparative Stock Pricing and Financial Data on Selected Companies
October 25, 1968

	Crawford & Co.	Wm. J. Burns Internat. Detective Agency Inc	Retail Credit Co.	Pinkertons Inc	Travelodge Corp
Fiscal Year End	12/31	12/31	12/31	12/31	1/31
Latest Complete Year	12/31/67	12/31/67	12/31/67	12/31/67	1/31/68
Sales (000)	$25,708	$66,518	$134,577	$82,921	$8,644
Net Income	956	2,178	8,229	2,891	1,187
Net Income/Sales	3.7%	3.3%	6.1%	3.5%	13.8%
Net Income/Net Worth	20.4%	25.1%	23.1%	26.0%	17.6%
Earnings per Share					
1967	$1.05	$1.98[1]	$2.64[3]	$2.08	$ .45
1966	1.29	1.48	2.63	1.40	.23
1965	1.01	1.33	2.56	1.15	.15
1964	.93	1.13	2.18	.97	.17
1963	.99	1.00	1.67	.62	.12
1967 vs. 5 yr. avg.	100%	143%	112%	168%	204%
Market Price[4]	—	85½	43	47	29⅛
Price Earnings—1967	—	43.1	16.3	22.6	64.6
Current Cash Dividend Rate	$ .26	$1.05	$1.75	$ .30	$ .25
Current Cash Yield	—	1.2%	4.1%	.64%	.86%
Common Shares					
Total Outstanding	153,219	1,077,866[2]	7,799,205	1,387,500	2,102,000
Traded	—	ASE	OC	OC	OC

[1]All years adjusted for 3 for 2 stock split in 1966.
[2]Includes A and B shares.
[3]All years adjusted for 25% stock dividend in 1961 and 100% stock dividend in 1964.
[4]Closing quotation October 25, 1968.

EXHIBIT 6

Crawford & Company
Description of Companies Listed in Exhibit 5

William J. Burns International Detective Agency, Inc.—One of the two largest private organizations in the United States furnishing protective services to industrial and commercial clients, usually on a continuing basis.

Retail Credit Company—Provides businesses throughout North America with facts on individuals for insurance, claim credit, employment, and marketing purposes.

Pinkerton's, Inc.—Company provides security and investigative services for industrial, commercial, and other clients, and makes various types of alarm equipment.

Travelodge Corporation—Company is in the motel industry, usually becoming partners in joint ventures which own and operate Travelodge motels.

Source: Standard & Poor's *Standard Corporation Descriptions.*

EXHIBIT 7

Crawford & Company
Selected Data on Principal and Selling Stockholders

		Number of Shares			Percent of Class Owned	
	Type of Ownership	Owned Before Sale	To Be Sold	Owned After Sale	Before Sale	After Sale
Trust Company of Georgia 36 Edgewood Avenue, N.E. Atlanta, Georgia	Record	863,730	215,933	647,797	96.0	72.0
Robert C. Crawford 1035 Old Powers Ferry Road, N.W. Atlanta, Georgia	Record & Beneficial	36,270	9,067	27,203	4.0	3.0

Source: Crawford & Company, Prospectus for offering of common stock, October 31, 1968.

EXHIBIT 8

Crawford & Company
Summarized Statements of Income for Periods Indicated

	(Unaudited) 3 Months Ended September 30,	
	1967	*1968*
Revenue from services	$6,378,036	$7,531,138
Net income	$ 221,404	$ 377,914
Net income per share of common stock	$ .25	$ .42

Source: Crawford & Company, Prospectus for offering of common stock, October 31, 1968.

EXHIBIT 9

Crawford & Company
Approximate Number of Claims Assigned to Company
1957-1967

Year	Claims	Year	Claims
1967	420,000	1961	254,000
1966	417,000	1960	234,000
1965	390,000	1959	214,000
1964	356,000	1958	186,000
1963	304,000	1957	164,000
1962	276,000		

Source: Crawford & Company, Prospectus for offering of common stock, October 31, 1968.

EXHIBIT 10

Crawford & Company
Data on Previous Offerings of Courts & Co.

Name of Firm	Offering Price to Public	Approximate Price in Subsequent Market
1. Davis Food Service	$ 8	$15
2. Cagle's, Inc.	$ 9	$12
3. Flowers Industries	$12½	$14
4. Golden Flake, Inc.	$ 8	$12

QUESTION

1. At what price should Mr. Caster issue the shares of Crawford & Company?

Case 34
Acme, Inc.

In January, 1974, Mr. Goodman, President of Acme, Inc., asked his Comptroller, Mr. Walter, to prepare an estimate of the company's need for external funds over the next 12 months, and make recommendations for how the funds should be obtained. Mr. Walter has handled the financing of Acme since the company was organized six years ago, in addition to his responsibilities as head of the accounting department. Since the company has grown substantially every year of its short life, Mr. Walter's primary consideration in making his financing decisions has been the availability of the funds needed rather than any attempt at a logical, consistent financial policy.

President Goodman knows that his company will have to raise a substantial amount of external capital in 1974, and he believes that the company should simultaneously revise its financial structure. The company's common stock, which is traded over the counter, declined from $6 per share to $4 per share during 1973, and Mr. Goodman feels that this was due in part to the patchwork nature of the company's financial structure.

In his request for recommendations from Mr. Walter, the President indicated that Mr. Walter should base his recommendations on the following assumptions.

A. Sales of existing product lines will increase 15% over the preceding year.
B. The firm's current negotiations to purchase a small local business in order to add to its product line will be successful and will be implemented during

This case was prepared by Professors James R. Longstreet and William G. Modrow of the University of South Florida as a basis for classroom discussion and not to illustrate either effective or ineffective handling of an administrative situation.

the year. The purchase price for the acquisition is summarized in Exhibit 1.

C. The proposal of the Production Manager of the main plant to automate and modernize his operations will be approved. A summary of his proposal is presented in Exhibit 2.

History

Acme, Inc., was organized in 1968 in order to provide a local firm that would both process and distribute the food products produced in the region. Their initial objective was to produce a variety of quality products that could be sold under their own label locally and under private labels outside their primary marketing area. The initial capital was raised locally through a group of individual investors and local financial institutions.

The company was almost immediately a success and began operating at a profit within its first six months of existence. Operations have increased every year since the firm opened for business, because the company has added to both its product lines and its marketing area each year.

Commercial Bank Lines

Acme has had a line of credit with the City Bank since 1969. They normally borrow from the bank in March and April and are out of debt to the bank by November. In 1973, however, they did not pay off their bank loans, and the City Bank has been pressing for some indication of the probability of principal payments in 1974.

The company currently has a $500,000 line of credit. They borrow on renewable 90-day notes at 1% above the prime bank rate—which is currently 12%. The City Bank requires its regular borrowers to carry a 10% compensating balance on the line as a whole, whether used or not, and an additional 10% for any amount actually borrowed.

7% Chattel Mortgage

The initial equipment purchased by Acme in 1968 for $400,000 was acquired subject to a chattel mortgage of $300,000. The company made a down payment of $100,000 and agreed to make principal payments of $30,000 a year. The company can make prepayment on principal without penalty.

Long-Term Lease

The initial plant for food processing was obtained via a long-term (15-year) lease of land and buildings from one of the original organizers. During the first two years of operation, the company spent more than $285,000 modernizing and adapting the building to fit their needs.

Annual lease payments are $60,000 a year, and Acme is responsible for paying all taxes, insurance, and the repairs and maintenance expenditures necessary to keep the property in good condition. The company has the option of renewing the lease on the same terms for another ten years in 1983.

6.5% Term Loan

In 1969, the company obtained $500,000 via a term loan. The loan had a ten-year maturity, and is convertible, at the option of the holder, into common stock at a price of $3.20 per share. The $500,000 face value of the term loan therefore represented a call on 156,250 shares of common stock. There are no sinking fund requirements and no call provision.

7.5% Convertible Debenture

In 1972, an issue of 7.5% convertible debentures was placed privately with a small group of individual investors. The debentures have a 20-year maturity and are callable at a price of $105 on 30 days' notice. They are convertible into common stock at a price of $6 per share. At the time of flotation, the common stock was trading on the over-the-counter market at about $5.00 per share. Mr. Walter believes that the debentures would have had to carry a 9% coupon rate if they had not contained the conversion option. The debentures have no sinking fund requirements.

8.0% Mortgage Notes

Ten-year notes requiring a $70,000 annual sinking fund payment beginning the second year were issued in 1971. They are callable, in whole or in part, on 30 days' notice at a price of $108 in 1974. The call price declines by 1% of face value each year after 1974 until it reaches 100. The mortgage notes are secured by fixed assets purchased during 1971.

9.25% Mortgage Notes

Ten-year notes requiring sinking fund payments of $30,000 a year beginning at the end of the second year were issued in 1972 as partial payment for a new warehouse. The warehouse, which cost $500,000, was pledged as collateral. Acme wanted at least a 20-year maturity on these notes, but could not find a lender willing to accept such a maturity date. The notes are callable at their face value on 30 days' notice.

9% Preferred Stock

The preferred stock was sold primarily to relatives of the founders when Acme was organized in 1968. The preferred has a prior claim to the common in regard to both income and assets. In the event of voluntary liquidation, preferred stockholders are entitled to $60 per share. In involuntary liquidation, they are entitled to $50 per share. The preferred stock is callable at $60 per share on 30 days' notice. There are no sinking fund requirements. Preferred stockholders are entitled to vote in the election of Directors and have one vote per share. Preferred stock dividends are fully cumulative. In the event that arrearages on preferred stock exceed $10 a share, preferred stockholders voting as a group are entitled to elect a majority of the Board of Directors.

Common Stock

The Corporate charter provides 1,000,000 shares of authorized common stock with a par value of 10¢ per share. Each share would have one vote in the election of Directors. The eight organizers subscribed to 500,000 shares at a price of $1 per share when the company was organized in 1968.

In 1970, with the company well established and showing a substantial profit, an additional issue of 200,000 shares of common stock was offered locally to public investors at a price of $3.50 per share. The net proceeds were $3.00 per share. The public issue was sold to more than 350 individual investors, and following the flotation, an active over-the-counter market was established by local brokerage firms. Within a few weeks of the public offering, the common stock of Acme was trading at $4 to $4¼ per share (bid). The earnings, dividends, and market price per share are summarized in Exhibit 5.

Treasury Stock

In 1972, one of the large stockholders, who had participated in organizing Acme, Inc., died of a heart attack. Lawyers for his estate notified the President, Mr. Goodman, that they intended to sell the entire 60,000 shares of Acme that were held by the estate. While there was a reasonably active market for the company's common stock in the over-the-counter market at that time, there was no doubt that such a large offering of common would have a significant adverse effect on the market price. Mr. Goodman therefore authorized the purchase of the entire block of common stock. A price 20% below the current market bid price at that time was negotiated with the estate.

Current Market Data

Based on discussions with bankers and members of the brokerage community, Mr. Walter believes that if he could consolidate the long-term debt into a single-issue 20-year mortgage bond, it would require a coupon rate of interest of at least 10.25% in order for the company to realize the face value of the new consolidating issue.

There is no current market for the outstanding preferred stock of the company. The dividend yield of preferred stocks reported by the *Federal Reserve Bulletin* in January, 1974, was 7.60%. Acme preferred stock would probably have to offer a yield of 9-10%, considering its poor quality and marketability.

The market price performance of Acme common stock is summarized in Exhibit 5. If additional shares of common stock must be sold to raise external capital, the flotation costs would probably be at least 15% of the gross proceeds from the sale of common. The latest market quotation of Acme common stock was $4.00-$4.375.

Mr. Walter intends to begin the preparation for his report to the President by estimating Acme's need for external funds during the next 12 months. He accepts the President's statement that sales of existing product lines will increase by 15% in the next 12 months, because this estimate was originated in his office. However, he plans to examine carefully the proposed acquisition and the automation proposal.

Once he has established the magnitude of external financing requirements, he will evaluate the alternative financial structures that may be adopted including the possible elimination of some of the outstanding securities.

EXHIBIT 1

Projected Financial Statements of Proposed Acquisition
Balance Sheet at Acquisition Price

Cash in bank	$ 20,000
Net Accounts Receivables	180,000
Inventory	200,000
Total Current Assets	$ 400,000
Accounts Payable	$ 130,000
Accruals	50,000
Total Current Liabilities	$ 180,000
Net Working Capital	$ 220,000
Net Fixed Assets	200,000
Proposed Purchase Price	$ 420,000

Expected Annual Income

Sales	$2,500,000
Cost of Sales*	2,300,000
Gross Profit	$ 200,000
Operating Expenses	125,000
Net Operating Income	$ 75,000

*Includes straight-line depreciation charges of $15,200 a year.

EXHIBIT 2

Estimated Cost and Benefits of Proposed Capital Expenditure

I. Required Capital Outlay

Price of Equipment	$230,000
Installation Costs	3,480
Total	$233,480

II. Estimated Life

Engineering Life	15 years
Economic Life Span	10 years
Life Span for Tax Purposes	10 years
Estimated Terminal Value	zero

III. Benefits

Year	Cost Savings	Depreciation	Added Income Taxes	Net Cash Flow
1	$80,652	$23,348	$28,652	$52,000
2	$80,652	$23,348	$28,652	$52,000
3	$80,652	$23,348	$28,652	$52,000
4	$80,652	$23,348	$28,652	$52,000
5	$80,652	$23,348	$28,652	$52,000
6	$80,652	$23,348	$28,652	$52,000
7	$80,652	$23,348	$28,652	$52,000
8	$80,652	$23,348	$28,652	$52,000
9	$80,652	$23,348	$28,652	$52,000
10	$80,652	$23,348	$28,652	$52,000
Total	$806,520	$233,480	$286,520	$520,000

IV. Performance Measures

1. Payback period	4.49 years
2. Average rate of return	25%
3. Internal Rate of Return	18%

EXHIBIT 3
Acme, Inc.
Comparative Balance Sheets

	1971	1972	1973
Current Assets			
Cash	$ 380,000	$ 410,000	$ 270,000
Notes Receivable	—	—	275,000
Accounts Receivable	1,010,000	1,180,000	1,290,000
Inventory	876,500	1,156,000	1,350,000
Prepaid Expenses	78,500	64,000	65,000
Total Current Assets	$2,345,000	$2,810,000	$3,240,000
Gross Plant and Equipment	1,950,000	2,490,000	2,950,000
Accumulated Depreciation	215,600	334,800	462,700
Net Plant and Equipment	$1,734,400	$2,155,200	$2,487,300
Leasehold Improvements, net	247,000	228,000	209,000
Total Assets	$4,326,400	$5,193,200	$5,936,300
Current Liabilities			
Bank Loans	$ —	$ —	$ 400,000
Accounts Payable	620,000	750,000	820,000
Accrued Liabilities	305,000	315,000	365,000
Accrued Taxes	198,000	242,000	278,000
Current Installment on L-T-D	30,000	100,000	130,000
Total Current Liabilities	$1,153,000	$1,407,000	$1,993,000
Long-Term Debt (L-T-D)			
7% Chattel Mortgage	$ 180,000	$ 150,000	$ 120,000
6.5% Term Loan	500,000	500,000	500,000
7.5% Convertible Debenture	—	300,000	300,000
8.0% Mortgage Notes	800,000	730,000	660,000
9.25% Mortgage Notes	—	400,000	370,000
	$1,480,000	$2,080,000	$1,950,000
Owner's Equity			
9% Preferred Stock, $50 Par	$ 200,000	$ 200,000	$ 200,000
Common Stock, 10¢ Par	70,000	70,000	70,000
Paid-in Capital	1,030,000	1,030,000	1,030,000
Retained Earnings	393,400	658,700	945,800
Less Treasury Stock 60,000 Shares at cost	—	(252,500)	(252,500)
Total Owner's Equity	$1,693,400	$1,706,200	$1,993,300
Total Liabilities and Owner's Equity	$4,326,400	$5,193,200	$5,936,300

EXHIBIT 4

Acme, Inc.

Comparative Income Statements

	1972	1973
Sales	$29,000,000	$32,100,000
Cost of Sales*	26,666,800	29,460,150
Gross Profit	$ 2,333,200	$ 2,639,850
Selling and Administrative	1,612,000	1,852,000
Net Operating Income	$ 721,200	$ 787,850
Interest Expense	154,600	177,650
Taxable Income	$ 566,600	$ 610,200
Income Taxes	283,300	305,100
Net Income	$ 283,300	$ 305,100
Preferred Stock Dividends	18,000	18,000
Available to Common	$ 265,300	$ 287,100
Common Stock Dividend	—	—
Addition to Retained Earnings	$ 265,300	$ 287,100

*Includes depreciation charges of $138,200 in 1972 and $152,000 in 1973.

EXHIBIT 5

Acme, Inc.

Summary of Operating and Market Data

	1969	1970	1971	1972	1973
Net Operating Income	$315,000	$420,000	$655,000	$721,200	$787,850
Net Income	$ 80,500	$144,000	$228,000	$283,300	$305,100
Dividends	$ 18,000	$ 18,000	$ 18,000	$ 18,000	$ 18,000
To Retained Earnings	$ 62,500	$126,000	$210,000	$265,300	$287,100
Per Share of Common					
Primary Earnings	$.125	$.21	$.30	$.42	$.45
Fully Diluted Earnings	$.12	$.188	$.264	$.336	$.372
Market (Bid) Prices					
High for year	NA	$4.50	$5.25	$6.25	$6.00
Low for year	NA	$3.50	$4.75	$5.00	$4.00

QUESTIONS

1. Evaluate the proposed acquisition and the capital expenditure proposal. Are both proposals acceptable? Why or why not?
2. Project Acme, Inc.'s need for external funds over the next 12 months both with and without the proposed acquisition and automation expenditures.
3. Based upon the acceptance of both, one, or neither of the capital expenditure proposals, what financial structure would you recommend for Acme?

Case 35
Boise Cascade

Company History

Stage I: 1957-1969

Boise Cascade Corporation was organized in April, 1957, with the merger of two medium-sized lumber companies: Boise Payette Company and Cascade Lumber Company. Prior to the merger, neither company processed a sufficient volume of lumber to operate a pulp and paper mill capable of utilizing the company's waste wood products.[1] The completion of the merger allowed the newly formed company to control sufficient timber resources in Oregon, Washington, and Idaho to justify construction of a 150-ton-per-day pulp and paper mill complex and thereby to increase the efficiency of the company's timber operations. The overall objective of the company in the late 1950's and early 1960's was to continue the company's integrated growth in the forest products industry, thereby increasing the company's operating efficiency and share of the market. Consistent with this goal, Boise Cascade acquired a number of building materials, paper, and packaging-related businesses from 1950 to 1966. The result was a spectacular growth in net sales, total assets, and net income (see Table 1).

Beginning in 1966, the company initiated plans to diversity its operations into three new markets that were not directly related to its forest-products businesses: (1) recreational land development; (2) urban development; (3) engineering and

This case was prepared by Professor Dennis B. Fitzpatrick of Boise State University as a basis for classroom discussion and not to illustrate either effective or ineffective handling of an administrative situation.

[1]Approximately two-thirds of each tree harvested in the Northwest consists of waste wood materials.

construction. Boise Cascade acquired substantial acreage of land in California, Nevada, and elsewhere for the purpose of developing recreational housing projects. The company subsequently became one of the largest land developers in the nation. The decision to invest in urban renewal and development projects was made in the wake of the 1968-1969 Watts, Detroit, and Newark riots, with the objective of promoting profit-making social progress. To meet this end, the Burnett-Boise Corporation, which began operations in 1968, was organized.

Boise Cascade's entrance into engineering and construction-related businesses was completed with the acquisition of Ebasco, Inc., in August, 1969. Ebasco, formerly one of the world's largest public utility holding companies, divested itself of all its American utilities in 1935. Ebasco subsequently exchanged a number of its Latin American utilities for foreign government-backed dollar securities. At the time of the Boise Cascade/Ebasco merger, Ebasco's assets totaled $680 million (book value) and consisted of (1) notes of Latin American governments; (2) cash, marketable securities and other short-term investments; (3) controlling ownership in engineering, chemical process, construction, and architectural companies; (4) controlling interest in four Latin American electric utilities; (5) other investments in Latin American manufacturing companies. Consequently, the culmination of the Boise Cascade/Ebasco merger left Boise Cascade with sizable investment in foreign government-backed securities and other Latin American investments.

Boise Cascade's diversification strategy resulted in continued rapid growth and a significant change in the company's sales mix (see Table 2). By late 1969, Boise Cascade had become the 55th largest American corporation[2] and was apparently well-positioned for future growth. This positive outlook for the company was reflected in the market price for its common stock, which was selling at almost 34 times earnings (i.e., approximately $80/share).

Stage II: 1969-1972

In 1970, Boise Cascade's fortunes soured as a result of the simultaneous impact of several factors. The American economy was entering a period of temporary stagnation coupled with conditions of high inflation and high interest rates. The resulting slowdown in the housing and construction sectors caught the company between rising operating costs and softening market conditions in its traditional product lines. At the same time, the company became exposed to environmentalist attacks concerning its recreational land developments in California and Nevada. Although management felt that the company's environmental standards were among the highest in the industry, the company responded by increasing expenditures for environmental safeguards. These circumstances resulted in delayed construction activities, higher development costs, and a further decline in sales. The land development business reported a net loss in the fourth quarter of 1970. The recreational land business was exposed to further negative pressures in 1971. The consumer advocate movement's crusade against the company resulted in an October, 1971, suit by the state of California accusing the company of improper sales procedures with regard to earlier recreational land development projects. Shortly thereafter, several class action suits with charges similar to the state's were also filed.

[2]According to Fortune magazine.

TABLE 1

Boise Cascade Corporation (a)

1958-1972 Pertinent Financial Data (Year End)

(expressed in thousands)

Year	Total Assets	Net Sales	Net Income	Current Assets	Current Liabilities	Long-Term Debt
1958	$ 57,974	$ 72,734	$ 3,036	$ 32,176	$ 16,331	$ 20,423
1960	74,570	131,182	3,365	47,132	13,808	27,441
1962	124,382	175,074	5,055	64,323	28,361	71,548
1964	293,475	361,608	14,947	122,537	47,896	126,979
1966	454,250	489,196	17,014	157,807	70,231	261,499
1968	1,773,809	764,787	58,738	502,304	273,852	679,300
1969	1,969,838	830,849	81,646	489,432	288,124	771,611
1970	2,196,394	846,540	33,590	539,598	258,156	960,731
1971	2,108,733	995,920	(85,150)	516,646	314,816	979,585
1972	1,782,040	1,130,780(b)	(170,610)	505,302	396,203	523,183

(a) Note: This table does not reflect data for discontinued operations.
(b) Restated in 1973 annual report.
Source: Robert L. Katz, *Cases and Concepts in Corporate Strategy,* (Englewood Cliffs, Prentice-Hall, Inc., 1970), pp. 400-401 and pp. 478-479 and 1972 annual reports.

TABLE 2

Sales Distribution by Major Markets—Boise Cascade Corporation (in %)

	1960	1962	1964	1966	1968	1969	1970	1971	1972
Building Materials	77	64	44	37	29	21	19	37	40
Housing	—	1	4	4	23	15	14	8	7
Recreation	—	—	—	—	6	12	9	—	—
Communication Papers	2	8	26	24	12	9	10	26	25
Packaging	9	14	14	18	15	10	11	14	14
Office	—	3	9	17	11	7	7	12	12
Engineering and Construction	—	—	—	—	—	17	22	—	—
Investment, Utilities and Other	12	10	3	—	4	9	8	3	2
Totals	100	100	100	100	100	100	100	100	100

Source: Goldman Sachs, *Research Report on Boise Cascade Corporation,* July, 1973, p. 2.

The company's investment in urban housing developments was also experiencing serious difficulties by 1971. The Burnett-Boise Corporation collapsed in financial ruin that year. This development coincided with the company's decision to discontinue on-site homebuilding projects and to significantly reduce the company's recreational land development activities.

As if Boise Cascade's recreational land and urban development problems were not enough, the company realized in 1970 and 1971 that some of its Latin American investments, although still profitable, had a sharply reduced market value. For example, the company held some government bonds originally yielding 6% while the current market yields were approximately 12%. Top management conducted a comprehensive review of its problems in early 1972, and concluded that the company's vital strength in its traditional businesses was being sapped by the difficulties it was encountering in the recreational land, urban development, and Latin American investments. At that time, management concluded that the company should discontinue its activities in these businesses and commenced to liquidate its investment in these operations. A summary of the results of the divestitute program is presented in Table 3.

As a result of these events, Boise Cascade reported an $85 million net deficit in 1971 (including a $48 million extraordinary charge against income) followed by a $170 million net loss in 1972 (see Table 1).

Stage III: 1973

Subsequent to the extraordinary charges of 1971 and 1972, John Fery, the newly appointed President of Boise Cascade, outlined five basic problems confronting the company: (1) the extraordinary charges necessitated modifying the company's many loan agreements; (2) debt had to be reduced quickly; (3) settlement of litigation involving the company's discontinued recreation land developments must be completed rapidly; (4) the company must operate its continuing businesses profitably; (5) top management must restore the company's lost credibility with the investment community. By summer, 1973, management felt that the first four problems were satisfactorily solved with the improvement of the company's tarnished image, just a matter of establishing a new track record. The divestiture program had netted the company approximately $400 million, and $500 million of total debt had been retired. The company had also settled the class action suits of some $500 million with the establishment of a settlement reserve of $25 million. The company's original businesses (building materials and paper) were extremely profitable for 1972 and 1973. These developments resulted in the company having an extraordinarily large net cash and marketable security position in excess of $200 million by July, 1973.

1974-1979 Capital Expenditure Program

With the problems of 1971 and 1972 mostly alleviated, top management turned its attention to the development of a capital budget for 1974 to 1979. After six months of deliberation and planning, the company tentatively decided to allocate approximately $1.1 billion for capital expenditures during these five years (see Table 4). Ed Cleary, Vice President and Treasurer, announced to the Board of Directors that estimated future cash flows from operations plus a modest increase in debt in addition to the company's present excess cash position would be sufficient to finance the $1.1 billion in capital expenditures.

Possible Repurchase of Common Stock*

After the capital expenditure program was tentatively approved by the Board of Directors, John Fery called a meeting with the Treasurer, the Assistant Treasurer,

*This section contains hypothetical conversations and does *not* represent actual conversations of Boise Cascade officials.

and a financial consultant, Max Hill. Mr. Fery opened the discussion by stating that since the company's 1974-1979 capital expenditure plans required very little in new long-term debt financing, he wondered if the company might have reduced its debt-to-equity ratio to the point where its marginal cost of capital might be adversely affected. Ed Cleary affirmed that this might well be the case and suggested that one way to solve this problem would be for the company to repurchase a portion of its 31.5 million shares of outstanding common stock. Cleary stated that some portion of its capital expenditures could be easily financed from new long-term debt sources. Max Hill, however, was skeptical about a common stock repurchase program at this time. Hill felt that such a program would not be well received by the investment community and would further depress the market value of Boise Cascade stock (the recent price history of the stock is presented in Table 5). Hill also noted that a repurchase program might prevent the company from using a "pooling of interests" accounting procedure for any new acquisitions for a period of at least two years.

On the other hand, Cleary argued that repurchasing stock would result in "reverse dilution" and cause the per share earnings to increase. This would have a positive influence on the market value of the stock. Cleary also noted that the terms of certain loan agreements still outstanding prohibited the payment of dividends in excess of $2 million in 1973 and $5 million in 1974. Repurchasing stock could be used as a vehicle by which stockholders could receive more current income from their investment in the company at a significant tax advantage. The net effect would most likely be a sharp increase in the price of the company's stock, according to Cleary.

Mr. Fery added that the company should always invest its capital in those investments that consistently yield the highest return. Fery noted that the P/E ratio had declined from a high of 34 in 1969 and it was presently felt that the low price multiple indicated that the company's stock represented an excellent investment for its excess working capital and should be included in the company's capital expenditure plans.

TABLE 3
Divestiture Program (a)

Divested Asset	Price(b) (millions)	Buyer	Date
Ebasco Services, Inc.	$ 65.0	Halliburton	Dec. 1972
Vernon Graphics, Inc. Chemical Construction Corp.	17.5	Aerojet-General	Feb. 1973
Mobile Homes and Recreational Vehicles Division	61.3	Bendix Corp.	Dec. 1972
Empresa Electrica De Guatemala	18.0	Government of Guatemala	May 1972
Panama Power & Light Co.	18.5	Government of Panama	June 1972
Argentina petrochemical plant	9.0	South American Consolidated Enterprises	Aug. 1972
Fort Bragg, California lumber operations	123.5 (c)	Georgia-Pacific and Louisiana-Pacific	Feb. 1973
Subtotal	$312.8		
Guatemalan, Brazilian, and Columbian bonds	47.0		
Subtotal	$359.8		
Metal Buildings Division		American Buildings	
Detroit Automotive	10.2 (d)	ASPRO, Inc.	
Detroit envelope plant		Seaman Patrick Paper	
Kansas City container plant		Hoerner-Waldorf	
Total	$370.0		

(a) Walter Kidde Constructors, Power Line Erectors, and Tyee Construction were liquidated.
(b) All transactions for cash.
(c) Georgia-Pacific, $119.3 million; Louisiana-Pacific, $4.2 million.
(d) Derived by subtraction; individual prices were not disclosed.

Source: Goldman Sachs, *Research Report on Boise Cascade Corporation,* July 30, 1973.

TABLE 4
Boise Cascade Capital Expenditure Plan 1974-1979

Expenditure Type	Dollar Amount (millions)	Percent of Total
Maintenance Expenditure	250.0	23.0
Pulp and Paper Manufacturing Facilities	270.0	25.0
Packaging and Office Products Distribution	135.0	12.0
Acquisition of Timberland and Manufacturing Fac.	125.0	11.0
Wood Produts Manufacture	160.0	14.5
Building Materials Fabrication	160.0	14.5
Totals	1,100.0	100.0

TABLE 5
Recent Price History of Boise Cascade Common Stock

Year	High	Low
1969	80¼	57½
1970	76⅞	40
1971	49⅞	15
1972	20⅝	9
1973 (first half)	12¼	8¼

QUESTIONS

1. Discuss the feasibility of the proposed stock reacquisition program.
2. What will be the impact of a stock reacquisition program on the firm's:
    (a) Capital structure?
    (b) Future dividend policy?
    (c) Financial risks?
    (d) Price to earnings multiple?
    (e) Future capital budgeting and financing plans?
    (f) Stockholder relations?
3. What recommendation would you make to Boise Cascade with respect to the reacquisition?

PART FIVE
CAPITAL STRUCTURE, COST OF CAPITAL, AND VALUATION

*

Case 36
American Telephone & Telegraph Company

In early 1971, Professor Stewart Myers, Associate Professor of Finance at the Sloan School of Management, Massachusetts Institute of Technology, was asked by the Federal Communications Commission to examine American Telephone & Telegraph's (AT&T) allowed rate of return. Since he had previously presented testimony in regulatory fields and had an active research interest in this area, Myers agreed to analyze AT&T and prepare testimony relating to the cost of capital.

Preliminary to his analysis, Myers decided to briefly review the background of utility regulation. In our economy, the forces of competition usually act to determine prices. In some industries, however, the economies of scale are such that only one or, at most, a few firms can operate efficiently. Since service is usually essential in these industries, demand is relatively inelastic. With inelastic demand and limited competition, the firms are in a position to exploit the consumer. For this reason, most industries in this situation are regulated with the allowed rate being just sufficient to allow companies a fair return on investment. That is, the company is allowed to set rates so as to earn its cost of capital.

The governing principle relating to fair rate of return was established by the Supreme Court in the Hope Natural Gas Company case in 1949:[1]

> The return to the equity owner should be commensurate with returns on investments in other enterprises having corresponding risks. That return, moreover, should be

This case was prepared by Professor George W. Trivoli of the University of Texas at Arlington and Professor J. Daniel Williams of the University of Akron as a basis for classroom discussion and not to illustrate either effective or ineffective handling of an administrative situation.

[1]*Federal Power Commission, et. al. v. Hope Natural Gas Company* (1949). 320 U. S. at 603.

sufficient to assure confidence in the financial integrity of the enterprise so as to maintain its credit and to attract capital.

The first sentence of the decision established a "comparable earnings" standard; the second, a standard of "capital attraction." Thus it is obvious that the allowed rate of return is quite similar to the cost of capital concept used in corporate finance.

Myers knows that the normal approach for a regulatory commission is to determine a utilities average cost of capital and then set prices so as to allow the company to earn this rate of return on its entire investment (referred to as rate base). The general procedure is to determine the component cost of the various portions of a firm's capital structure (e.g., debt, preferred stock, and equity) and then find the overall weighted average cost of capital. Although he thought a strong argument could be made for using current market values as weights, Myers knew that regulation typically employed book values and embedded interest costs in calculating the cost of capital. He estimated that AT&T's embedded interest cost in early 1971 is approximately 6 percent. The AT&T capital structure is represented by the balance sheets for 1969 and 1970 illustrated in Exhibit 1. Dr. Myers also felt that the risk faced by AT&T (and hence its cost of equity capital) was lower than most industrial companies and, at most, equal to that of a typical well-established utility.

The cost of debt and preferred stock is seldom a controversial issue, but the cost of equity, Myers knew, was open to various interpretations. He felt that the basic tenet of cost of capital is that at any point in time securities are priced so that all securities of equivalent risk offer the same expected rate of return. For a given utility, the problem is to determine the expected rate of return for the risk class in which the stock falls. This is then defined as a cost of equity capital.

Although there is no unique way to make this judgment, Myers felt that several factors should be examined in order to estimate the cost of equity capital for AT&T. Interest rates on corporate bonds and other instruments provide a minimum floor for cost of equity estimates. Myers prepared the information in Exhibit 2 to illustrate recent bond yields. A second approach is to use past rates of return to investors in similar companies as a guide. Exhibit 3 illustrates average rates of return on New York Stock Exchange common stocks. Exhibit 4 shows the recent earnings-to-price ratios which Myers felt might be helpful in calculating the cost of equity. Another approach that has received a great deal of attention in recent financial literature is the discounted cash flow approach (DCF). This method relates the cost of equity capital to the expected future dividends paid by the firm. One of the simplest formulations of this theory is a format popularized by Myron Gordon: $K = D_1 P_0 + G$ where K is the required rate of return, D_1 the dividends expected in the next period, P_0 the current market price, and G the expected rate of growth. Although this model assumes growth will be constant, it can easily be modified to handle other assumptions relating to the rate of growth. Myers assembled the data in Exhibit 5 to help him estimate the cost of equity capital using the DCF approach.

The FCC hearings were to begin in approximately a month, and Dr. Myers must be prepared to submit his recommendation at that time.

EXHIBIT 1

American Telephone & Telegraph Company and Its Telephone Subsidiaries
Consolidated Balance Sheets

	(Thousands of Dollars)	
	Dec. 31, 1970	*Dec. 31, 1969*
ASSETS		
Telephone Plant and Other Investments		
Telephone Plant—at cost		
Land, buildings and equipment		
In service	$52,150,445	$47,482,327
Under construction	2,584,619	1,708,638
Held for future use	78,138	53,524
	$54,813,202	$49,244,489
Less: Accumulated depreciation	12,262,989	11,235,038
	$42,550,213	$38,009,451
Other investments		
Investment in subsidiaries not consolidated	2,631,908	2,159,759
Other	406,811	190,499
	$45,588,932	$40,359,709
Current Assets		
Cash and temporary cash investments	$ 1,083,790	$ 848,132
Receivables—less allowance for uncollectibles:		
1970, $27,712,000; 1969, $20,577,000	2,186,727	2,053,129
Material and supplies	287,629	226,681
	$ 3,558,146	$ 3,127,942
Prepaid Expenses and Deferred Charges	$ 494,431	$ 415,470
Total Assets	$49,641,509	$43,903,121

(Balance Sheet continues on following page)

EXHIBIT 1 (continued)
American Telephone & Telegraph Company and Its Telephone Subsidiaries
Consolidated Balance Sheets

	(Thousands of Dollars)	
	Dec. 31, 1970	*Dec. 31, 1969*

LIABILITIES AND CAPITAL

Equity

American Telephone & Telegraph Company

Common shares—par value $16-2/3 per share Authorized 600,000,000 shares Outstanding at December 31, 1970, 549,275,000 shares	$ 9,154,586	$ 9,154,401
Premium on shares	5,294,506	5,288,923
Proceeds on excess of par value		
Reinvested earnings	9,845,653	9,085,508
	$24,294,745	$23,528,832
Minority interests	798,276	785,504
	$25,093,021	$24,314,336

Debt

Long-term	$18,248,326	$14,149,000
Notes payable—interim financing	2,205,335	1,719,029
	$20,453,661	$15,868,029

Current Liabilities

Accounts payable	$ 1,565,595	$ 1,348,407
Advance billing and customers' deposits	423,628	388,648
Dividends payable	369,142	369,137
Taxes accrued	728,582	769,381
Interest accrued	283,613	211,863
	$ 3,370,560	$ 3,087,436

Deferred Credits

Unamortized investment credit	$ 591,294	$ 571,492
Deferred income taxes	114,358	37,966
Other	18,615	23,862
	$ 724,267	$ 633,320
Total Liabilities and Capital	$49,641,509	$43,903,121

EXHIBIT 2

AT&T Cost of Capital Study
Stewart C. Myers

	Moody's Aaa Utilities	Moody's Average Utility
March, 1970	8.08	8.35
April, 1970	8.03	8.36
May, 1970	8.05	8.71
June, 1970	8.80	9.09
July, 1970	8.67	9.00
August, 1970	8.43	8.83
September, 1970	8.39	8.80
October, 1970	8.31	8.75
November, 1970	8.33	8.75
December, 1970	7.94	8.32
January, 1971	7.67	8.13
February, 1971	7.49	7.95

Source: Standard & Poor's *Bond Guide,* Moody's *Public Utility News Reports.*

EXHIBIT 3

AT&T Cost of Capital Study
Stewart C. Myers

Past Average Rates of Return on
New York Stock Exchange Common Stocks

From	To	Compound Rate of Return	Compound Rate of Return from Date in "From" Column to December 1965
Jan. 1926	Dec. 1930	-2.3	9.3
Dec. 1930	Dec. 1935	9.3	12.0
Dec. 1935	Dec. 1940	-1.1	12.6
Dec. 1940	Dec. 1945	33.6	16.0
Dec. 1945	Dec. 1950	7.8	12.6
Dec. 1950	Dec. 1955	18.5	14.5
Dec. 1955	Dec. 1960	11.2	12.5
Dec. 1960	Dec. 1965	15.9	15.9

Assumptions
(1) Equal investment in all NYSE stocks at the start of each year.
(2) Dividends reinvested.
(3) Returns calculated before tax.

Source: L. Fisher and J. H. Lorie, "Rates of Return on Investments in Common Stock: The Year-by-Year Record, 1926-65," *Journal of Business,* Vol. 41 (July, 1968), 291-316.

EXHIBIT 4
AT&T Cost of Capital Study
Stewart C. Myers

Recent Financial Data for AT&T Stock

Period	Price Range	Closing Price at Month-end	Dividend Yield[1]	Earnings/ Price Ratio[2]
October 1970	42⅛-45¾	43⅜	.06	.092
November 1970	43-46	45⅜	.057	.088
December 1970	45½-50½	48⅜	.054	.083
January 1971	48⅜-53⅝	53½	.049	.075
February 1971	47¾-53⅞	49	.053	.082

[1]Current dividend is $2.60; closing price used in calculation.
[2]1970 earnings per share were $3.99; closing price used in calculation.

Source: The Wall Street Journal, various issues.

EXHIBIT 5
AT&T Cost of Capital Study
Stewart C. Myers

Growth in Earnings, Dividends, Etc.,
Per Share of AT&T Stock

Year	Earnings Per Share	Dividends Per Share	Book Value Per Share
1960	$2.77	$1.65	$27.66
1961	2.76	1.76	29.19
1962	2.90	1.80	30.58
1963	3.03	1.80	31.94
1964	3.24	2.00	34.08
1965	3.41	2.05	35.80
1966	3.69	2.20	37.43
1967	3.79	2.25	39.00
1968	3.75	2.40	40.54
1969	4.00	2.45	42.10
1970	3.99	2.60	43.52

Source: Bell System *Statistical Manual;* Supplemental Statement of J. J. Scanlon, Bell Statement 7A, Attachment M.

EXHIBIT 6
AT&T Cost of Capital Study
Stewart C. Myers

Past Growth of the Bell System

Year	Total Assets (millions)	Percent Increase in Total Assets from Previous Year	Operating Revenues (millions)	Operating Income (millions)
1957	$ 17,678	—	$ 6,314	$ 880
1958	19,494	10.3	6,771	1,056
1959	20,807	6.7	7,393	1,223
1960	22,558	8.4	7,920	1,318
1961	24,618	9.1	8,414	1,430
1962	26,717	8.5	8,980	1,525
1963	28,275	5.8	9,569	1,655
1964	30,906	9.3	10,306	1,797
1965	32,819	6.2	11,062	1,951
1966	35,218	7.3	12,138	2,159
1967	37,608	6.8	13,009	2,317
1968	40,151	6.8	14,100	2,358
1969	43,903	9.3	15,684	2,575
1970	49,642	13.1	16,955	2,822
Growth Rate, 1957-70	7.8%		7.7%	8.6%
Growth Rate 1960-69	7.4%		7.8%	7.9%

Source: Bell System *Statistical Manual,* AT&T 1970 *Annual Report.*

QUESTIONS

1. Discuss the importance of cost of capital as it relates to rate of return regulation.
2. Calculate AT&T's overall cost of capital using (a) book value and (b) market value weights.
3. Discuss the pros and cons of using market versus book value weights.
4. What rate of return should AT&T be allowed?

Case 37
The Green Meadows Project (A)

On a rainy day in August, 1973, Roger Lund sat at his desk, trying to analyze the data he had gathered to make an initial recommendation concerning financial compensation to a private contractor. His aim was to recommend a maximum allowable rate of return figure that would ultimately be incorporated in a contract between the Lightning Aircraft Corporation (LAC) and the Central Region Development Agency (CRDA).

Mr. Lund was a recently graduated MBA from a major southeastern university. As his first task on joining the staff of the development agency some three months ago, he had been assigned to work on some of the financial aspects of the preliminary contract negotiations currently under way with LAC. These negotiations concerned Green Meadows, a proposed community for which the aircraft company might become the prime private developer in partnership with CRDA.

Early History of the Project

The Central Region Development Agency, headquartered near the Ozark Mountains, had considerable experience in various aspects of regional economic development and was considered by many as a model for such a government agency. Certainly, it was one of the earliest, having been established in the late 1930's. The agency's development activities had grown and now encompassed a

This case was prepared by Professor David J. Springate of Southern Methodist University as a basis for classroom discussion and not to illustrate either effective or ineffective handling of an administrative situation.

wide front. Examples included both infrastructure activity such as dam building and maintenance, power generation, management of recreation areas and waterfronts, and forestry activities and also attempts to aid local economic developments more directly through such means as identification of target industries, aid to local industrial promotion activites, and economic planning for urban renewal. These economic and development activities were carried out for an area of approximately 35,000 sq. miles encompassing six mid-western states. Total staff numbered about 18,000. CRDA was funded by annual government appropriations passed by Congress and by individual state legislatures. To partially repay past government appropriations, CRDA made annual payments to its sponsoring organizations of millions of dollars. Although a government agency, CRDA had considerable freedom and autonomy from sister governmental organizations and from its sponsors in pursuing its activities.

The idea of Green Meadows itself had arisen some ten years earlier when plans for damming the Kokomo River were first formulated. The site of the dam and subsequent lake on the Kokomo seemed to Mr. Jim Colbeck, then a regional planner, to be a logical spot for a new town—one where CRDA could profitably use its expertise gained in past development and also develop additional expertise in an area new to the agency, that of planning and development for a completely new community.

The idea lay dormant for several years at CRDA but was revived in 1970 after Mr. Colbeck became Head Regional Planner. As the idea became accepted and somewhat modified at the higher levels of CRDA management, the Green Meadows project seemed to offer the chance to reach previously identified economic and social objectives relating to better job opportunities and to a wider range of housing availability for area residents. It also allowed the attainment of additional objectives relating to the private sector. Specifically, if a private concern was made a partner or major contractor in developing the new town, it was hoped that new, useful concepts in joint management of residential and industrial development would evolve. It was held by some professionals at CRDA that as land became scarcer near other metropolitan centers and as government entered the planning and regulating frameworks in increasing intensity, the apparent need for closer collaboration and for new, proven modes of joint public-private action would increase. In this sense, CRDA could make a contribution to national

In 1971, LAC contacted CRDA and asked if the latter might be interested in exploring the possibility of LAC's participation in developing the new town. LAC was a giant in the aerospace industry, being active in military and civilian aircraft and advanced space vehicles. Lately, the company had become more active in its attempts to diversify. These attempts had taken LAC into alternate forms of ground transportation, electronic services and systems management. It was the combination of a desire to diversity and to use its corporate systems management skills that led LAC to consider working with CRDA in new town development.

After a preliminary examination of CRDA's ideas, lasting several months, LAC decided to try to continue developing the Green Meadows concept. At the same time, CRDA had by open contest determined that there were no other suitable private partners seriously interested in exploring the possibility of joining CRDA in developing Green Meadows.

During the last half of 1972 and in early 1973, the two parties worked together to gather basic economic, financial, and physical data on which to base preliminary plans for the possible new town. The planning framework envisioned a twenty-year town development period once all plans were finalized. Not only did the basic physical conceptualization of the town and its waterfront have to be carried out, but coordination and exploratory work were entailed with various state agencies and local governments and some federal agencies. Additionally, the economics behind the new town, its likely population and attraction for industry, a "time line" for its possible development, a tentative financing plan, and a tentative development plan—all had to be determined if the potential partners were to make an intelligent individual investment decision.

The Problem at Hand

By the summer of 1973, the two organizations were approaching the point where formalization of a planning and development contract between them was becoming a goal that had appeal for both parties. A split of project management, planning and financial responsibility, at least on major points, was required. One unresolved area that remained, blocking the execution of a preliminary agreement which would assign major responsibilities and allow teams to proceed with more detailed contract drafting for subsequent adoption, was the lack of agreement over appropriate compensation for LAC. It was at this point that Mr. Ben Harris, who headed CRDA's ad hoc Green Meadows investigation team under Mr. Colbeck added Roger Lund to his staff. The latter's first task would be to advise Mr. Harris and his superiors on some of the financial arrangements between the two prospective parties to the Green Meadows agreement.

The specific task that confronted Mr. Lund was to recommend a maximum rate of return that LAC might earn on the funds it committed to the Green Meadows project. It was anticipated that LAC would make investments to develop some of the residential properties in the new town and prepare them for sale to subdevelopers. These sales would provide project revenues. Delayed reimbursement to LAC would prove necessary, since revenues in the initial years would not match anticipated outlays. Exhibit 1 provides a summary of one early projection of the anticipated cash flows for LAC under certain assumptions relating to town development costs, revenues, and the effective tax rate.

Earlier in 1973, it had been agreed that LAC's maximum earnings rate would be limited in return for its first call on project revenues. Further, LAC would be reimbursed on the basis of an allowed percent annual return, after tax, on each dollar invested. Thus, as Roger Lund began his task, he knew that LAC might earn up to X percent, after tax, a year on each dollar the corporation had remaining invested in Green Meadows. However, how large X was to be was still open to question. It was anticipated that returns above the set X percent would go to CRDA to be held in public trust for eventual return to the new community.

If agreement on certain major items, including return, was reached between the negotiators for CRDA and LAC, a twenty-page preliminary agreement would be reviewed and ultimately signed by the respective top managements. Work would then start on a larger, much more detailed contract and on further joint planning for the town of Green Meadows. LAC expected to use basically the small team of negotiators and analysts it had supported at CRDA headquarters for the past eighteen months.

Cost of Capital Approach

Mr. Lund's first thought was to find what past achieved rates of return on individual investment projects in LAC had been. This did not prove practical, however, for two reasons. First, LAC did not have much information readily available. Second, since LAC would naturally prefer a relatively high limit to be set, Mr. Lund felt that any information he did obtain on past achieved rates of return might be slanted in favor of projects that had proved successful.

Mr. Lund next turned to a consideration of cost of capital. He had available to him past balance sheets and income statements for LAC for the years 1968-72 (see Exhibits 2 and 3). Further, he had compiled a matrix of annual rates of return actually achieved by stockholders of Lightning Aircraft in the past (Exhibit 4). For assumed holding periods of differing lengths with starting years and ending years between 1958 and 1972, he had computed the annual rates of return realized taking into account starting stock prices, ending stock prices, and interim dividends. The mean figure was 8.1 percent, which Mr. Lund proposed to use as his basic cost of equity. To be conservative, he adjusted this cost to 8.1/.9 or 9 percent. This last refinement allowed for underpricing of 10 percent should LAC decide to provide new equity investment through stock flotation.

Knowing that long-term debt for a company with LAC's current bond rating was priced in the market to yield 7.6 percent, Mr. Lund wondered if he could reasonably measure the cost of capital for LAC using the information he had at hand and what the relevance of the resulting calculation would be. His thoughts were that he could take the cost of equity as 9 percent (the average of the entries in the matrix of rates of return achieved by shareholders, modified for underpricing as above), that 7.6 percent could be taken as a measure of the cost of debt, and that the current proportions of debt and equity in the LAC corporate capital structure could be used to compute a weighted cost of capital.

If he did proceed in this manner, Mr. Lund was unsure how taxes should be taken into account. His inclination was to use the average of percentage figures over fifteen previous years for income taxes as a percent of reported net earnings before taxes. However, considering income taxes as a percent of operating income reported in past years or looking at taxes actually payable "in cash" in any year as a percent of earnings before tax in that year gave substantially different figures, as seen on the next page.

	Tax Rates for Previous 15 Years		Tax Rates for Previous 5 Years		
	Average	Standard Deviation	Average	Standard Deviation	1972 Tax Rate
Income tax as a percent of year's operating income.	.20	.21	-.35	.64	-.04
Income tax as a percent of net earnings before tax (extraordinary items not considered)	.29	.51	-.26	.96	-.22
Tax currently payable as a percent of current earnings before tax in any year.	.47	.29	.58	.35	.40

Note: Most of the negative entries in the above table were due to tax credits.

As a partial check on the applicability of any calculation he might make above, Mr. Lund thought he might to able to use returns attained by a sample of firms in the real estate industry and reported in Moody's *Handbook for Investors*. Using industry data provided on average share prices and dividends for a representative sample of firms, he was able to compute annual rates of return in a manner similar to Exhibit 4. The results of his computations are given in Exhibit 5. A cost of capital figure of about 11 percent was calculated.

Other Considerations

As stated, Mr. Lund was not sure that the cost of capital approach was the correct one to use. Some other information he had assembled included:

1. Data from the Federal Trade Commission and Securities and Exchange Commission.

Using the FTC-SEC Quarterly Financial Reports for Manufacturing Companies, Mr. Lund determined that for aircraft manufacturers the average for 1965-72 of achieved quarterly rates of profit after tax as a percent of total equity was 11.6. Over the same period, the average return on fixed assets and inventory before taxes for six durable goods industries was 20.5 percent.

2. First National City Bank Data

The monthly letter of April, 1973, showed a 1972 average rate of return on net worth of 12.1 percent for 2,414 diversified manufacturing concerns. The average reported rate of return on net worth over the last 25 years averaged 11.3 percent. For 44 aero-space companies, the 1972 industrial average was 8.8 percent.

3. A Report in the May, 1973, Issue of *Fortune*

About one-third of the largest 500 domestic corporations earned more than 12 percent on the book value of corporate equity in 1972. The median realized return was 10.3 percent.

As a final consideration, Mr. Lund was mulling over the use of the so-called "Capital Asset Pricing Model," a one-period model developed using assumptions of perfect capital markets. One expression of the model holds that the expected return of any security above a "riskless" rate of interest (a hypothetical construct) is related to the volatility of the security (a measure of the tendency of any security to vary compared to swings in some overall market index) and expected market rates of return int he following manner:

$$E(r_i) - R_f = \beta \ (E(R\ ) - R\ )$$

where, E(ri) = expected return on the security being considered.

R_f = riskless rate of return.

β_i = index of volatility for the security, that is the ratio of its change in value for a given change in the value of the market index.

$E(R_I)$ = expected rate of return for the market index, commonly the 425 industrial stocks used as an index by Standard and Poor's.

If he used this concept, Mr. Lund intended to use the following facts:

1. A leading stock analyst's handbook had recently judged LAC to have a β of 1.45.
2. Current long-term government debt was selling for 7.2 percent.
3. A study by Fisher and Lorie had shown that over the years 1926-60 the average annual rate of return of stock listed on the New York Stock Exchange assuming the investment of dividends and tax exemptions, was 9.0 percent.[1]
4. The average β of four real estate companies in the business of assembling undeveloped real estate and providing for some development was found to be 1.58 using data from the stock analyst's handbook.

In talking with Mr. Albert Fry, a member of the local LAC analysis and negotiating team, Mr. Lund learned that in LAC's opinion a 15 percent return on capital employed represented the lowest figure for which the company should settle with CRDA. Apparently, aircraft manufacturing returned "about 30 percent" per year, and new town development was felt to be "half as risky." At the same time, Mr. Fry showed Roger Lund some literature relating to one British new town and one in the United States. In these cases, rates of return on equity between 10 and 20 percent had been achieved by the private developers. In Mr. Lund's view, however, this latter data had limited direct application to his current problem. The literature referred to towns where a developer had carried out all development functions and been responsible for complete development. In the present case, CRDA would provide financing for nearly $30 million of infrastructure to be ultimately installed. Furthermore, at a cost of about $5 million, CRDA had already assembled the land that would ultimately be used for the Green Meadows project. LAC's anticipated cumulative investment was $58.2 million (see Figure 1). At any moment, its

[1]Lawrence Fisher and James Lorie, "Rates of Return on Investments in Common Stock," *Journal of Business,* January, 1964.

investment exposure would be less than this due to the generation of ongoing project returns for LAC.

EXHIBIT 1

The Green Meadows Project (A)

A Projected LAC Cash Flow for Green Meadows Project
(Dollars in Thousands)

Project Year	Cash Flows From Revenues Before Tax	Cash Flows for Taxes	Cash Flows to Cover Expenditures	Total Incremental Net Cash Flows Due to Project
(Col. 1)	(Col. 2)	(Col. 3)	(Col. 4)	(Col. 5 = 2+3+4)
1 (1972)	$ —	$ 115	$ (231)	$ (115)
2	—	104	(209)	(105)
3	—	104	(209)	(105)
4	—	213	(426)	(213)
5	744	(53)	(2,641)	(1,950)
6	1,767	(291)	(2,533)	(1,057)
7	2,555	(208)	(2,652)	(306)
8	2,969	(279)	(2,094)	595
9	2,969	(293)	(1,937)	738
10	2,839	(178)	(2,330)	332
11	3,107	(233)	(2,653)	212
12	3,581	(368)	(2,500)	713
13	3,581	(368)	(3,107)	106
14	3,940	(364)	(2,404)	1,173
15	3,813	(367)	(3,410)	(47)
16	3,834	(377)	(2,774)	684
17	4,112	(509)	(3,007)	596
18	4,112	(509)	(2,744)	859
19	4,260	(517)	(3,093)	650
20	4,112	(525)	(2,734)	852
21	4,113	(526)	(3,514)	73
22	5,026	(725)	(3,000)	1,300
23	5,026	(725)	(3,000)	1,300
24	5,026	(742)	(2,886)	1,398
25	5,026	(742)	(2,863)	1,421
26	5,175	(935)	107	4,347

Note: Numbers may not add due to rounding.

EXHIBIT 2

The Green Meadows Project (A)

Balance Sheets of Lightning Aircraft Corporation

(Dollars in Thousands)

	1972	1971	1970	1969	1968
ASSETS					
Cash	$ 39,741	$ 68,844	$ 49,347	$ 63,340	$ 45,515
Notes and accounts receivable	112,728	115,920	79,923	82,161	47,659
Receivables under federal government contracts	99,632	86,912	79,231	67,712	77,725
Refundable income taxes	—	1,760	3,488	7,525	—
Inventories	884,011	1,068,850	1,162,640	1,088,541	798,833
Prepayments	5,320	4,999	5,385	9,344	10,047
Total current assets	$1,141,433	$1,347,284	$1,380,013	$1,318,612	$ 979,780
Long-term notes receivable	$ 195,933	$ 193,296	$ 201,952	$ 177,492	$ 161,875
Leased aircraft	20,250	28,177	44,685	55,303	70,457
Property, plant, and equip.	826,211	840,261	861,469	862,371	804,773
Less: Depreciation reserve	527,936	490,085	446,367	387,182	315,218
Net property account	$ 298,275	$ 350,176	$ 415,102	$ 475,189	$ 489,555
Other assets	$ 3,417	$ 3,318	$ 3,266	$ 3,310	$ 3,506
Total Assets	$1,659,369	$1,922,251	$2,045,019	$2,029,906	$1,705,173

(Balance Sheet continues on following page)

EXHIBIT 2

The Green Meadows Project (A) *(continued)*

Balance Sheets of Lightning Aircraft Corporation

(Dollars in Thousands)

LIABILITIES AND EQUITY	1972	1971	1970	1969	1968
Notes payable to banks	$ 83,499	$ 196,322	$ 89,661	$ 115,637	$ —
Notes & accts. payable	253,709	410,926	592,695	574,197	463,330
Accrued wages, taxes, etc.	116,067	101,537	104,706	121,451	133,501
Provision for income taxes	959	—	—	—	7,230
Current portion/long-term debt	111,140	96,562	80,790	31,163	11,458
Total current liabilities	$ 565,374	$ 805,347	$ 914,651	$ 842,448	$ 615,519
Deferred income taxes	$ 1,560	$ 13,260	$ 13,416	$ 19,578	$ 37,392
Deferred investment credit	25,818	34,632	45,864	53,664	53,196
Long-term debt	392,058	411,495	486,530	493,324	366,984
Capital stock (par $5)	348,788	348,691	348,691	348,691	347,581
Retained earnings	325,776	308,825	282,667	272,201	284,500
Total stockholder's equity	$ 674,559	$ 657,517	$ 631,357	$ 620,892	$ 632,082
Total Liabilities and Equity	$1,659,369	$1,922,251	$2,045,019	$2,029,906	$1,705,173
Note: Equity Market Value (in thousands) on December 31.	$ 422,276	$ 314,995	$ 240,971	$ 475,760	$ 909,409

EXHIBIT 3

The Green Meadows Project (A)
Income Statements of Lightning Aircraft Corporation
(Dollars in Thousands)

	1972	1971	1970	1969	1968
Sales, less discounts, returns and allowances	$1,848,272	$2,371,056	$2,868,117	$2,210,976	$2,553,704
Less: (Cost of goods sold, Selling and admin. expenses)	$1,743,824	$2,268,515	$2,743,418	$2,116,729	$2,350,795
Depreciation and amortization	59,217	69,895	76,730	82,154	73,192
Operating profit	$ 45,231	$ 32,646	$ 47,968	$ 12,094	$ 129,717
Other income	18,132	20,920	19,118	14,797	13,041
Total income	$ 63,363	$ 53,566	$ 67,086	$ 26,891	$ 142,758
Interest & debt expense	44,015	44,072	59,762	38,021	26,093
Balance	$ 19,348	$ 9,494	$ 7,324	$ (11,131)	$ 116,666
Federal income tax	Cr 4,368	Cr 8,001	Cr 9,906	Cr 19,110	51,948
Net Income before extraordinary items	$ 23,716	$ 17,495	$ 17,230	$ 7,979	$ 64,578
Extraordinary item	—	Cr 15,428	—	—	—
Net income	$ 23,716	$ 32,924	$ 17,230	$ 7,979	$ 64,578
Retained earnings, beginning	308,825	282,667	272,201	284,500	240,032
Dividends	$ 6,776	$ 6,765	$ 6,765	$ 20,271	$ 20,252
Retained earnings, end	$ 325,776	$ 308,825	$ 282,667	$ 272,201	$ 284,500

EXHIBIT 4

The Green Meadows Project (A)

Percent Annual Return on Equity Purchase of Lightning Aircraft Corporation Stock for Holding Period of Various Lengths

Starting Year	Ending Year													
	1959	1960	1961	1962	1963	1964	1965	1966	1967	1968	1969	1970	1971	1972
1958	-31	-10	6	-6	-7	10	20	16	19	12	6	1	3	4
1959		23	32	12	9	22	31	27	28	19	11	6	8	9
1960			42	6	5	21	33	27	29	19	10	4	6	7
1961				-24	-15	4	30	24	27	16	6	-9	7	-4
1962					2	41	56	41	41	24	11	11	6	8
1963						98	95	58	54	30	13	-8	6	8
1964							94	41	41	16	-6	16	-12	-7
1965								2	19	-5	-20	-27	-21	-15
1966									40	-7	-25	-32	-24	-16
1967										-36	-44	-46	-34	-24
1968											-48	-49	-32	-20
1969												-45	-20	-5
1970													34	35
1971														36

Notes: Average Annual Return = 8.1%
Adjustments made for stock dividends and stock splits.

Example: Adjusted stock price Dec. 31, 1958 = $23.04
Adjusted stock price Dec. 31, 1960 = $18.38
Dividend per share in 1959 = $.49
Dividend per share in 1960 = $.58

Solution to $(18.38 + .58) = \dfrac{\$.49}{(1 + x)} + \dfrac{\$23.04}{(1 + x)^2}$

is x = -10%

EXHIBIT 5

The Green Meadows Project (A)

Computed Cost of Capital for Representative Sample of
Firms in Real Estate Industry

I. Computed Recent Annual Return on Equity Purchases of Firms for Varying Holding Period Lengths

Ending Year

Starting Year	1966	1967	1968	1969	1970	1971
1965	9	33	51	47	30	27
1966		64	79	64	37	32
1967			95	64	28	24
1968				37	3	7
1969					-22	-8
1970						13
1971						

Average of above entries = 33.6%

II.	Capital Component	Assumed proportion of capital structure	After-Tax Cost (Percent)	Weighted Average Cost (Percent)
	Debt	.8	5*	4
	Equity	.2	33.6	6.8
				10.8

Basic Data Source Moody's *Handbook for Investors*

*Reflects the fact that long-term business loans from banks in August, 1973, were being charged an average of 9.5% before tax in 35 financial centers.

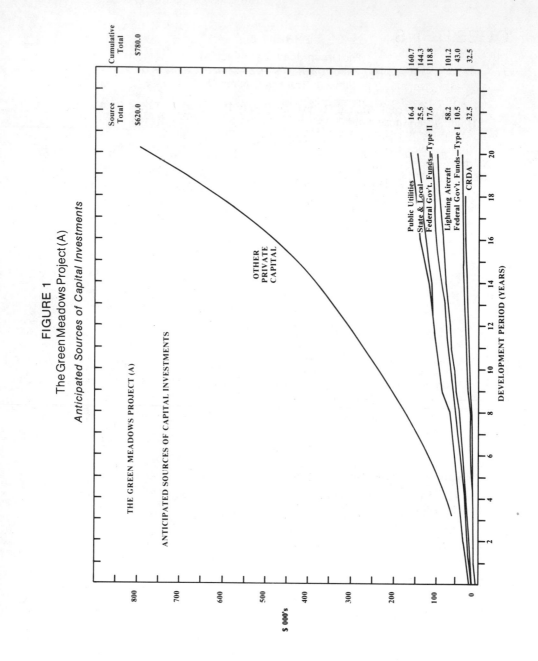

FIGURE 1
The Green Meadows Project (A)
Anticipated Sources of Capital Investments

THE GREEN MEADOWS PROJECT (A)

ANTICIPATED SOURCES OF CAPITAL INVESTMENTS

OTHER PRIVATE CAPITAL

DEVELOPMENT PERIOD (YEARS)

$ 000's

	Source Total	Cumulative Total
	$620.0	$780.0
Public Utilities	16.4	160.7
State & Local	25.5	144.3
Federal Gov't. Funds—Type II	17.6	118.8
Lightning Aircraft	58.2	101.2
Federal Gov't. Funds—Type I	10.5	43.0
CRDA	32.5	32.5

QUESTIONS

1. Compare and contrast the applicability of the two alternate approaches for estimating the maximum rate of return allowed for LAC, i.e., (a) cost of capital and (b) capital asset pricing model.
2. Using each of these approaches and the data presented in the case, determine and recommend the appropriate rate of return for LAC.
3. In light of your findings in Question 2, consider these allowed rates in light of LAC's opportunity cost.
4. Discuss why it might be argued by LAC that estimates of its maximum return should include a substantial risk premium.

Case 38
Idaho Power Company

I. Background Information

Idaho Power Company, a large electric utility operating in southern Idaho, northern Nevada, and eastern Oregon, has experienced a 7 percent average growth rate in operating revenues during the past 11 years (see Table 1). The company's service area is primarily an agriculture-dominated economy. However, the economic base of the area has been strengthened in recent years with the emergence of several light manufacturing industries. The company's generating capacity is characterized by an almost total reliance on hydroelectric generating facilities. Idaho Power operates 14 hydroelectric plants located principally in the Snake River Valley of southern and western Idaho (see Table 2). Approximately 90 percent of the company's load requirements are presently satisfied with power produced from these facilities. The remaining 10 percent has been supplied by neighboring utilities via interchange agreements. Idaho Power experiences a peak power demand during the summer months, while neighboring utilities' power requirements peak in the winter. This enables Idaho Power to readily purchase power from other utilities when demand exceeds generating capacity.

In order to meet the growing demand for power in its service area, the company has spent a total of $231.1 million on capital expenditures since 1968. In addition, top management anticipates that capital expenditures will exceed $186 million during the next three years (see Table 3). In the late 1960's, these expenditures largely consisted of capital allocations associated with the completion

This case was prepared by Professor Dennis B. Fitzpatrick of Boise State University as a basis for classroom discussion and not to illustrate either effective or ineffective handling of an administrative situation.

of the Hell's Canyon Dam project. The high volume of capital expenditures for the 1971-1976 period reflects the construction of the coal-fired JimBridger Power Plant near Rock Springs, Wyoming. Idaho Power is building the facility jointly with the Pacific Power and Light Company. One 500-kw generating unit is scheduled to start producing electricity for Idaho Power's customers by late 1974.

II. Idaho Power's Rate of Return, Forecasted Cash Flows, and Future Financial Requirements

From 1968 to 1973, Idaho Power has earned an average rate of return on rate base of 6.63 percent (see Table 4), and management has forecasted that the net internal generation of cash will increase from $14.8 million in 1973 to $22.2 million in 1976. This cash flow will only partially offset the heavy construction outlays during these years, resulting in a new external cash requirement of approximately $230 million for the 1973-1976 period (see Table 5).

III. Long-Range Financial Strategy

Since the costs of raising these large sums of capital are critical to the company's future success, Al Carlsen, Idaho Power President, directed Bob Klumpp, Financial Vice President, to prepare a detailed analysis of the company's cost of capital and capital structure for a special meeting of the Board of Directors. Klumpp, who has been employed by Idaho Power since 1972, decided that a thorough review of the company's embedded cost of capital and capital structure policy be made. Idaho Power presently has a goal of maintaining a long-term capital structure consisting of 55 percent debt, 35 percent comon stock, and 10 percent preferred stock.

In preparation for the meeting, Mr. Klumpp compiled the embedded costs of outstanding long-term debt and preferred stock based on book values and estimated costs on bonds and preferred stock that will be issued in the next three years (see Tables 6 and 7). As a result of his analysis, Klumpp predicted that the percentage increase in the company's embedded costs of debt will be 30 percent, and the cost of preferred stock will increase by almost 60 percent from 1971 to 1976 (see Table 8). Klumpp's projections were based on the assumption that the company will be able to issue bonds and preferred stock at 8 percent yields for the next three years. Klumpp also noted that the return on average common equity had increased from 9.7 percent to 12.8 percent over the last five years, but was still significantly less than a select group of other Aa rated utilities (see Table 9). Finally, Klumpp compiled a chart showing that although the company's dividend payments have almost doubled since 1963, the payout ratio has declined to approximately 60 percent (see Table 10).

Klumpp presented this information at the special Board of Directors meeting and announced that management should consider changing the firm's stated capital structure objectives by increasing the percentage of common equity to 40 percent of the capital structure. Al Carlsen questioned the wisdom of such a change in company policy and suggested that the tax advantages of debt were significant and consideration should be given to increasing long-term debt. Sam Jensen, a recent

MBA graduate and Special Assistant to Carlsen, asserted that changes in the company's capital structure would have little impact on the price of Idaho Power stock. Jensen said that several recent academic studies conclude that changes in an electric utility's capital structure have no direct bearing on stock valuation. Hence, discussions of capital structure policies are academic and a waste of time.

Klumpp strongly disagreed and suggested that increasing the debt to equity ratio to more than 1.25 would result in increased risk exposure to the firm's creditors and stockholders, resulting in negative market pressure on Idaho Power common stock. Board member Harold Johnson presented a comparison of Idaho Power's interest coverage ratios with those of similar utilities (see Table 11). Johnson suggested that increasing the company's financial leverage would result in lower interest coverage ratios and possibly lower bond ratings. Johnson argued that a downgrading of the company's securities by the rating agencies would increase the cost of future bond financing by 20 basis points.

Mr. Carlsen terminated the meeting and stated that more study of the company's capital structure should be made, and scheduled another board meeting in two weeks.

TABLE 1
Operating Revenues (1962-1973)
(in thousands of $)

Year	Operating Revenue	Percent Change in Operating Revenue from Preceding Year
1962	44,326	—
1963	48,456	9.32
1964	50,644	4.52
1965	52,572	3.81
1966	57,255	8.91
1967	60,679	5.98
1968	66,926	10.31
1969	69,377	3.66
1970	74,735	7.72
1971	81,810	9.47
1972	89,809	9.78
1973	90,707	1.00
		Average 6.77

TABLE 2
List of Idaho Power Company's Power Plants

Plant	Estimated Maximum Capacity	Plant	Estimated Maximum Capacity
1. American Falls	27,500 Kw	8. Lower Malad	15,000 Kw
2. Twin Falls	10,000 Kw	9. Bliss	80,000 Kw
3. Shoshone Falls	12,500 Kw	10. C. J. Strike	89,000 Kw
4. Thousand Springs	8,000 Kw	11. Swan Falls	12,000 Kw
5. Upper Salmon	39,000 Kw	12. Brownlee	450,000 Kw
6. Lower Salmon	70,000 Kw	13. Oxbow	220,000 Kw
7. Upper Malad	9,000 Kw	14. Hell's Canyon	450,000 Kw

Total Smaller Plants	2,700 Kw
Total System	1,494,700 Kw

UNDER CONSTRUCTION

15. Jim Bridger   500,000 Kw

Transmission Lines	4,070 miles
Distribution Lines	15,035 miles
Total Lines	19,105 miles

TABLE 3
Idaho Power Company Capital Expenditures
(Actual 1968-1972: Estimated 1973-1976)
(in thousands of $)

Year	Construction Expenditures
1968	12,146
1969	12,737
1970	11,858
1971	22,696
1972	55,907
1973	115,799
1974	61,622
1975	55,931
1976	69,309

TABLE 4
Rate of Return on Average Rate Base
(Actual 1968-1972; Estimated 1973-1976)
(In thousands of $)

Line No.		1968	1969	1970	1971	1972	1973	1974	1975	1976
				Before Proposed Rate Increase						
	Beginning and End of Year Average									
1.	Electric plant in service	$466,966	$477,663	$487,511	$497,860	$510,170	$534,475	$651,835	$770,143	$824,392
	Deductions:									
2.	Accumulated provision for depreciation & amortization	66,217	71,947	77,808	83,972	90,226	96,242	103,197	113,182	125,626
3.	Contributions in aid of construction	798	837	884	1,156	1,442	1,526	1,610	1,702	1,800
4.	Contributions in deferred credits	1,952	1,984	1,999	1,746	1,605	1,819	1,930	1,941	1,864
5.	Net plant investment	$397,999	$402,868	$406,820	$410,986	$416,897	$434,888	$545,098	$653,318	$695,102
	Add—Working capital:									
6.	45 days' operation and maintenance expenses, excluding purchased power and fuel cost	1,559	1,641	1,814	2,199	2,322	2,412	2,673	3,093	3,186
7.	Materials and supplies	1,456	1,389	1,459	1,605	1,815	1,700	1,800	2,400	2,500
8.	Total working capital	$ 3,015	$ 3,030	$ 3,273	$ 3,804	$ 4,137	$ 4,112	$ 4,473	$ 5,493	$ 5,686
9.	Rate base	$401,014	$405,898	$410,093	$414,790	$421,034	$439,000	$549,571	$658,811	$700,788
10.	Operating income	$ 23,898	$ 25,265	$ 27,395	$ 29,433	$ 30,284	$ 34,634	$ 39,784	$ 41,803	$ 42,757
11.	Rate of return	5.96%	6.22%	6.68%	7.10%	7.19%	7.21%	7.24%	6.35%	6.10%

TABLE 5

Projected Internal Cash Flows and External Cash Requirements

(in thousands of $)

Year	Net Internal Cash Generation	Construction Expenditures	External Cash Requirements
1973	14,823	115,799	100,976
1974	13,926	61,622	47,696
1975	22,644	55,931	33,287
1976	22,240	69,309	47,069
Total	73,633	302,661	229,028

TABLE 6

Idaho Power Company
Cost of Long-Term Debt
Outstanding as of December 31, 1973
Estimated 1974-1976

Description of Security	Date Issue	Date Maturity	Original Issue	Currently Outstanding	Annual Cost	Effective Rate
Outstanding as of December 31, 1973:						
First Mortgage Bonds:						
3⅛% Series due 1973	11-15-43	11-15-73	$ 18,000,000	$ 18,000,000	$ 562,500	3.13%
3⅛% Series due 1973			(18,000,000)	(18,000,000)	(562,500)	(3.13)
2¾% Series due 1977	2- 1-47	2- 1-77	5,000,000	5,000,000	137,500	2.75
3 % Series due 1978	5- 1-48	5- 1-78	10,000,000	10,000,000	300,000	3.00
2¾% Series due 1979	11- 1-49	11- 1-79	12,000,000	12,000,000	330,000	2.75
3¼% Series due 1981	10- 1-51	10- 1-81	15,000,000	15,000,000	487,500	3.25
4½% Series due 1987	1- 1-57	1- 1-87	20,000,000	20,000,000	900,000	4.50
4¾% Series due 1987	11-15-57	11-15-87	15,000,000	15,000,000	712,500	4.75
4 % Series due April 1988	4- 1-58	4- 1-88	10,000,000	10,000,000	400,000	4.00
4½% Series due October 1988	10-15-58	10-15-88	15,000,000	15,000,000	675,000	4.50
5 % Series due 1989	5-15-59	5-15-89	15,000,000	15,000,000	750,000	5.00
4⅞% Series due 1990	11-15-60	11-15-90	15,000,000	15,000,000	731,250	4.88
4½% Series due 1991	11- 1-61	11- 1-91	10,000,000	10,000,000	450,000	4.50
5¼% Series due 1996	4- 1-66	4- 1-96	20,000,000	20,000,000	1,050,000	5.25
6⅛% Series due 1996	10- 1-66	10- 1-96	30,000,000	30,000,000	1,837,500	6.13
7¾% Series due 2002	9- 1-72	9- 1-02	30,000,000	30,000,000	2,325,000	7.75
Total first mortgage bonds			$222,000,000	$222,000,000	$11,086,250	4.99%
Other Long-Term Debt:						
4¼% Sinking Fund Debentures, due April 1983	4- 1-58	4- 1-83	10,000,000	7,274,000	309,145	4.25
Pollution Control Revenue Bonds, 5.90% Series due 2003	9- 1-73	9- 1-03	27,000,000	27,000,000	1,593,000	5.90
Total debt as of December 31, 1973			$259,000,000	$256,274,000	$12,988,395	5.07%

TABLE 7

Idaho Power Company

Cost of Preferred Stock
Actual as of December 31, 1973
Estimated 1974-1976

Description	Date of Issue	Number of Shares	Par Value	Annual Cost	Effective Rate
Outstanding as of December 31, 1973:					
4% Preferred Stock	8-1-44	60,587	$ 6,058,700	$ 242,348	4.00%
" " "	8-1-45	39,413	3,941,300	157,652	4.00
" " "	1947- 48	35,000	3,500,000	140,000	4.00
" " "	5- 6-49	10,000	1,000,000	40,000	4.00
" " "	1950	20,000	2,000,000	80,000	4.00
" " "	1951	11,000	1,100,000	44,000	4.00
" " "	1952	5,000	500,000	20,000	4.00
" " "	1953	3,000	300,000	12,000	4.00
" " "	1954	16,000	1,600,000	64,000	4.00
" " "	1955-56	15,000	1,500,000	60,000	4.00
7.68% Serial Preferred Stock, First Series	9-27-72	150,000	$15,000,000	$1,152,000	7.68%
Total preferred stock as of December 31, 1973		365,000	$36,500,000	$2,012,000	5.51%

TABLE 8

Percentage Increase in Effective Cost of Long-Term Debt and Preferred Stock

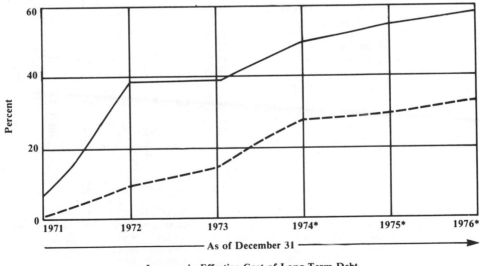

————— **Increase in Effective Cost of Long-Term Debt**
– – – **Increase in Effective Cost of Preferred Stock**

*estimates.

TABLE 9

Comparison of Return on Average Common Equity
with Aa-Rated Utilities

1968-1972 and Twelve Months Ended September 30, 1973

Company	1968	1969	1970	1971	1972	Twelve Months Ended 9/30/73
IDAHO POWER COMPANY	9.7%	10.4%	11.5%	12.8%	12.8%	12.0%
Aa Electric Utilities:						
Oklahoma Gas and Electric Company	15.1%	16.5%	17.4%	15.8%	15.4%	14.8%
Kansas City Power and Light Company	12.5	11.7	11.3	11.5	11.4	9.5
Columbus and Southern Ohio Electric Company	12.4	12.1	12.1	9.9	12.1	12.0
Tampa Electric Company	14.1	14.7	14.5	9.4	14.2	14.8
Atlantic City Electric Company	15.1	14.8	13.1	12.9	13.5	14.3
Southwestern Public Service Company	14.8	15.6	18.0	16.8	15.7	16.2
Kentucky Utilities Company	11.9	12.7	12.9	12.1	11.3	12.5
Kansas Gas and Electric Company	11.6	12.6	12.9	12.9	12.9	11.1
Average for Aa electric utilities	13.4	13.9	14.0	12.7	13.3	13.2
Aa Combination Electric and Gas Utilities:						
San Diego Gas and Electric Company	12.2	13.0	12.1	11.6	10.6	11.9
Central Illinois Public Service Company	14.9	14.8	14.4	14.8	12.8	11.0
Indianapolis Power and Light Company	15.1	15.6	13.9	14.1	17.1	16.2
Delmarva Power and Light Company	13.7	14.5	11.8	13.2	12.2	14.3
Iowa-Illinois Gas and Electric Company	13.4	13.5	12.3	9.1	14.6	12.9
Wisconsin Power and Light Company	12.1	12.9	12.2	10.9	10.1	12.1
Kansas Power and Light Company	12.5	13.2	14.9	14.7	13.3	12.4
Toledo Edison Company	15.2	15.6	15.2	14.5	15.3	14.5
Central Illinois Light Company	11.7	12.0	13.7	13.8	13.1	11.1
Iowa Electric Light and Power Company	11.6	10.5	11.3	9.9	12.6	11.1
Iowa Power and Light Company	13.7	13.5	10.6	10.8	11.4	13.5
Montana Power Company	14.6	16.4	16.7	16.2	16.4	13.6
Central Hudson Gas and Electric Corporation	12.0	11.6	8.2	12.7	14.6	12.9
Southern Indiana Gas and Electric Company	14.4	14.9	15.4	14.9	15.9	15.1
Average for Aa combination utilities	13.4%	13.7%	13.1%	12.9%	13.6%	13.0%
Average for Aa electric and combination utilities	13.4%	13.8%	13.4%	12.8%	13.5%	13.1%

Notes: Years 1968-1972 calculated from Moody's *Public Utility Manual,* 1973.
  Twelve months ended September 30, 1973 obtained from Moody's Investors Service, Inc., and
  Investors Management Sciences, Inc. (Subsidiary of Standard & Poor's Corporation), to the
  extent the data was available in their files; for those companies whose data were not available
  from the foregoing sources, such data were obtained by direct contact with the companies by
  telephone.

TABLE 10
Idaho Power Company
Dividends Paid Out Ratio
for Years 1963-1973
(in thousands of $)

Year	Dividends Paid Per Share	Earnings Available for Common	Dividends Paid Out	% Dividends Paid Out
1963	$1.05	$ 9,577	$ 6,668	69.6
1964	1.15	10,779	7,303	67.7
1965	1.25	12,250	8,175	66.7
1966	1.35	13,813	8,910	64.5
1967	1.45	14,630	9,570	65.4
1968	1.55	12,744	10,230	80.3
1969	1.60	13,913	10,560	75.9
1970	1.60	15,903	10,560	66.4
1971	1.65	18,547	10,890	58.7
1972	1.73	19,495	11,418	58.6
1973	1.81	21,487	12,974	60.4
Total 1963-1973		$163,138	$107,258	65.7
Total 1971-1973		$ 59,529	$ 35,282	59.3

TABLE 11

Idaho Power Company

Comparison of Times Interest Charges Earned with Aa-Rated Utilities
1968-1972 and Twelve Months Ended September 30, 1973

Company	Times Charges Earned Before Taxes						Times Charges Earned After Taxes					
	1968	1969	1970	1971	1972	12 Mo. Ended 9/30/73	1968	1969	1970	1971	1972	12 Mo. Ended 9/30/73
IDAHO POWER COMPANY	3.43	3.55	3.79	4.20	4.03	3.52	2.43	2.39	2.56	2.87	2.82	2.68
Aa Electric Utilities:												
Oklahoma Gas and Electric Co.	5.38	5.57	4.89	5.19	4.82	4.85	3.55	3.56	3.28	3.47	3.24	3.45
Kansas City Power and Light Co.	4.99	4.09	3.41	3.11	2.90	3.45	3.32	2.87	2.51	2.41	2.33	2.05
Columbus & Southern Ohio Electric Co.	4.46	3.33	2.51	2.05	2.37	2.48	2.97	2.45	2.20	1.93	2.20	2.23
Tampa Electric Co.	4.10	3.56	3.15	2.51	3.15	3.36	2.77	2.56	2.41	2.04	2.34	2.50
Atlantic City Electric Co.	3.79	3.84	2.73	2.34	2.73	2.65	3.04	3.28	2.57	2.37	2.53	2.53
Southwestern Public Service Co.	5.05	5.54	5.57	4.73	4.55	4.39	3.27	3.47	3.60	3.36	3.21	3.13
Kentucky Utilities Co.	10.16	7.58	4.47	3.72	3.32	3.41	5.47	4.33	3.05	2.67	2.41	2.51
Kansas Gas and Electric Co.	6.37	5.97	4.56	3.47	2.97	2.86	3.76	3.78	2.64	2.55	2.36	2.16
Average for Aa electric utilities	5.54	4.94	3.91	3.39	3.35	3.43	3.52	3.29	2.78	2.60	2.58	2.57

TABLE 11
Idaho Power Company (continued)
Comparison of Times Interest Charges Earned with Aa-Rated Utilities
1968-1972 and Twelve Months Ended September 30, 1973

Company	Times Charges Earned Before Taxes						Times Charges Earned After Taxes					
	1968	1969	1970	1971	1972	12 Mo. Ended 9/30/73	1968	1969	1970	1971	1972	12 Mo. Ended 9/30/73
Aa Combination Electric & Gas Utilities:												
San Diego Gas and Electric Co.	4.24	3.99	3.16	2.88	2.27	2.33	3.14	2.97	2.60	2.49	2.24	2.29
Central Illinois Public Service Co.	5.88	5.70	4.97	4.35	3.36	3.06	3.53	3.46	3.23	2.98	2.49	2.21
Indianapolis Power and Light Co.	5.52	5.12	4.31	4.18	4.36	3.93	3.47	3.35	2.86	2.85	3.02	2.85
Delmarva Power & Light Co.	5.30	4.38	3.15	2.98	2.87	3.03	3.39	3.23	2.67	2.74	2.63	2.85
Iowa-Illinois Gas and Electric Co.	4.93	3.90	2.99	2.36	3.76	3.86	3.10	2.61	2.21	1.86	2.45	2.45
Wisconsin Power and Light Co.	6.70	4.74	2.77	2.86	2.65	2.69	3.97	3.18	2.66	2.25	2.14	2.25
Kansas Power and Light Co.	8.69	7.85	6.91	5.94	6.14	6.43	5.03	4.61	4.37	3.84	3.79	3.78
Toledo Edison Co.	5.75	5.67	4.53	3.57	3.64	3.29	3.65	3.62	3.26	2.75	2.91	2.76
Central Illinois Light Co.	4.44	4.74	4.27	3.61	3.54	3.25	2.83	2.95	2.85	2.48	2.40	2.21
Iowa Electric Light and Power Co.	4.42	3.98	3.27	2.88	3.01	2.03	2.78	2.46	2.25	2.19	2.25	1.93
Iowa Power and Light Co.	5.37	5.37	3.65	3.41	3.69	3.60	3.24	3.29	2.51	2.30	2.49	2.43
Montana Power Co.	5.95	5.97	5.96	5.91	5.75	4.95	3.98	3.68	3.83	3.96	3.85	3.41
Central Hudson Gas & Electric Corp.	3.63	3.08	2.00	2.62	2.83	2.86	2.85	2.58	1.91	2.28	2.46	2.44
Southern Indiana Gas & Electric Co.	6.86	5.91	5.38	5.01	4.72	5.32	4.13	3.63	3.45	3.33	3.10	3.38
Average for Aa combination Utilities	5.55	5.03	4.17	3.75	3.76	3.62	3.51	3.26	2.90	2.74	2.73	2.66
Average for Aa electric & combination utilities	5.54	4.99	4.07	3.62	3.61	3.55	3.51	3.27	2.86	2.69	2.67	2.63

Notes: Years 1968-1972 compiled from Moody's *Public Utility Manual*, 1973. Twelve months ended September 30, 1973 obtained from Moody's Investors Service, Inc., and Investors Management Sciences, Inc. (Subsidiary of Standard & Poor's Corporation), to the extent the data were available in their files; for those companies whose data were not available from the foregoing sources, such data were obtained by direct contact with the companies by telephone.

QUESTIONS

1. Evaluate Idaho Power Company's existing capital structure, and comment on the disagreement between Klumpp, Carlsen, and Jensen.
2. Discuss the factors relating to cost of capital, capital expenditures, dividend policy, bond ratings, and market value that should be considered in making the decision.
3. Suggest a plan for obtaining the needed financing, and comment on its impact on the factors mentioned in Question 2.
4. Would your analysis and recommendations have been the same had the company not been a public utility? Explain.

Case 39
Sparkling Water

I. Background Information

The Sparkling Water Company, a medium-sized water utility (with a rate base of approximately $10 million) serving southwestern Idaho, is a wholly owned subsidiary of a large public utility holding company. The holding company owns some seventy water, sewer, and steam heating subsidiaries operating in eastern and western states. It is the policy of the holding company to finance 100% of each subsidiary's capital requirements with equity investments made by the parent company. The capital structures of the subsidiaries therefore do not contain long-term debt. The parent company in turn is wholly owned by a large multinational firm whose stock is actively traded on the New York Stock Exchange, while Sparkling Water Company itself owns two other water companies located in the Pacific Northwest. Consequently, Sparkling Water is only one member of a vast four-tiered holding company. As a result, there is no market value data available for either Sparkling Water's common stock or that of its immediate parent company.

II. 37% Rate Increase Request

Early in 1974, the Sparkling Water Company made a formal application for an across-the-board rate increase of 37% to all its customers. The company cited the

This case was prepared by Professor Dennis B. Fitzpatrick of Boise State University as a basis for classroom discussion and not to illustrate either effective or ineffective handling of an adminstrative situation.

very rapid rise in its operating costs and record high interest rates as being the primary causes for the rate increase.

Privately owned water utilities are regulated by the state Public Utilities Commissions that have jurisdiction over all public utilities operating in their respective states. The Idaho Public Utilities Commission[1] (I.P.U.C.) therefore has complete discretion over the rate requests of Sparkling Water Company. Public utilities can appeal a decision that they feel is inequitable to the judicial system.

The I.P.U.C. received upon request a written testimony from Mr. George Smith, Sparkling Water's financial vice president, detailing the economic and financial rationale for the company's steep rate request. Mr. Smith stated that the severe inflationary conditions of recent years were putting water companies at a severe operating disadvantage. Smith suggested that the demand for water services is relatively inelastic, while water utilities are subjected to the "extreme price elasticity of unregulated suppliers of goods and services which the utility must obtain in order to function. Without immediate corresponding increases in water rates (which, under regulation, do not occur) to compensate for the increased costs of doing business, there is a constant erosion in the rate of return." To prove this point, Mr. Smith demonstrated that the fixed capital investment, in relation to revenues, is much higher for water companies than other types of public utilities (see Table 1). According to Smith, Sparkling Water received only $17 in revenues per $100 of gross investment in capital assets. This contrasted with $60 in revenues for gas companies, $27 for telephone companies, and $21 for electric utilities.

In actually determining his company's fair rate of return,[2] Smith decided not to determine the cost of capital for Sparkling Water itself. Instead, he felt that since the holding company provided 100% of Sparkling Water's financing needs, the proper estimate of its fair rate of return is actually the cost of capital of the parent company. Accordingly, Smith decided that the various capital costs (i.e., cost of debt and cost of equity capital) should be weighted by using the parent company's capital structure (see Table 2) in determining Sparkling Water's fair rate of return. Smith feels strongly that the cost of debt for the parent company (and hence for Sparkling Water as well) is simply the embedded or historical debt of the parent company, which is approximately 7.6% (see Table 3).

Smith acknowledged that the cost of equity capital is much more difficult to quantify. He consequently employed three separate approaches in his determination of the parent's equity costs: (1) comparable earnings approach; (2) earnings-to-market value approach; (3) discounted cash flow analysis. Using the comparable earnings method, Smith calculated the earnings-to-book value ratios for fifteen large publicly traded utilities from 1968 through 1972. Smith adjusted the resulting five-year earnings-to-book value ratio of 12.0% (see Table 4) for such additional factors as inflationary expectations, expected real growth, regulatory

---

[1]The Idaho Public Utilities Commission consists of three members appointed by the governor of Idaho.

[2]In order to determine a utility's revenue requirements, Public Utility Commissions typically calculate: (1) the effective asset base of the company (rate base); (2) the fair rate of return the company should earn for its investors (cost of capital). The estimated fair rate of return is multiplied by the rate base to determine net operating income. Finally, required revenues are estimated by adding operating expenses, property taxes, state and federal income taxes to net operating income.

lag, and earnings attrition (due to higher debt costs) and arrived at an overall equity cost of 13.68%. Similarly, Smith calculated the five-year average earnings-to-market price ratios for the same fifteen sample utilities to be 8.92% (see Table 5). After again correcting for real growth, inflationary factors, and the like, the adjusted earnings-to-market price ratio came to 13.96%.

In contrast to the first two approaches, the discounted cash flow (D.C.F.) approach normally requires knowledge of the market value of a company's common stock. The D.C.F. equity costs are then determined by calculating the effective rate of return based on dividend and capital appreciation expectations. Since market value data for Sparkling Water Company and its immediate parent company were not available, Smith calculated the D.C.F. equity costs for three different assumptions: (1) market price of the common stock is equal to book value; (2) market price of the common stock is equal to 114% of book value; (3) market price of common stock is 141% of book value. Smith felt that this range of assumptions was conservative, since the market value of the average publicly traded water company was slightly less than book value in 1973. With these assumptions, the D.C.F. aproach yielded equity costs ranging from 12.4% to 14.5% (see Table 6).

Based on the results of all three equity cost approaches, Smith decided that the best estimate of Sparkling Water's three equity costs was 13.5%. This rate coupled with the embedded debt costs of 7.6% produced a fair and reasonable rate of return of 10.2% (see Table 7). When this rate of return is multiplied by Sparkling Water's rate base, it becomes evident that the company needs a 37% rate hike.

Upon receiving Smith's written testimony, the Idaho Public Utilities Commission staff members become concerned with the validity of Smith's rate of return calculations. Their concern boiled down to the following four questions: (1) Should the parent company's capital structure and capital costs be used in calculating Sparkling Water's cost of capital? (2) Does Sparkling Waer have the same business and financial risks as its parent? (3) What is the *real* significance of the high fixed capital investment to revenues ratio for water utilities? (4) Is it really appropriate to adjust earnings-to-book value and earnings-to-price ratios for factors such as real growth and inflationary expectations?

TABLE 1
Fixed Capital Investment to Revenue
Ratios for Public Utility Companies

Gas Distribution Companies	165%
Telephone Companies	385%
Electric Companies	465%
Water Companies	545%

TABLE 2
The Parent Company's Capital Structure
(as of December 31, 1973)

Line No.	Security	Principal Amount	Sinking Fund Provisions	Net of Current Portion at 12/31/73 Dollars	Percent
	Long-Term Debt				
1	Revolving Cr. Notes, due 1980 (9.07%)	$10,000,000	$ —	$10,000,000	
2	Revolving Cr. Notes, due 1979 (9.08%)	10,000,000	—	10,000,000	
3	8.5% Bonds, due 1996	24,500,000	250,000	24,250,000	
4	5⅜% Bonds, due 1987	9,968,000	112,000	9,856,000	
5	4⅝% Bonds, due 1981	9,600,000	240,000	9,360,000	
6	5⅞% Debentures, due 1981	8,580,000	360,000	8,220,000	
7	5% Notes, due 1979	263,870	45,102	218,770	
8	Subsidiaries Debt at Acquisition	8,475,293	137,431	8,342,860	
	Total Long-Term Debt	$81,387,163	$1,144,533	$80,252,630	
10	Minority Interest in Subsidiaries			$ 1,288,919	
11	Total Senior Capital			$81,531,549	57.2%
	Common Equity				
12	Common Stock			$ 1,000	
13	Capital Surplus			19,300,348	
14	Earned Surplus			41,737,733	
15	Total Common			$61,039,081	42.8
16	TOTAL CAPITAL			$142,570,630	100.0%

TABLE 3
Parent Company Weighted Cost of Long-Term Debt
(as of December 31, 1973)

Line No.		Principal Net of Sinking Fund Provisions	% of Total	Cost Rate (%)	Weighted Cost
	Parent Company				
1	Revolving Credit Notes due 1980	$10,000,000	13.91	0.0695[1]	1.2616%
2	Revolving Credit Notes due 1979	10,000,000	13.91	9.0779[1]	.2627
3	1st Mortgage Bonds 8½% Series, due 1996	24,250,000	33.73	8.8714[1]	2.9923
4	1st Mortgage Bonds 5⅜% Series, due 1987	9,856,000	13.71	5.4758[1]	0.7507
5	1st Mtg. & Coll. Tr. Bonds 4⅝% Series, due 1981	9,360,000	13.02	4.7742[1]	0.6216
6	Sinking Fund Debentures 5⅞%, due June 1, 1981	8,220,000	11.43	5.9800[1]	0.6835
7	5% Note Payable in Quarterly Installments to 1979	218,770	0.30	5.0000[2]	0.0150
8	Total Long-Term Debt	$71,904,770	100.00%		7.5874%
9	Add for Annual Trustee Fees ($14,000 fees ÷ $51,686,000)				0.0271
10	Weighted Cost of Long-Term Debt				7.6145%
11	Use				7.6 %

Notes:
[1] As developed in Table 3.
[2] Nominal rate used.

TABLE 4
Earnings to Book Value Ratios
15 Nonwater Utilities
(Return Rates 1968-1972)

Company	1968	1969	1970	1971	1972	5-Year Average
Arkansas-Louisiana Gas	17.4%	16.2%	15.1%	13.2%	12.9%	15.0%
Carolina Power & Light	12.1	12.4	7.6	9.8	11.5	10.7
Utah Power & Light	10.6	11.2	10.5	11.5	11.4	11.0
Pacific Power & Light	10.7	10.8	10.5	12.5	12.5	11.4
Washington Water Power	10.1	9.8	10.1	10.1	10.3	10.1
Indiana Gas	11.3	11.6	15.9	4.5	11.7	13.0
Central Maine Power	10.2	10.1	10.8	9.4	10.7	10.2
Interstate Power	10.7	11.1	11.1	11.1	11.4	11.1
Minnesota Power & Light	13.2	12.7	12.7	14.1	13.4	13.2
St. Joseph's Light & Power	11.8	11.0	10.5	11.7	11.2	11.2
New Jersey Natural Gas	16.1	15.3	16.1	17.1	16.8	16.3
Niagara Mohawk Power	9.4	9.8	8.4	9.1	10.8	9.5
Rochester Gas & Electric	11.7	11.9	10.7	9.7	9.2	10.6
Piedmont Natural Gas	18.3	16.5	13.1	13.9	14.3	15.2
Equitable Gas	11.2	12.2	11.6	12.0	13.3	12.0
15 Company Average	12.3%	12.2%	11.7%	12.0%	12.1%	12.0%

TABLE 5
Earnings to Market Price Ratios, 1968-1972
12 Investor-Owned Nonwater Utilities

Company	1968	1969	1970	1971	1972	5-Year Averages
Arkansas Louisiana Gas	6.75%	8.02%	9.65%	9.33%	10.04%	8.76%
Utah Power & Light	7.35	8.56	9.47	9.64	10.15	9.03
Washington Water Power	7.25	7.29	9.14	8.43	8.81	8.18
Indiana Gas	7.06	8.41	12.04	10.79	9.70	9.60
Central Maine Power	7.02	7.84	9.66	7.63	9.21	8.27
Interstate Power	6.62	7.67	8.77	8.32	8.77	8.03
St. Joseph's Light & Power	7.71	7.78	9.48	9.61	9.98	8.91
New Jersey Natural Gas	6.45	7.05	11.00	10.43	11.44	9.27
Niagara Mohawk Power	6.83	7.97	8.69	8.84	10.85	8.64
Rochester Gas & Electric	7.99	8.53	9.33	8.36	9.18	8.68
Piedmont Natural Gas	8.62	8.69	8.91	9.67	11.71	9.52
Equitable Gas	7.95	9.26	10.60	10.23	12.53	10.11
Group Average (All "A" Rated)	7.30%	8.09%	9.73%	9.27%	10.20%	8.92%

TABLE 6

Parent Company Equity Cost Analysis

Summary of Cost of Common Equity at December 31, 1973
Using Discounted Cash Flow Analysis (D.C.F.)

Line
No.

Basic Formula:

1 (K) is purported to be the cost in % of common equity.
2 (D) is the actual dividend paid by Parent Company.
3 (P) is the derived market price of Parent Company common stock.
4 (g) is the real earnings growth rate of Parent Company from operations.
5 (m) is the percentage the market price of a new issue is of the existing market price for the same stock before issue (market pressure).[1]

6
$$K = (D/P + g)m$$

Values in Formula:

7   Case I: (P) Market Price of Common assumed equal to book value.
8   Case II: (P) Market Price of Common assumed equal to 114% of book value.[2]
9   Case III: (P) Market Price of Common assumed equal to 141% of book value.[2]
10 Real Parent Company earnings growth rate (g) from operations is 6.5% per year (given).
11 Parent Company dividends from normal earnings paid in 1973 (D) = $3,833,000 (Excludes $1,228,000 Prior Yrs. and $210,000 from Sale of Subsidiaries).
12 Book value of Parent Company common at 12/31/73 = $61,039,081 (given).
13 Market pressure (m) = 13%.[1]
14 114% of book value = $69,584,550; 141% of book value = $86,065,101.

	Case I	*Case II*	*Case III*
15	$K = (D/P + g)m$	$K = (D/P + g)m$	$K = (D/P + g)m$
16	$K = \left(\dfrac{\$\ 3{,}833{,}000}{\$61{,}039{,}081} + 6.5\%\right)m$	$\left(\dfrac{\$\ 3{,}833{,}000}{\$69{,}584{,}550} + 6.5\%\right)m$	$K = \left(\dfrac{\$\ 3{,}833{,}000}{\$86{,}065{,}101} + 6.5\%\right)m$
17	$K = (6.3\% + 6.5\%)m$	$K = (5.5\% + 6.5\%)m$	$K = (4.5\% + 6.5\%)m$
18	$K = (12.8\%)(113\%)$	$K = (12.0\%)(113\%)$	$K = (11.0\%)(113\%)$
19	$K = 14.5\%$	$K = 13.6\%$	$K = 12.4\%$

Notes:
[1]Based on 9 issues of water company common stock between 1960 and 1970—none recorded since.
[2]5-year average market to book ratios of 5 "A"-rated water utilities = 114%. For 12 "A"-rated nonwater utilities = 141%.

TABLE 7
Parent Company and Subsidiaries Cost of Capital and Fair Rate of Return
at December 31, 1973 (1)

Line No.		Senior Capital		Common Equity		Total Capital
1	Capital Ratio	57.9%(2)		43.0%		100.0%
2	Cost Rate	x 7.6		x 13.5		
3	Cost of Capital	4.33	+	5.81	=	10.14
4	Other Rate of Return Elements				+	0.06
5	Minimum Fair Rate of Return					10.20%

Notes:

(1) Pro forma February 1974 long-term revolving credit notes included.

(2) Includes approximately one percentage point of Minority Interest in Subsidiaries for ratio purposes but not for cost rate purposes. Cost rate applied is solely that of debt, shown in Table 3.

QUESTIONS

1. Answer the four questions posed by the Idaho Public Utilities Commission's staff.

2. Comment on the procedures and resulting minimum "fair rate of return" as determined by Mr. Smith.

3. Discuss the problems associated with determining the cost of capital for a 100% equity financed subsidiary.

4. As a consultant for I.P.U.C., determine Sparkling Water Company's cost of capital and consequent rate of return.

Case 40
Midwestern Food Corporation

In the summer of 1969, the financial staff of Midwestern Food Corporation (MFC), a leading diversified food processor, is examining the capital expenditure proposals of the company's International Division. The International Division had expanded substantially in recent years, largely as the result of the acquisition of several existing foreign companies. Now the Division is supporting substantial capital expenditures by these acquired companies.

In discussions concerning the minimum acceptable rate of return on a proposed capital expenditure, MFC financial staff members advocate the use of a corporate-wide cost-of-capital estimate. Such a cost-of-capital estimate includes the cost of long-term capital from all sources, using the mix of funds in the most recent consolidated balance sheet (Exhibit 1). This practice resulted in a 10 percent after-tax discount rate being used for U.S. projects.

Because of the recent and projected rapid growth of MFC's business abroad, the International Division is developing a manual of capital investment procedures. A draft of this document had reached MFC's home office, and part of this is reproduced as Exhibit 2. In accordance with this draft, the International Division is supporting an expansion of the production capacity of the British affiliate, Masons, Ltd. The proposed capital expenditures total $3,500,000, to be spent in 1969-70. The International Division recommendation for this expenditure includes an estimated discounted cash flow return slightly above 9 percent and an assessment that the proposal is consistent with the long-term corporate goals of MFC.

This case was prepared © 1973 by Professor Roger B. Upson of the Graduate School of Business Administration, University of Minnesota at Minneapolis, as a basis for classroom discussion and not to illustrate the effective or ineffective handling of an administrative situation. This case was made possible by an anonymous corporation.

EXHIBIT 1

Midwestern Food Corporation
Balance Sheet
April 30, 1969

Current Assets	$302,645,923
Current Liabilities	140,225,445
Net Current Assets	$162,420,478
Net Fixed Assets	148,313,832
Patents, trademarks	15,005,981
Goodwill	75,180,678
	$400,920,969
Deferred Income Taxes	$ 4,713,707
Long-Term Debt[1]	138,513,487
Minority Interests	2,924,731
Common Stock	254,769,044
	$400,920,969

[1]Long-Term Debt:

Notes and Debentures issued by MFC and predecessor companies, varying maturities	$ 95,150,000
Debentures of Foreign Subsidiaries	12,674,417
Eurodollar loans guaranteed by MFC	30,689,070
	$138,513,487

EXHIBIT 2

MFC International Division

Excerpt from Draft of Capital Investment Procedures

The Relevant Discount Rate

We have adopted for each country a relevant discount rate equal to the weighted average cost of capital of the subsidiary considered. A weighted average cost of capital approach has been preferred as more convenient, and more consistent with the domestic practices of MFC.

The 10 percent after-tax discount rate used in the U.S. is not, as such, relevant when we consider foreign subsidiaries. This 10 percent rate reflects the particular environment of a business operating in the U.S., with its accepted capital structure and its interest rate.

When we consider a foreign subsidiary, we may discover that a much heavier or lighter debt is allowable, and that the interest rates on the country's money market are higher or lower than in the U.S.: the cost of money for the subsidiary is then different from the U.S. 10 percent after-tax discount rate.

Our investment in the equity of our subsidiary is made up of U.S. funds (a mix of equity and debt), and we borrow locally on the strength of this mix, as well as on the credit standing of the local subsidiary, thus modifying the cost of capital of each subsidiary, through the leveraging of some of our domestic debt.

Furthermore, the investment opportunities in the country considered do not necessarily follow the U.S. pattern, their average return being either higher or lower than for domestic opportunities. Thus it would be illogical to penalize or excessively support our subsidiary by asking for a 10 percent after-tax return. This is particularly true in the case of a joint venture where we have to consider the interests of our local partner(s).

For the computation of the recommended discount rate (see Attachment), we need to obtain the following elements: interest rate, cost of equity, capital structure, and local tax rate.

1) The interest rate is equal to the subsidiary's borrowing rate on the country's money market.

2) The cost of equity is assumed to be 10 percent after tax. This figure represents MFC's required return on the investment of domestic funds, and, therefore, is realistic for MFC's share of equity in a foreign subsidiary. It is thus assumed that our local partners, if any, will be content to achieve the same return on their share of equity.

3) The capital structure used to weight the costs of debt and equity should be that of the subsidiary's last closing balance sheet. Each year, or oftener if the subsidiary's financial structure is substantially modified, the weighted average cost of capital would thus be brought up to date. This method ignores the existence of any goodwill figure recorded on MFC books as an equity investment, for the following reasons:

    a If goodwill is included, the subsidiary and MFC would be investing goodwill in every capital project. This is unrealistic as goodwill has already been paid for, once and for all.

b The inclusion of goodwill in the subsidiary's capital structure would amount in most cases to penalizing unduly the subsidiary in comparison to its competitors through a higher cost of capital (presumably, the goodwill was paid because of the subsidiary's pre-existing promising profitability).

4) The local tax rate is used in order to obtain the actual after-tax cost of debt and the actual after-tax cost of capital.

Treatment of Risk

There are two kinds of risks attached to an International capital project: one is the "project" risk, the other is the "country" risk. The location of the investment has no bearing on the project risk, which is directly related to the nature of the investment considered. As this risk must be appreciated on a "shot-by-shot" basis, no attempt has been made to deal with its treatment in this report.

On the other hand, the "country" risk represents the relative risk of doing business in a given country, compared to the United States. Political situation, stability, economic growth . . . , all are significant factors in this respect, and can and should be provided for explicitly, in order to sensitize the personnel involved in the evaluation of International's projects to this factor.

The countries in which the International Division has subsidiaries will be classified in three categories—high, medium, and low "country risk"—but no attempt will be made to integrate that risk factor into the mechanism of quantitative evaluation of the projects. Such an inclusion, whether by means of an uncertainty factor affecting inflows, or by means of a higher required present value ratio, would be meaningless because of day-to-day changes in the countries' situation, and the difficulty of having all concerned agree on a quantitative factor.

Other Intangible Factors

Still other intangible factors—such as a strategic decision to go into a given market regardless of profitability, or a strong unsupported hunch—will, of course, bear on the eventual decision. These cannot, in any case, be quantified, or provided for in a formal procedure, which does not attempt to be a decision rule, but to provide the decision maker with some of the quantitative factors which he will need to reach a decision.

Attachment to Exhibit 2

Case Example: Computation of the weighted average cost of capital for Masons, Ltd., for the fiscal year 1969-1970.

Elements of Computation

1. The Before-Tax long-term borrowing rate of Masons, Ltd., is 5.75%.
2. The After-Tax cost of equity for Masons, Ltd., is the MFC 10 percent after taxes.
3. According to its 1969 closing balance sheet, Masons Ltd.'s capital structure is:

Equity:	73.3%
Debt:	26.7%

4. The British corporate tax rate is 45%.

Formula

The local weighted average cost of capital is given by:

r = (% equity x after-tax cost of equity) + [(% debt x interest rate before tax) x (1 − tax rate)]

Computation

Masons Ltd.'s cost of capital for fiscal 1969-1970 is:

$$r = [(.733) \times (.1)] + [(.267) \times (.0575) \times (1 - .45)]$$
$$r = .0733 + .0084 = .0817$$
$$\text{or } \underline{8.17\%}$$

QUESTIONS

1. Evaluate and discuss the excerpt from Midwestern Food Corporation's Draft of Capital Investment Procedures.
2. Discuss the pros and cons of using a single companywide cutoff rate to evaluate capital expenditures.
3. What factors favor the use of multiple cutoff rates when dealing with subsidiary decisions?
4. Which approach would you recommend that MFC use for making Masons, Ltd.'s capital expenditures decisions?

Case 41
General Delivery Services, Inc.

In August 1975, William Marsh, Vice President of General Delivery Services, Inc., commented as he was preparing a stock prospectus that in order for GDS to take advantage of the available market opportunities it must expand its capital base. See Exhibit 1 for a copy of GDS's prospectus. Planning projections called for sales to double in its Dallas market within the next 12 months. Entry into a new market area, Houston, Texas, appeared imminent as negotiations were under way to buy out a small delivery operation there. This acquisition would result in some $120,000 immediate sales increase for GDS.

Commenting further on GDS's need for additional capital, he offered:

> We [referring to himself and Jim Ashford as co-owners] need and would like to have some outside money in GDS. GDS can continue to grow at a reduced pace from internally generated funds but we feel that we must seize opportunities as they come along. It's simply a trade-off between faster and, possibly, more growth and total ownership and control. As long as we retain control and the terms are reasonable we are prepared to make the trade. In view of our personal credit capacity and GDS's excellent cash flow, an additional $20,000 infusion of equity should handle the expected growth over the next year or so. Our major concern is not finding investors, as several potential investors have already expressed active interest in GDS, but in placing a realistic value on what we have today and may have in the intermediate term. We don't want to run the investor off by asking too much for our stock but we don't want to leave any on the table either.

This case was prepared by Professor Charles W. Mohundro of East Texas State University at Texarkana as a basis for classroom discussion and not to illustrate either effective or ineffective handling of an administrative situation.

EXHIBIT 1
Confidential Prospectus for
General Delivery Services, Inc.

The Company

General Delivery Services, Inc., was incorporated in Texas, during May 1974, and on July 1, 1974, began corporate operation of the delivery business which had been started some two months earlier by Jim Ashford as a proprietorship.

The business purpose of General Delivery Services, Inc. (GDS), at its inception as it remains today, is to provide its customers with a highly reliable, competitive, and professionally managed delivery service. To accomplish its purpose, GDS now operates a fleet of radio-equipped vehicles from a central location near downtown Dallas, Texas.

The Nature of the Business

In general, the delivery business consists of picking up customer directed parcels from one location and transporting and delivering the parcels at other designated locations. The efficiency of this procedure is enhanced through the use of radio-equipped delivery vehicles and a central dispatcher as well as with the use, for heavier parcels, of power lift gates on the vehicles. In addition, GDS operates "rolling warehouses" in the downtown area for one of its customers from which deliveries are made to that customer's employees.

GDS now furnishes what might be termed "general delivery services" for numerous firms in the Dallas area. In addition, GDS furnishes somewhat specialized delivery services to Cromwell Industries, one of its major customers. Cromwell Industries has somewhat unique delivery needs in the downtown areas of the larger cities. Because of the number of service personnel, cost of service vehicles, parking problems, and other factors, Cromwell has found private delivery services better serve some of its needs that its own inhouse services. When various items are needed, Cromwell's personnel advise GDS's central dispatcher, which in turn routes a delivery vehicle to a central warehouse where the requested item is picked up and delivered to the serviceman at curbside at the desired location. (Items may also be returned to the warehouse.)

For the smaller and more commonly needed items by the Cromwell's service personnel, GDS makes deliveries with "rolling warehouses." The rolling warehouses are specially equipped van trucks which have literally been turned into small warehouses. These are routed to the requesting service personnel by GDS's central dispatcher and deliveries are almost "instant." Once the delivery is made, the rolling warehouse is ready for dispatch to other points.

Facilities

General Delivery Services, Inc., is located approximately two blocks from access to the major Dallas freeway exchanges and five blocks from the downtown area of Dallas, Texas. The leased premises consist of an office building and fenced vehicle storage yard. Gasoline pumps are also available on the premises. The terms of the one-year lease, which has recently been renewed, are considered favorable and the premises adequate for the current level of business.

Equipment

General Delivery Services, Inc., is currently operating the following delivery equipment:

2 passenger vehicles
7 ½- to ¾-ton pickups with power lift gates
2 1-ton vans (rolling warehouses)

This equipment is presently leased from B & C Leasing, Inc., under finance equipment leases. It is anticipated that this arrangement will continue for the near term because of tax and financial considerations. The lease rates are competitive with those generally available.

The investment in radio equipment is expected to grow as additional delivery vehicles are added. The present equipment consists of a base unit and seven mobile units.

Market Factors

The general economic conditions in the Dallas, Texas, area are quite good in spite of recent national recessionary trends. GDS's rate of growth and an analysis of the basic need for delivery services demonstrates the industry's apparent immunity to most recessionary complications. It appears that as other industries are tightening their economic belts, independent delivery services can assist them in accomplishing their goal by providing their delivery services more efficiently than can be accomplished inhouse.

Market Structure

The light delivery industry in Dallas is composed of numerous small operations. The typical delivery business starts out as a one-vehicle operation with an owner/driver. As the business grows, an additional vehicle is purchased and an employee/driver hired, and the process repeated until the owner's managerial talent and financial capacity are strained to the breaking point. The reliability and quality of service deteriorates and generally one of two things happens: the business fails, or the size of the business is reduced to coincide with the owner's managerial talent and financial capacity. In general, the typical person who starts a delivery business and who may have an opportunity to expand it usually does not have the managerial talent, nor the financial capacity, and ability necessary to create a large, viable and profitable organization.

The small two- to five-vehicle operation is the typical competition GDS faces in its non-Cromwell Industries related business. Competitors make little or no effort to market their services through a sound and aggressively directed marketing program. GDS, within the next 12 to 14 months, through aggressive marketing techniques anticipates tripling its non-Cromwell Industries sales.

Cromwell Industries alone constitutes a sizable delivery market. From conversation with their representatives, GDS has learned that their yearly delivery expenditure is approximately $565,000, or $47,000 per month. Presently, GDS services approximately 22 to 25% of their delivery needs. GDS's major competitor for their business is estimated to have approximately 20% of the available total. With reasonable marketing efforts, it is anticipated that GDS can, within the next 12 to 14 months, double its present Cromwell-related business. GDS is expected to achieve annualized sales at the $325,000 to $350,000 level by May 1976, in the Dallas area. A 50% growth rate in the Dallas market is projected for 1976, and a 20 to 30% annual growth rate thereafter.

Presently, GDS is investigating the establishment of a branch operation in Houston, Texas. Preliminary discussions have been held with an existing delivery service for possible buy-out. This company is currently operating six vehicles and is marginally profitable with average monthly sales of approximately $10,000. (See Figures A and B.) It currently does some business with Cromwell; however, a significant portion of its business is with other companies. Conversations with Cromwell in Houston have assured us that GDS would retain their business and, quite probably, greatly increase the volume by providing service similar to that now provided them in Dallas. Cromwell's delivery expenditures in Houston is believed to be approximately $1.5 million to $2 million annually (based upon information supplied by Cromwell's employees). In addition, the general delivery business market appears to be about double that of Dallas.

It is anticipated that the present owner would remain as city manager. Investigation has indicated that the owner has reached and exceeded his total enterprise management and financial limits but does have good potential for a more limited operational manager's position. The purchase price for the Houston business is expected to be nominal. Little, if any, of the equipment now used by this business is desirable, and most will not be purchased by GDS. However, GDS will have to make capital expenditures for vehicles, radio equipment, and initial deposits (lease, telephone, etc.) as well as provide sufficient working capital. (See Table A.)

The Marketing Plan

The basic ingredients in GDS's marketing plan are: quality service at a reasonable competitive price, aggressive selling of services, which is not being done by most of our competitors, and professional management, which makes the first two ingredients possible.

With aggressive marketing and professional management, which would include strong financial management and control, delivery operations can be established in other major cities such as Houston, New Orleans, Atlanta, etc. The optimum size for a city's operation has not yet been determined. It now appears, however, that a plateau of optimum operations occurs at approximately the $450,000 to $500,000 sales level. This level of operations would entail:

> 1 city manager
> 1 assistant city manager/salesman
> 1 dispatcher
> 1 clerk/dispatcher
> 20 drivers & vehicles
> 1 mechanic

and would result in a city operational gross profit of $80,000 to $100,000.

GDS's current level of sales has been achieved with what may be best described as limited marketing efforts. The President, Ashford, and City Manager, Hamilton, have been able to devote only a small portion of their time and effort to sales promotion. However, GDS has now reached a level of sales and profit which will permit a greater concentration of corporate energies toward market development.

Ashford, on July 1, 1975, began to devote all his energies to GDS. In addition, the Vice President, Marsh, will assume a broader role in planning, capital budgeting, and financial control. These developments will permit a major emphasis on market expansion by both Ashford and Hamilton.

Management

Officers and Directors

The executive officers and directors of the company are as follows:

Jim Ashford	President, Treasurer, and Director
William Marsh	Vice President, Secretary, and Director

Jim Ashford is 36 years old and has been in the automobile rental, leasing, and selling business since 1958. Prior to July 1975, Ashford developed and managed Cooper Leasing Co. of Dallas. Ashford had primary development and operational responsibility, with Cooper supplying the capital. Prior to the formation of Cooper Leasing Co. of Dallas, Ashford owned a minority interest in and served as Vice President, Director, and General Sales Manager for Roadside Ford, Inc., of Waxahachie, Texas, for approximately one year.

From 1963 to 1972, Ashford was connected with Brown Enterprises of Dallas, Texas, where at the time of departure he was Vice President of Brown Leasing and Truck Rental with responsibility for some $2,750,000 annual revenue. He also was Vice President in charge of operations for Brown's Avis franchises throughout Texas, with responsibility for annual revenue in excess of $7 million. In addition, he served as a member of the Executive Committee for Brown Enterprises. Brown Enterprises is a small family-owned mini-conglomerate with 1973 sales of approximately $60 million.

Marsh is 37 years old and has been involved with various aspects of small business management and organizations for the past 11 years. He served as Vice President, General Counsel, and Director for Brown Properties, Inc., now Brown Enterprises, Inc., from 1963 through 1969. Since that time he has been an Assistant Professor of Management at Texas A&M University and has served as a consultant and director to numerous small businesses. He has a Master of Business degree from North Texas State University and a JD degree from the University of Texas.

Ray Hamilton, Dallas city manager for G D S , has been involved in various phases of the delivery business for more than 20 years, including having owned his own business.

Remuneration

Set forth below is the annualized remuneration which is now being paid to the directors and officers of the company as well as to its Dallas, Texas, City Manager.

Jim Ashford   President, Treasurer, and Director
William Marsh   Vice President, Secretary, and Director
Ray Hamilton   City Manager

Ashford was paid a minimal remuneration in the form of consulting fees, increased lease cost, and a company-supplied automobile prior to July 1, 1975. Ashford's total remuneration, as he now devotes full time to GDS, is $1,500 per month. His total compensation is expected to increase, as GDS's growth permits, to a salary of $25,000.

Marsh is paid at normal legal and consulting rates for services rendered to the corporation. It is anticipated that he will be paid on a par with Ashford as he assumes direct management responsibility in the Dallas and anticipated Houston operatoins and as GDS's growth permits.

Hamilton is paid on a salary and a bonus based upon a percentage of the gross revenue of the Dallas operation. This arrangement will result in anticipated annual remunerations to Hamilton, assuming the projected growth is reached, of approximately $18,000.

Capitalization

The capitalization of the company as of July 31, 1975, was as follows:

Capital Stock	Authorized	Outstanding
Class A no par common stock	100,000	40,000
Class B no par common stock[1]	200,000	0

[1]Of the authorized Class B no par common stock, 5,000 shares are reserved for a stock option now held by Ray Hamilton for 5,000 shares or 5% of the outstanding capital stock.

EXHIBIT 1 *(continued)*
Confidential Prospectus for
General Delivery Services, Inc.

Principal Shareholders

The company had the following shareholders as of July 31, 1975.

Capital Stock	Class A Common	Class B Common[1]
Jim Ashford	20,000	0
William Marsh	20,000	0
New Stockholders	—	0

Description of Capital Stock

The shares of capital stock of the company are divided into two classes: Class A Common Stock and Class B Common Stock, both classes without par value.

Holders of common stock are entitled to dividends in cash, property, in shares of common stock when and as declared by the Board of Directors. Each holder of Class A common stock is entitled to one vote for each share of stock held. The holders of Class B common stock do not have the right to vote for members of the Board of Directors.

The holders of both Class A common and Class B common stock are entitled on liquidation, dissolution, and winding up the affairs of the company to share ratably in the distribution of the assets of the company.

The holders of both classes of common stock have preemptive stock subscription rights.

All outstanding shares of the common stock are fully paid and are not liable for further calls or subject to assessment.

Stock Offering

GDS is offering to selected investors a total of _____ shares of the no par Class A Common Stock of the Company. This number of shares represents an amount equal to ___ percent of the no par Class A Common Stock authorized and, after this offering, outstanding. The offering price is _____ per share.

This is a private stock offering made to selected investors only. The contents of this prospectus are to be treated as private and confidential between GDS and the investor.

Proceeds of Sale

The proceeds received from the sale of stock will be used for the start-up of its anticipated Houston operations, for expansion of the Dallas market, and for increased working capital. See Table A capital requirements of Houston operations start-up.

FIGURE A
Net Sales
(Monthly)

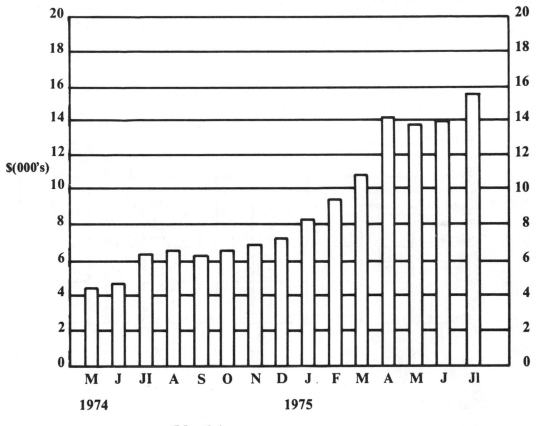

FIGURE B
Average Daily Sales Per Month

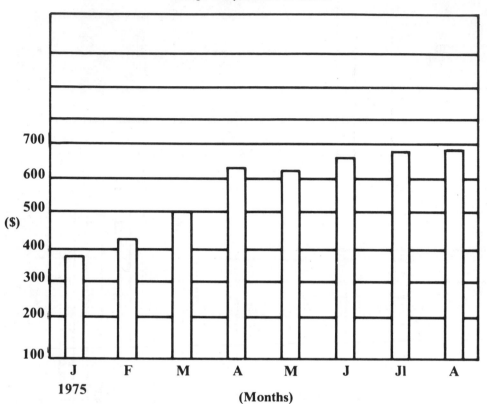

TABLE A
General Delivery Services, Inc.
Initial Houston Capital Requirements

Trucks (4) lease deposit	$ 1,200
Radios (4 mobile units plus base)[1]	5,000
Lift gates (4)[1]	4,000
Deposits	300
Lease deposits	700
Working capital	8,000
Estimated Initial Capital Requirements	$18,500

[1]A portion of radio and lift gate cost may be financed if desirable.

TABLE B

General Delivery Services, Inc.
Comparative Balance Sheets

	May-Dec. 1974	Jan. 1975	Feb. 1975	March 1975	April 1975	May 1975	June 1975	July 1975
Assets								
Cash	$ 991	$ 45	$ 1,686	$ 1,221	$ 856	$ 4,624	$ 4,390	$ 2,511
Accounts Receivable	5,205	6,400	7,538	8,320	10,398	9,449	9,768	12,180
Notes	5,857	6,438	6,398	7,019	7,148	4,595	4,716	4,931
Deposits	31	31	31	31	168	67	67	67
Equipment (Net of Depreciation)	5,848	6,652	6,512	7,426	7,735	8,551	8,509	8,678
Prepaid Items	—	—	—	256	565	210	632	510
Total Assets	$17,932	$19,566	$22,215	$24,373	$26,870	$27,501	$28,082	$28,877
Liabilities								
Accounts Payable	$ 3,197	$ 4,941	$ 2,506	$ 3,048	$ 3,960	$ 3,490	$ 3,559	$ 3,791
Accrued Taxes	1,253	1,229	1,183	1,628	2,104	1,633	1,590	2,173
Notes Payable	8,908	8,800	8,692	9,462	9,763	9,590	9,418	8,796
Notes Payable– Ashford & Marsh	3,200	3,200	—	—	—	—	—	—
Total Liabilities	$16,557	$18,170	$12,331	$14,138	$15,807	$14,713	$14,567	$14,760
Capital Stock Outstanding	1,800	1,800	10,000	10,000	10,000	10,000	10,000	10,000
Earned Surplus	(425)	(404)	(138)	(235)	1,043	2,788	3,515	4,117
Net Worth	$ 1,375	$ 1,396	$ 9,862	$10,235	$11,043	$12,788	$13,514	$14,117
Total Liabilities and Net Worth	$17,932	$19,566	$22,215	$24,373	$26,870	$27,501	$28,082	$28,877

TABLE C
General Delivery Services, Inc.
Comparative Income Statements

	May-Dec. 1974	Jan. 1975	Feb. 1975	March 1975	April 1975	May 1975	June 1975	July 1975
Sales	$48,220	$8,441	$9,415	$11,037	$14,070	$13,834	$13,834	$15,763
Cost of Services Sold								
Fleet expense	$ 8,461	$1,793	$2,646	$ 2,364	$ 2,788	$ 1,730	$ 3,400	$ 3,500
Insurance expense	1,166	220	250	303	322	366	300	300
Payroll expense[1]	31,624	5,068	4,695	6,284	7,861	8,245	7,039	10,231
Gross Profit	$ 6,969	$1,360	$1,824	$ 2,086	$ 3,099	$ 3,493	$ 2,207	$ 1,677
General and Administrative Expense								
Legal and professional[2]	$ 3,500	$ 660	$ 860	$ 960	$ 1,110	$ 810	$ 500	$ —
Telephone	596	74	67	74	87	141	155	174
Rent	1,300	200	200	200	200	300	300	300
Equipment repairs	24	11	—	—	86	51	—	45
Interest	258	111	—	36	134	—	—	102
Radio depreciation	629	220	220	226	263	319	319	319
Advertising	54	—	—	—	63	—	38	—
Travel and entertainment	405	4	42	6	244	48	115	17
Office Supplies	564	33	5	18	71	27	25	108
Miscellaneous	62	26	164	193	33	2	28	10
Net Profit	($ 425)	$ 21	$ 266	$ 373	$ 808	$ 1,745	$ 727	$ 602

[1]Includes Ashford's salary of $1,000 for July 1975 and $1,500 for later months.
[2]Consists of sums paid to Ashford and Marsh.

QUESTIONS

1. Evaluate the past performance of General Delivery Services, Inc., using the financial statements presented. Comment on the firm's outlook for the future in light of the data presented.
2. Using several different methods, determine a fair value for GDS to be used by Marsh and Ashford.
3. As a potential investor in GDS, what value would you place on the company? What, if any, additional information would you desire?
4. Discuss any problems you find in valuing a nonpublic firm such as GDS as opposed to large publicly traded firms.

Case 42
Virginia Foundry and Manufacturing

Vernon Hayes sat in his office looking at the papers on which he had been working. The familiar sounds and smells of the foundry were reassuring to him as he tried to grapple with his decision. Eleven years ago, Mr. Hayes had come to Virginia Foundry and Manufacturing (VFM) as Plant Manager in 1963, after ten years in a similar capacity at another foundry in Ohio. Now after eleven years with VFM, Vernon was considering buying his division from the parent company, MICOM Mfg., of Richmond City, Indiana.

As Vernon pondered his decision, he could look around his plant with justifiable satisfaction. He had turned a consistently money-losing division into a most profitable component of MICOM. As a result, Mr. Hayes was named a Vice President of MICOM in mid-1974; from this new vantage, he was able to obtain a better picture of the overall corporate situation. Mr. Hayes had developed VFM into a consistently profitable enterprise in spite of two factors. First, the main products of VFM are cast iron and bronze fittings that are used primarily in new construction; hence, sales volume is heavily dependent on the level of construction—and 1975 was a poor year in this cyclical business. Second, the parent company periodically subcontracted its least profitable foundry work to VFM because it knew "Hayes could handle it."

Probably the crowning point in the career of the 61-year-old Hayes was the development of a new pollution control device called a "Low-Energy Wet Scrubber." Hayes had initiated the project to help his plant meet the ever more stringent air quality standards. This new scrubber was developed at a cost of

This case was prepared by Professor Brian Belt of the Univesity of Missouri, Kansas City, and Professor Bill D. Fortune of Texas A&M University as a basis for classroom discussion and not to illustrate either effective or ineffective handling of an administrative situation.

$150,000 (half the cost of comparable existing commercial systems); but most important, it worked well enough to meet both existing and upcoming air quality (particulate emissions) requirements. All Research and Development (R & D) costs on the scrubber system could be produced, marketed, delivered, and placed on an operating basis for about 80% of the average proposed market price of $250,000. The market size east of the Mississippi River alone for these scrubbers was at least several hundred units between now and 1980. With this proven technology—Mr. Hayes had received several patents for various important components—VFM could expect a significant share of this market if this "Scrubber Program" was pursued actively. Exhibit 1 contains an article on "Scrubbers" that appeared in a local newspaper.

EXHIBIT 1
Foundry "Air Scrubber" May Join Product Line

An antipollution device initially built by the Virginia Foundry and Manufacturing Co. for use in its plant has proved so successful that it has been patented and installed in yet another plant.

The device, the Company's Low-Energy Wet Scrubber system, has met particulate emission standards of the state and city, the foundry's patent firm, MICOM Manufacturing Co. of Richmond City, Ind., said.

Vernon Hayes, Manager of the Foundry, said the board of MICOM now is considering whether to add the device to the company's product line and sell it to other customers. If so, it probably would be manufactured here, he said.

Dust, Grit Problems

Virginia Foundry began work on the wet scrubber in 1971 to combat the dual problems of heavy dust and grit associated with cast metal processes, according to Hayes.

A search for a commercial pollution control system showed there were basically two types, the "wet scrubber" and the "bag-house," in which the air is cleaned by sending it through a series of filtering bags.

The scrubber "washes" dirty air and gases of their impurities by passing the air and gases through water.

Neither system, however, was found to be completely satisfactory, and both were costly, according to Hayes.

So Hayes and Don Roberts, the plant's engineer, began to design their own system. They first designed a pilot system based on the "wet scrubber" technique, refining the technology to fit their own needs. That included a special system to clean and recycle water used in cleaninig the air of pollutants.

Larger Version

When the pilot system proved successful, they went to a larger one to clean the in-plant air and developed a similar one to take care of emissions from the firm's two cupolas, the furnaces used to melt scrap metal to produce the foundry's plumbing products.

The system requires about a third of the horsepower needed by similar systems built elsewhere, the company said. In addition, recycled water is used to scrub the cupola discharge.

Also, the company said, the cupola's scrubber system can be used to recover much of the heat normally lost in the metal melting process. A heat transfer unit in the settling tanks can provide hot water for a circulating heating system for the plant.

According to presently accepted standards, wet scrubbers in foundry cupola operations normally removed about 17 to 21 pounds of pollutants per ton of metal melted. Virginia Foundry's system has reached a level in excess of 30 pounds per ton melted, according to Hayes.

Mr. Hayes reviewed the profit picture for the last five years (see Exhibit 2). Experience had made Mr. Hayes painfully aware of the variability of both sales and profits. In spite of the stodgy image of the foundry business, this capital-intensive industry was quite risky, with business failures not at all uncommon. In addition to the profits generated, depreciation averaged about $39,000 per year over the five-year interval. However, Mr. Hayes knew that with the relatively old fixed assets of VFM, the depreciation expense barely covered the cash costs of replacing and overhauling VFM's fixed assets. Exhibit 3 shows the most recent VFM balance sheet provided to Mr. Hayes by his accountant.

Mr. Hayes had asked for an outside evaluation of VFM by persons experienced in corporate purchases. As a result, a report was made by White-First Securities (WFS), a regional investment banker. Exhibit 4 illustrates a summary of WFS's comments on the valuation of VFM.

Deliberations had proceeded to the point where Mr. Hayes had considered different alternative ways of raising the necessary capital. Other top VFM management and marketing personnel had agreed, in principle, to assist Mr. Hayes with an employee "buy-out" of VFM from MICOM.

Three alternative financial plans were considered. First, VFM could be purchased from the accumulated savings of the group. However, the group was unwilling or unable to put more than $400,000 into VFM at this time. Second, the group could borrow some capital and provide the balance from accumulated savings. Also, a Small Business Administration (SBA) loan might be available in the future to help finance the proposed "Scrubber Program." However, in mid-1975, capital providers were quite selective in their loans. Last, VFM could be purchased through an Employee Stock Ownership Plan/Trust (commonly known as ESOP/ESOT). White-First Securities felt that an ESOP plan might work quite well for VFM; however, no company in Virginia had yet set up an ESOP/ESOT, and the laws of Virginia differed somewhat from those states where ESOPs were successfully implemented (Hayes had just read an article on the ESOP/ESOT used for South Bend Lathe in *Business Week,* August 11, 1975).

Mr. Hayes already had discussed a possible employee "buy-out" with MICOM's Financial Vice President, Mr. L. C. Becker. Mr. Becker seemed agreeable and mentioned a figure of $3,000,000 for VFM and the associated patents—a value Mr. Hayes knew corresponded to the amount of a short-term debt that MICOM had to pay in the near future. MICOM would be willing to sell VFM at a substantially lower price if MICOM kept the "Scrubber Program"; however, the value of the "Scrubber Program" was problematic at best if Mr. Hayes was no longer associated with the program.

Two difficult questions face Vernon Hayes today. First, did he and the group really want to buy VFM? He was keenly aware of the number of persons in the buy-out group who were over 60 years of age. Second, what price was VFM worth to the group? The sooner he dealt with these questions, the quicker he could return to the day-to-day management of VFM.

EXHIBIT 2

Sales and Profits for VFM

Fiscal Year Ending May 31	Sales ($)	Profit Using LIFO Inventory Valuation*	"Mgt. Fee" Paid to MICOM**	Assumed VFM Earnings Before Taxes***	Assumed VFM Earnings After Taxes ****
1975	$3,259,000	$ 38,000	$48,000	$ 74,000	$ 45,000
1974	3,559,000	378,000	48,000	414,000	222,000
1973	3,042,000	53,000	48,000	89,000	53,000
1972	3,115,000	189,000	48,000	225,000	124,000
1971	2,682,000	43,000	48,000	79,000	48,000
				5-Year Aver. =	$ 98,000

*Including management fee paid to MICOM.

**Management fee paid to MICOM covers corporate overhead costs that the parent company charges back to various operating divisions.

***Assuming VFM were run separately from MICOM; if VFM were separate from MICOM, the management fee costs are assumed to be $12,000—not $48,000.

****Assuming tax rate of 22% on the first $25,000 of earnings before taxes and 48% on all earnings before taxes over $25,000.

EXHIBIT 3

MICOM Manufacturing Company
VFM Division
Balance Sheet
May 31, 1975

ASSETS

Cash	$ 4,108	
Accounts Receivable—Net	237,386	
Miscellaneous Receivable—Other	187	
Advance—Officers & Employees	282	
Inventories—Net	291,533	
Prepaid & Other Current Accounts	18,598	
Total Current Assets		$552,094
Machinery & Equipment	$405,161	
Patterns	40,163	
Furniture & Fixtures	8,880	
Leasehold Improvement	131,979	
Autos & Trucks	2,275	
Construction in Progress	5,993	
Total	$594,451	
Less: Accumulated Depreciation	(354,853)	
Total Fixed Assets		$239,598
Noncurrent Prepaid Ins.		$ 5,223
Goodwill Patents & Trademarks		0
Other Assets & Deferred Charges		0
TOTAL ASSETS		$796,915

LIABILITIES

Accounts payable	$195,981	
Notes Payable—Current	139,538	
Loan on Inventory	165,358	
Estimated Fed. Income Tax	—	
Accrued Salaries, Wages & Commissions	64,051	
Accrued Payroll, Fringes & Deductions	11,963	
Accrued Taxes, Interest & Other	15,019	
Total Current Liabilities		$591,910
Notes Payable—Long Term		$ 10,071

NET WORTH

Home Office Account	($959,924)	
Retained Earnings of May 31, 1974	1,082,319	
Current Earnings*	72,439	
Total Net Worth		$194,934
TOTAL LIABILITIES & NET WORTH		$796,915

*This value differs from that shown in Exhibit 2; the above value is calculated using MICOM accounting methodologies which differ from those used in Exhibit 2 for several items.

EXHIBIT 4

Summary of VFM by White-First Security Evaluation Report

Real Property—the present real property is in a good location for possible future development—probably in the Industrial category—although there are several other adjacent properties up for sale; the character of the area could take on a Commercial or even a high-density, Residential direction. This will probably be influenced by the movement of the adjacent property in the next year or two. The estimated valuation of the property was $285,000 to $400,000. the property is currently leased from MICOM.

Machinery & Equipment, etc.—on a disposal basis, would probably bring $100,000 to $150,000. Net after sales expenses.

Inventory—value estimated at $400,000 to $450,000, depending upon the time available for disposing of the inventory.

Summary—Since VFM assets have substantial liens against the Property, Machinery, Equipment, Inventory, and Receivables (most liens are direct against MICOM), the book values must be reduced by the amount of the liens. With these corrections, the liquidation value of the property would be in the $500,000 to $750,000 area, based upon a disposal arrangement. Some of these liens are separate from the liabilities illustrated on VFM "balance sheets."

Unquestionably the greatest value of the assets of the Company is on a continuing business arrangement as a Foundry, or a Manufacturing operation, requiring foundry operations.

The one area of valuation that is most difficult to determine is the worth of the "Scrubber Program." In this area, the principal value of the company may well be found. This area needs careful analysis and evaluation before determining the value of this part of the business, but the batting average of new products coming on the market, and making a payoff, within one or two years, is very low.

QUESTIONS

1. Evaluate the financial performance and condition of Virginia Foundry and Manufacturing in 1975 as well as in earlier years.
2. Determine the value of VFM that you believe would be fair to both parties (i.e., Hayes' group and MICOM).
3. Discuss the problems associated with valuation as a result of the unknown market potential of the product.
4. As a consultant, what recommendations would you give Mr. Hayes?
    (a) Buy or don't buy?
    (b) If buy, how should he finance the purchase?

*

PART SIX
SELECTED TOPICS IN
FINANCIAL MANAGEMENT

*

Case 43
J. I. Case Company

The merger negotiations between the J. I. Case Company and the American Tractor Corporation held the attention of the financial community during the Spring and Summer of 1956. The first announcement of the merger had aroused considerable interest and speculation as to the chances of an agreement on mutually acceptable terms. Financial analysts agreed that there was a logical basis for the merger from an operating standpoint; however, wide differences in previous management policies raised questions concerning the likelihood of reaching a compromise that is inevitably required for successful merger consummation.

The management of J. I. Case had initiated the merger talks in April 1956, and it was generally thought that the Case Company might especially benefit from the combined operations, should a satisfactory merger plan be worked out. In initiating the merger talks, Case had three primary objectives: (1) to broaden its product line into light and medium crawler tractors; (2) to gain the automatic tractor transmission developed by American Tractor; and (3) to acquire American Tractor's management, which had demonstrated both an ability to develop new products and aggressive markéting technique.

J. I. Case could offer to American Tractor several things of value. American Tractor, a relatively small but expanding company, had been faced with a chronic shortage of working capital and plant space. At this time in its history, J. I. Case had both substantial liquid assets and excess plant capacity. Its extensive marketing organization would also be useful in permitting an even more rapid expansion of American Tractor, whose recent growth had been impressive.

Permission for use of this case was provided by the Northwestern University Graduate School of Management. The case was prepared as a basis for classroom discussion and not to illustrate either effective or ineffective handling of an administrative situation.

In 1956, J. I. Case, like other farm machinery manufacturers, was facing the problems created by a slump in the farm machinery industry. Since 1952, the sale of agricultural equipment had been steadily declining, wages had been rising, and raw materials cost had been moving upwards. Coupled with low-capacity operation, these factors produced an unbroken decline in earnings. The basic cause of these declines was a falling farm income which is closely correlated to farm expenditures for durable agricultural equipment.[1] J. I. Case, the fifth-largest full-line producer of farm equipment, had been greatly affected by these developments. Sales and earnings declined to a point where in 1954 and 1956, the company recorded net losses from its operations. Cash dividends on Case common stock had been discontinued after the fourth-quarter payment in 1954. The Case management had already closed two factories, and employment, which reached 13,000 in the peak years of 1949, had fallen to 5,500 by mid-1955. (A financial summary of J. I. Case's operations is presented in Table 1.)

In addition, the management policies of the Case Company reflected the age and the conservatism of the Board of Directors. The Board of Directors, whose average age was 67 in 1951, often delayed decisions for months and did not provide dynamic leadership. Between 1951 and 1954, the control of the company drifted as the position of President and Board Chairman changed three times. Case's plant managers, who had always had considerable independence, became practically autonomous. Each pursued his own design and styling ideas, so that tractors made in one plant bore little family resemblance to those manufactured in another. The overall effect of this situation, coupled with a minimum provision for research expenditures, resulted in only a slight improvement in Case's farm equipment since 1946.

Morgan Stanley and Company, investment bankers who had underwritten Case's $9,200,000 common stock issue in 1952, considered the situation to be in need of adjustment. One result of Morgan Stanley's firm stand toward the Case Directors was that in June 1953, Mr. John T. Brown, age 50, was elected President and was subsequently made Board Chairman.

One of Mr. Brown's first actions as president was to bring younger men into the company and revise the organizational structure in an effort to gain more support for the policy changes he intended to make. An executive committee composed of younger Board members was formed, and it began meeting twice a month. Board action on policy matters gradually accelerated, numerous cost-cutting activities were instituted, and the research budget steadily increased to $2,500,000 by mid-1955. The effects of these policy changes were overshadowed,

[1]The farm income statistics as reported by U.S. Department of Agriculture are as follows:

Year	Cash Farm Income	Government Payments	Total	Farmers' Net Income
1950	$28,773	$283	$29,056	$12,344
1951	32,800	283	33,083	14,299
1952	32,373	275	32,648	14,319
1953	31,200	247	31,447	12,747
1954	30,200	247	30,447	12,500
1955	29,264	229	29,493	11,340
1956 (est.)	29,849	537	30,386	11,750

however, by the generally unfavorable conditions which prevailed in the farm machinery industry. The new management believed that some other method had to be used to rebuild the 114-year-old concern, and they decided that J. I. Case should try to acquire other companies having good future prospects.

This policy was a departure from that previously used by the J. I. Case Company. Prior to 1956, J. I. Case had grown largely through retained earnings. Mergers had been used infrequently and only for the acquisition of companies having large plant capacity and engine-producing facilities. Case acquired the Pierce Motor Company in 1912, the Grand Detour Company in 1919, the implement plant of Emerson-Brantingham in 1928, and the rights to the J. I. Case Plow Works, also in 1928. J.I. Case's greatest period of growth had been in the late 1940's. The company emerged from World War II in a strong liquid position and with a large plant capacity. Faced with the large unfilled postwar demand for new farm equipment, J. I. Case had little trouble selling its products, and sales and earnings reached record heights.

with the Oliver Corporation and the Minneapolis-Moline Company. These companies looked for mergers to help lower production costs and to strengthen distribution. Case management broke off negotiations, realizing that mergers with either Oliver or Minneapolis-Moline would be a "marriage of first cousins." Their problems were similar, and they did not promise a basic solution to either Case or the other companies. The Case management preferred a merger that would give the company a growth product, and attention was subsequently turned toward the American Tractor Corporation.

The American Tractor Corporation was founded in 1948 by Mr. Marc B. Rojtman, an exporter of farm equipment. Originally, the company assembled tractor parts manufactured by the American Steel Dredge company and sold the finished tractor through foreign and domestic outlets. By 1950, the company's sales had grown to $821,000; the next year sales reached $3,000,000. To continue the expansion of operations, more tractor parts were needed; however, the American Steel Dredge Company would not produce the parts at the rate American Tractor wanted.

An opportune purchase of inventory established American Tractor as a leading tractor producer, but later inventory purchases presented major problems. With money raised from friends and through the use of bank loans, Mr. Rojtman purchased the parts inventory of a liquidating farm implement company for $400,000 or 25% of its replacement value. This inventory of cheaply acquired parts enabled American Tractor to assume the role of a leading producer of gasoline and diesel crawler tractors. During the Korean War, the parts inventory was exhausted, and because of the tight supply conditions and the lack of a steel quota, the company was forced to enter the "gray" market. Even at double the mill price, American Tractor could only purchase inferior grades of steel. Product quality deteriorated, and American Tractor paid substantial sums for repairs on its guaranteed equipment. The company's reputation suffered and sales declined.

Mr. Rojtman believed the company could recover if it had the additional long-term capital needed to develop a superior product. He enlisted the aid of a New York investment banker, making him a director and granting him warrants for

American Tractor Common stock. The investment banker, in turn, helped to arrange bank loans secured by the company's fixed assets.

In 1953, American Tractor began to develop an automatic tractor transmission, the terramatic, which consisted of a torque convertor combined with a hydraulic power shift transmission. It was designed to improve tractor operation by avoiding the down-shifting necessary in vehicles equipped with conventional gear shifts. The idea was not new; similar transmissions had been used in Russian and German tanks during World War II. Commercial tractor manufacturers, however, had avoided using the transmission because they feared maintenance difficulties.

Mr. Rojtman hired the chief development engineer of the Allis-Chalmers' Crawler Tractor Division. This policy of hiring engineering talent away from other companies had been used before. Although the executives usually had to accept a reduction in salary, they were attracted by the greater opportunity to develop new products that Rojtman offered. Technical problems were worked out, and in 1955 American Tractor began selling tractors equipped with terramatic drive.

By mid-1956, American Tractor's dealerships had grown to 175 from 80 in 1950, and floor space at the company's Churubusco, Indiana, plant was increased from 6,900 to 250,000 square feet. Furthermore, sales, which were $2,500,000 in 1954, rose to $10,000,000 by 1956. (A summary of American Tractor's operations appears in Table 2.)

When J. I. Case negotiators first approached American Tractor with the idea of merging the two companies, the response was not very favorable. Several American Tractor Directors did not favor a merger with Case because they were not certain that it would be in the best interest of American Tractor to be allied with a company whose future prospects were not promising. These objections were later modified to the position that favorable merger terms might offset the risks of combination with the larger, less successful, company.

By the time the merger talks became serious, American Tractor had a book value of $1.15 per share and was being traded on the American Stock Exchange in a range of $12 to $15 per share. J. I. Case, with assets of $146,000,000 and a book value of $37 per share, was being traded in the range of $11 to $16 per share on the New York Stock Exchange. Whereas Case management wanted to base the exchange on book value, American Tractor's financial advisors suggested an exchange of shares based upon market price, since they felt American Tractor's low book value did not accurately represent the company's worth. American Tractors' earnings had been reduced by large maintenance and repair expenditures, and accelerated amortization and the resulting small additions to net worth, it was claimed, did not therefore represent the real value of the company's capital assets. Also American Tractor's officers had been exercising stock options at $4 a share for common stock with a $.25 par value. By basing the exchange on book value, it was argued, the value of stockholders' claims would be diluted.

The J. I. Case management stated that a share-for-share exchange would allow American Tractor stockholders too large a lien on future earnings and book value. They also noted that Rojtman and his wife owned 42% of the outstanding American Tractor common stock, and so control of the merged companies would be questionable were an even exchange to be made.

With merger negotiations at a standstill, it became a question of whether a reexamination of the financial statements and the arguments of the two companies would yield clues to formulate a feasible compromise plan.

TABLE 1

J. I. Case Company
Financial Summary

Year ended Oct. 31	Net Sales (Millions)	Net Income (Millions)	Earnings per Share	Dividends per Share	Book Value per Share[1]	Range of Market Price per Share (High-Low)
1946	$ 38.2	$ 1.48	$ 0.44	$ 0.83	$ 20.04	23 - 13
1947	81.2	4.92	2.28	0.66	21.66	19 - 12
1948	154.2	10.38	5.18	0.83	24.83	22 - 14
1949	170.3	17.61	9.03	0.91	33.58	21 - 14
1950	142.3	15.14	7.71	2.30	40.97	26 - 16
1951	165.4	9.79	4.86	2.50	43.34	39 - 26
1952	153.2	7.05	2.83	2.50	40.68	36 - 22
1953	111.5	0.78	0.06	2.00	38.74	25 - 14
1954	92.4	d(0.55)	d(0.53)	0.50	37.71	20 - 41
1955	94.9	0.90	0.11	N.L.	37.75	19 - 14
1956[2]	59.6	d(3.70)	d(1.85)	N.L.	37.00 (est.)	18 - 11

[1]Based on 2,262,766 shares of common stock outstanding.
[2]Seven months ended July 31, 1956.

TABLE 2

American Tractor Corporation
Sales and Earnings Summary

Year Ended	Net Sales (Thousands)	Net Income or (Loss) (Thousands)	Earnings or (Loss) per Share[1]	Dividends per Share[2]	Book Value per Share[1]	Market Price per Share
1950[3]	$ 800	$ 23	$.03	—	$ .62	—
1951[3]	3,100	26	.03	—	.64	—
1952[3]	3,500	(40)	(.05)	—	.68	—
1953[4]	1,700	(89)	(.09)	—	.60	—
1954[4]	2,300	(167)	(.16)	—	.46	—
1955[4]	5,300	347	.32	—	.88	18 - 6
1956[5]	9,200	306	.25	—	1.15	16 - 12

[1]Based on 1,107,704 shares of common stock outstanding.
[2]Cash dividends on common stock prohibited under terms of bank loan. Preferred dividends of $26,000 were paid in 1956.
[3]Year ended December 31.
[4]Year ended August 31.
[5]Eleven months ended July 31 (unaudited).

TABLE 3

J. I. Case Company

Balance Sheets
for Year Ended

	Oct. 31, 1954	Oct. 31, 1955	July 31, 1956 (unaudited)
ASSETS			
Current Assets	$100,649,414	$ 99,058,707	$113,802,175
Other Assets	1,117,112	792,361	264,354
Plant, Property, and Equipment (net)	32,601,668	33,506,280	31,992,224
Patents, Designs, Devices	1	1	1
Prepaid Expenses	662,695	904,071	909,653
Total Assets	$135,030,890	$134,261,420	$146,968,407
LIABILITIES AND CAPITAL			
Current Liabilities	$ 15,413,541	$ 14,554,169	$ 31,452,302
Funded Debt	25,000,000	25,000,000	25,000,000
Preferred Stock	9,290,600	9,290,600	9,290,600
Common Stock	28,284,575	28,284,575	28,284,575
Paid-in Surplus	10,008,314	10,008,314	10,008,314
Earned Surplus	47,033,860	47,123,762	42,932,616
Total Liabilities and Capital	$135,030,890	$134,261,420	$146,968,407

TABLE 4

American Tractor Corporation

Balance Sheets
for Year Ended

	Oct. 31, 1954	Oct. 31, 1955	July 31, 1956 (unaudited)
ASSETS			
Current Assets	$1,090,695	$2,504,339	$3,757,459
Noncurrent Assets	5,158	7,134	8,971
Property, Plant, and Equipment (net)	406,957	778,955	1,418,168
Deferred Charges	168,773	219,585	492,178
Total Assets	$1,671,584	$3,510,013	$5,676,776
LIABILITIES AND CAPITAL			
Current Liabilities	$ 598,151	$1,667,202	$2,350,123
Long-Term Debt	558,982	875,016	801,000
Commitments and Contingent Liabilities[1]	—	—	—
Total Liabilities	$1,157,133	$2,542,218	$3,151,123
Preferred Stock	—	—	1,250,000
Common Stock (par value $0.25 per share)	$ 261,348	$ 274,848	$ 276,926
Paid-in Surplus	500,404	593,466	619,076
Earned Surplus	(247,301)	99,481	379,651
Total Liabilities and Capital	$1,671,584	$3,510,013	$5,676,776

[1]No provision is made for approximately $95,000 in liabilities at August 31, 1955, and approximately $50,000 in liabilites at July 31, 1956, under new building construction contracts for work not completed on these respective dates. No liability is reflected for the balance of approximately $542,000 owing at July 31, 1956, or $712,000 at September 30, 1956, due in future periods under leases of machinery and equipment, which leases also contain options to purchase. Fixed rentals paid in 11 months ended July 31, 1956 have been charged to operating expenses.

QUESTIONS

1. Using the financial data presented in the tables, evaluate the financial condition of J. I. Case Company and American Tractor Corporation.
2. List and discuss the subjective advantages and disadvantages of merging, from the viewpoint of the stockholders of each company.
3. Determine the value of each company using the limited data provided, and determine a fair ratio of exchange for the proposed merger.
4. What arguments would you give the management of each company in support of your response in Question 3?

Case 44
Coburn Industries, Inc.—
Equity National Industries, Inc.

Nature of the Problem

In April 1969, R. A. McGilvary, President and Chairman of the Board of Coburn
Industries, Inc., a small mobile home manufacturing company, was faced with
making the decision of either accepting or rejecting a proposal for merging Coburn
Industries, Inc., into Equity National Industries, Inc. McGilvary had been
approached by several companies during the past year concerning the possibility of
a merger of his company but none of these contacts had reached the serious
negotiation stage, with the exception of the current negotiations with Equity
National Industries.

    Realizing that his company would need a substantial amount of new capital
soon if it was to take advantage of the tremendous growth opportunity which the
mobile home industry was currently offering, McGilvary thought that merger with
a larger company was one way to get access to the "public" funds market. Although
he knew of several mobile home manufacturers which had "gone public" recently,
McGilvary was convinced by Courts & Co., an Atlanta-based investment banking
house, that Coburn Industries was not mature enough to "go public" at that time. It
was after a conference with the underwriting department of Courts & Co. that
McGilvary decided that if the "right candidate" made a "sweet enough" merger
offer, he would give it favorable consideration.

    Courts & Co. indicated that they would be happy to seek an acceptable
merger candidate for Coburn Industries, and McGilvary signed an agreement

This case was prepared by Professor Albert H. Clark of Georgia State University, Atlanta, as a basis for
classroom discussion and not to illustrate either effective or ineffective handling of an administrative
situation.

making that investment banking firm the exclusive agent in seeking a possible merger situation for Coburn Industries. This agreement provided that in the event a merger was consummated, Courts & Co. would receive a finders' fee of 5% of the first million of consideration and 2% of the balance of the consideration up to $5 million.

Shortly after the conference with Courts & Co., John Meuller, one of the merger representatives of the investment banking firm, presented the Coburn Industries file to Charles H. Childs, President of Equity National Industries, Inc. Equity National was a small, aggressive Atlanta-based diversified holding company which had made five acquisitions during 1968. These acquisitions were all closely held companies in the fields of art crafts and art supplies, pleasure boat original equipment, photographic processing, and life insurance.

After receiving the file on Coburn Industries, Inc., Mr. Childs expressed an immediate interest in the possibility of a merger between Equity National and Coburn, and during the first week in April 1969, he and Mr. Meuller flew to Nashville, N.C., to visit with Mr. McGilvary and to view the facilities and operations of Coburn Industries. As a result of this visit, Mr. Childs later mailed a proposal of merger to McGilvary (see Exhibit 1).

Description and History of Coburn Industries, Inc.

Description of Business

Coburn Industries was engaged in the design, manufacture, and sale of mobile homes, office units, classrooms, retail shops, laboratory units, etc. Mobile homes contributed approximately 90% of total sales. The company's two wholly owned subsidiaries were Coburn Realty, Inc., and Diamond Sales, Inc. Coburn Realty owned the real estate which was leased to the parent company. Diamond Sales was set up as a sales agency for Coburn Industries primarily for a tax advantage; however, it was also used for direct, large-volume sales as well as an occasional direct sale to a retail customer.

The company offered its dealers a complete line of mobile homes in the low- to medium-price range. The company's Coburn line featured the brand names "Coburn Homes" and "Ebb Tide." These virtually identical brand-named units ranged in size from 12 feet by 44 feet to 12 feet by 60 feet, with a base wholesale price range[1] from $2,800 to $4,500. A new line brand-named "Empire" was introduced in mid-March 1969. Although the Empire line featured a completely new floor plan, it was of the same quality and price bracket as the Coburn line. Dealer franchises were only brand-name distributor rights; therefore, the new Empire line resulted in greater market penetration by facilitating sales to a completely different set of dealers. By late April 1969, Coburn planned to introduce its Castle units, base-priced between $4,400 and $5,500, and with a size range of between 12 feet by 60 feet and 12 feet by 65 feet. In addition to facilitating the granting of dealer franchises in market areas overlapping existing dealer territories, the new line would generate an approximate 18% gross profit margin versus the average of 14% realized on the company's other lines.

[1]Normally 30% may be added to determine the retail price range.

In March 1969, Coburn had 36 active dealers with 64 total locations. Five of these dealers were multi-lot operators with five or more lots covering wide geographical areas. While Coburn's limited past production had not been sufficient to provide any real volume to these dealers, relations were excellent and future business seemed assured.

The company's policy was to not allow over 25% of total production to any one dealer or group. Geographically, 50% of Coburn's production was sold in North Carolina, 10% in South Carolina, 35% in Virginia, with the balance sold in close surrounding areas. North Carolina was normally the third-ranking state in dealer sales, following only Florida and California, yet there were only nine other manufacturers in the state. Neighboring Virginia ranked fourth in dealer sales and had only three manufacturers.

The successive assembly steps in manufacturing mobile homes include the construction and/or installation of the (1) metal frame, (2) wood floor frame, (3) partitions and flooring, (4) side walls, (5) end walls and roof, (6) the completion of electrical wiring, hanging of wall cabinets, connection of interior plumbing, the start of exterior metal application, and the start of interior plumbing, (7) the hanging of doors and light fixtures, installation of refrigerator and stove, and completion of interior trim, and (8) the installation of drapes and furniture. The units undergo a thorough final inspection before being shipped.

Facilities

Located near U.S. Highway 64 just east of Nashville, North Carolina, on a 14-acre site, Coburn Industries occupied two new modern sprinklered-equipped steel buildings with a combined size of 48,000 square feet. The plant's condition was excellent, and the main building, which was a 140-foot by 325-foot clear span, was designed and located adjacent to the main building and railroad spur. The new office building, which was constructed on Coburn's own production line in January 1968, was a 1,440-square-foot heated and air conditioned building with seven offices, reception room, and supply room. Another office building containing 700 square feet was added in November 1968.

Personnel and Management

Coburn's employee breakdown was as follows:

Description	Number
Factory:	
Direct	85
Indirect—Supervision, truck drivers,	
service, etc.	20
Clerical:	3
Executive—Including sales and purchasing	4
Total	112

Employee relations were very good. No union activity or indication of such activity was in evidence. The average factory hourly wage was $1.60 to $1.70. The foremen's salaries averaged $125 per week. A factory-wide bonus system, allocated pro rata to every factory employee, was currently paying an average of $.65 per hour ($25 to $30 per week for foremen). The bonus system was based on a factory wage budget of 9% of the list price of units produced with any savings passed on to the employees. Employee benefits included five paid holidays plus a one-week paid vacation to all employees with at least one full year of employment.

The executive officers of the company were as follows:

R. A. McGilvary, age 44, was President and Chief Executive Officer of the Company. Mr. McGilvary was formerly Executive Vice President of Troy Lumber Co., a $15 million company located in Troy, North Carolina, and comprised of three mobile home factories, a furniture factory, a millwork factory, and a hardware supply house. Prior to this, he was employed 14 years with Coleman Industries (Wichita, Kansas), where he was National Sales Manager of the mobile home division before leaving.

Don L. Cramer, age 43, Vice President, was responsible for sales, purchasing and office management. Mr. Cramer was formerly General Manager of Taylor Mobile Homes, Inc., of Green Cove Springs, Florida (an affiliate of Troy Lumber Company). Prior to this, he was a design consultant and represented United Draperies, Inc., of Chicago in the Southeast. Mr. Cramer originally designed many of the most successful models still produced by several major southeastern mobile home manufacturers. His original start in the mobile home industry was in 1951 as manufacturers' representative for Preway, Inc., a major appliance supplier.

C. C. Smith, age 44, Production Superintendent. Mr. Smith, regarded as one of the most competent production men in the industry, was Production Superintendent of Taylor Mobile Homes, Troy division of Troy Lumber Co., for four years immediately preceding his move to Coburn.

Luther Barbee, age 41, Assistant Secretary, was the company's accountant. Prior to joining Coburn in 1964, Mr. Barbee was an accountant with a C.P.A. firm in Rocky Mount, North Carolina.

Jim Bryan, age 41, was in charge of sales inspection, delivery, and also handled a few dealers. Mr. Bryan was a former retired Air Force Master Sergeant.

George Nihart, Jr., age 39, Salesman. Mr. Nihart had been with Coburn three years.

History

Coburn Industries, Inc., organized and incorporated in 1964, was primarily engaged in the design, manufacture, and sale of mobile homes. The company was organized by the following group of mobile home dealers:

(1) A & U Mobile Homes—Blacksburg, Virginia
(2) G. W. G. Mobile Homes—Rocky Mount, North Carolina
(3) George's Mobile Homes—High Point, North Carolina
(4) Colonial Compact Homes—Atlanta, Georgia

The organizers hired George Nihart, Sr., to manage the company. Mr. Nihart (also a stockholder) was previously employed as a mobile home salesman with the General Coach division of Divco Wayne. By October 31, 1967, the company's accumulated losses totaled $166,000. In the opinion of Coburn's present management, the company's unsuccessful experience to that date was due to (1) the lack of experienced personnel and (2) the fact that the mobile home dealers (the stockholders) divided up the company's production as to territory but did not adequately sell its products. The company's management was not allowed to sell to other dealers. It is estimated that A & U Mobile Homes took two-thirds of Coburn's production during that period.

On October 26, 1967, Coburn Industries was purchased by R. A. McGilvary and the principals of A & U Mobile Homes, Herbert Alcom and Alfred Underwood. The new owners invested, in exchange for a promissory note, $30,000 in working capital. They also agreed to an unsecured obligation of Coburn Industries to pay the original stockholders according to the following schedule:

October 27, 1970	$11,183.33
October 27, 1971	11,183.33
October 27, 1972	61,508.34
Total	$83,875.00

Since this acquisition, Net Sales increased from $852,000 in the fiscal year ended October 31, 1967, to $2,295,000 in fiscal 1968. Net Income Before Taxes recovered from a loss of $81,956 in fiscal 1967 to a profit of $133,963 in 1968.[2] This dramatic turn-around was due primarily to new management in production, sales, and administrative areas plus complete re-layout of the plant, new jigs and fixtures, more than doubling the amount of machinery and maintaining adequate raw material inventories.

Stock Ownership

As of March 1969, the outstanding 124,566.7 shares of common stock were held as follows:

Stockholder	Shares	Percent
R. A. McGilvary	62,283.3	50.0%
Herbert Alcom	31,141.7	25.0%
Alfred Underwood	31,141.7	25.0%
Total	124,566.7	100.0%

Operating Record and Projections

The very substantial operating gains achieved since the change in ownership and management in 1967 are evident in the summary of operating results shown in Exhibit 2. Coburn was currently producing homes at the rate of 30 to 35 per week (approximately $90,000 to $100,000 per week) on a one-shift five-day basis.

Management expected to increase its production to 40 to 45 units per week (approximately $125,000) in mid-summer 1969. The production line had an output

[2]Projections for fiscal 1969 and 1970 are provided in Exhibit 2.

capacity of 50 homes per week. The projected operating results for fiscal 1969 and 1970 are shown in Exhibit 2.

Financial Condition

The company's March 31, 1969, financial statements are shown in Exhibits 2 and 3. Coburn had a deficit Net Worth of $40,145 on October 31, 1967, when the new owners and management assumed control. Although the present and projected levels of cash flow were adequate to finance the company's operation, it was felt by management that an additional investment of $250,000 for working capital purposes would be desirable.

Homes were sold to dealers either on a cash or floor-plan basis. If a dealer requested a floor-plan purchase, Coburn checked with the finance company suggested by the dealer to determine whether the dealer had unused financing capacity. The finance company paid Coburn when the dealer accepted delivery. Coburn was obligated under a repurchase agreement with the finance company only on a wholesale basis and only if the dealer defaulted. Such obligation was released when the home was sold by the dealer.

Coburn was currently taking the larger purchase discounts available. Additional working capital would enable the company to take all discounts.

Description and History of Equity National Industries, Inc.

Nature of the Company

Equity National Financial Corporation was an Atlanta-based diversified holding company. Some people referred to Equity National as a "mini-conglomerate" since its history and mode of operation somewhat resembled those of the so-called large "conglomerate" companies such as Ling-Temco-Vought, Inc., Gulf and Western Industries, Litton Industries, etc. Unlike these larger diversified companies, which have a great number of subsidiaries and divisions, Equity National had only six subsidiaries operating in four major industries at the end of February 1969. Equity National was, however, presently negotiating for the acquisition of companies in several other industries. The industries in which the company was presently operating were as follows:

> *Life Insurance:* Equity National Life Insurance Company (Atlanta, Ga.)
> *Photography Processing:* Hewitt Studios, Inc. (Atlanta, Ga.)
> *Art Crafts and Art Suppliers:* Cunningham Art Products, Inc., and Craft Shack, Inc. (Atlanta, Ga.)
> *Pleasure Boat Original Equipment:* Water Bonnet, Inc., and Akers Marine Supply, Inc. (Orlando, Fla.)

History of the Company

Charles H. Childs, Jr., founded Equity National Life Insurance Company in 1964 and had been President of the company since that time. Prior to 1964, he was Executive Vice President of a small regional life insurance company which had its home office in Atlanta.

Equity National Life Insurance Company was formed for the purpose of writing individual reducing-term mortgage redemption life insurance policies to be sold exclusively through savings and loan associations mainly in the southeastern United States. In order to form the company, Mr. Childs was able to get 17 investment banking houses in Atlanta and the Southeast to offer 300,000 shares of common stock to the public at $3 per share. Although the issue was handled on a "best efforts" basis by the investment bankers, the issue was "sold out" almost immediately. Several of the regional houses continued to make a market for the stock after the initial offer, and the stock, although not highly active, was quoted daily in the Atlanta newspapers on the over-the-counter stock market page.

Since 1964, Equity National Life Insurance Company had been moderately successful. By 1968, approximately 115 savings and loan associations and several mortgage banking firms in Georgia and Alabama were selling insurance policies of the company. At the end of 1968, the company had $80 million of insurance in force and the gross premium value for 1968 was $771,470. Because of the accounting methods prescribed by state laws for life insurance companies, it is normal for new life insurance companies to show a net loss from operations for the first six to eight years that they are in the business. Although Equity National Life Insurance Company had shown a loss for each of the years it had been in existence, including 1968, Mr. Childs indicated that the projections for the company indicated that it would "turn around" in 1969 and show a small profit. He explained that because of the special nature of the policies written by the company and the way the policies were sold, it would allow Equity National Life to show a profit earlier than the more traditional-type life insurance company.

The business of life insurance is rather rigidly regulated by state statutes and, as a result of this, life insurance companies may not expand their activity into other lines of business. Many life insurance companies in recent years have established parent holding companies in order to diversify into other fields, mainly in areas of financial services and "mutual funds" share sales.

Seeing this trend develop, Mr. Childs decided in the summer of 1967 that this was the course that Equity National should take. However, after much deliberation and discussion with the personnel in the underwriting department of Courts & Co., an Atlanta-based regional investment banking firm, it was decided that a Delaware corporate charter should be obtained for the holding company, so that the company could, if it desired, diversify into a broader range of activity. It was the opinion of Courts & Co. that Equity National should think of acquiring companies outside the life insurance field and other financially-oriented industries. The more Mr. Childs pursued the idea of a broad diversification program, the more it appealed to him.

In the fall of 1967, preparations were made to organize a new Delaware-chartered corporation named Equity National Financial Corporation and to propose a one-for-one stock exchange between Equity National Life Insurance Company and Equity National Financial Corporation. The result of this so-called reorganization was that Equity National Life Insurance Company would become a wholly owned subsidiary of the newly organized parent company, Equity National Financial Corporation.

A formal proxy statement proposing this corporate reorganization and the new proposed diversification program was prepared and sent to the stockholders in

February 1968, stating that the matter would be voted upon at the annual stockholders' meeting in mid-March.

The stockholders overwhelmingly approved the proposed diversification program and the corporate reorganization at the annual meeting. All of the legal work was performed during the next three months, and after the Internal Revenue Service ruling on the tax-free transfer aspect of the reorganization was received on July 1, 1968, the reorganization was completed. At that point, the stockholders of Equity Naitonal Life Insurance Company automatically became the stockholders of Equity National Financial Corporation.

Operations of the Company

In Equity National's 1968 annual report, Mr. Childs made the following statements concerning the philosophy and progress of the company:

> The year 1968 has truly been a year of dynamic growth and change in your company. At the beginning of 1968 your company was a progressive, small, regional life insurance company. Equity National Industries, Inc., is now a fast-growing diversified holding company having five wholly-owned subsidiaries operating in the fields of life insurance, art crafts and art supplies, photo finishing-and pleasure boat original equipment.
>
> During 1967, operating as a life insurance company only, your company recorded a net loss of $78,297 on a net premium sales volume of $365,308. Assets at the same time totaled $666,949. For 1968, the combined after-tax net profit of Equity National Financial Corporation was $346,396 on net sales of $6,599,055. Assets on December 31, 1968, reached $3,338,184.
>
> The new direction of Equity National began officially on March 12, 1968, when you, the stockholders, approved our plan of reorganization for the formation of the holding company, Equity National Financial Corporation. Earlier in 1968, however, we began our planning and research program in order to determine the criteria and standards for our new venture of growth and diversification through mergers and acquisitions. Early in the spring of 1968, we began to seek fast-growing, well-managed, closely held companies in growth-oriented industries as possible merger candidates. After viewing in excess of 200 possible candidates during 1968, we found four companies which met our criteria and desired to become part of Equity National's family of fast-growing companies.
>
> Equity National's philosophy centers around the concept of making acquisitions only in industries in which substantial future growth potential is projected. Our acquisition program is based upon obtaining the best management people available in a selected industry or product line who have a proven success pattern with a profitable company. This requires extensive research and analysis of hundreds of potential candidates before we find a company with the right combination of good management and strong growth product lines. Our philosophy is to acquire companies only if their key successful management personnel commit themselves to remain and continue to manage the companies. In our acquisition program, we are not seeking "bargains" since our concept is to form a successful management team within the Equity National's family of fine companies.
>
> We encourage these successful management teams to expand their companies through internal and external growth means and by utilizing Equity National's financial, management, and planning resources. As the companies grow, these key men receive larger rewards than would have been possible before they joined Equity

National, since they own a substantial portion of Equity National stock. This, we feel, is an attractive, built-in incentive for outstanding performance.

Our plan is especially attractive to the owners of medium-size, closely held companies because it allows them to obtain all of the advantages of a publicly held corporation with an actively traded stock. These advantages, which include marketability and liquidity of their stock as well as greater opportunity for "capital gains" appreciation, can be obtained while, at the same time, the autonomy of their operations is preserved.

Although our acquisitions in 1968 were primarily related to the leisure-time industry, we are not restricting our negotiations only to this field. There are several other industries which we think are very attractive such as educational and institutional services and products, convenience foods, data and document processing, waste and water handling, and personal services.

Our philosophy of diversification gives us flexibility to act swiftly when areas of unusual opportunity appear. At the same time, this diversification also protects the Equity National family of companies against cyclical movements in the economy.

Through Equity National's management structure we are able to maintain control while preserving flexibility. The executives of our subsidiary companies meet frequently to plan Equity National's progress and set individual company goals. The key personnel of the parent company constantly monitor the subsidiary companies' progress toward attainment of their goals. This system forms the essential link between the corporate headquarters and the individual companies.

In summary, we refer to our acquisition program and corporate philosophy as "Planned Parenthood, Corporate Style."

Marketability of the Company's Stock

In 1964, when Equity Naitonal Life Insurance Company stock was first offered to the public, it was sold under a full Securities and Exchange Commission registration statement and prospectus. Although the original offering was handled by 17 stock brokerage firms on a "best efforts" basis in 1964, only 2 regional firms made an "after market" in the stock from 1964 until mid-1968. During this period of time, the monthly average number of shares traded was only approximately 2,000 shares. At the beginning of 1968, Equity National had approximately 800 shareholders, and the number of outstanding shares was approximately 400,000. During January of 1968, the share bid price ranged from $1\frac{1}{2}$ to $1\frac{7}{8}$.

In the spring of 1968, the price and activity in Equity National's stock increased somewhat, when it was announced that a holding company was being formed. It was not until July, when the first acquisition was announced, that the price of the stock and number of shares traded increased greatly. See Exhibit 4.

By the fall of 1968, several additional local brokerage firms were "making a market" in Equity National's stock, and by the end of 1968, there were also two investment banking firms in New York City and one in Dallas, Texas, shown in the "pink sheets" as making a market in the stock. By the end of 1968, the number of shareholders had grown to over 1,600, and the residences of the stockholders had fanned out to include other sections of the country besides the Southeast.

Although the number of shares outstanding had grown from approximately 400,000 to over 800,000 by the end of 1968, this increase was brought about by the number of shares delivered in consideration from the acquisitions. These additional shares were nonregistered shares and therefore were not traded in the market.

Beginning in December 1968, Equity National's stock began being shown in the daily national over-the-counter stock list in the *Wall Street Journal*. This was the result of the increased activity in the stock and the fact that the company had attained 1,600 shareholders.

EXHIBIT 1
Proposal for Merger of
Coburn Industries, Inc., with Equity National Industries, Inc.
Exchange of the Common Stock (Voting) of Equity National for the Business
and Assets of Coburn Industries, Inc.

The following proposal is contingent upon Coburn Industries, Inc., recording net pre-tax audited earnings of at least $400,000, excluding extraordinary income items for the period 10/31/68 to 10/31/69. The total number of Equity National shares offered also depends upon Coburn's earnings during this same period. The formula is that Equity National will deliver to Coburn one share of its common stock for every $2.3333 of pre-tax earnings recorded by Coburn for the period 10/31/68 through 10/31/69 up to a maximum of $670,000 in earnings, or up to a maximum of 287,142 Equity National shares. These shares will be delivered to Coburn at the closing date.

The number of contingent shares shall be the same number of shares as those delivered at closing, and they will be delivered over a 3½-year period, contingent upon Coburn's increased future earnings.

Summary of the Proposal

One share of Equity National common stock for every $2.3333 of pre-tax audited earnings to be delivered at the closing up to a maximum of 287,142 shares.

PLUS

An equal number of shares of Equity National common stock with delivery over a 3½-year period contingent upon Coburn's increased future earnings.

Details of the Proposal

1. One share of Equity National common stock will be delivered to Coburn for every $2.333 of pre-tax audited earnings upon the completion of an audit of the books of Coburn performed as of October 31, 1969, and the receipt by Equity of an unqualified auditor's opinion for the past three years, provided, however, that the number of shares shall not exceed 287,142.

2. An equal number of additional shares of Equity National common stock may be delivered to Coburn over a 3½-year period, based upon increased pre-tax earnings of Coburn. The delivery dates of these contingent shares will be March 31 of each year beginning March 31, 1971, and ending March 31, 1973. The amount of shares to be distributed each year will depend upon the amount by which Coburn's pre-tax earnings exceed the pre-tax earnings for the year ending 10/31/69 or the pre-tax earnings for the calendar year ending 12/31/70 or 12/31/71, whichever annual amount is higher.

Contingent Shares Earnings Schedule

Maximum number of shares Coburn shall receive in any one year is equal to the number of shares issued at the closing, less the number of contingent shares previously received by Coburn.

EXHIBIT 1 *(continued)*

Calendar Year 1970:

For each $2.3333 of additional pre-tax earnings *above* an amount equal to the pre-tax earnings of the fiscal year ending 10/31/69, Coburn will receive one share of Equity stock.

Calendar Year 1971:

For each $2.3333 of additional pre-tax earnings *above* an amount equal to the pre-tax earnings of the fiscal year ending 10/31/69 or the calendar year ending 12/31/70, whichever amount is larger, Coburn will receive on share of Equity stock.

Calendar Year 1972:

For each $2.3333 of additional pre-tax earnings *above* an amount equal to the pre-tax earnings of the fiscal year ending 10/31/69 or the calendar year ending 12/31/70 or the calendar year ending 12/31/71, whichever is largest, Coburn will receive one share of Equity stock.

This proposal is made on
April 9, 1969, and will
remain in effect until
May 1, 1969.

_____

Charles H. Childs, Jr.
President
Equity National Industries, Inc.
44 Broad Street
Atlanta, Georgia

We, the following shareholders of Coburn Industries, Inc., agree in principle to the above proposal:

_____

_____

_____

_____

EXHIBIT 2
Coburn Industries, Inc.
Condensed Operating Record and Projections
for Fiscal Years Ended October 31

	1965	1966	1967	1968	Projected 1969	Projected 1970
Net Sales	$295,367	$820,153	$852,822	$2,295,325	$5,500,000	$6,500,000
Cost of Sales	264,395	781,804	840,448	2,045,501	4,746,500	5,512,000
Gross Profit	$ 30,972	$ 38,349	$ 12,374	$ 249,824	$ 753,500	$ 988,000
Sales Expense	—	—	52,329	48,115	110,000	136,500
General and Administrative Expense	—	—	60,765	79,147	132,000	143,000
Total Operating Expense	$ 77,884	$ 81,748	$113,094	$ 127,262	$ 242,000	$ 279,500
Operating Profit	(46,912)	(43,399)	(100,720)	122,562	511,500	708,500
Other Income	4,423	1,601	18,764	11,402	27,500	32,500
Net Income Before Taxes	(42,489)	(41,798)	(81,956)	133,964	539,000	741,000
Federal and State Income Taxes	—	—	—	9,359	269,000	371,000
Net Income	$(42,489)	$(41,798)	$(81,956)	$ 124,605	$ 270,000	$ 370,000
COST OF MANUFACTURING						
Cost of Materials Used	$207,079	$672,035	$582,377	$1,644,690	$3,905,000	$4,550,000
Direct Labor	33,030	99,600	132,742	227,521	495,000	572,000
Manufacturing Overhead	24,296	60,170	80,965	173,761	346,500	390,000
Total Cost of Manufacturing	$264,405	$831,805	$796,084	$2,045,972	$4,746,500	$5,512,000

EXHIBIT 3
Coburn Industries, Inc.
and Its Wholly Owned Subsidiaries
Nashville, North Carolina

Balance Sheet
March 31, 1969

ASSETS

Current Assets:

Petty Cash	$ 200.00	
Peoples Bank & Trust Company	14,352.23	
Cash in Escrow	9,493.88	
Payroll Accounts	200.00	
Reserve Peoples Bank	1,212.86	
Notes Receivable	1,000.00	
Accounts Receivable	429,621.82	
Inventory—Raw Materials	316,285.55	
Inventory—Work in Process	12,335.40	
Inventory—Finished Coaches	55,844.80	
Total Current Assets		$840,546.54

Fixed Assets:

Buildings	$177,522.11	
Mobile Office Units	20,882.64	
Machinery and Equipment	58,419.82	
Furniture and Fixtures	6,149.71	
Automobile Equipment	52,496.81	
Railroad, Parking Lot, etc.	23,382.95	
Prepaid Interest	8,893.47	
Prepaid Insurance	3,940.40	
Organization Cost	207.23	
Loan Cost	1,950.68	
Leasehold Improvements	15,617.54	
Lease Cost	2,497.73	
Accumulated Depreciation	(50,196.18)	
Provision Income Tax	2,200.00	
Total Fixed Assets		$ 323,964.39
Total Assets		$1,164,510.93

(Balance Sheet continues on following page)

EXHIBIT 3
Coburn Industries, Inc. *(continued)*
and Its Wholly Owned Subsidiaries
Nashville, North Carolina

Balance Sheet
March 31, 1969

LIABILITIES AND NET WORTH

Current Liabilities:

Accounts Payable	$421,470.54	
Provision for Sales Allowances	11,550.00	
Christmas Savings	1,109.80	
Notes Payable Due Within One Year	49,546.66	
Notes Payable—Factor—Peoples Bank & Tr. Co.	216,459.24	
Interest Payable	2,106.33	
Accrued Payroll	13,333.89	
Payroll Tax Payable	13,484.08	
Sales Tax Payable	4,319.09	
Other Current Liabilities	485.42	
Total Current Liabilities		$ 734,065.05
Long-Term Liabilities:		
Notes Payable—Long-Term		$ 213,976.24
Total Liabilities		$ 948,041.29
Net Worth:		
Capital Stock Common	$124,574.70	
Retained Earnings	(38,438.94)	
Capital Contributed in Excess of Par	76.18	
Profit or Loss Year to Date	130,257.70	
Total Net Worth		$ 216,469.64
Total Liabilities and Net Worth		$1,164,510.93

EXHIBIT 4
Equity National Industries, Inc.
Stock Market Data

Shares of Stock Transferred in 1968

Month	Number	Month	Number
January	9,801	July	53,871
February	3,703	August	65,570
March	26,136	September	89,257
April	4,380	October	87,165
May	11,245	November	46,353
June	30,079	December	53,775

Monthly Stock Price Range
High and Low Bid Prices 1968-1969

Date	High	Low
January 1968	1⅞	1½
February 1968	1⅞	1½
March 1968	1⅝	1½
April 1968	1⅝	1½
May 1968	3	1⅝
June 1968	4½	2¾
July 1968	6½	4¼
August 1968	8	4¾
September 1968	11¾	7¾
October 1968	14½	10¾
November 1968	16¾	13¼
December 1968	17½	14½
January 1969	17	13¼
February 1969	18½	14¼
March 1969	14¼	11¾
April 1969	14¼	13¾

EXHIBIT 5

Equity National Industries, Inc., and Consolidated Subsidiaries
Consolidated Balance Sheet, December 31, 1968

ASSETS
Current Assets:

Cash	$ 164,586
Accounts receivable, less reserve for doubtful accounts	773,381
Current portion of long-term notes receivable	19,967
Inventories, at the lower of cost (first-in, first-out) or market	928,118
Prepaid expenses, etc.	24,233
Total current assets	$1,019,595
Investment in Equity National Life Insurance Company (Wholly owned), at equity in underlying net assets	$ 323,070

Property and Equipment, at cost:

Land and land improvements	$ 162,745
Buildings	406,869
Machinery and equipment	555,283
Furniture and fixtures	88,157
Autos and trucks	129,576
Leasehold improvements	46,249
Gross Plant and Equipment	$1,388,879
Less reserve for depreciation	369,284
Net Plant and Equipment	$1,910,285

Other Assets:

Long-term notes receivable from officers of subsidiaries, less current portion above	$ 42,629
Cash surrender value of life insurance ($1,440,000 face amount)	30,020
Deposits, etc.	11,585
Total Other Assets	$ 84,234
Total Assets	$3,337,184

LIABILITIES AND STOCKHOLDERS' INVESTMENT
Current Liabilities:

Notes payable, 7% to 7½%	$ 379,008
Current portion of long-term debt	119,220
Accounts payable and accrued liabilities	895,690
Accrued income taxes	270,302
Total current liabilities	$1,664,220
Long-Term Debt, less current portion above	$ 250,758

Stockholders' Investment:

Preferred stock, no par value, authorized 250,000 shares, no shares outstanding	
Common stock, $1 par value, authorized 2,000,000 shares, outstanding 872,867 shares	$ 872,867
Paid-in surplus	156,485
Retained earnings	392,854
Total stockholders' investment	$1,422,206
Total Liabilities and Stockholders Investment	$3,337,184

EXHIBIT 6

Equity National Industries, Inc., and Consolidated Subsidiaries

Consolidated Statement of Income
for the Year Ended December 31, 1968

Net Sales	$6,599,055
Cost and Expenses:	
Materials and supplies	$3,151,142
Salaries and wages	1,555,798
Depreciation (principally straight-line)	129,357
Other expenses	994,635
Total Costs	$5,830,932
Gross Profits	$ 768,123
Provision for Income Taxes:	$ 394,000
Profits After Taxes	$ 374,123
Loss of Equity National Life Insurance Company	27,727
Net Income	$ 346,396
Net Income per Share:	
Based on the 872,867 shares presently outstanding	$ .40
Assuming conversion of all stock options and warrants	$ .35

QUESTIONS

1. Using the financial data presented, evaluate the past and projected performance of Coburn Industries, Inc.
2. From the viewpoint of Coburn's stockholders, evaluate the overall desirability of becoming part of Equity National Industries, Inc.
3. Analyze the merger proposal (Exhibit 1) submitted to Coburn by Equity National.
4. What recommendation would you make to McGilvary with respect to both the desirability of merging with Equity and the necessary terms of such a merger?

Case 45
Alpha Dynamics, Ltd.

In the afternoon of May 14, 1974, Ken Semenoff—the recently appointed treasurer of Alpha Dynamics, Ltd.—received an urgent call summoning him to the executive vice-president's office. Roger Turnbull—the executive vice-president—was impatiently awaiting Ken's appearance. "Come in Ken . . . take a seat," said Roger, "I've just heard at lunch from a friend that there were rumors of an imminent devaluation of the Australian dollar—some people say probably by 15 or even 20 percent. I want to know what effect this would have on our position in Australia and what we're doing to avert any negative effects." "I wish it was the Australian dollar only," responded Ken. "Right now, the floating Sterling couldn't make up its mind whether to go up or down, and the Germans are apparently resisting pressures to upvalue their Mark. I know that our investments in these countries are basically sound; but their currencies—God knows—have been lively actors in this money circus . . ." As Ken was about to continue, Roger interrupted, "Look Ken, I don't want to appear to be breathing down your neck, but I want to make darn sure that we don't get caught again with our pants down in currency markets, as happened a few months ago." Roger paused for a few seconds, wondering whether to remind Ken that the ex-treasurer had lost his job on account of what happened, but decided against it. Instead, he said, "I am confident that you will do your level best to keep us from getting into the same kind of trouble again; but I want some action to be taken now."

This case was prepared by Professor T. Abdel-Malek of the College of Commerce, University of Saskatchewan as a basis for classroom discussion and not to illustrate either effective or ineffective handling of an administrative situation. It was made possible by the cooperation of a firm that wishes to remain anonymous and by research grants from the Principal's Fund, and the Banff School of Advanced Management Fund administered by the College of Commerce, University of Saskatchewan.

"Well, Roger," Ken replied, "I've been reviewing the latest balance sheets of our three subs, and I was going to ask for a meeting of the Foreign Exchange Committee for some time tomorrow. I'd prefer early afternoon, as I need a few hours in the morning to complete my review of our overall position and to check with a few people on the latest market developments." "Good, ... I'll call a meeting for 1:30 p.m. tomorrow. I just hope we won't get caught between now and then. . . Oh, incidentally, Ken, once we deal with the present situation, I want the committee to establish the operating guidelines we talked about the other day, as soon as possible. I'll feel better when we have some regular procedures to follow in dealing with our foreign exchange exposure. We mustn't wait until we have a crisis on hand." Ken nodded in agreement.

On his way back to his office, Semenoff began to draw together in his mind the basic facts and issues bearing on Alpha's position—a process which took up the remainder of that afternoon. Alpha produced abroad more or less the same product line of industrial equipment which it manufactured at home. Whereas the German subsidiary bought virtually all its production requirements from German suppliers, both the British and Australian affiliates imported about 50 percent of the required raw materials and components from the Canadian parent company. These imports represented between 20 and 25 percent of the selling prices of equipment in these two markets at present. All three subsidiaries were encouraged to borrow locally. within limits set by the parent, whenever local interest rates were not significantly higher than those in international money markets. The Australian company had an outstanding loan of 1.2 m. Canadian dollars (C$) at 9 percent, due to be repaid at end of 1976, and the British subsidiary had borrowed DM 15 m. from a German bank at 8½% to be repaid in DM on June 30, 1976. All other loans outstanding were in local currencies. The three companies exported to varying degrees, primarily to neighboring markets: the Australian company to New Zealand and a few South East Asian countries, the German subsidiary to other Common Market countries, and the British firm to a number of Commonwealth markets. All export proceeds were in £ (Pounds Sterling) except in the case of the German subsidiary, which received DM (Deutschmarks) for approximately 80 percent of its exports and £ for the remainder.

The Australian subsidiary—which was the smallest and most recent of Alpha's—was a joint venture with a local group of investors who held 25 percent of the equity. The other two subsidiaries were wholly owned by Alpha.

Next, Ken Semenoff revised the balance sheet figures he received last month from the subsidiaries, in order to show their latest position according to information his office had since obtained. The revised balance sheets are shown in Exhibit 1.

Semenoff spent a good part of the following morning talking with Alpha's bankers and a few financial observers whose judgment he respected. He made the following notes for himself, which briefly summed up the latest assessments of £, DM, and A$:

Pound Sterling: The Pound's appreciation in recent weeks was due primarily to improved economic outlook following the end of the miners' strike and the resumption of the 5-day working week, as well as to heavy purchases of £ by oil

EXHIBIT 1

Balance Sheet of Alpha (U.K.), Ltd.
as of May 15, 1974

		£ 000
ASSETS		
Cash and Short-term Local Investments		1,800
Accounts Receivable		8,250
Inventories:*		
Raw Materials and Components	840	
Work in Process	1,230	
Finished Goods	2,400	4,470
Prepaid Expenses		510
Deferred Expenses		240
Land, Buildings, and Equipment	15,750	
Depreciation	5,250	10,500
Total Assets		25,770
LIABILITIES AND EQUITY		
Accounts Payable†		6,840
Notes Payable		2,940
Accrued Expenses		1,200
Income Tax Payable		780
Long-term Debt‡		6,300
Minority Interest		—
Capital Stock		6,000
Retained Earnings		1,710
Total Liabilities and Equity		25,770

*Half the raw materials and components shown were imported; work in process and finished goods included imported inputs amounting to approximately 40 percent and 30 percent of the values shown, respectively.
†35 percent of this amount at existing exchange rate is payable to parent company in Canadian dollars.
‡Includes a German loan of DM 15 m. payable in DM, in June 1976.

EXHIBIT 1 *(continued)*

Balance Sheet of Alpha (Germany)
as of May 15, 1974

		DM 000
ASSETS		
Cash and Short-Term Local Investments		4,300
Accounts Receivable*		13,500
Inventories:		
Raw Materials and Components	2,000	
Work in Process	6,800	
Finished Goods	6,600	15,400
Prepaid Expenses		1,600
Deferred Expenses		—
Land, Buildings, and Equipment	42,000	
Depreciation	9,200	32,800
Total Assets		67,600
LIABILITIES AND EQUITY		
Accounts Payable		21,800
Notes Payable		6,300
Accrued Expenses		2,900
Income Tax Payable		4,100
Long-Term Debt		5,000
Minority Interest		—
Capital Stock		17,000
Retained Earnings		10,500
Total Liabilities and Equity		67,600

*Includes export proceeds equivalent to DM 2.8 m. receivable in £.

EXHIBIT 1 *(continued)*

Balance Sheet of Alpha (Australia), Ltd.
as of May 15, 1974

		A$ 000
ASSETS		
Cash and Short-Term Local Investments		420
Accounts Receivable		2,860
Inventories:*		
Raw Materials and Components	1,000	
Work in Process	2,200	
Finished Goods	1,520	4,720
Prepaid Expenses		360
Deferred Expenses		140
Land, Buildings, and Equipment	7,600	
Depreciation	1,800	5,800
Total Assets		14,300
LIABILITIES AND EQUITY		
Accounts Payable†		2,340
Notes Payable		700
Accrued Expenses		1,360
Income Tax Payable		1,140
Long-Term Debt		2,400
Minority Interest ‡		1,500
Capital Stock		4,500
Retained Earnings		360
Total Liabilities and Equity		14,300

*A$ 800,000 worth of the raw materials and components shown were imported; work in process and finished goods included imported inputs amounting to approximately 40 percent and 30 percent of the values shown, respectively.

†40 percent of this amount at existing exchange rate is payable to parent company in Canadian dollars.

‡Includes a loan of C$ 1.2 m., payable in Canadian dollars, in December 1976.

EXHIBIT 2
Average Spot Rates for £, DM, and A$ in Terms of the Canadian Dollar (C$)
(1970-1974)

	£/C$	DM/C$	A$/C$
1970	2.5016	0.2863	1.1583
1971	2.4687	0.2900	1.1459
1972	2.4797	0.3108	1.1794
1973	2.4533	0.3782	1.4283
1973 May	2.5311	0.3586	1.4113
June	2.5723	0.3874	1.4140
July	2.5369	0.4291	1.4190
Aug.	2.4858	0.4140	1.4244
Sept.	2.4383	0.4154	1.4958
Oct.	2.4322	0.4147	1.4874
Nov.	2.3856	0.3879	1.4874
Dec.	2.3170	0.3763	1.4814
1974 Jan.	2.2062	0.3520	1.4686
Feb.	2.2213	0.3600	1.4408
Mar.	2.2766	0.3714	1.4461
Apr.	2.3126	0.3833	1.4410

Sources: Bank of Canada, *Bank of Canada Review* (various issues) for £ and DM rates, and Reserve Bank of Australia, *Statistical Bulletin* (various issues) and I.M.F., *International Financial Statistics* (1973 Supplement) for A$ rates.

QUESTIONS

1. Discuss the importance of Alpha Dynamics, Ltd.'s concern with changing currency valuations.
2. Determine Alpha's foreign exchange exposure on May 15, 1974.
3. What recommendations would you suggest that Semenoff make to the Foreign Exchange Committee in order to deal with the situation?
4. Identify the main costs and benefits associated with your recommendations given for Question 3.

Case 46
Global Enterprises

In preparation for the next monthly meeting of his company's Foreign Exchange Committee in July 1974, Don Kroner—the treasurer—was examining a summary statement of the forward Sterling contracts which Global Enterprises had transacted since January 1971, when the company started keeping detailed records of these transactions (Exhibit 1). Kroner had asked a member of his staff to prepare the statement, as he felt it would be useful in evaluating the company's actual experience in forward coverage. The Foreign Exchange Committee had recently decided that such evaluation was necessary as part of the process of reviewing Global's foreign exchange policies.

The company produced a number of industrial commodities which were sold under standard specifications in world markets. Each commodity commanded a fairly uniform price which prevailed in a relatively barrier-free world market. The United Kingdom was one of Global's main export markets. All sales to the U.K. were made in £ (Pound Sterling), amounting to about £40 million in 1973. Approximately two-thirds of this volume was sold on cash or spot basis. The remainder was exported under agreements for future delivery at fixed prices. Agreements typically extended over five to six months. Once invoiced, payments were received within two or, at most, three months. Global's practice had been to arrange for a full coverage of net exposure in £ (Pound Sterling) (i.e., receivables + estimated receipts under fixed-price agreements — estimated disbursements in £

This case was prepared by Professor T. Abdel-Malek of the College of Commerce, University of Saskatchewan as a basis for classroom discussion and not to illustrate either effective or ineffective handling of an administrative situation. It was made possible by the cooperation of a company that wishes to remain anonymous and by research grants from the Principal's Fund, and the Banff School of Advanced Management Fund administered by the College of Commerce, University of Saskatchewan.

[Pound Sterling] during a given period) through forward £ (Pound Sterling) contracts which in virtually all cases carried a maturity date of 180 days.

Kroner recalled that he found himself in the midst of a debate at last month's committee meeting about the foreign exchange practices which had been in effect for several years now. Some members were advocating the continuation of present policy of full coverage at all times. Others believed that this approach was too conservative and perhaps too costly, and argued instead that the company should first make greater effort to anticipate the future rate of £ (Pound Sterling) and should then consider revising its full coverage practice, with a view to reducing the cost of coverage or even to taking advantage of whatever opportunities of making profit may present themselves.

Kroner, as well as other members of the committee, was fully aware that practices of other firms varied widely and that some firms had been reported as "highly successful" in that they were able to exploit profitable opportunities in the foreign exchange market. Others had "gambled" and, not infrequently, lost considerable sums of money. Others still, like his company, had faithfully adhered to the principle of full coverage against exchange risk at all times.

Partly because of this diversity of experiences and options and partly due to the greater variability and uncertainty of exchange rates in the past three years or so under the floating system, Global's top management recently set up the Foreign Exchange Committee and charged it with the task of reviewing present policies and recommending any changes it deemed desirable.

In the circumstances, Kroner did not expect the committee to automatically endorse existing policy. But while he wanted to keep an open mind and consider alternatives which might be put forward, he did not see any serious shortcomings in present practices.

As he perused the figures in the statement in front of him, he was satisfied that he was right when he contended at the meeting that Global had made a net gain under £ (Pound Sterling) forward contracts during the past 3½ years—a rather turbulent period for £ (Pound Sterling). Meanwhile, the pound's recent behavior and its short-term outlook were by no means reassuring, as indicated in the following excerpts from a recent *Bank Review* he regularly consulted.

"Last month [May 1974], the pound against the Canadian dollar (C$) traded between $2.2938 and $2.3518. Against the U.S. dollar, sterling eased from a high of $2.4380 to approximately $2.3950 by the end of the month. Sterling's weaknesses against the dollar reflects the continuing decline in United Kingdom interest rates at a time when U.S. rates are buoyant. . . .

The pound traded erratically against the major continental European currencies, registering net gains for the month. Other factors that influenced the spot sterling rate included the sudden settlement of the Engineering Union dispute, rumors of a summer election, new North Sea oil estimates and an improved United Kingdom visible trade deficit for April. . . .

The pound trading near the U.S. $2.40 level belies sterling's intrinsic weakness. Large (Arab) capital inflows into the United Kingdom, oil company demand for sterling, and market attention being focused on other currencies (the mark and lire) are having the effect of preventing sterling from weakening. However, on interest rate considerations alone, it is expected that the pound will weaken in the short term. If there is a major upheaval sterling could weaken sharply."

EXHIBIT 1
Summary of Forward Sterling's Transactions
January 1971-June 1974

Delivery	Month	Amount in £ 000	Spot Rate on Contract Date	Forward Contract Rate C$/£	Spot Rate at Delivery C$/£
1971	January	1,100	2.4672	2.4100	2.4210
	February	640	2.4390	2.4275	2.4300
	March	1,570	2.4230	2.4275	2.4315
	April	60	2.4395	2.4230	2.4325
	May	160	2.4320	2.4200	2.4400
	June	100	2.4318	2.4215	2.4712
	July	340	2.4340	2.4175	2.4718
	August	1,490	2.4362	2.4190	2.4910
	September	900	2.4338	2.4000	2.5000
	October	370	2.4370	2.4150	2.4905
	November	630	2.4400	2.4160	2.5010
	December	600	2.4710	2.4490	2.5015
	Total	7,960			
1972	January	600	2.4720	2.4365	2.5700
	February	580	2.4710	2.4938	2.5990
	March	1,420	2.5020	2.4920	2.6112
	April	400	2.5030	2.5045	2.5905
	May	600	2.5060	2.5132	2.5650
	June	1,200	2.5690	2.5712	2.4018
	July	1,100	2.6120	2.6132	2.4000
	August	1,000	2.6100	2.6156	2.3908
	September	1,000	2.5920	2.5965	2.3810
	October	1,300	2.5925	2.5970	2.3200
	November	600	2.5690	2.5788	2.3210
	December	800	2.3880	2.3706	2.3298
	Total	10,600			
1973	January	1,000	2.3990	2.3694	2.3502
	February	800	2.3662	2.3456	2.4500
	March	700	2.3660	2.2958	2.4618
	April	1,600	2.2968	2.2776	2.4808
	May	2,000	2.3115	2.2962	2.4949
	June	600	2.3206	2.3012	2.5754
	July	700	2.3898	2.3750	2.5210
	August	1,000	2.4006	2.3840	2.4774
	September	1,400	2.4018	2.3806	2.4304
	October	2,000	2.4805	2.4670	2.4319
	November	900	2.5110	2.4985	2.3995
	December	500	2.5500	2.5343	2.3124
	Total	13,200			
1974	January	1,800	2.5072	2.4875	2.2560
	February	1,750	2.3788	2.3591	2.2875
	March	2,400	2.3910	2.3738	2.3279
	April	2,000	2.4198	2.3935	2.3094
	May	1,900	2.2902	2.2600	2.2999
	June	1,100	2.3396	2.3234	2.3005
	Total	10,950			

QUESTIONS

1. Evaluate Global Enterprises' existing policy of fully covering their net foreign exchange exposures.
2. Compute the gains/losses made under the forward contracts using the data given in Exhibit 1.
3. Specifically identify the main policy options available for Global in relation to its transactions.
4. If you were a member of Global's Foreign Exchange Committee, what course of action would you recommend? Why?

Case 47
The American Aluminum Corporation

By the end of July, 1974, Charles M. Hall, a recent MBA graduate from a leading U.S. business school, had been on his first assignment with American Aluminum Corporation (AMAL) for only two weeks, and he found himself facing the first important problem of his very brief career. Hall's boss had assigned him the responsibility for the petroleum coke aspects of the primary aluminum production process and with this responsibility came two related problems of important long-run consequences. The first problem was whether or not to accept an offer from British Columbia Aluminum, Ltd., a Canadian company, to supply 50,000 tons of petroleum coke at a delivered price of 10% less than the delivered price of the best alternative source of petroleum coke from U.S. sources. AMAL used large quantities of petroleum coke and was interested in purchasing 50,000 tons in order to tide it over the next six months. The second problem was to establish and justify a price at which a new long-run source of petroleum coke should be transferred from AMAL's recently formed Canadian subsidiary. But before deciding what to do about these two problems, Hall reviewed what he knew about AMAL operations.

The Company Structure

American Aluminum Corporation, a U.S. corporation located on the West Coast of the Pacific Northwest, refines high-quality aluminum ingot from aluminum oxide (alumina) which was transported in bulk ocean carriers from bauxite mines

This case was prepared by Professor J. Frederick Truitt of the University of Washington and Mr. Rex Loesby as a basis for classroom discussion rather than to illustrate the effective or ineffective handling of an administrative situation.

in Western Australia to AMAL's smelter. The aluminum smelting process combines a few basic raw materials (alumina, cryolite, aluminum floride, pitch, and petroleum coke) with large quantities of electric power to produce aluminum ingot. (See Exhibit 1.) AMAL's smelter was located so that it had access to a deep-water harbor for unloading the alumina, as well as convenient rail service and relatively inexpensive hydroelectric power.

AMAL was owned by two U.S. corporations, Eastern Metals Corporation and North American Metals Corporation. Each owned 50% of AMAL. Eastern Metals Corporation was in turn 40% owned by European Resources, Ltd., a French corporation. (See Exhibit 2.)

The Petroleum Coke Supply Problem

During the two years immediately preceding Hall's assignment, AMAL had been experiencing problems securing dependable supplies of petroleum coke[1] at a stable and reasonable price. AMAL used a maximum of 110,000 tons of petroleum coke per year, and between late 1973 and June, 1974, the delivered price of petroleum coke had increased from $45 per ton to $90. This dramatic increase in price along with interruptions in supply and decrease in the quality of petroleum coke available from U.S. West Coast refineries led AMAL to seek an alternative source of supply for a substantial portion of its petroleum coke requirements.

Canada Coke, Ltd.

AMAL management decided in late 1973 to procure their petroleum coke from Canada and had entered into a venture with British Columbia Aluminum, Ltd. (BCA, Ltd.), to construct a petroleum coke processing facility near the petroleum refineries in Edmonton, Alberta. Canada Coke, Ltd., was formed as a wholly owned Canadian subsidiary to carry out the details of the venture with BCA, Ltd. Canada Coke was a corporate facade or "nonfirm" in the sense that no management personnel were employed by Canada Coke, Ltd., in Canada. All managerial decisions involving Canada Coke, Ltd., were made by AMAL personnel in the U.S.

Hall found the nature of the agreement between AMAL's Canada Coke, Ltd., and BCA, Ltd., interesting because it did not seem to fit into any of the familiar categories (wholly-owned subsidiary, joint venture, licensing arrangement, etc.) he had studied in his MBA program. AMAL (through Canada Coke, Ltd.) and BCA, Ltd., shared the output of the newly constructed petroleum coke processing facility proportional to the contribution each partner made to financing the construction of the facility. The arrangement was in many ways similar to a joint venture between AMAL and BCA, Ltd., but was in fact termed a "co-tenancy" agreement. The petroleum coke producing facility had no separate legal identity and the "co-tenancy" form allowed each of the participating companies to write down their respective shares in the asset at different depreciation schedules. AMAL had

[1]Petroleum coke is the last product resulting from the petroleum refining process after all the higher-grade fuels and chemicals are taken off. Before the coke is suitable for use in the aluminum smelting process, it must go through a calcining process which removes the impurities in the coke.

decided to write down its share in the new facility using the straight-line method of depreciation over a twenty-year period.

BCA, Ltd., contributed 61% of the cost of constructing the petroleum coke processing facility and was scheduled to take 61% of its annual 180,000-ton production. AMAL, through Canada Coke, Ltd., contributed 39% of the construction cost and was scheduled to take 39% of the annual 180,000-ton production when the facility came on stream some time in the next six months. (See Exhibits 2 and 3.) BCA, Ltd., was the operating partner in the "co-tenancy" arrangement and was to provide coke to AMAL through Canada Coke, Ltd., at a cost determined by the following schedule:

Actual operating cost of calcining process (does not include depreciation)	$ 5.00 per ton[1]
Management fee	.50 per ton
Coke purchasing commission	.40 per ton
	$ 5.90 per ton
Cost of green coke from refineries	40.00 per ton
Total cost charged by BCA, Ltd., the operating company of the "co-tenancy" arrangement, to Canada Coke, Ltd.	$45.90 per ton

[1]All figures are in U.S. dollars.

Transporting the refined Canadian coke from the Edmonton facility to the AMAL's smelter will cost $13.00 per ton. The U.S. tariff on petroleum coke imports is 7.5% ad valorem F.O.B.[2]

Canada Coke, Ltd., was financed with $850,000 in capital stock and $2,000,000 in loans at the prime rate of 12% from a major Canadian bank. That is, AMAL's 39% participation in the Edmonton coke facility was through Canada Coke, Ltd., in the amount of $2,850,000.

The Transfer Pricing Decision

The decision to go to Canada in this particular arrangement had been put into motion before Hall had joined AMAL. What remained for Hall to decide was the price at which Canada Coke, Ltd., sold its 39% share of the petroleum coke output from the calcining facility to AMAL. Since Canada Coke, Ltd.'s profits, and hence Canadian income tax liability, were dependent almost entirely on this transfer price, Hall saw the need to proceed carefully, lest AMAL run afoul of Canadian (let alone U.S.) income tax authorities. Therefore, he sought the assistance of tax lawyers on the corporate staff. Summarized, this assistance told Hall the following:

A. Since AMAL is a subsidiary of two large, complex U.S. corporations, the tax rates of the parent corporations must be taken into account when calculating AMAL's effective tax rate. The effective rate of U.S. income tax for AMAL turns out to be in the 30% to 35% range.

B. The effective tax rate for Canada Coke, Ltd., is 41%.

C. Canadian tax authorities' judgment on the propriety transfer pricing decisions would be based upon the "arm's length" guideline, i.e, the

[2]F.O.B. stands for "Free on Board," which means that the buyer must pay the shipping cost.

transfer price had to be close to the price that would be used by two unrelated organizations. The two basic methods for determining an "arm's length" transfer price favored by Canadian authorities are:

1. *a market* price between unrelated organizations, or if a market price is not available as a guideline;
2. *comparison* of rates of return on total assets,

$$\text{i.e., RTA} = \frac{\text{Net profit before interest and tax}}{\text{Total assets}}$$

of similar independent operations with the expectation that a foreign-owned subsidiary in transfer pricing relationships with its parent company should earn a return on assets comparable to independent firms.

Earlier in the week, Hall took a day off from the smelter and drove down to a large university library in order to look up some more information on the petroleum coke industry in Canada. He found that the RTA (return on total assets) for petroleum coke operations in Canada averaged a surprisingly low 5% to 6%. Later, he verified this figure by telephone with the Canadian Consulate nearest AMAL's smelter. He also found that to the best of his and the consulate's knowledge, there was no market price for petroleum coke in Western Canada, because there were no sales of petroleum coke between independent companies in Western Canada.

It was Friday morning, the weather was promising, and Hall was looking forward to a good, relaxing weekend. But the weekend would be all the more relaxing if in the next couple of hours he could make the decisions on the BCA, Ltd., offer and Canada Coke, Ltd., transfer price, write the two-page justification for his decisions, and wrap up these two problems before leaving for the weekend.

EXHIBIT 1

The Aluminum Refining Process: Raw Materials Required

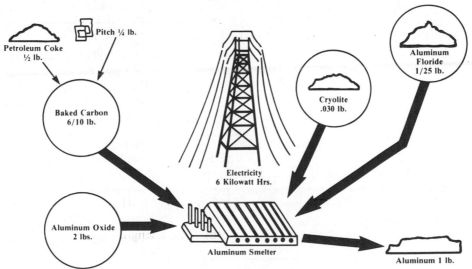

EXHIBIT 2

Corporate Ownership Structure: American Aluminum Corporation

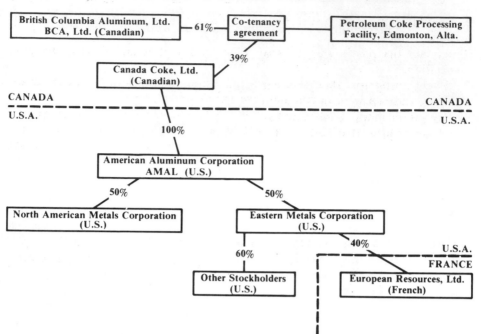

EXHIBIT 3

Flow of Petroleum Coke from Edmonton

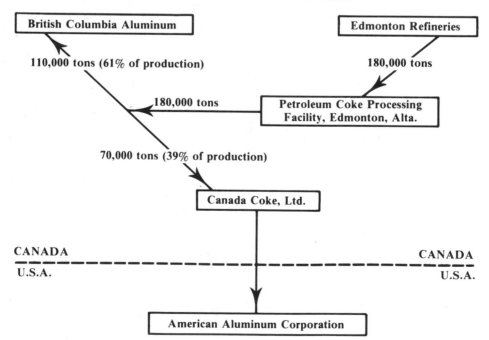

QUESTIONS

1. Should Hall accept British Columbia Aluminum, Ltd.'s offer? Explain why or why not.
2. Explain the relationship between BCA, Ltd.'s offer and the transfer price decision.
3. What transfer price should the American Aluminum Corporation use in Canada Coke, Ltd.—American Aluminum transactions? Why?
4. Discuss the moral issue: "Can a good Canadian corporate citizen" fairly arrange a transfer price that puts all of the income in the parent company's country?

*

APPENDIX
MATHEMATICAL TABLES

*

A-1 Compound Sum of One Dollar

Period	1.00%	2.00%	3.00%	4.00%	5.00%	6.00%	7.00%	8.00%	9.00%	10.00%
1	1.010	1.020	1.030	1.040	1.050	1.060	1.070	1.080	1.090	1.100
2	1.020	1.040	1.061	1.082	1.102	1.124	1.145	1.166	1.188	1.210
3	1.030	1.061	1.093	1.125	1.158	1.191	1.225	1.260	1.295	1.331
4	1.041	1.082	1.126	1.170	1.216	1.262	1.311	1.360	1.412	1.464
5	1.051	1.104	1.159	1.217	1.276	1.338	1.403	1.469	1.539	1.611
6	1.062	1.126	1.194	1.265	1.340	1.419	1.501	1.587	1.677	1.772
7	1.072	1.149	1.230	1.316	1.407	1.504	1.606	1.714	1.828	1.949
8	1.083	1.172	1.267	1.369	1.477	1.594	1.718	1.851	1.993	2.144
9	1.094	1.195	1.305	1.423	1.551	1.689	1.838	1.999	2.172	2.358
10	1.105	1.219	1.344	1.480	1.629	1.791	1.967	2.159	2.367	2.594
11	1.116	1.243	1.384	1.539	1.710	1.898	2.105	2.332	2.580	2.853
12	1.127	1.268	1.426	1.601	1.796	2.012	2.252	2.518	2.813	3.138
13	1.138	1.294	1.469	1.665	1.886	2.133	2.410	2.720	3.066	3.452
14	1.149	1.319	1.513	1.732	1.980	2.261	2.579	2.937	3.342	3.797
15	1.161	1.346	1.558	1.801	2.079	2.397	2.759	3.172	3.642	4.177
16	1.173	1.373	1.605	1.873	2.183	2.540	2.952	3.426	3.970	4.595
17	1.184	1.400	1.653	1.948	2.292	2.693	3.159	3.700	4.328	5.054
18	1.196	1.428	1.702	2.026	2.407	2.854	3.380	3.996	4.717	5.560
19	1.208	1.457	1.753	2.107	2.527	3.026	3.616	4.316	5.142	6.116
20	1.220	1.486	1.806	2.191	2.653	3.207	3.870	4.661	5.604	6.727
21	1.232	1.516	1.860	2.279	2.786	3.399	4.140	5.034	6.109	7.400
22	1.245	1.546	1.916	2.370	2.925	3.603	4.430	5.436	6.658	8.140
23	1.257	1.577	1.974	2.465	3.071	3.820	4.740	5.871	7.258	8.954
24	1.270	1.608	2.033	2.563	3.225	4.049	5.072	6.341	7.911	9.850
25	1.282	1.641	2.094	2.666	3.386	4.292	5.427	6.848	8.623	10.834
30	1.348	1.811	2.427	3.243	4.322	5.743	7.612	10.062	13.267	17.449

A-1 Compound Sum of One Dollar (continued)

Period	11.00%	12.00%	13.00%	14.00%	15.00%	16.00%	17.00%	18.00%	19.00%	20.00%
1	1.110	1.120	1.130	1.140	1.150	1.160	1.170	1.180	1.190	1.200
2	1.232	1.254	1.277	1.300	1.322	1.346	1.369	1.392	1.416	1.440
3	1.368	1.405	1.443	1.482	1.521	1.561	1.602	1.643	1.685	1.728
4	1.518	1.574	1.630	1.689	1.749	1.811	1.874	1.939	2.005	2.074
5	1.685	1.762	1.842	1.925	2.011	2.100	2.192	2.288	2.386	2.488
6	1.870	1.974	2.082	2.195	2.313	2.436	2.565	2.700	2.840	2.986
7	2.076	2.211	2.353	2.502	2.660	2.826	3.001	3.185	3.379	3.583
8	2.305	2.476	2.658	2.853	3.059	3.278	3.511	3.759	4.021	4.300
9	2.558	2.773	3.004	3.252	3.518	3.803	4.108	4.435	4.785	5.160
10	2.839	3.106	3.395	3.707	4.046	4.411	4.807	5.234	5.695	6.192
11	3.152	3.479	3.836	4.226	4.652	5.117	5.624	6.176	6.777	7.430
12	3.498	3.896	4.334	4.818	5.350	5.936	6.580	7.288	8.064	8.916
13	3.883	4.363	4.898	5.492	6.153	6.886	7.699	8.599	9.596	10.699
14	4.310	4.887	5.535	6.261	7.076	7.987	9.007	10.147	11.420	12.839
15	4.785	5.474	6.254	7.138	8.137	9.265	10.539	11.974	13.589	15.407
16	5.311	6.130	7.067	8.137	9.358	10.748	12.330	14.129	16.171	18.488
17	5.895	6.866	7.986	9.276	10.761	12.468	14.426	16.672	19.244	22.186
18	6.543	7.690	9.024	10.575	12.375	14.462	16.879	19.673	22.900	26.623
19	7.263	8.613	10.197	12.055	14.232	16.776	19.748	23.214	27.251	31.948
20	8.062	9.646	11.523	13.743	16.366	19.461	23.105	27.393	32.429	38.337
21	8.949	10.804	13.021	15.667	18.821	22.574	27.033	32.323	38.591	46.005
22	9.933	12.100	14.713	17.861	21.644	26.186	31.629	38.141	45.923	55.205
23	11.026	13.552	16.626	20.361	24.891	30.376	37.005	45.007	54.648	66.247
24	12.239	15.178	18.788	23.212	28.625	35.236	43.296	53.108	65.031	79.496
25	13.585	17.000	21.230	26.461	32.918	40.874	50.656	62.667	77.387	95.395
30	22.892	29.960	39.115	50.949	66.210	85.849	111.061	143.367	184.672	237.373

Period	21.00%	22.00%	23.00%	24.00%	25.00%	26.00%	27.00%	28.00%	29.00%	30.00%
1	1.210	1.220	1.230	1.240	1.250	1.260	1.270	1.280	1.290	1.300
2	1.464	1.488	1.513	1.538	1.563	1.588	1.613	1.638	1.664	1.690
3	1.772	1.816	1.861	1.907	1.953	2.000	2.048	2.097	2.147	2.197
4	2.144	2.215	2.289	2.364	2.441	2.520	2.601	2.684	2.769	2.856
5	2.594	2.703	2.815	2.932	3.052	3.176	3.304	3.436	3.572	3.713
6	3.138	3.297	3.463	3.635	3.815	4.001	4.196	4.398	4.608	4.827
7	3.797	4.023	4.259	4.508	4.768	5.042	5.329	5.629	5.945	6.275
8	4.595	4.908	5.239	5.589	5.960	6.353	6.767	7.206	7.669	8.157
9	5.560	5.987	6.444	6.931	7.451	8.004	8.595	9.223	9.893	10.604
10	6.727	7.305	7.926	8.594	9.313	10.086	10.915	11.806	12.761	13.786
11	8.140	8.912	9.749	10.657	11.642	12.708	13.862	15.112	16.462	17.921
12	9.850	10.872	11.991	13.215	14.552	16.012	17.605	19.343	21.236	23.298
13	11.918	13.264	14.749	16.386	18.190	20.175	22.359	24.759	27.395	30.287
14	14.421	16.182	18.141	20.319	22.737	25.420	28.395	31.691	35.339	39.373
15	17.449	19.742	22.314	25.195	28.422	32.030	36.062	40.565	45.587	51.185
16	21.113	24.085	27.446	31.242	35.527	40.357	45.799	51.923	58.808	66.541
17	25.547	29.384	33.758	38.740	44.409	50.850	58.165	66.461	75.862	86.503
18	30.912	35.848	41.523	48.038	55.511	64.071	73.869	85.070	97.862	112.454
19	37.404	43.735	51.073	59.567	69.389	80.730	93.813	108.890	126.242	146.190
20	45.258	53.357	62.820	73.863	86.736	101.720	119.143	139.379	162.852	190.047
21	54.762	65.095	77.268	91.591	108.420	128.167	151.312	178.405	210.079	247.061
22	66.262	79.416	95.040	113.572	135.525	161.490	192.165	228.358	271.002	321.178
23	80.178	96.887	116.899	140.829	169.407	203.477	244.050	292.298	349.592	417.531
24	97.015	118.203	143.786	174.628	211.758	256.381	309.943	374.141	450.974	542.791
25	117.388	144.207	176.857	216.539	264.698	323.040	393.628	478.901	581.756	705.627
30	304.471	389.748	497.904	634.810	807.793	1025.904	1300.477	1645.488	2078.208	2619.936

Period	31.00%	32.00%	33.00%	34.00%	35.00%	36.00%	37.00%	38.00%	39.00%	40.00%
1	1.310	1.320	1.330	1.340	1.350	1.360	1.370	1.380	1.390	1.400
2	1.716	1.742	1.769	1.796	1.822	1.850	1.877	1.904	1.932	1.960
3	2.248	2.300	2.353	2.406	2.460	2.515	2.571	2.628	2.686	2.744
4	2.945	3.036	3.129	3.224	3.321	3.421	3.523	3.627	3.733	3.842
5	3.858	4.007	4.162	4.320	4.484	4.653	4.826	5.005	5.189	5.378
6	5.054	5.290	5.535	5.789	6.053	6.328	6.612	6.907	7.213	7.530
7	6.621	6.983	7.361	7.758	8.172	8.605	9.058	9.531	10.025	10.541
8	8.673	9.217	9.791	10.395	11.032	11.703	12.410	13.153	13.935	14.758
9	11.362	12.166	13.022	13.930	14.894	15.917	17.001	18.151	19.370	20.661
10	14.884	16.060	17.319	18.666	20.106	21.646	23.292	25.049	26.924	28.925
11	19.498	21.199	23.034	25.012	27.144	29.439	31.910	34.567	37.425	40.495
12	25.542	27.982	30.635	33.516	36.644	40.037	43.716	47.703	52.020	56.694
13	33.460	36.937	40.745	44.912	49.469	54.451	59.892	65.830	72.308	79.371
14	43.832	48.756	54.190	60.181	66.784	74.053	82.051	90.845	100.509	111.119
15	57.420	64.358	72.073	80.643	90.158	100.712	112.410	125.366	139.707	155.567
16	75.220	84.953	95.857	108.061	121.713	136.968	154.002	173.005	194.192	217.793
17	98.539	112.138	127.490	144.802	164.312	186.277	210.983	238.747	269.927	304.911
18	129.086	148.022	169.561	194.035	221.822	253.337	289.046	329.471	375.198	426.875
19	169.102	195.389	225.517	260.006	299.459	344.537	395.993	454.669	521.525	597.625
20	221.523	257.913	299.937	348.408	404.270	468.571	542.511	627.443	724.919	836.674
21	290.196	340.446	398.916	466.867	545.764	637.256	743.240	865.871	1007.637	1171.343
22	380.156	449.388	530.558	625.601	736.781	866.668	1018.238	1194.900	1400.615	1639.878
23	498.004	593.192	705.642	838.305	994.653	1178.668	1394.986	1648.961	1946.854	2295.829
24	652.385	783.013	938.504	1123.328	1342.781	1602.988	1911.129	2275.564	2706.125	3214.158
25	854.623	1033.577	1248.210	1505.258	1812.754	2180.063	2618.245	3140.275	3761.511	4499.816
30	3297.081	4142.008	5194.516	6503.285	8128.426	10142.914	12636.086	15716.703	19517.969	24201.043

Period	1.00%	2.00%	3.00%	4.00%	5.00%	6.00%	7.00%	8.00%	9.00%	10.00%
1	1.000	1.000	1.000	1.000	1.000	1.000	1.000	1.000	1.000	1.000
2	2.010	2.020	2.030	2.040	2.050	2.060	2.070	2.080	2.090	2.100
3	3.030	3.060	3.091	3.122	3.152	3.184	3.215	3.246	3.278	3.310
4	4.060	4.122	4.184	4.246	4.310	4.375	4.440	4.506	4.573	4.641
5	5.101	5.204	5.309	5.416	5.526	5.637	5.751	5.867	5.985	6.105
6	6.152	6.308	6.468	6.633	6.802	6.975	7.153	7.336	7.523	7.716
7	7.214	7.434	7.662	7.898	8.142	8.394	8.654	8.923	9.200	9.487
8	8.286	8.583	8.892	9.214	9.549	9.897	10.260	10.637	11.028	11.436
9	9.368	9.755	10.159	10.583	11.027	11.491	11.978	12.488	13.021	13.579
10	10.462	10.950	11.464	12.006	12.578	13.181	13.816	14.487	15.193	15.937
11	11.567	12.169	12.808	13.486	14.207	14.972	15.784	16.645	17.560	18.531
12	12.682	13.412	14.192	15.026	15.917	16.870	17.888	18.977	20.141	21.384
13	13.809	14.680	15.618	16.627	17.713	18.882	20.141	21.495	22.953	24.523
14	14.947	15.974	17.086	18.292	19.598	21.015	22.550	24.215	26.019	27.975
15	16.097	17.293	18.599	20.023	21.578	23.276	25.129	27.152	29.361	31.772
16	17.258	18.639	20.157	21.824	23.657	25.672	27.888	30.324	33.003	35.949
17	18.430	20.012	21.761	23.697	25.840	28.213	30.840	33.750	36.973	40.544
18	19.614	21.412	23.414	25.645	28.132	30.905	33.999	37.450	41.301	45.599
19	20.811	22.840	25.117	27.671	30.539	33.760	37.379	41.446	46.018	51.158
20	22.019	24.297	26.870	29.778	33.066	36.785	40.995	45.762	51.159	57.274
21	23.239	25.783	28.676	31.969	35.719	39.992	44.865	50.422	56.764	64.002
22	24.471	27.299	30.536	34.248	38.505	43.392	49.005	55.456	62.872	71.402
23	25.716	28.845	32.452	36.618	41.430	46.995	53.435	60.893	69.531	79.542
24	26.973	30.421	34.426	39.082	44.501	50.815	58.176	66.764	76.789	88.496
25	28.243	32.030	36.459	41.645	47.726	54.864	63.248	73.105	84.699	98.346
30	34.784	40.567	47.575	56.084	66.438	79.057	94.459	113.282	136.305	164.491

A-2 Sum of an Annuity of One Dollar (continued)

Period	11.00%	12.00%	13.00%	14.00%	15.00%	16.00%	17.00%	18.00%	19.00%	20.00%
1	1.000	1.000	1.000	1.000	1.000	1.000	1.000	1.000	1.000	1.000
2	2.110	2.120	2.130	2.140	2.150	2.160	2.170	2.180	2.190	2.200
3	3.342	3.374	3.407	3.440	3.472	3.506	3.539	3.572	3.606	3.640
4	4.710	4.779	4.850	4.921	4.993	5.066	5.141	5.215	5.291	5.368
5	6.228	6.353	6.480	6.610	6.742	6.877	7.014	7.154	7.297	7.442
6	7.913	8.115	8.323	8.535	8.754	8.977	9.207	9.442	9.683	9.930
7	9.783	10.089	10.405	10.730	11.067	11.414	11.772	12.141	12.523	12.916
8	11.859	12.300	12.757	13.233	13.727	14.240	14.773	15.327	15.902	16.499
9	14.164	14.776	15.416	16.085	16.786	17.518	18.285	19.086	19.923	20.799
10	16.722	17.549	18.420	19.337	20.304	21.321	22.393	23.521	24.709	25.959
11	19.561	20.655	21.814	23.044	24.349	25.733	27.200	28.755	30.403	32.150
12	22.713	24.133	25.650	27.271	29.001	30.850	32.824	34.931	37.180	39.580
13	26.211	28.029	29.984	32.088	34.352	36.786	39.404	42.218	45.244	48.496
14	30.095	32.392	34.882	37.581	40.504	43.672	47.102	50.818	54.841	59.196
15	34.405	37.280	40.417	43.842	47.580	51.659	56.109	60.965	66.260	72.035
16	39.190	42.753	46.671	50.980	55.717	60.925	66.648	72.938	79.850	87.442
17	44.500	48.883	53.738	59.117	65.075	71.673	78.978	87.067	96.021	105.930
18	50.396	55.749	61.724	68.393	75.836	84.140	93.404	103.739	115.265	128.116
19	56.939	63.439	70.748	78.968	88.211	98.603	110.283	123.412	138.165	154.739
20	64.202	72.052	80.946	91.024	102.443	115.379	130.031	146.626	165.417	186.687
21	72.264	81.698	92.468	104.767	118.809	134.840	153.136	174.019	197.846	225.024
22	81.213	92.502	105.489	120.434	137.630	157.414	180.169	206.342	236.436	271.028
23	91.147	104.602	120.203	138.295	159.274	183.600	211.798	244.483	282.359	326.234
24	102.173	118.154	136.829	158.656	184.166	213.976	248.803	289.490	337.007	392.480
25	114.412	133.333	155.616	181.867	212.790	249.212	292.099	342.598	402.038	471.976
30	199.018	241.330	293.192	356.778	434.738	530.306	647.423	790.932	966.698	1181.865

A-2 Sum of an Annuity of One Dollar (continued)

Period	21.00%	22.00%	23.00%	24.00%	25.00%	26.00%	27.00%	28.00%	29.00%	30.00%
1	1.000	1.000	1.000	1.000	1.000	1.000	1.000	1.000	1.000	1.000
2	2.210	2.220	2.230	2.240	2.250	2.260	2.270	2.280	2.290	2.300
3	3.674	3.708	3.743	3.778	3.813	3.848	3.883	3.918	3.954	3.990
4	5.446	5.524	5.604	5.684	5.766	5.848	5.931	6.016	6.101	6.187
5	7.589	7.740	7.893	8.048	8.207	8.368	8.533	8.700	8.870	9.043
6	10.183	10.442	10.708	10.980	11.259	11.544	11.837	12.136	12.442	12.756
7	13.321	13.740	14.171	14.615	15.073	15.546	16.032	16.534	17.051	17.583
8	17.119	17.762	18.430	19.123	19.842	20.588	21.361	22.163	22.995	23.858
9	21.714	22.670	23.669	24.712	25.802	26.940	28.129	29.369	30.664	32.015
10	27.274	28.657	30.113	31.643	33.253	34.945	36.723	38.592	40.556	42.619
11	34.001	35.962	38.039	40.238	42.566	45.030	47.639	50.398	53.318	56.405
12	42.141	44.873	47.787	50.895	54.208	57.738	61.501	65.510	69.780	74.326
13	51.991	55.745	59.778	64.109	68.760	73.750	79.106	84.853	91.016	97.624
14	63.909	69.009	74.528	80.496	86.949	93.925	101.465	109.611	118.411	127.912
15	78.330	85.191	92.669	100.815	109.687	119.346	129.860	141.302	153.750	167.285
16	95.779	104.933	114.983	126.010	138.109	151.375	165.922	181.867	199.337	218.470
17	116.892	129.019	142.428	157.252	173.636	191.733	211.721	233.790	258.145	285.011
18	142.439	158.403	176.187	195.993	218.045	242.583	269.885	300.250	334.006	371.514
19	173.351	194.251	217.710	244.031	273.556	306.654	343.754	385.321	431.868	483.968
20	210.755	237.986	268.783	303.598	342.945	387.384	437.568	494.210	558.110	630.157
21	256.013	291.343	331.603	377.461	429.681	489.104	556.710	633.589	720.962	820.204
22	310.775	356.438	408.871	469.052	538.101	617.270	708.022	811.993	931.040	1067.265
23	377.038	435.854	503.911	582.624	673.626	778.760	900.187	1040.351	1202.042	1388.443
24	457.215	532.741	620.810	723.453	843.032	982.237	1144.237	1332.649	1551.634	1805.975
25	554.230	650.944	764.596	898.082	1054.791	1238.617	1454.180	1706.790	2002.608	2348.765
30	1445.111	1767.044	2160.459	2640.881	3227.172	3941.953	4812.891	5873.172	7162.785	8729.805

A-2 Sum of an Annuity of One Dollar (continued)

Period	31.00%	32.00%	33.00%	34.00%	35.00%	36.00%	37.00%	38.00%	39.00%	40.00%
1	1.000	1.000	1.000	1.000	1.000	1.000	1.000	1.000	1.000	1.000
2	2.310	2.320	2.330	2.340	2.350	2.360	2.370	2.380	2.390	2.400
3	4.026	4.062	4.099	4.136	4.172	4.210	4.247	4.284	4.322	4.360
4	6.274	6.362	6.452	6.542	6.633	6.725	6.818	6.912	7.008	7.104
5	9.219	9.398	9.581	9.766	9.954	10.146	10.341	10.539	10.741	10.946
6	13.077	13.406	13.742	14.086	14.438	14.799	15.167	15.544	15.930	16.324
7	18.131	18.696	19.277	19.876	20.492	21.126	21.779	22.451	23.142	23.853
8	24.752	25.678	26.638	27.633	28.664	29.732	30.837	31.982	33.167	34.395
9	33.425	34.895	36.429	38.028	39.696	41.435	43.247	45.135	47.103	49.152
10	44.786	47.062	49.451	51.958	54.590	57.351	60.248	63.287	66.473	69.813
11	59.670	63.121	66.769	70.624	74.696	78.998	83.540	88.335	93.397	98.739
12	79.167	84.320	89.803	95.636	101.840	108.437	115.450	122.903	130.822	139.234
13	104.709	112.302	120.438	129.152	138.484	148.474	159.166	170.606	182.842	195.928
14	138.169	275.299	161.183	174.063	187.953	202.925	219.058	236.435	255.151	175.299
15	182.001	197.996	215.373	234.245	254.737	276.978	301.109	327.281	355.659	386.418
16	239.421	262.354	287.446	314.888	344.895	377.690	413.520	452.647	495.366	541.985
17	314.642	347.307	383.303	422.949	466.608	514.658	567.521	625.652	689.558	759.778
18	413.180	459.445	510.792	567.751	630.920	700.935	778.504	864.399	959.485	1064.689
19	542.266	607.467	680.354	761.786	852.741	954.271	1067.551	1193.870	1334.683	1491.563
20	711.368	802.856	905.870	1021.792	1152.200	1298.809	1463.544	1648.539	1856.208	2089.188
21	932.891	1060.769	1205.807	1370.201	1556.470	1767.380	2006.055	2275.982	2581.128	2925.862
22	1223.087	1401.215	1604.724	1837.068	2102.234	2404.636	2749.294	3141.852	3588.765	4097.203
23	1603.243	1850.603	2135.282	2462.669	2839.014	3271.304	3767.532	4336.750	4989.379	5737.078
24	2101.247	2443.795	2840.924	3300.974	3833.667	4449.969	5162.516	5985.711	6936.230	8032.906
25	2753.631	3226.808	3779.428	4424.301	5176.445	6052.957	7073.645	8261.273	9642.352	11247.063
30	10632.543	12940.672	15737.945	19124.434	23221.258	28172.016	34148.906	41357.227	50043.625	60500.207

A-3 Present Value of One Dollar

Period	1.00%	2.00%	3.00%	4.00%	5.00%	6.00%	7.00%	8.00%	9.00%	10.00%
1	.990	.980	.971	.962	.952	.943	.935	.926	.917	.909
2	.980	.961	.943	.925	.907	.890	.873	.857	.842	.826
3	.971	.942	.915	.889	.864	.840	.816	.794	.772	.751
4	.961	.924	.888	.855	.823	.792	.763	.735	.708	.683
5	.951	.906	.863	.822	.784	.747	.713	.681	.650	.621
6	.942	.888	.837	.790	.746	.705	.666	.630	.596	.564
7	.933	.871	.813	.760	.711	.665	.623	.583	.547	.513
8	.923	.853	.789	.731	.677	.627	.582	.540	.502	.467
9	.914	.837	.766	.703	.645	.592	.544	.500	.460	.424
10	.905	.820	.744	.676	.614	.558	.508	.463	.422	.386
11	.896	.804	.722	.650	.585	.527	.475	.429	.388	.350
12	.887	.789	.701	.625	.557	.497	.444	.397	.356	.319
13	.879	.773	.681	.601	.530	.469	.415	.368	.326	.290
14	.870	.758	.661	.577	.505	.442	.388	.340	.299	.263
15	.861	.743	.642	.555	.481	.417	.362	.315	.275	.239
16	.853	.728	.623	.534	.458	.394	.339	.292	.252	.218
17	.844	.714	.605	.513	.436	.371	.317	.270	.231	.198
18	.836	.700	.587	.494	.416	.350	.296	.250	.212	.180
19	.828	.686	.570	.475	.396	.331	.277	.232	.194	.164
20	.820	.673	.554	.456	.377	.312	.258	.215	.178	.149
21	.811	.660	.538	.439	.359	.294	.242	.199	.164	.135
22	.803	.647	.522	.422	.342	.278	.226	.184	.150	.123
23	.795	.634	.507	.406	.326	.262	.211	.170	.138	.112
24	.788	.622	.492	.390	.310	.247	.197	.158	.126	.102
25	.780	.610	.478	.375	.295	.233	.184	.146	.116	.092
30	.742	.552	.412	.308	.231	.174	.131	.099	.075	.057
35	.706	.500	.355	.253	.181	.130	.094	.068	.049	.036
40	.672	.453	.307	.208	.142	.097	.067	.046	.032	.022
45	.639	.410	.264	.171	.111	.073	.048	.031	.021	.014
50	.608	.372	.228	.141	.087	.054	.034	.021	.013	.009

A-3 Present Value of One Dollar (continued)

Period	11.00%	12.00%	13.00%	14.00%	15.00%	16.00%	17.00%	18.00%	19.00%	20.00%
1	.901	.893	.885	.877	.870	.862	.855	.847	.840	.833
2	.812	.797	.783	.769	.756	.743	.731	.718	.706	.694
3	.731	.712	.693	.675	.658	.641	.624	.609	.593	.579
4	.659	.636	.613	.592	.572	.552	.534	.516	.499	.482
5	.593	.567	.543	.519	.497	.476	.456	.437	.419	.402
6	.535	.507	.480	.456	.432	.410	.390	.370	.352	.335
7	.482	.452	.425	.400	.376	.354	.333	.314	.296	.279
8	.434	.404	.376	.351	.327	.305	.285	.266	.249	.233
9	.391	.361	.333	.308	.284	.263	.243	.225	.209	.194
10	.352	.322	.295	.270	.247	.227	.208	.191	.176	.162
11	.317	.287	.261	.237	.215	.195	.178	.162	.148	.135
12	.286	.257	.231	.208	.187	.168	.152	.137	.124	.112
13	.258	.229	.204	.182	.163	.145	.130	.116	.104	.093
14	.232	.205	.181	.160	.141	.125	.111	.099	.088	.078
15	.209	.183	.160	.140	.123	.108	.095	.084	.074	.065
16	.188	.163	.141	.123	.107	.093	.081	.071	.062	.054
17	.170	.146	.125	.108	.093	.080	.069	.060	.052	.045
18	.153	.130	.111	.095	.081	.069	.059	.051	.044	.038
19	.138	.116	.098	.083	.070	.060	.051	.043	.037	.031
20	.124	.104	.087	.073	.061	.051	.043	.037	.031	.026
21	.112	.093	.077	.064	.053	.044	.037	.031	.026	.022
22	.101	.083	.068	.056	.046	.038	.032	.026	.022	.018
23	.091	.074	.060	.049	.040	.033	.027	.022	.018	.015
24	.082	.066	.053	.043	.035	.028	.023	.019	.015	.013
25	.074	.059	.047	.038	.030	.024	.020	.016	.013	.010
30	.044	.033	.026	.020	.015	.012	.009	.007	.005	.004
35	.026	.019	.014	.010	.008	.006	.004	.003	.002	.002
40	.015	.011	.008	.005	.004	.003	.002	.001	.001	.001
45	.009	.006	.004	.003	.002	.001	.001	.001	.000	.000
50	.005	.003	.002	.001	.001	.001	.000	.000	.000	.000

Per-iod	21.00%	22.00%	23.00%	24.00%	25.00%	26.00%	27.00%	28.00%	29.00%	30.00%
1	.826	.820	.813	.806	.800	.794	.787	.781	.775	.769
2	.683	.672	.661	.650	.640	.630	.620	.610	.601	.592
3	.564	.551	.537	.524	.512	.500	.488	.477	.466	.455
4	.467	.451	.437	.423	.410	.397	.384	.373	.361	.350
5	.386	.370	.355	.341	.328	.315	.303	.291	.280	.269
6	.319	.303	.289	.275	.262	.250	.238	.227	.217	.207
7	.263	.249	.235	.222	.210	.198	.188	.178	.168	.159
8	.218	.204	.191	.179	.168	.157	.148	.139	.130	.123
9	.180	.167	.155	.144	.134	.125	.116	.108	.101	.094
10	.149	.137	.126	.116	.107	.099	.092	.085	.078	.073
11	.123	.112	.103	.094	.086	.079	.072	.066	.061	.056
12	.102	.092	.083	.076	.069	.062	.057	.052	.047	.043
13	.084	.075	.068	.061	.055	.050	.045	.040	.037	.033
14	.069	.062	.055	.049	.044	.039	.035	.032	.028	.025
15	.057	.051	.045	.040	.035	.031	.028	.025	.022	.020
16	.047	.042	.036	.032	.028	.025	.022	.019	.017	.015
17	.039	.034	.030	.026	.023	.020	.017	.015	.013	.012
18	.032	.028	.024	.021	.018	.016	.014	.012	.010	.009
19	.027	.023	.020	.017	.014	.012	.011	.009	.008	.007
20	.022	.019	.016	.014	.012	.010	.008	.007	.006	.005
21	.018	.015	.013	.011	.009	.008	.007	.006	.005	.004
22	.015	.013	.011	.009	.007	.006	.005	.004	.004	.003
23	.012	.010	.009	.007	.006	.005	.004	.003	.003	.002
24	.010	.008	.007	.006	.005	.004	.003	.003	.002	.002
25	.009	.007	.006	.005	.004	.003	.003	.002	.002	.001
30	.003	.003	.002	.002	.001	.001	.001	.001	.000	.000
35	.001	.001	.001	.001	.000	.000	.000	.000	.000	.000
40	.000	.000	.000	.000	.000	.000	.000	.000	.000	.000
45	.000	.000	.000	.000	.000	.000	.000	.000	.000	.000
50	.000	.000	.000	.000	.000	.000	.000	.000	.000	.000

A-3 Present Value of One Dollar (continued)

Per-iod	31.00%	32.00%	33.00%	34.00%	35.00%	36.00%	37.00%	38.00%	39.00%	40.00%
1	.763	.758	.752	.746	.741	.735	.730	.725	.719	.714
2	.583	.574	.565	.557	.549	.541	.533	.525	.518	.510
3	.445	.435	.425	.416	.406	.398	.389	.381	.372	.364
4	.340	.329	.320	.310	.301	.292	.284	.276	.268	.260
5	.259	.250	.240	.231	.223	.215	.207	.200	.193	.186
6	.198	.189	.181	.173	.165	.158	.151	.145	.139	.133
7	.151	.143	.136	.129	.122	.116	.110	.105	.100	.095
8	.115	.108	.102	.096	.091	.085	.081	.076	.072	.068
9	.088	.082	.077	.072	.067	.063	.059	.055	.052	.048
10	.067	.062	.058	.054	.050	.046	.043	.040	.037	.035
11	.051	.047	.043	.040	.037	.034	.031	.029	.027	.025
12	.039	.036	.033	.030	.027	.025	.023	.021	.019	.018
13	.030	.027	.025	.022	.020	.018	.017	.015	.014	.013
14	.023	.021	.018	.017	.015	.014	.012	.011	.010	.009
15	.017	.016	.014	.012	.011	.010	.009	.008	.007	.006
16	.013	.012	.010	.009	.008	.007	.006	.006	.005	.005
17	.010	.009	.008	.007	.006	.005	.005	.004	.004	.003
18	.008	.007	.006	.005	.005	.004	.003	.003	.003	.002
19	.006	.005	.004	.004	.003	.003	.003	.002	.002	.002
20	.005	.004	.003	.003	.002	.002	.002	.002	.001	.001
21	.003	.003	.003	.002	.002	.002	.001	.001	.001	.001
22	.003	.002	.002	.002	.001	.001	.001	.001	.001	.001
23	.002	.002	.001	.001	.001	.001	.001	.001	.001	.000
24	.002	.001	.001	.001	.001	.001	.001	.000	.000	.000
25	.001	.001	.001	.001	.001	.000	.000	.000	.000	.000
30	.000	.000	.000	.000	.000	.000	.000	.000	.000	.000
35	.000	.000	.000	.000	.000	.000	.000	.000	.000	.000
40	.000	.000	.000	.000	.000	.000	.000	.000	.000	.000
45	.000	.000	.000	.000	.000	.000	.000	.000	.000	.000
50	.000	.000	.000	.000	.000	.000	.000	.000	.000	.000

Period	1.00%	2.00%	3.00%	4.00%	5.00%	6.00%	7.00%	8.00%	9.00%	10.00%
1	.990	.980	.971	.962	.952	.943	.935	.926	.917	.909
2	1.970	1.942	1.913	1.886	1.859	1.833	1.808	1.783	1.759	1.736
3	2.941	2.884	2.829	2.775	2.723	2.673	2.624	2.577	2.531	2.487
4	3.902	3.808	3.717	3.630	3.546	3.465	3.387	3.312	3.240	3.170
5	4.853	4.713	4.580	4.452	4.329	4.212	4.100	3.993	3.890	3.791
6	5.795	5.601	5.417	5.242	5.076	4.917	4.767	4.623	4.486	4.355
7	6.728	6.472	6.230	6.002	5.786	5.582	5.389	5.206	5.033	4.868
8	7.652	7.326	7.020	6.733	6.463	6.210	5.971	5.747	5.535	5.335
9	8.566	8.162	7.786	7.435	7.108	6.802	6.515	6.247	5.995	5.759
10	9.471	8.983	8.530	8.111	7.722	7.360	7.024	6.710	6.418	6.145
11	10.368	9.787	9.253	8.760	8.306	7.887	7.499	7.139	6.805	6.495
12	11.255	10.575	9.954	9.385	8.863	8.384	7.943	7.536	7.161	6.814
13	12.134	11.348	10.635	9.986	9.394	8.853	8.358	7.904	7.487	7.103
14	13.004	12.106	11.296	10.563	9.899	9.295	8.746	8.244	7.786	7.367
15	13.865	12.849	11.938	11.118	10.380	9.712	9.108	8.560	8.061	7.606
16	14.718	13.578	12.561	11.652	10.838	10.106	9.447	8.851	8.313	7.824
17	15.562	14.292	13.166	12.166	11.274	10.477	9.763	9.122	8.544	8.022
18	16.398	14.992	13.754	12.659	11.690	10.828	10.059	9.372	8.756	8.201
19	17.226	15.679	14.324	13.134	12.085	11.158	10.336	9.604	8.950	8.365
20	18.046	16.352	14.878	13.590	12.462	11.470	10.594	9.818	9.129	8.514
21	18.857	17.011	15.415	14.029	12.821	11.764	10.836	10.017	9.292	8.649
22	19.661	17.658	15.937	14.451	13.163	12.042	11.061	10.201	9.442	8.772
23	20.456	18.292	16.444	14.857	13.489	12.303	11.272	10.371	9.580	8.883
24	21.244	18.914	16.936	15.247	13.799	12.550	11.469	10.529	9.707	8.985
25	22.023	19.524	17.413	15.622	14.094	12.783	11.654	10.675	9.823	9.077
30	25.808	22.397	19.601	17.292	15.373	13.765	12.409	11.258	10.274	9.427
35	29.409	24.999	21.487	18.665	16.374	14.498	12.948	11.655	10.567	9.644
40	32.835	27.356	23.115	19.793	17.159	15.046	13.332	11.925	10.757	9.779
45	36.095	29.490	24.519	20.720	17.774	15.456	13.606	12.108	10.881	9.863
50	39.197	31.424	25.730	21.482	18.256	15.762	13.801	12.234	10.962	9.915

Period	11.00%	12.00%	13.00%	14.00%	15.00%	16.00%	17.00%	18.00%	19.00%	20.00%
1	.901	.893	.885	.877	.870	.862	.855	.847	.840	.833
2	1.713	1.690	1.668	1.647	1.626	1.605	1.585	1.566	1.547	1.528
3	2.444	2.402	2.361	2.322	2.283	2.246	2.210	2.174	2.140	2.106
4	3.102	3.037	2.974	2.914	2.855	2.798	2.743	2.690	2.639	2.589
5	3.696	3.605	3.517	3.433	3.352	3.274	3.199	3.127	3.058	2.991
6	4.231	4.111	3.998	3.889	3.784	3.685	3.589	3.498	3.410	3.326
7	4.712	4.564	4.423	4.288	4.160	4.039	3.922	3.812	3.706	3.605
8	5.146	4.968	4.799	4.639	4.487	4.344	4.207	4.078	3.954	3.837
9	5.537	5.328	5.132	4.946	4.772	4.607	4.451	4.303	4.163	4.031
10	5.889	5.650	5.426	5.216	5.019	4.833	4.659	4.494	4.339	4.192
11	6.207	5.938	5.687	5.453	5.234	5.029	4.836	4.656	4.487	4.327
12	6.492	6.194	5.918	5.660	5.421	5.197	4.988	4.793	4.611	4.439
13	6.750	6.424	6.122	5.842	5.583	5.342	5.118	4.910	4.715	4.533
14	6.982	6.628	6.303	6.002	5.724	5.468	5.229	5.008	4.802	4.611
15	7.191	6.811	6.462	6.142	5.847	5.575	5.324	5.092	4.876	4.675
16	7.379	6.974	6.604	6.265	5.954	5.669	5.405	5.162	4.938	4.730
17	7.549	7.120	6.729	6.373	6.047	5.749	5.475	5.222	4.990	4.775
18	7.702	7.250	6.840	6.467	6.128	5.818	5.534	5.273	5.033	4.812
19	7.839	7.366	6.938	6.550	6.198	5.877	5.585	5.316	5.070	4.843
20	7.963	7.469	7.025	6.623	6.259	5.929	5.628	5.353	5.101	4.870
21	8.075	7.562	7.102	6.687	6.312	5.973	5.665	5.384	5.127	4.891
22	8.176	7.645	7.170	6.743	6.359	6.011	5.696	5.410	5.149	4.909
23	8.266	7.718	7.230	6.792	6.399	6.044	5.723	5.432	5.167	4.925
24	8.348	7.784	7.283	6.835	6.434	6.073	5.747	5.451	5.182	4.937
25	8.422	7.843	7.330	6.873	6.464	6.097	5.766	5.467	5.195	4.948
30	8.694	8.055	7.496	7.003	6.566	6.177	5.829	5.517	5.235	4.979
35	8.855	8.176	7.586	7.070	6.617	6.215	5.858	5.539	5.251	4.992
40	8.951	8.244	7.634	7.105	6.642	6.233	5.871	5.548	5.258	4.997
45	9.008	8.283	7.661	7.123	6.654	6.242	5.877	5.552	5.261	4.999
50	9.042	8.305	7.675	7.133	6.661	6.246	5.880	5.554	5.262	4.999

A-4 Present Value of an Annuity of One Dollar (continued)

Period	21.00%	22.00%	23.00%	24.00%	25.00%	26.00%	27.00%	28.00%	29.00%	30.00%
1	.826	.820	.813	.806	.800	.794	.787	.781	.775	.769
2	1.509	1.492	1.474	1.457	1.440	1.424	1.407	1.392	1.376	1.361
3	2.074	2.042	2.011	1.981	1.952	1.923	1.896	1.868	1.842	1.816
4	2.540	2.494	2.448	2.404	2.362	2.320	2.280	2.241	2.203	2.166
5	2.926	2.864	2.803	2.745	2.689	2.635	2.583	2.532	2.483	2.436
6	3.245	3.167	3.092	3.020	2.951	2.885	2.821	2.759	2.700	2.643
7	3.508	3.416	3.327	3.242	3.161	3.083	3.009	2.937	2.868	2.802
8	3.726	3.619	3.518	3.421	3.329	3.241	3.156	3.076	2.999	2.925
9	3.905	3.786	3.673	3.566	3.463	3.366	3.273	3.184	3.100	3.019
10	4.054	3.923	3.799	3.682	3.570	3.465	3.364	3.269	3.178	3.092
11	4.177	4.035	3.902	3.776	3.656	3.544	3.437	3.335	3.239	3.147
12	4.278	4.127	3.985	3.851	3.725	3.606	3.493	3.387	3.286	3.190
13	4.362	4.203	4.053	3.912	3.780	3.656	3.538	3.427	3.322	3.223
14	4.432	4.265	4.108	3.962	3.824	3.695	3.573	3.459	3.351	3.249
15	4.489	4.315	4.153	4.001	3.859	3.726	3.601	3.483	3.373	3.268
16	4.536	4.357	4.189	4.033	3.887	3.751	3.623	3.503	3.390	3.283
17	4.576	4.391	4.219	4.059	3.910	3.771	3.640	3.518	3.403	3.295
18	4.608	4.419	4.243	4.080	3.928	3.786	3.654	3.529	3.413	3.304
19	4.635	4.442	4.263	4.097	3.942	3.799	3.664	3.539	3.421	3.311
20	4.657	4.460	4.279	4.110	3.954	3.808	3.673	3.546	3.427	3.316
21	4.675	4.476	4.292	4.121	3.963	3.816	3.679	3.551	3.432	3.320
22	4.690	4.488	4.302	4.130	3.970	3.822	3.684	3.556	3.436	3.323
23	4.703	4.499	4.311	4.137	3.976	3.827	3.689	3.559	3.438	3.325
24	4.713	4.507	4.318	4.143	3.981	3.831	3.692	3.562	3.441	3.327
25	4.721	4.514	4.323	4.147	3.985	3.834	3.694	3.564	3.442	3.329
30	4.746	4.534	4.339	4.160	3.995	3.842	3.701	3.569	3.447	3.332
35	4.756	4.541	4.345	4.164	3.998	3.845	3.703	3.571	3.448	3.333
40	4.760	4.544	4.347	4.166	3.999	3.846	3.703	3.571	3.448	3.333
45	4.761	4.545	4.347	4.166	4.000	3.846	3.704	3.571	3.448	3.333
50	4.762	4.545	4.348	4.167	4.000	3.846	3.704	3.571	3.448	3.333

A-4 Present Value of an Annuity of One Dollar (continued)

Period	31.00%	32.00%	33.00%	34.00%	35.00%	36.00%	37.00%	38.00%	39.00%	40.00%
1	.763	.758	.752	.746	.741	.735	.730	.725	.719	.714
2	1.346	1.331	1.317	1.303	1.289	1.276	1.263	1.250	1.237	1.224
3	1.791	1.766	1.742	1.719	1.696	1.673	1.652	1.630	1.609	1.589
4	2.130	2.096	2.062	2.029	1.997	1.966	1.935	1.906	1.877	1.849
5	2.390	2.345	2.302	2.260	2.220	2.181	2.143	2.106	2.070	2.035
6	2.588	2.534	2.483	2.433	2.385	2.339	2.294	2.251	2.209	2.168
7	2.739	2.677	2.619	2.562	2.508	2.455	2.404	2.355	2.308	2.263
8	2.854	2.786	2.721	2.658	2.598	2.540	2.485	2.432	2.380	2.331
9	2.942	2.868	2.798	2.730	2.665	2.603	2.544	2.487	2.432	2.379
10	3.009	2.930	2.855	2.784	2.715	2.649	2.587	2.527	2.469	2.414
11	3.060	2.978	2.899	2.824	2.752	2.683	2.618	2.555	2.496	2.438
12	3.100	3.013	2.931	2.853	2.779	2.708	2.641	2.576	2.515	2.456
13	3.129	3.040	2.956	2.876	2.799	2.727	2.658	2.592	2.529	2.469
14	3.152	3.061	2.974	2.892	2.814	2.740	2.670	2.603	2.539	2.477
15	3.170	3.076	2.988	2.905	2.825	2.750	2.679	2.611	2.546	2.484
16	3.183	3.088	2.999	2.914	2.834	2.757	2.685	2.616	2.551	2.489
17	3.193	3.097	3.007	2.921	2.840	2.763	2.690	2.621	2.555	2.492
18	3.201	3.104	3.012	2.926	2.844	2.767	2.693	2.624	2.557	2.494
19	3.207	3.109	3.017	2.930	2.848	2.770	2.696	2.626	2.559	2.496
20	3.211	3.113	3.020	2.933	2.850	2.772	2.698	2.627	2.561	2.497
21	3.215	3.116	3.023	2.935	2.852	2.773	2.699	2.629	2.562	2.498
22	3.217	3.118	3.025	2.936	2.853	2.775	2.700	2.629	2.562	2.498
23	3.219	3.120	3.026	2.938	2.854	2.775	2.701	2.630	2.563	2.499
24	3.221	3.121	3.027	2.939	2.855	2.776	2.701	2.630	2.563	2.499
25	3.222	3.122	3.028	2.939	2.856	2.776	2.702	2.631	2.563	2.499
30	3.225	3.124	3.030	2.941	2.857	2.777	2.702	2.631	2.564	2.500
35	3.226	3.125	3.030	2.941	2.857	2.778	2.703	2.632	2.564	2.500
40	3.226	3.125	3.030	2.941	2.857	2.778	2.703	2.632	2.564	2.500
45	3.226	3.125	3.030	2.941	2.857	2.778	2.703	2.632	2.564	2.500
50	3.226	3.125	3.030	2.941	2.857	2.778	2.703	2.632	2.564	2.500

INDEX OF CASES

†